DRAW MANGA

Keroko James

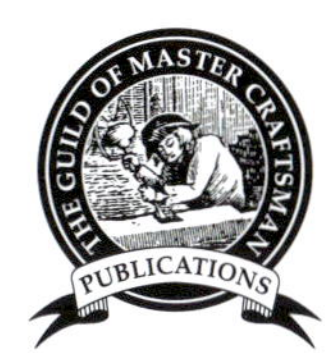

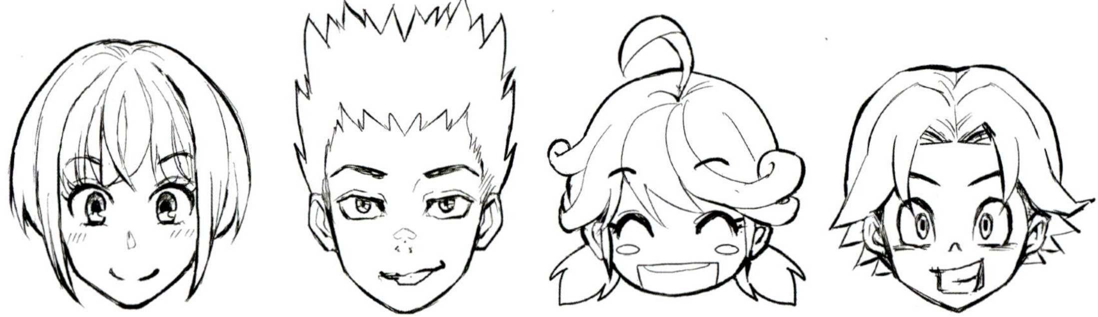

Contents

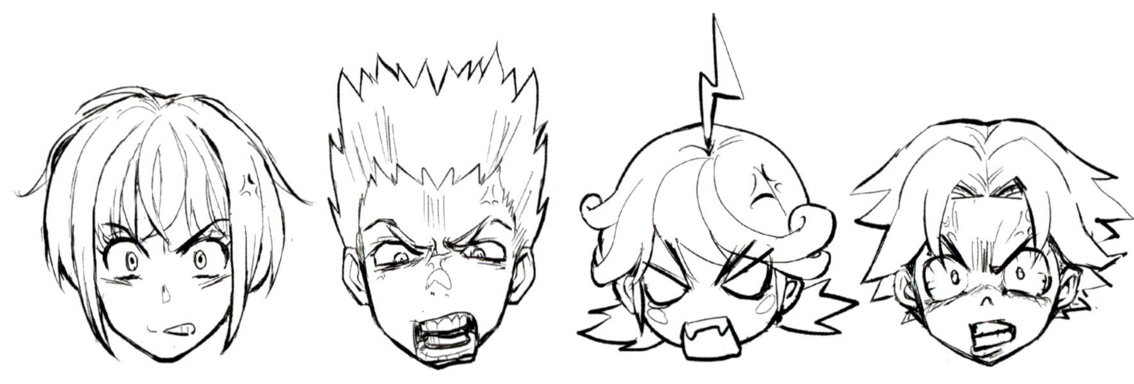

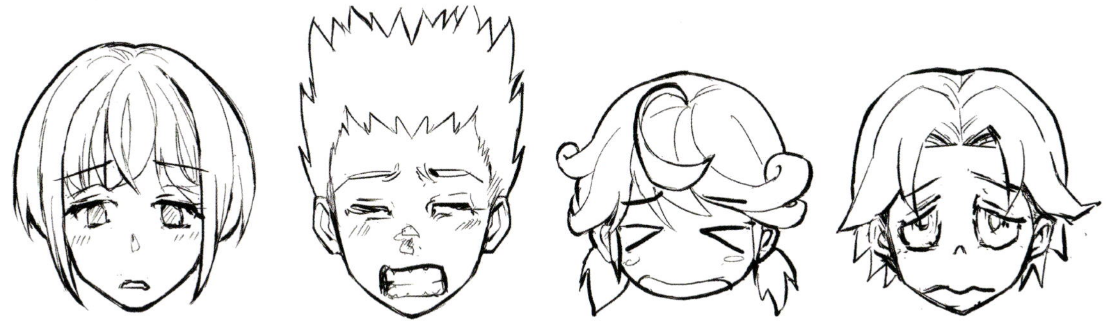

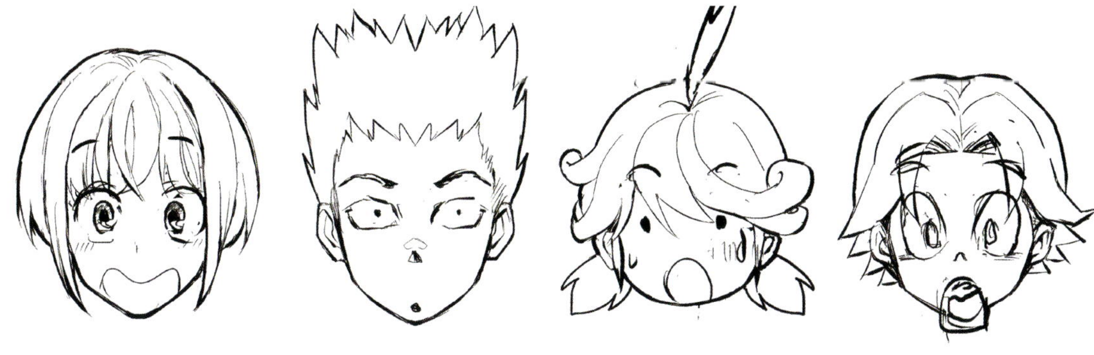

INTRODUCTION

Would you like to draw manga but don't where to begin? Do you wish you could create your own characters and poses? If so, you've found the right book to help you make a good start – and all you will need is a pencil and paper!

WHAT IS MANGA?

Manga is a traditional Japanese style of drawing that appears in comic books and graphic novels. It used to be aimed at children, but it has become very popular with all ages. Numerous manga magazines are published weekly and monthly in Japan, and Japanese animation, or 'anime', has reached a worldwide audience.

Manga covers every genre, from drama to fiction, sci-fi, everyday life, horror, crime or anything else. It is noted for characters with strong expressions and exaggerated emotions, the use of close-up framing – similar to that used in films – and uses stylized text to express sounds.

Manga art style varies depending on the artists and authors. However, cute 'chibi' (tiny) characters that have large eyes staring from a large head is the most well-known style.

Many people become interested in the world of manga after watching anime. Today, the internet has made it possible to view a diverse range of manga and anime titles, both old and new. In addition, manga culture has become a varied media, with live-action films, stage performances, game collaborations, toys and other manufactured goods, and cosplay (where people dress up in the costumes of their favourite characters).

MANGA COMPARED TO WESTERN COMICS

The two images here show the differences between typical Japanese and Western comic book characters. Both have good points: the style you prefer is a matter of personal taste.

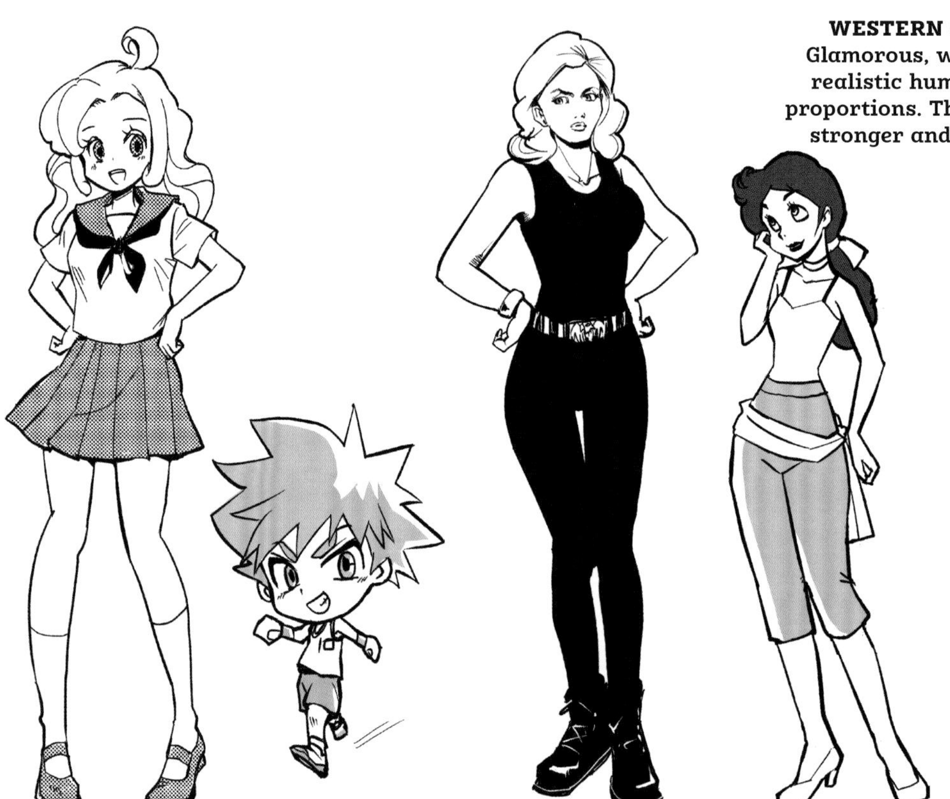

WESTERN COMIC
Glamorous, with more realistic human body proportions. The lines are stronger and simpler.

JAPANESE MANGA
A large head and eyes, but a small face and impossibly stylized hair. A youthful build with long, slender limbs.

Types of manga

There are different manga magazines for different ages and preferences that could be classified as genres in their own right. Here are just a few examples.

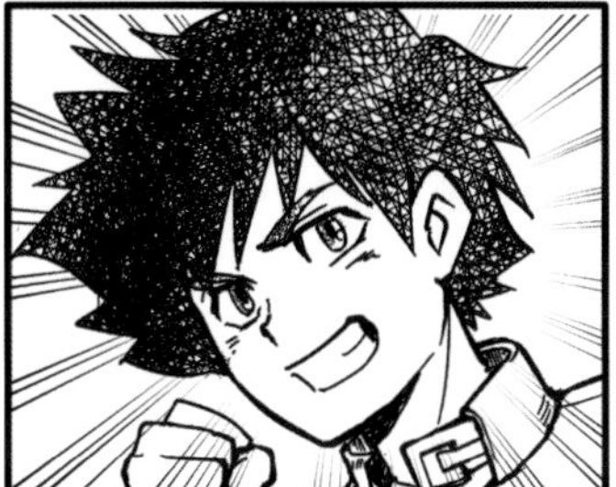

SHONEN
Shonen means 'boy' in Japanese. Shonen manga is popular among different genders and ages. Action and combat-based manga are among the most loved.

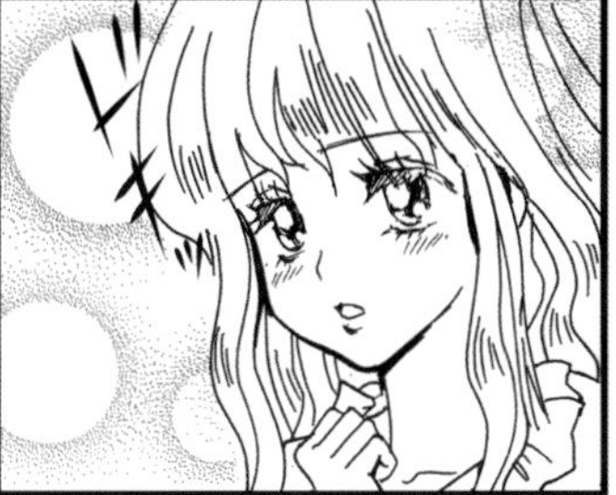

SHOJO
Meaning 'girl', shojo manga features more delicate lines than shonen manga, and many shojo manga series focus on romance or drama rather than action.

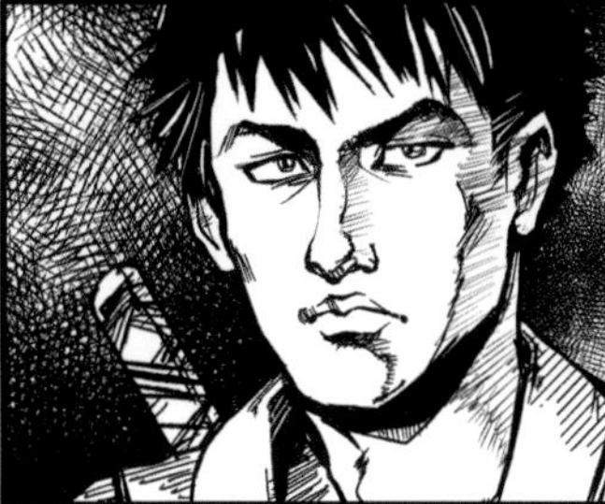

SEINEN
Seinen means 'youth', and this style of manga is for young people, roughly equivalent to the content of a 12A film. Seinen manga is more realistic and detailed.

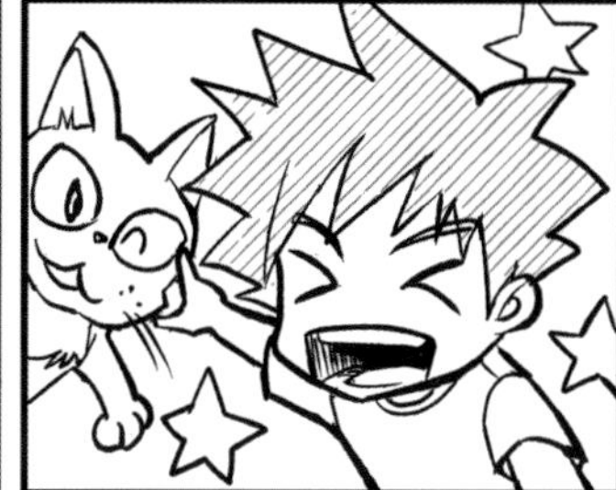

GYAGU
Gyagu is a translation of 'gag'. It is a style of comedy manga, with four-frame strips and quite simple character art.

History of manga

Manga art has quite a long history. You can see some of the features found in manga in the Choju-giga scrolls (c.12th/13th centuries). It doesn't have speech bubbles, but the scroll tells a unique story using a sequence of pictures.

The word 'manga' was created by Katusika Hokusai, a famous *ukiyo-e* artist in the 19th century. He drew the *Hokusai Manga* and woodblock-printed copies of this work were popular during Japan's Edo era.

The 1920s saw the establishment of typical comic book expressions such as comic panels and speech bubbles. Later, they started being drawn with a pen instead of a brush.

The most recent manga style was formed in the 1940s under the influence of Western comics. However, the drawing style remains distinctive and has evolved in its own way through exaggeration and variety.

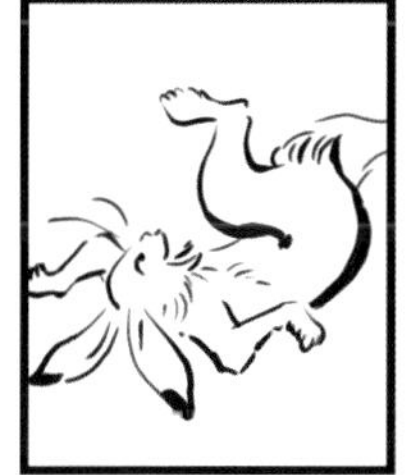

12TH CENTURY

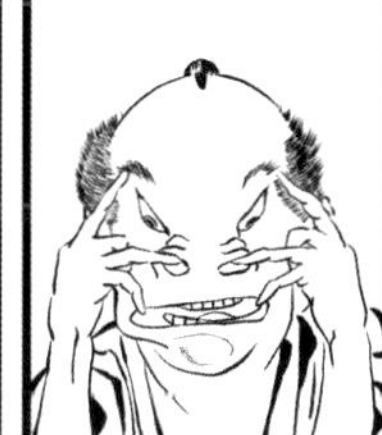

19TH CENTURY

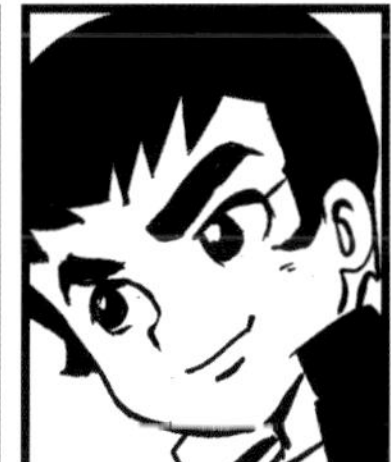

1960s

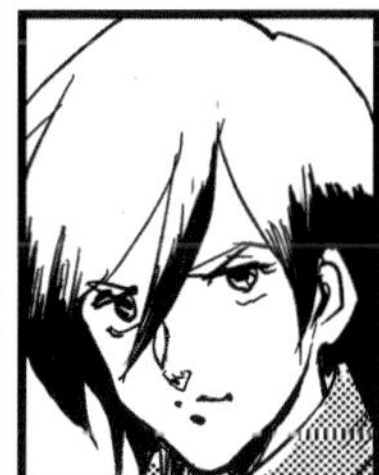

1980s

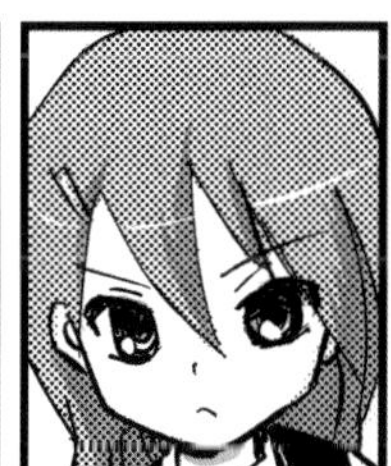

2000s

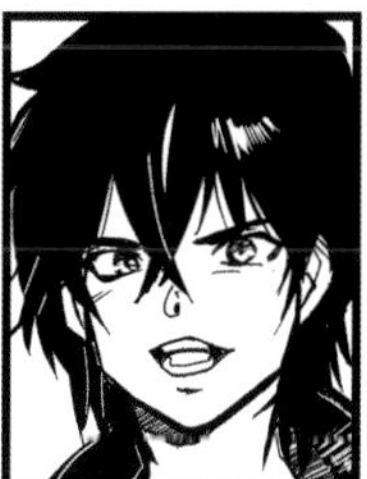

2010s

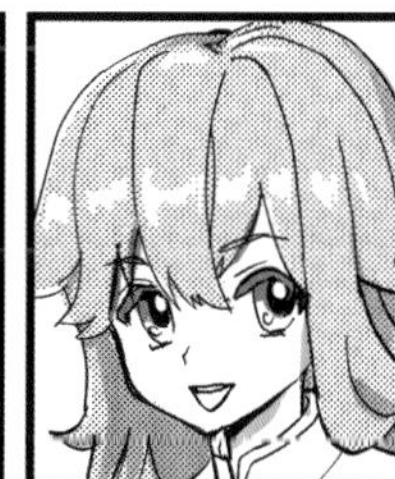

2020s

TOOLS AND MATERIALS

One advantage of manga is that you don't need much to draw it. It's likely that you will already have a notepad and pencil at hand to get started, and you can add to these at a later stage.

BEGINNER'S BASIC KIT

PENCIL AND PENCIL SHARPENER

You don't need to buy special art pencils when you're starting out – use whatever you usually use for writing. However, it will be easier to draw lines that can be erased with a soft 2B pencil than a hard pencil or mechanical pencil (B pencils are soft, H pencils are hard). Use a pencil sharpener to keep the point sharp for making crisp lines.

ERASER

Use a large, good-quality eraser, even if your pencil has an eraser at the end of it.

RULER

Any ruler marked with measurements and that has a straight edge for drawing a straight line is fine.

PAPER

A4 (or letter) paper will do the job. You can use the back of unwanted sheets of paper for exercises and warm-up practices – keep a stack at hand. If you find it hard to draw a circle or parallel lines, use 5mm (¼in) graph paper with grid lines.

CARD STOCK

Copier paper is not the best paper for ink and colour finishes. Slightly thicker paper – so the ink doesn't bleed through – is better. There are specialist comic and colour marker papers available, but I recommend 160–200gsm (60–110lb) card stock, which is inexpensive and easy to find.

LIGHT PAD

Also called a lightbox, a light pad is used to transfer a rough sketch to another sheet of paper. LED light pads are now cheap, so I recommend you get one. A4 light pads are relatively small and easy to use. If you wish to draw a lot of larger art, consider investing in an A3 light pad.

INKING AND COLOURING TOOLS

Once you are confident with the quality of your pencil drawing, you may want to ink it and colour it. Here are some examples of entry-level inking and colouring equipment.

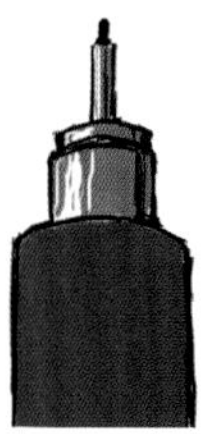

FINELINERS
Black pens with pigmented ink are ideal for drawing fine, even lines; it will be helpful to have a set of several of these in widths that range from 0.01mm to 1.0mm. A set of five pens with 0.1mm, 0.2mm, 0.3mm, 0.5mm and 0.8mm widths is a good place to start.

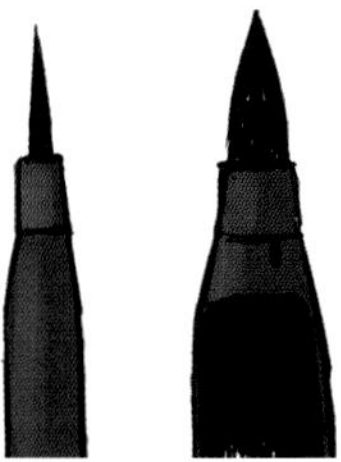

BRUSH PENS
These pens have brush-like tips that allow you to change from fine to thick dynamic lines as you draw, depending on the amount of force you apply to the tip. Mastering them takes practice, but your lines will be more fluid and live. Thick brush pens are also suitable for filling in.

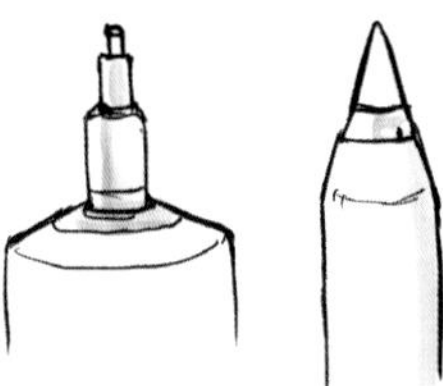

CORRECTION PENS AND WHITE ACRYLIC PENS
These are used to make corrections to ink lines and to add white highlights and patterns. I recommend getting a pen-shaped acrylic version, which will be easier to control. If you are intending to use them to add white on top of another colour, wait until the base ink has dried, otherwise they can cause the drawing to be smudged.

COLOUR MARKERS FOR MANGA

When it comes to adding colour to manga drawings by hand, colour markers are the most popular option. They are easy to use and dry quickly, and there is a wide selection of colours to choose from. Choose alcohol-based markers because they can be blended together.

There are various brands of alcohol markers on the market, from reasonable to expensive, including sets with lots of different colours. When you are starting out, it is better to buy a wider selection of cheaper markers rather than a smaller selection of more expensive pens. To minimize having to mix different markers to create new colours, I would recommend getting a set with 40 or more colours.

Some markers aimed at professional artists can be refilled with ink, but it is best to get them only after you have mastered colouring your work with standard markers.

Don't worry if you don't have colour markers. You can also use any other colouring tools, such as coloured pencils or acrylic paint.

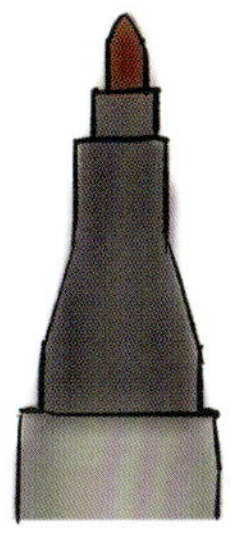

FINE-TIP MARKERS
For drawing thin lines or filling areas with small details. It's a good idea to start colouring from the edge using a fine tip.

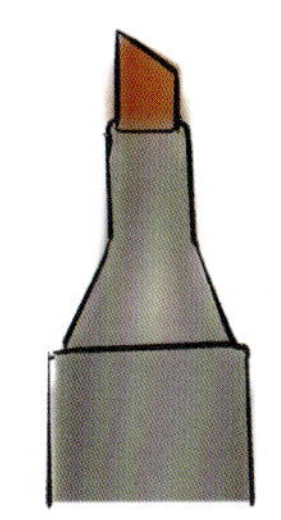

FLAT-TIP MARKERS
A broad nib is perfect for filling large areas, but it can't handle details, for which you'll need a fine-tip marker.

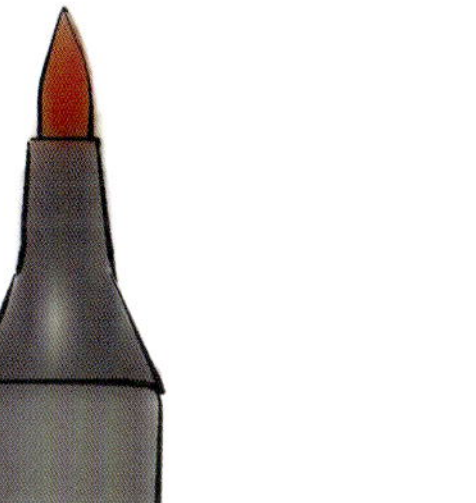

BRUSH-TIP MARKERS
Brush-tip markers are my favourite pens to draw with: you can draw both thick and thin lines without changing pens, and fill in the colour with it easily like a paintbrush.

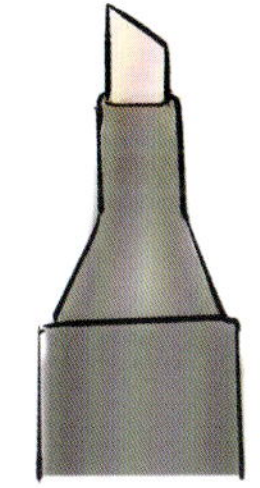

TRANSPARENT BLENDER
A blender marker, which is usually the no. 0 marker, has transparent ink. You can use it to fade a colour into transparency or for mixing colours (see page 113).

DUAL-TIP MARKERS
Many markers that are intended for manga art are designed so that you can use both ends, which have different tips. You can use them for different purposes.

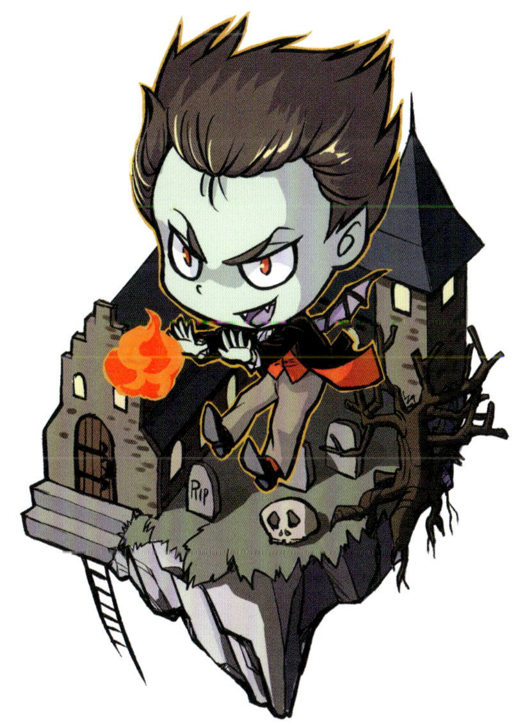

Optional tools

Although these tools are not always necessary, they can be very helpful aids, especially when creating your own images.

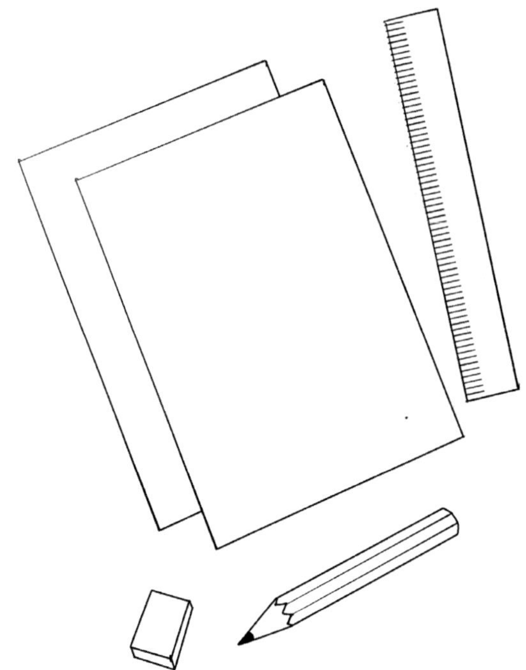

NOTEPAD

Not only is a notepad ideal for practising doodles and rough sketches, but it will also be useful for jotting down new ideas. It should be fun to follow your progress as you fill in the pages, which will motivate you to practise even more.

SCANNER/PRINTER

Photocopiers are useful for duplicating, enlarging or reducing sketches. Choose a printer with a scanner, so you can digitize your illustrations to upload on a computer or laptop.

CAMERA

A smartphone camera is fine for this purpose. Use it to photograph the poses you wish to draw and to gather reference material to help you draw scenery and props.

THE INTERNET

Access to the internet will assist you in finding images to use as references. Having a tablet or laptop with a screen larger than a smartphone and access to an image search tool will come in handy.

REFERENCE BOOKS

It is a good idea to have printed references from different genres. I have a number of reference books on my bookshelves at home to make art.

KNEADED ERASER

This is a soft, malleable eraser favoured by artists. You can press it into different shapes to erase fine details and to white out pencil grey tones.

FRENCH AND FLEXIBLE CURVES

Available in sets of different sizes, plastic or metal, French curves are templates designed with various curves. There is also a long, thin flexible curve that can be adjusted to change its shape. These templates are good for people who wish to draw precise lines or who find it tricky to draw curves.

GEOMETRIC TEMPLATES

Various sizes of circles, ovals, triangles, squares and other shapes are cut out of the templates to be used as guides for drawing these shapes. They are suitable for artists who want to finish their drawings with precise lines.

Computers and drawing tablets

When starting out, I recommend using pencils and paper rather than drawing on a computer, which involves different skills. By using a pencil, you can concentrate strictly on your drawings. Furthermore, it's very hard to draw lines on a computer without investing in an expensive drawing tablet.

However, if you already have a computer and the appropriate software, you can use it to add and correct colours. In this case, I recommend drawing lines by hand on paper, then scanning your drawing and using your computer to add and correct colours.

Getting Ready to Draw Manga

Drawing is as much a skill as it is a talent, and with practice and effort, you can learn more and improve over time, just like you can with other skills such as cooking, swimming or playing a piano.

Ten Tips for Improving Your Drawing Skills

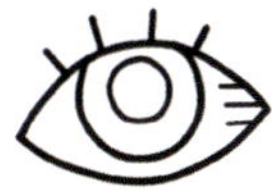

1 LEARN TO SEE

It is important that you are aware of what you can see, both in observing and understanding life around you, and in assessing your drawings and thinking about how to improve them.

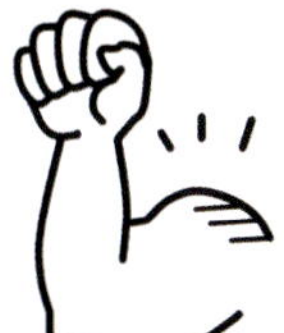

2 WORK ON YOUR MUSCLE MEMORY

Practise making marks and lines regularly so that you learn how to control your pen and pencil accurately.

3 POSITIVE MINDSET

A positive mindset is always important when you study a new skill. Do not say 'I can't' – it is a negative attitude that could stop your growth. Never give up: if you keep trying and don't give up, before you know it, you will be able to do it. If you find you are getting frustrated, then set what you're doing aside for now and come back to it when you have more confidence.

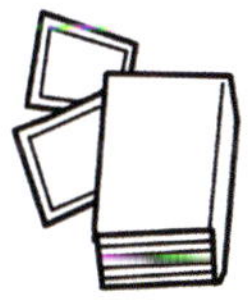

4 BUILD AN IMAGE LIBRARY

The secret to creating great art is filling your memories with images. Observe everything around you, and look at art in books and visit galleries.

5 PASSION AND PATIENCE

As with any skill, it takes time to develop – no magic will allow you to master it overnight. Be patient even if you are frustrated with yourself. Practise, and passion, makes perfect.

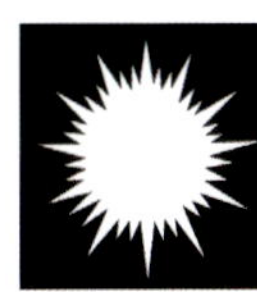

6 CONCENTRATION

It is essential to concentrate while creating art, so it is important to know how to sustain it for a long time. Find a good location where you can concentrate such as a quiet place where you will be alone and undisturbed.

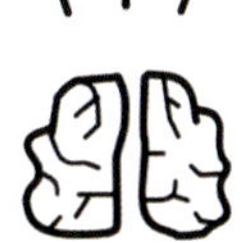

7 LEARN NEW DRAWING SKILLS

A good knowledge of different drawing techniques will enable you to improve your art.

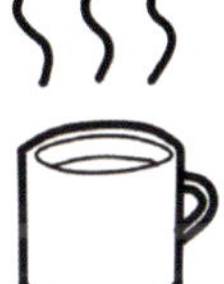

8 RELAX

Don't be a perfectionist: you are still learning. Not even the greatest artists drew perfect work from the start. Don't compare yourself with others. Everyone works and improves at a different pace.

9 TRY NEW THINGS

Experience is a treasure trove of ideas. Never be afraid of failure or of trying something new – if you only draw what you can already draw, your skills will stop improving.

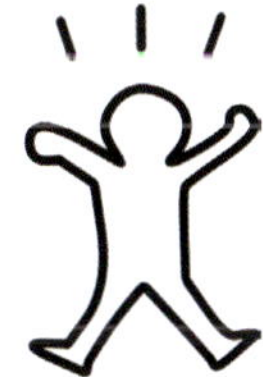

10 ENJOY YOURSELF

You may feel frustrated or depressed because you can't draw as well as you would like but you will get better with time. Meanwhile, don't forget to find fun in drawing manga. Give yourself a pat on the back for being that little bit better at drawing than you were the day before.

Drawing basics

Knowing how to hold and draw with a pencil or pen will help you to draw clean lines with confidence, but it takes practice, practice, practice – and more practice. When drawing with a pencil, always use one with a sharp point for creating crisp lines.

Holding your pencil

Use the same grip when drawing that you use to write. This is important because a writing grip allows your wrist to move freely and will give you greater control over making long strokes and curved lines. Practise drawing lines using your writing grip until you can control them with ease.

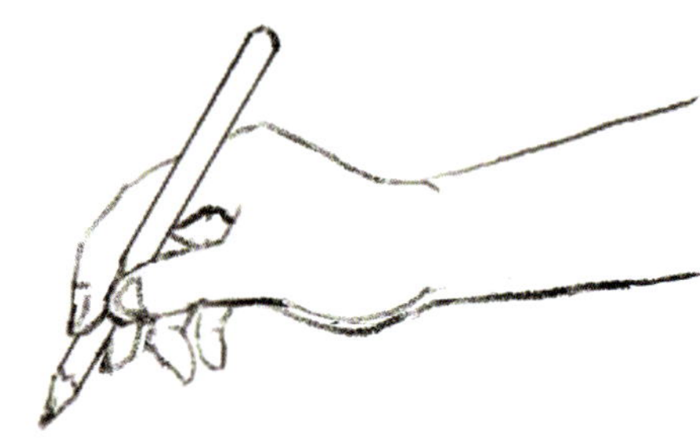

For a pencil grip, use three fingers: place the pencil between your index and middle fingers and stabilize it with your thumb.

Pressure and speed

Strong black lines will look good on paper because they provide a strong contrast. However, if you make a mistake, it's hard to completely erase them, and you could damage the paper when trying to do so. Instead, start with soft, light lines that you can easily erase without damaging the paper – you can redraw them later once you are happy with the drawing. Depending on what section you are drawing and the overall theme you are trying to express, you can use either slow, neat lines or quick, dynamic lines.

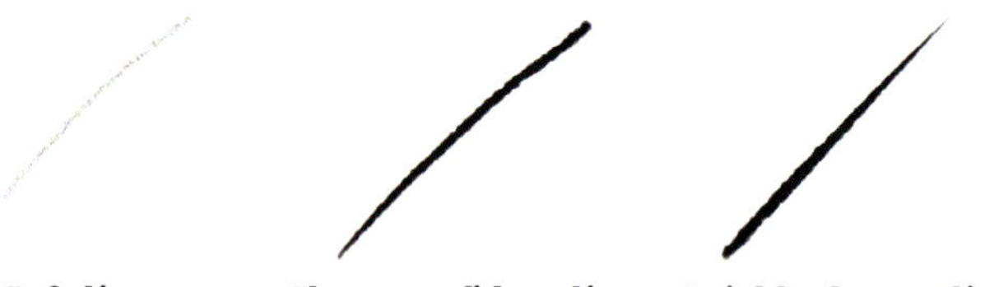

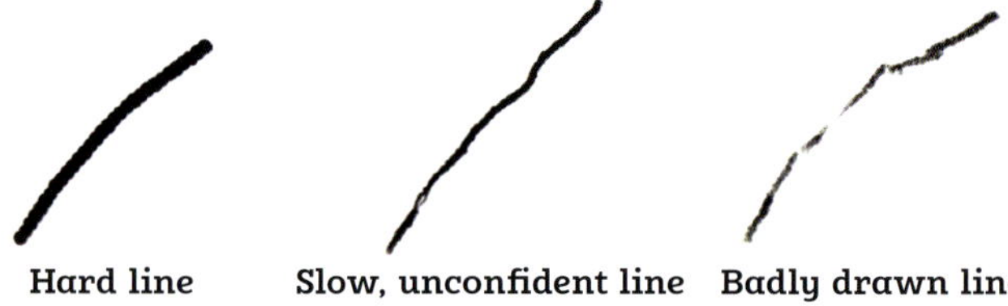

Let's practise lines

Lines are important in manga. Practise drawing them regularly so that you can make them reliably.

DRAW SIMPLE LINES

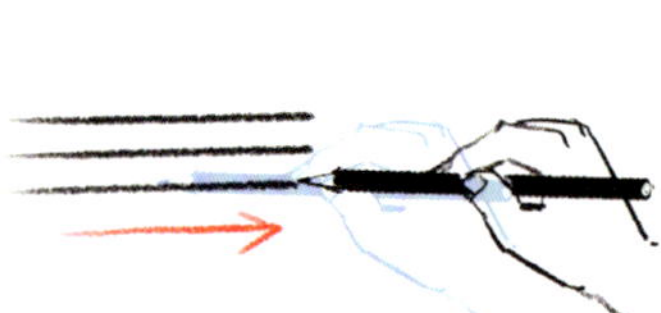

1 Draw some parallel horizontal lines, using the whole of the paper's width. Check they are straight, parallel and the same distance from each other. Move your arm to draw instead of your fingers.

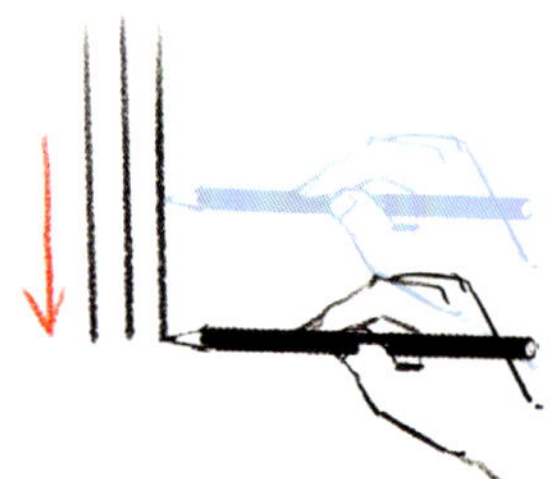

2 Draw some parallel vertical lines. Check they are straight, parallel and the same distance from each other. To see how you can achieve the most control, try different speeds, strengths and directions.

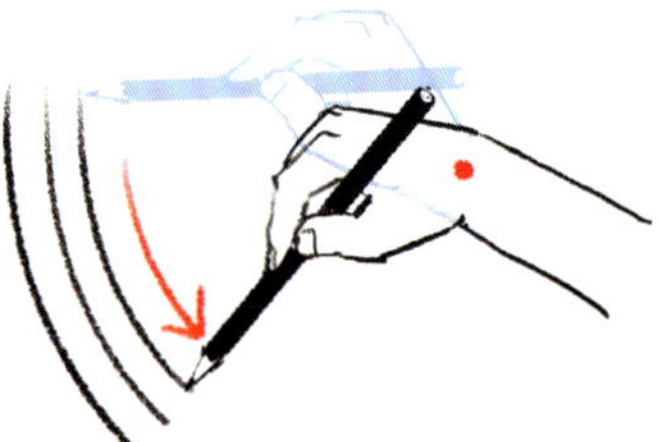

3 Draw some curved lines by bending your wrist. You can draw a smooth, curving line when using your wrist like a compass. Switch to your elbow if you wish to make bigger arcs.

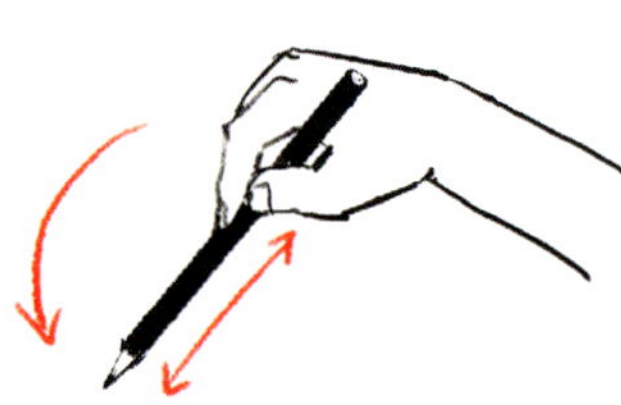

4 Try gripping the pencil a little higher up and then draw some larger circles.

Let's practise shapes

You will need to draw squares and rectangles often, so it's important to master the ability to draw them. Let's practise drawing them here.

DRAWING SQUARES

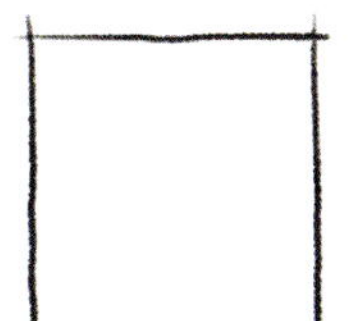

1 Drawing freehand rather than using a ruler, draw a square with approximately 2in (5cm) sides. Correct the lines using an eraser if you need to and make them perfect.

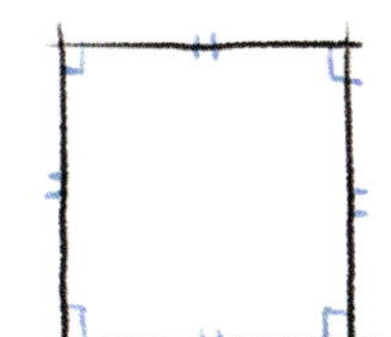

2 Use a ruler to check all the sides are straight and the same length. Opposite sides should be parallel, and all the corners should be 90 degrees.

Caution

BAD EXAMPLES

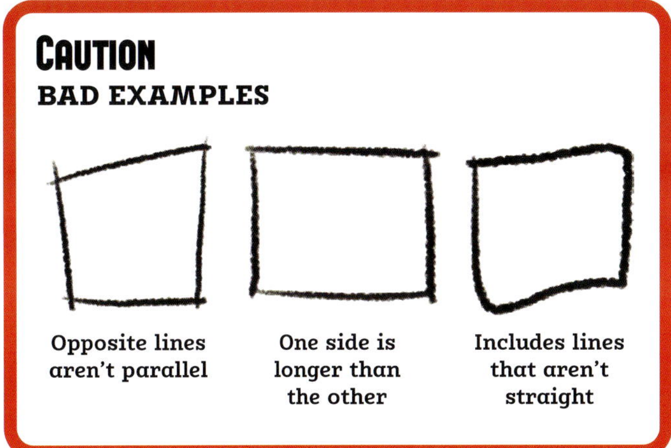

Opposite lines aren't parallel

One side is longer than the other

Includes lines that aren't straight

DRAWING CUBES

Practise these cubes until you can draw them confidently, then try drawing other cubes at different sizes and angles.

FROM THE FRONT

1 Draw a square.

2 Draw another square behind the first one.

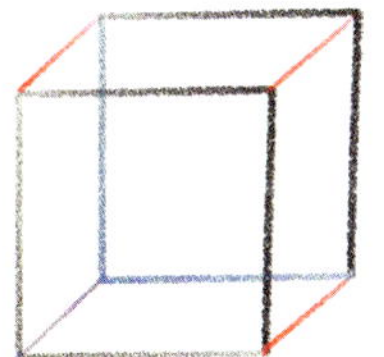

3 Make the sides by drawing lines between the matching corners.

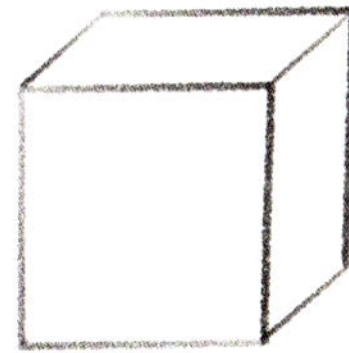

4 Erase any lines that should no longer be visible.

FROM THE TOP

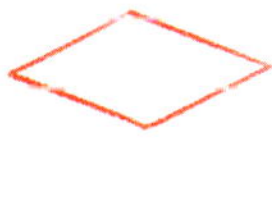

1 Draw a diamond shape for the top.

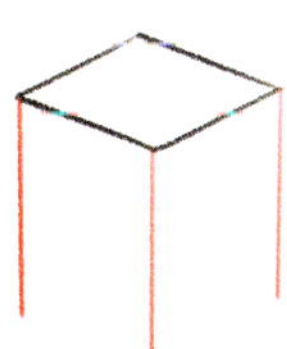

2 Draw vertical lines down from the three lower corners.

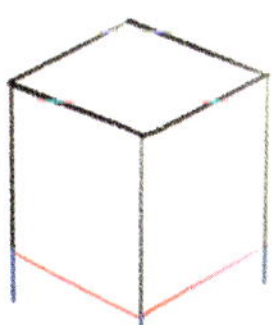

3 Draw a base parallel to the two lower edges of the diamond. Make sure the vertical lines are the same length as the diagonal lines.

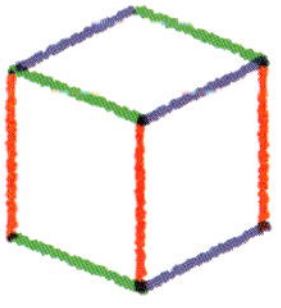

4 Erase any lines that should no longer be visible.

DRAWING CIRCLES

A manga face begins as a circle, so being able to draw a good circle is very important for achieving a nice result. You can start by drawing lines slowly and concentrating on your control. Then gradually practise drawing circles faster without losing any quality.

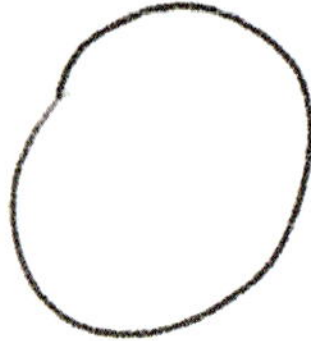

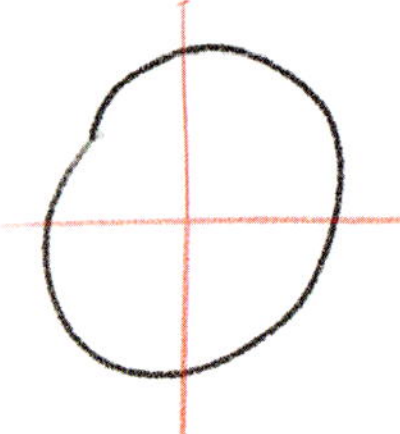

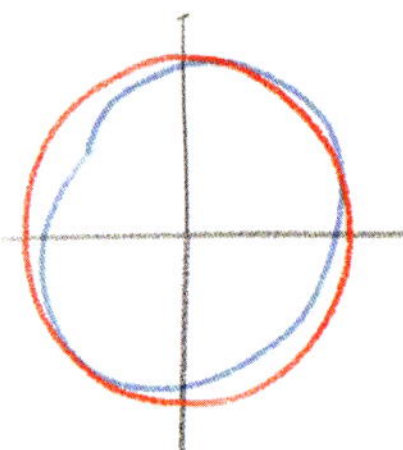

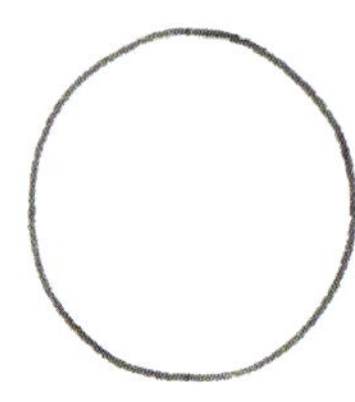

1 Draw a circle at least 2in (5cm) in radius, using one or two rounded strokes. Avoid drawing heavy lines or having any gaps in them.

2 To check how accurate your circle is, add a vertical and a horizontal line to divide it into exact quarters.

3 Using a ruler, check that the Step 2 lines are straight and perfectly perpendicular, then check that all your curved shapes are even and symmetrical. Correct them with an eraser.

4 Erase the straight lines.

DRAWING CYLINDERS

The most important shape for drawing a body will be the cylinder. Arms, legs, fingers and the neck can all be simplified into a cylinder. Let's practise! Draw cylinders based on various shapes of ovals and at different angles.

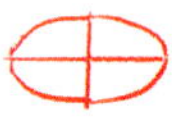

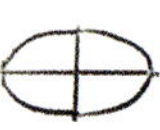

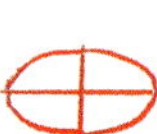

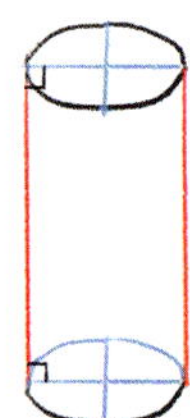

1 Draw an oval. You can start with a cross shape, as a guide for drawing a symmetrical oval (see below).

2 Make another one exactly the same directly below the first one.

3 Draw straight lines between the two ovals, connecting them at the sides.

4 Erase the hidden lines.

DRAWING SYMMETRICAL OVALS

Manga faces come in different shapes, so practise drawing different ovals in various sizes. Practise drawing symmetrical ovals using the steps below. Be aware that the arcs of an oval are gradual curves with peaks in the middle.

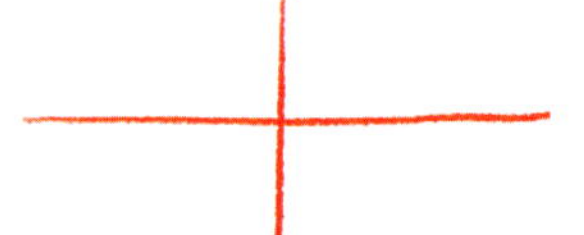

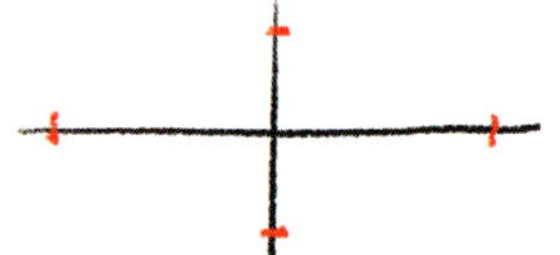

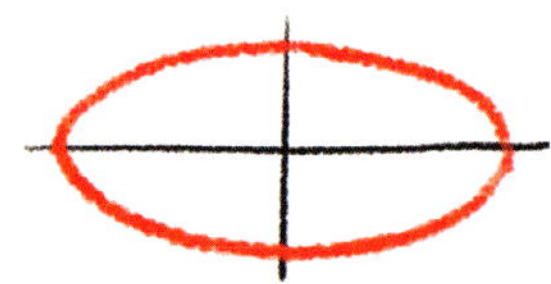

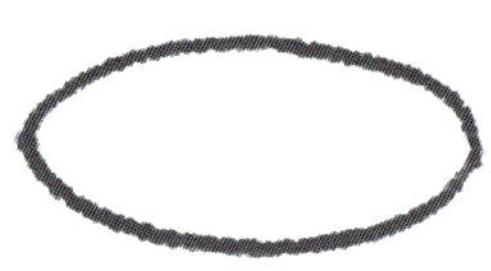

1 Draw a cross. One line should be longer than the other, and they should meet in the middle of each line.

2 Mark the opposite ends of the lines at the same distance from the centre.

3 Draw a symmetrical oval using these marks.

4 Erase the cross shape.

How to sit correctly

Having a correct posture and a table or chair at the right height for your body are important when drawing. You should sit with a straight back, not hunched over. A drafting table or artist's workstation that allows the work surface to tilt up can help improve your posture. Alternatively, use some books to prop up a board.

Ensure the room you will be drawing in is bright enough for seeing your work without straining your eyes. To see the colours you will be using more accurately, choose a light bulb with a natural colour temperature.

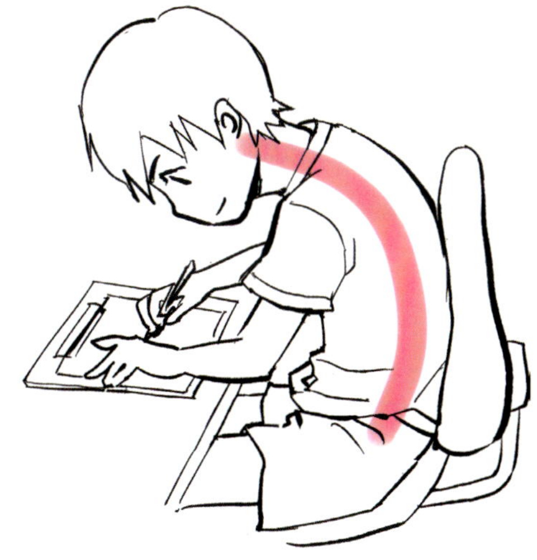

BAD POSTURE

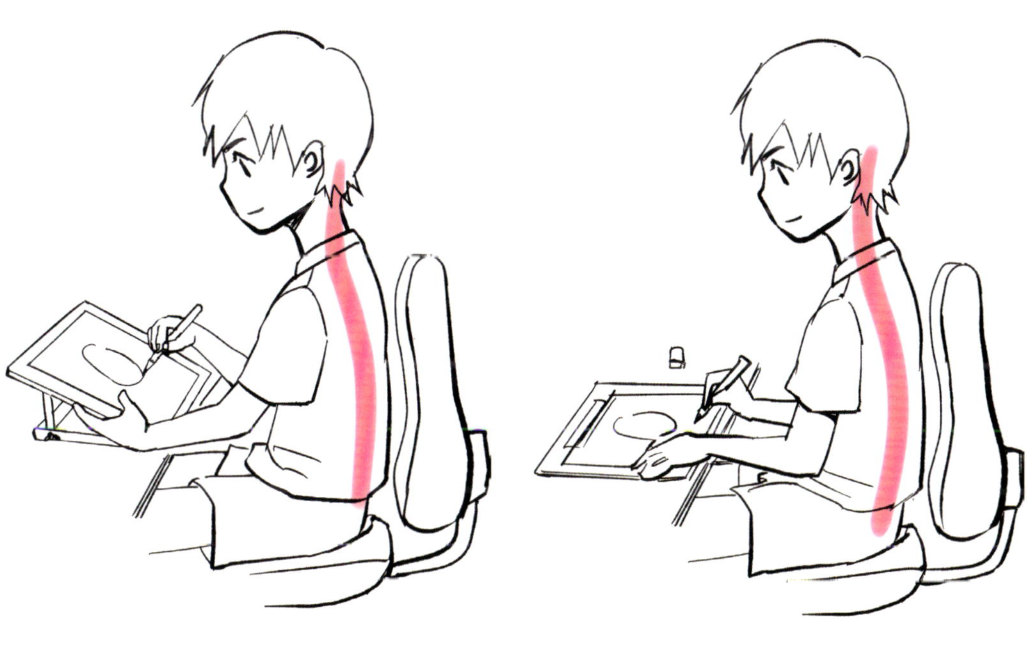

GOOD POSTURE **GOOD POSTURE**

How to use this book

This book contains ten projects to provide you with the most important skills you will need to draw your own manga art. The first project shows you how to draw a cute chibi – one of the simplest manga styles to draw – from start to finish to give you a sense of achievement. I recommend that you then work your way through the remaining projects in the order presented to build up your skills.

The projects

Each of the projects will focus on teaching you a different level of drawing manga art, taking you from drawing basic stick figures to colouring in your finished ink figure set in a scene. Unless you are already an experienced artist, master one project first before moving on to the next section.

The main section of each project is a series of step-by-step instructions that will take you from the first lines to a finished piece of art. The projects also have tutorials on various topics such as body proportions, facial emotions, foreshortening, observation, colour theory, background effects and composition. Along the way you will find 'focus on' sections, where I will look in more detail at the key techniques and subjects that arise in the project, such as how to draw hair, hands and shadows. In some projects there is an extra 'practice' section. These will help to reinforce what you have learned by drawing different variations on the theme, allowing you to develop your own particular art style.

The best approach to drawing manga

The secret to drawing manga is to start by simplifying the shape of your subject and using light lines that are easy to erase and correct, then build up your drawing gradually. It is a good idea to draw a stick figure with good proportions first – this way you can modify the character's pose and size very easily. Avoid focusing on only one area of the drawing, and instead work on it as a whole, so you can see the balance of the entire piece.

A common mistake is to focus on adding details before fully establishing a character's pose and form. This can lead to wasted effort, since you may need to erase your character, and therefore also any details you've added, several times before you get your pose and forms right. Instead, adding details should be the last stage of your drawing before introducing tones and colour.

FOLLOWING THE STEPS

The basic step-by-step approach to drawing that I recommend and use in this book is as follows. For the first few projects, stop at the end of stage 3 and practise to master the essentials. Once you are confident with your new skills, you can finish off your drawing. You will be introduced to using ink, adding colour and drawing backgrounds in the later projects.

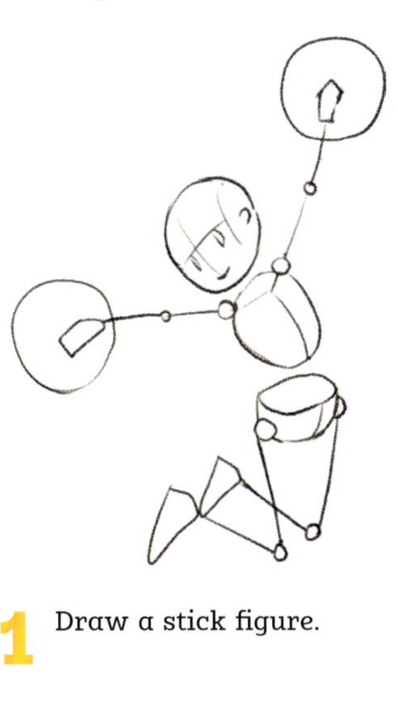

1 Draw a stick figure.

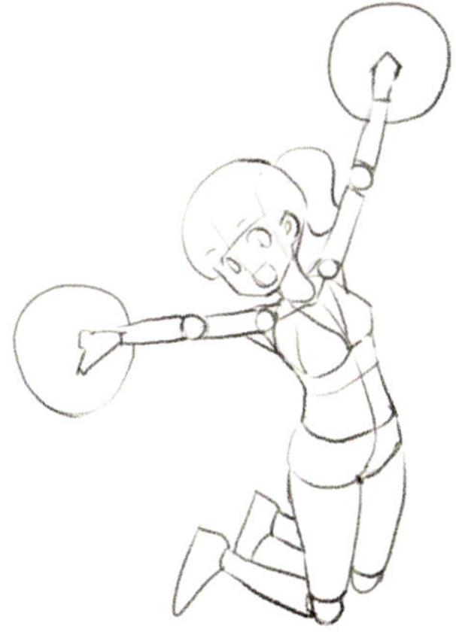

2 Turn your stick figure into a three-dimensional doll figure.

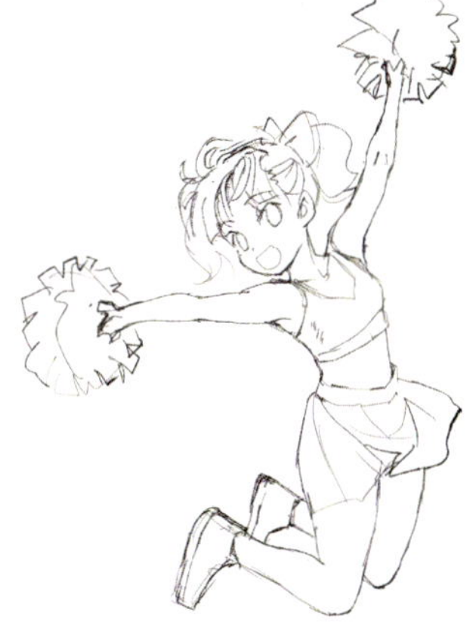

3 Add the details and clean up your lines.

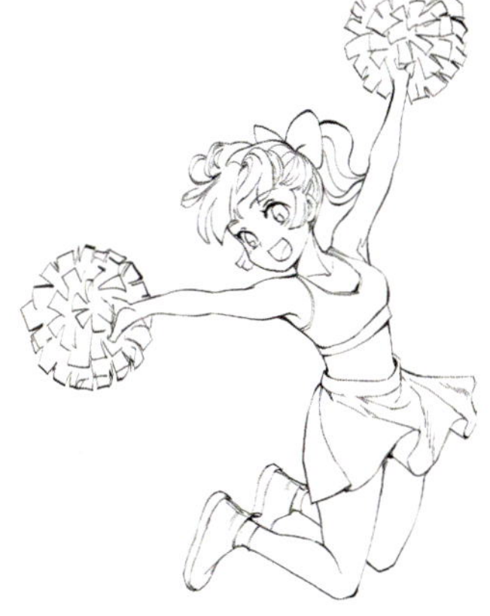

4 Ink the art.

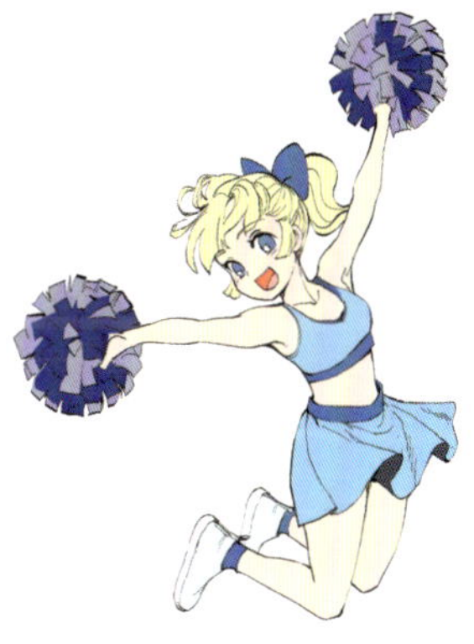

5 Add your base colours.

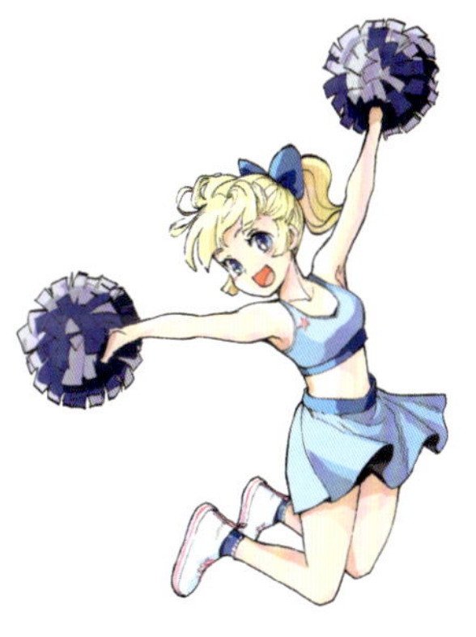

6 Add the tones.

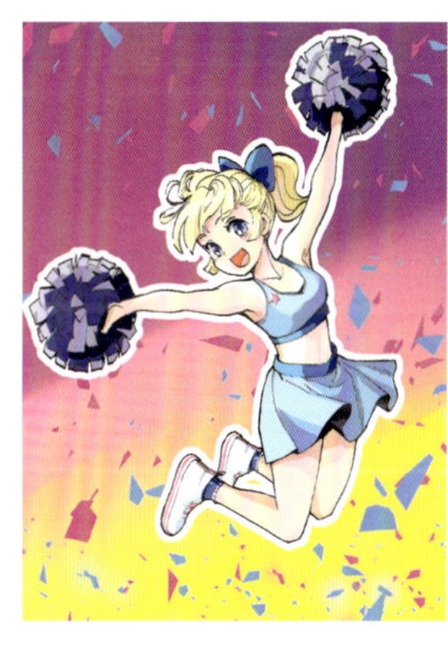

7 Add the background.

DRAW AT AN APPROPRIATE SIZE

Manga illustrations that will be professionally printed and published are usually drawn at a larger size than they will appear in print. That way, a higher resolution can be achieved, and the final print quality will be better.

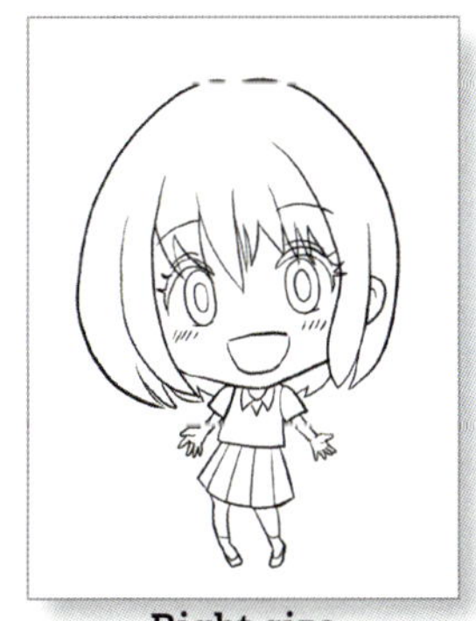

Right size

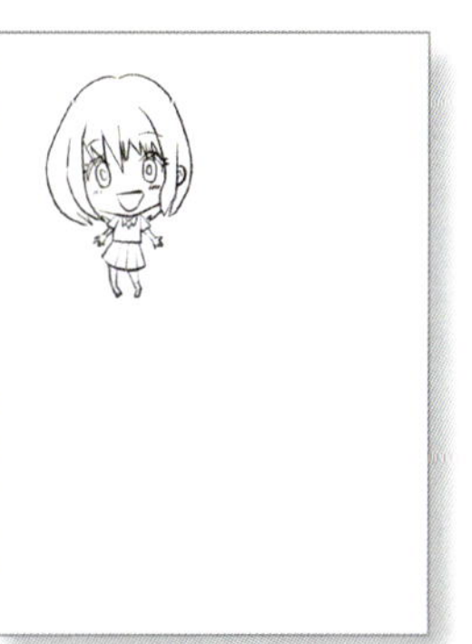

Too small

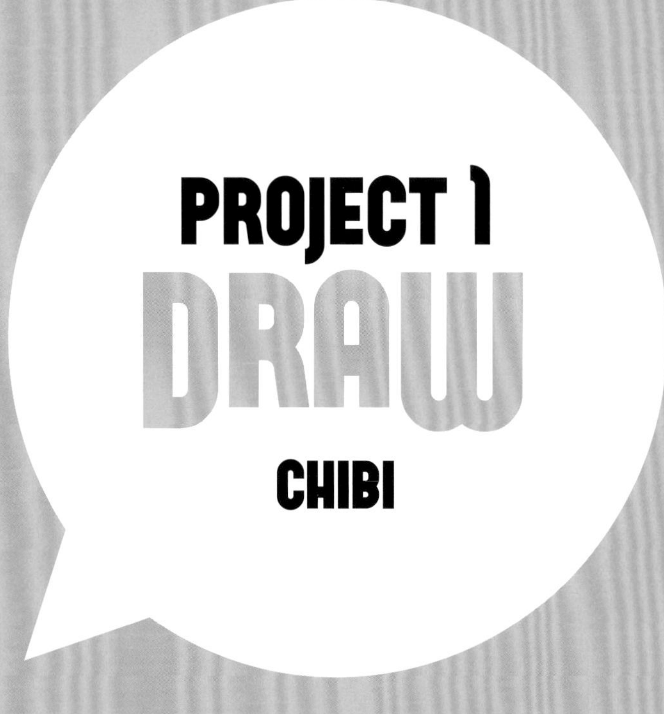

PROJECT 1
DRAW
CHIBI

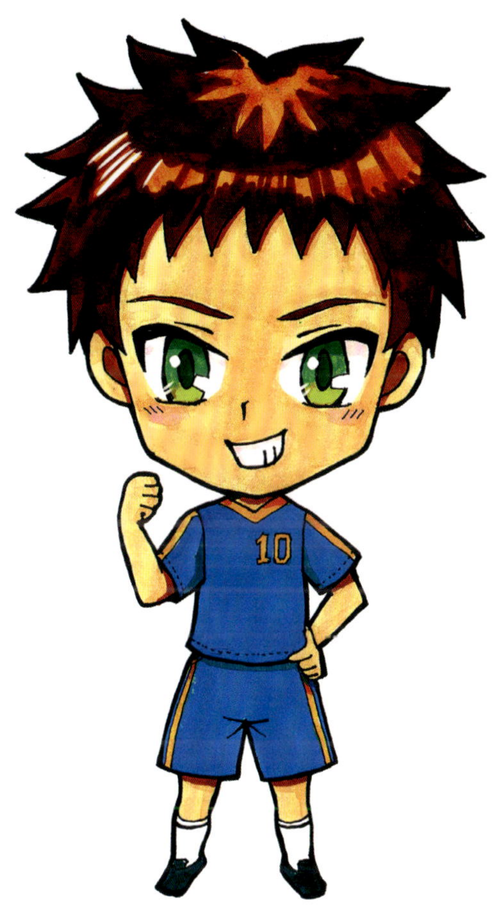

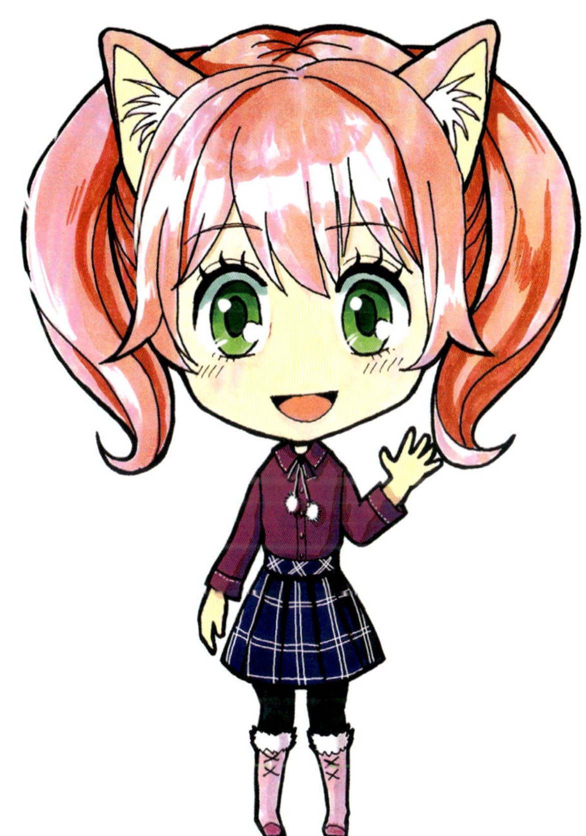

It's time to start drawing manga! In this project, I will show you how to draw a chibi character. This is a very popular style of manga in which the characters have a huge head, but it's on a tiny body. The chibi style is also well known for the character's huge eyes. Drawing a chibi is a fun and easy way to get to know manga style.

STAGE 1

DRAWING THE HEAD

Start off by drawing a circle and making lines and marks to guide you. Aim to get a well-balanced face shape and facial parts. Use faint lines and marks, so they will be easier to remove after completing the steps.

Making a neat circle is essential for drawing faces freehand, so practise drawing them if you need to **(see page 12).**

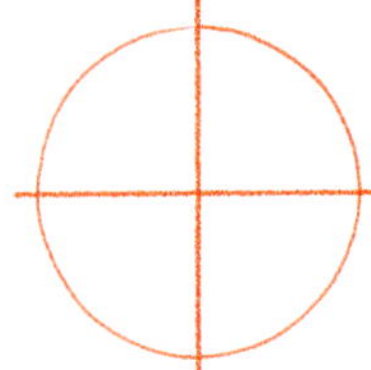

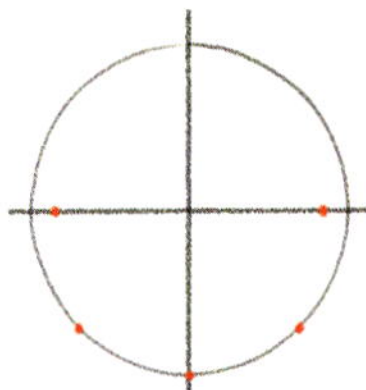

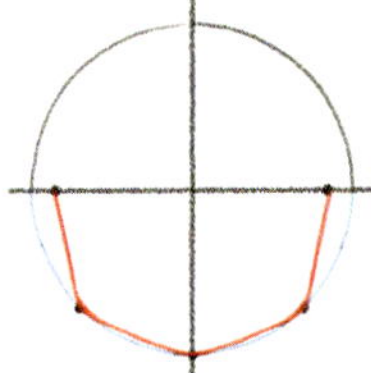

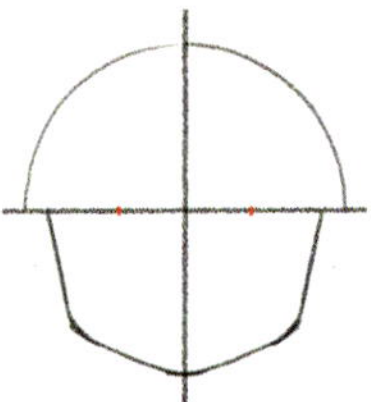

1 Draw a circle on the upper half of the paper. Add vertical and horizontal central lines to divide it into exact quarters. Use a ruler to keep the lines straight and at right angles. Check your shapes to ensure they are exactly the same (you can use an eraser if you need to fix them).

2 Add marks just inside the horizontal line, in the middle of the curve on the two bottom quarters and where the vertical line meets the base of the circle.

3 Connect these marks with a straight line to make a jaw shape. Make slightly rounded corners for the cheeks and a thin chin.

4 Erase the bottom circle and check again to ensure the shape is symmetrical. On each side of the face, add an eye position mark on the horizontal line, halfway between the vertical line and edge of the face.

BOY

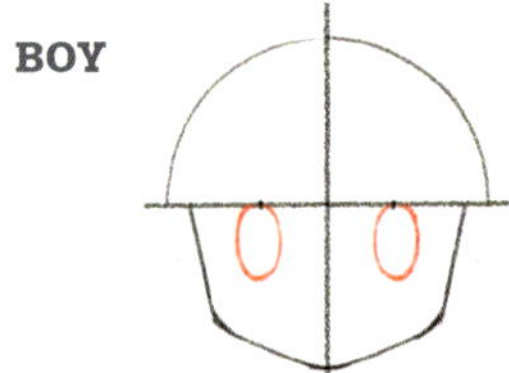

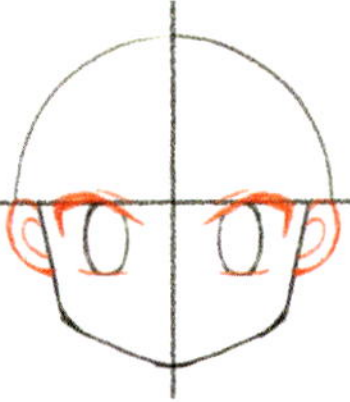

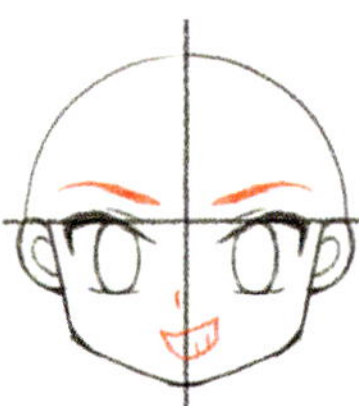

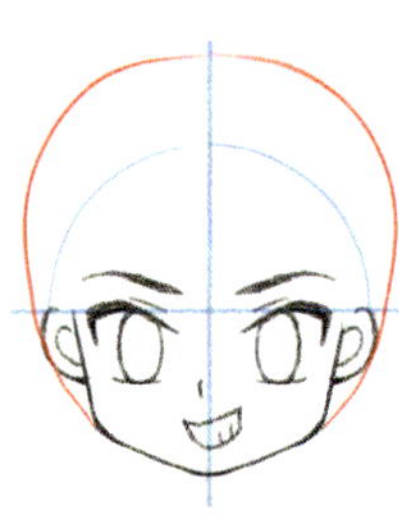

GIRL

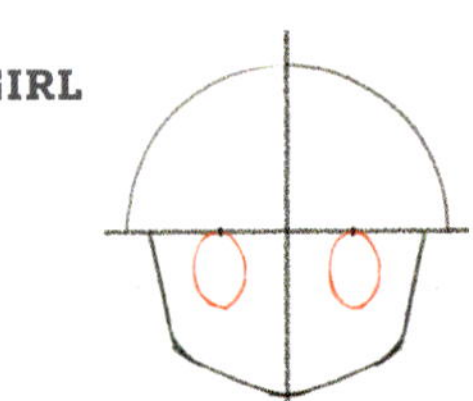

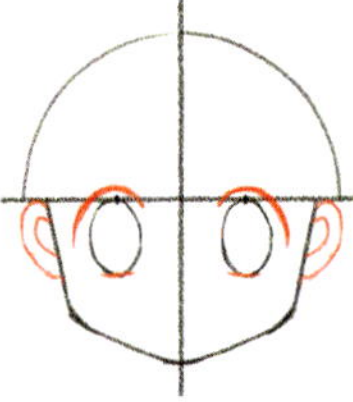

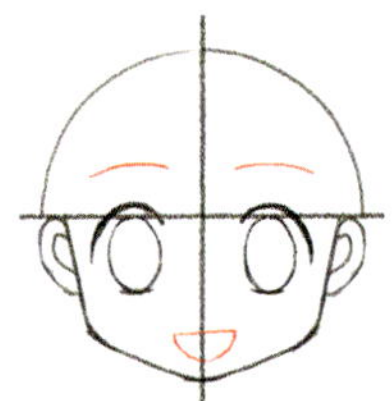

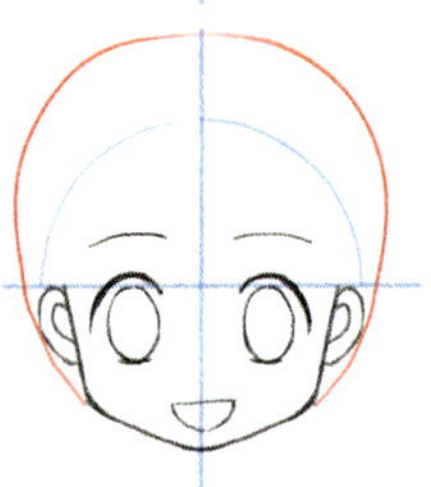

5 Draw ovals underneath each of the two marks. Check that they are the same size and height, and they should be the same distance from the vertical line. Bigger ovals are good for girls.

6 Draw the eyelids, making the lines mirror images of each other. Take care that both start and end at the same height. Straighter eyelids are best for boys and rounder ones are suitable for girls. Add ears, placing them at the same height as the eyes.

7 Add eyebrows above the eyelids. Typically, eyebrows on boys are thicker than those on girls. Next, add a mouth. A dot nose or no nose at all is fine for chibi.

8 Add a helmet shape above the upper circle by drawing a half-circle. (This will be the shape of the skull.) Erase the original circle and two central lines.

HAIR

To help you draw hair, divide it into three parts: the fringe (aka 'bangs'), the sides and the top. Make neat outlines of the small tufts (shapes representing clumps of hair) and avoid trying to draw individual hairs randomly.

BOY

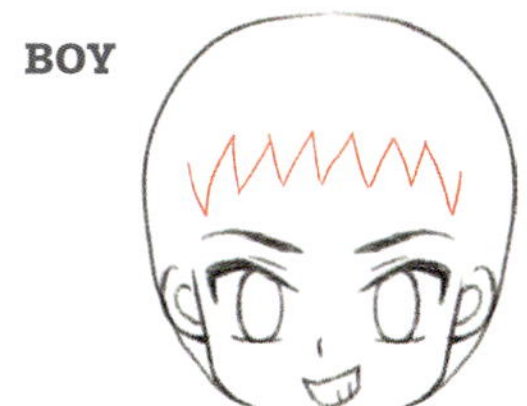

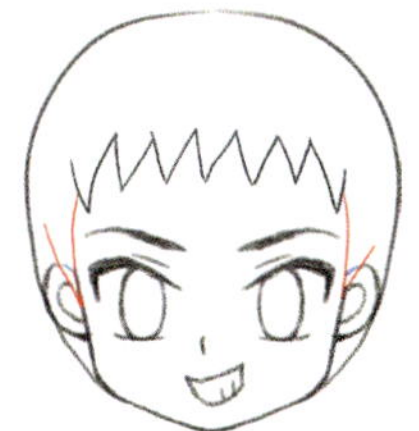

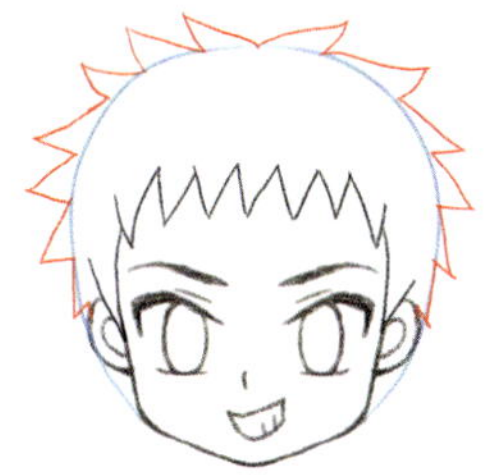

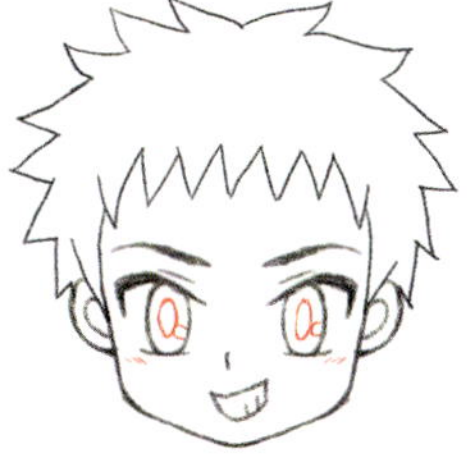

GIRL

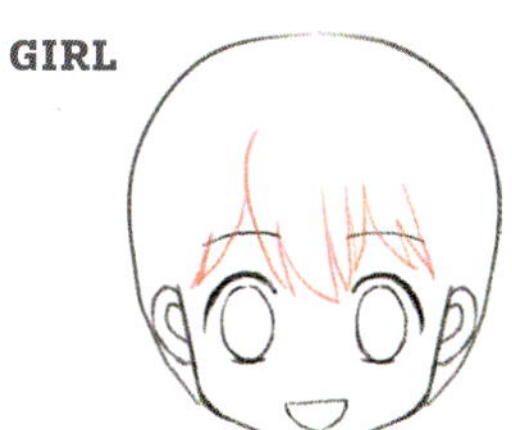

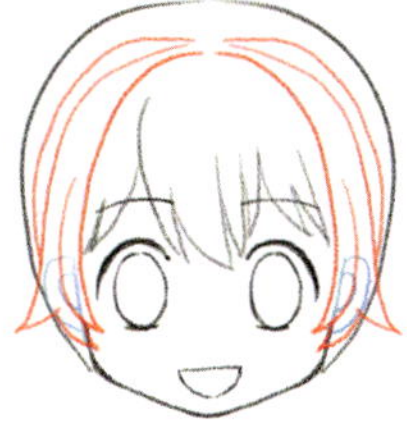

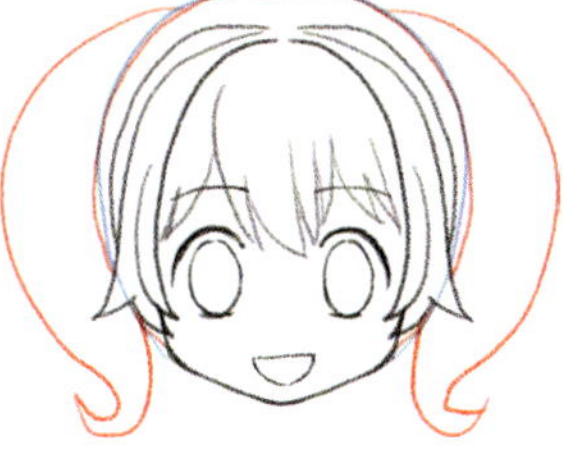

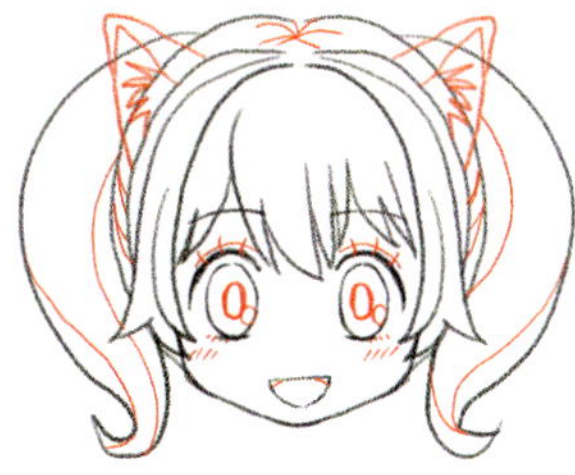

1 Draw the fringe as tufts, not individual hairs. Make these tufts a similar length, but add a little variation to make the fringe look more natural.

2 Add the hair along the sides of the face. The tufts should go halfway down and slightly in front of the ear. You may also wish to draw some tufts in front of the ears for girls.

3 Now add the hair at the top of the head. For short hair, draw triangular shapes neatly above the helmet circle (to keep the head shape round). You can add pigtails or a ponytail for girls. Keep both sides the same height and shape.

4 Erase the helmet line. Your chibi head is now ready to add the final details such as pupils in the eyes and teeth. See below for some suggestions.

ADD THE DETAILS

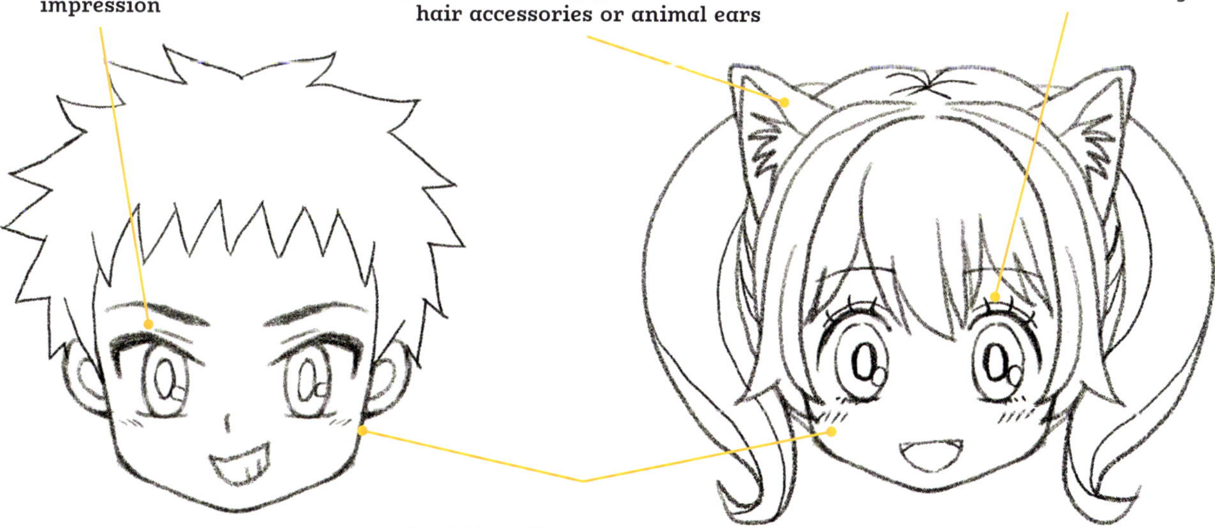

STAGE 2

DRAWING THE BODY

The proportions for chibi figures are based on being two to three heads tall – the height of the head I use is the same as the body.

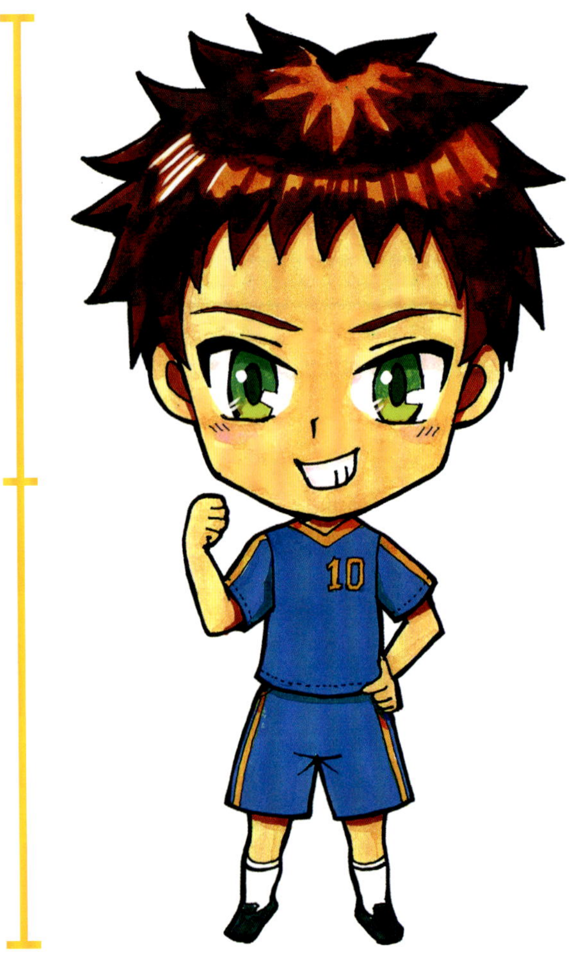

STEPS 1—4 (THESE ARE THE SAME FOR THE BOY AND GIRL)

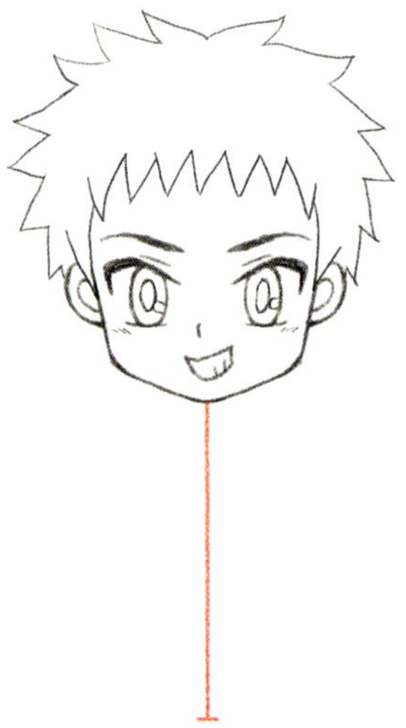

1 Measure the height of the head and draw a vertical line of the same length down from the centre of the chin. Mark a base line for the feet.

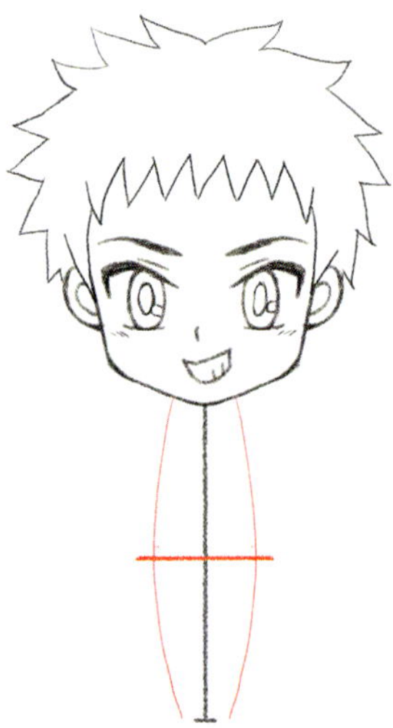

2 Draw a cucumber-like shape and halve it horizontally. Check carefully that both sides are the same width from the vertical line.

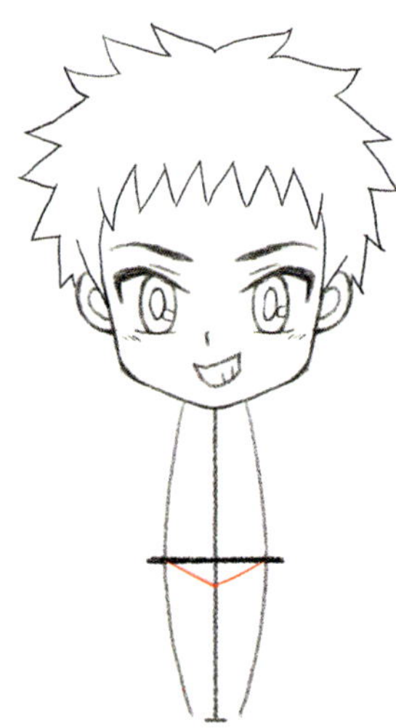

3 Add an upside-down triangle under the horizontal line to mark the joints where the body's torso meets the legs.

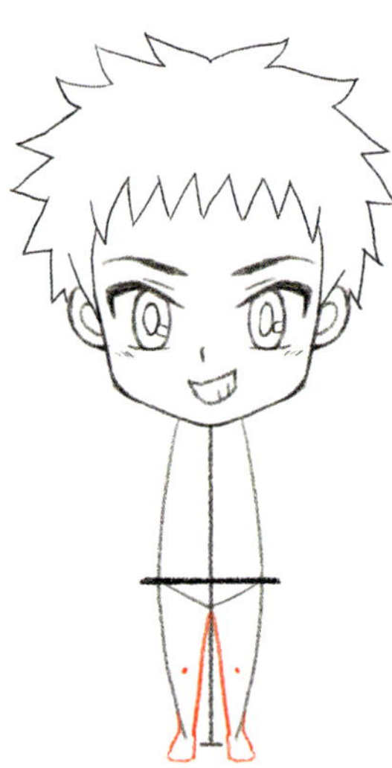

4 Draw two diagonal lines to create the shape of the character's legs. Add the feet at the end of the legs, as well as dots for the knees.

CAUTION

Check the angle of the feet: are they perfectly side on? People don't normally turn their ankles to 180 degrees unless they're a ballet dancer! Create a front view (see step 4) or a three-quarter view instead.

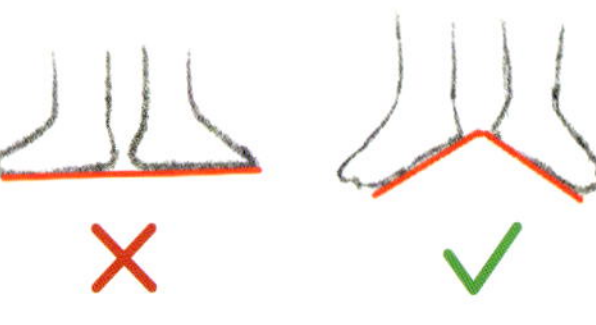

BOY

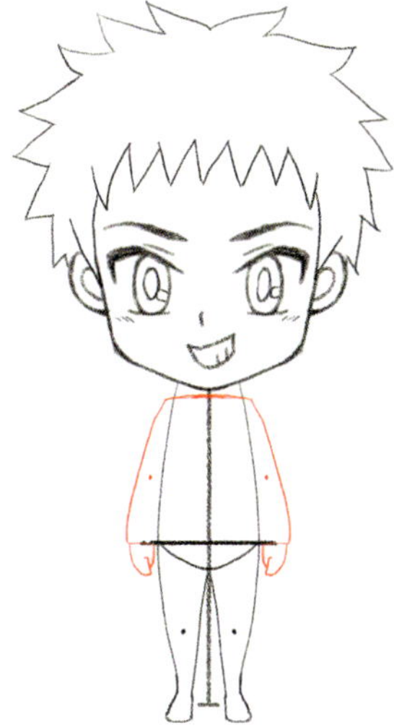

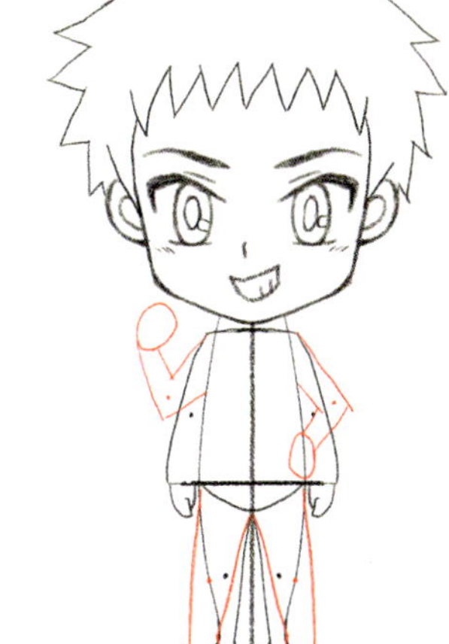

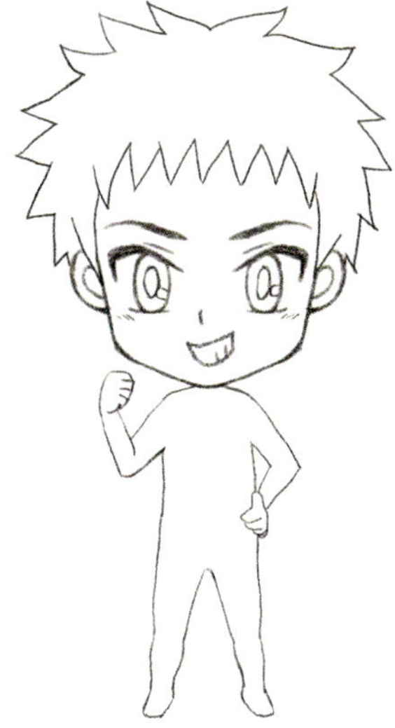

GIRL

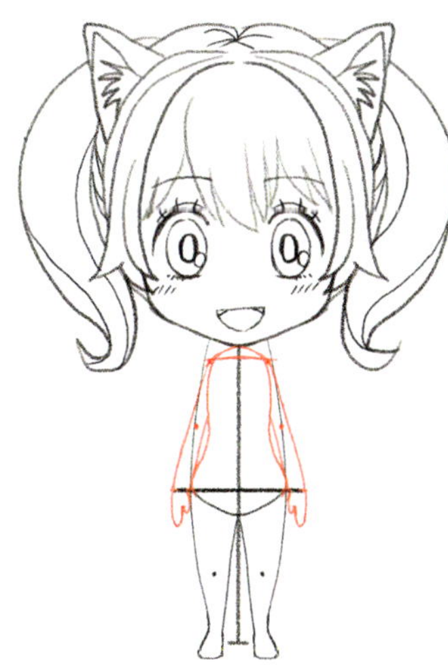

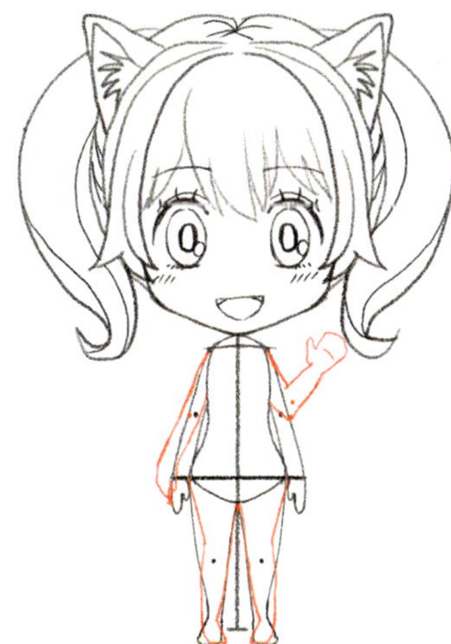

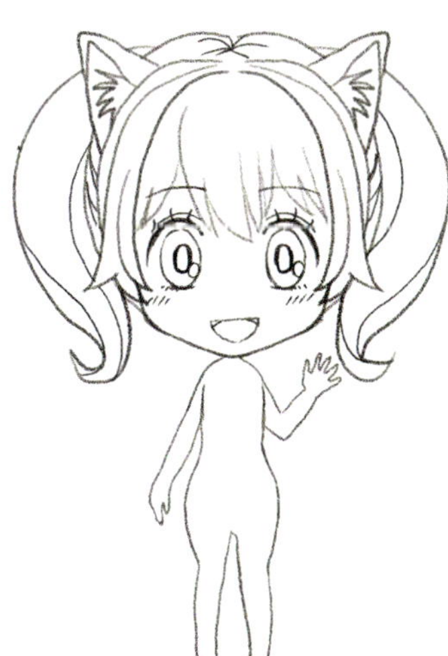

5 Draw a horizontal line for the shoulders, and then add a line at each end to start the arms. The final shape for your arms will be a trapezoid. For girls, draw narrower shoulders and make the body pear shaped. Add arm lines from the shoulders to the body's horizontal line. Add hands at the end of the arms, and dots halfway up the arms for the elbows.

6 At this point you can modify your character to strike a pose. You can make the limbs bend at the dots added for the knees and elbows. Be careful to keep limbs at their original length and avoid stretching or shrinking them.

7 Erase all the guide lines and marks and clean up the body so it is ready to add clothing.

STAGE 3

DRESSING YOUR CHIBI

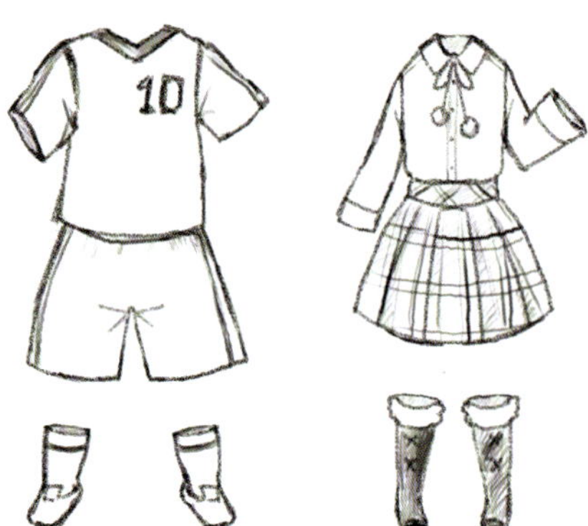

The final stage of creating your sketch is to add the clothing. Will your character be wearing shorts, trousers (aka 'pants'), a skirt or dress? Will the tops have long or short sleeves, and what will be on your chibi's feet? As you put together your fashion-forward chibi's outfit, don't forget to think about colours and any patterns on the fabric.

TOP

T-SHIRT

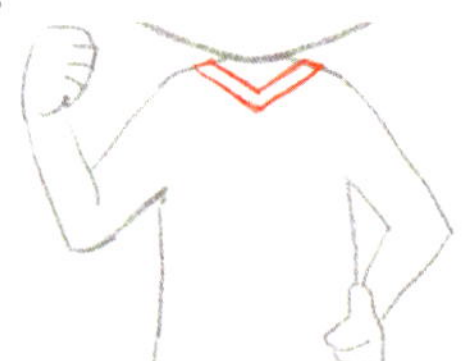

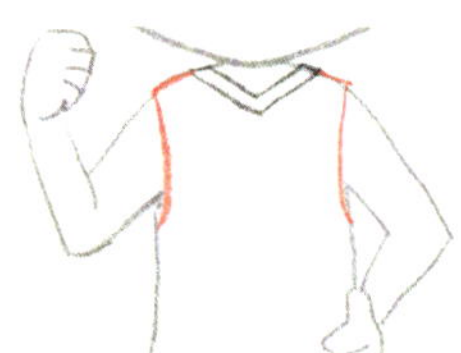

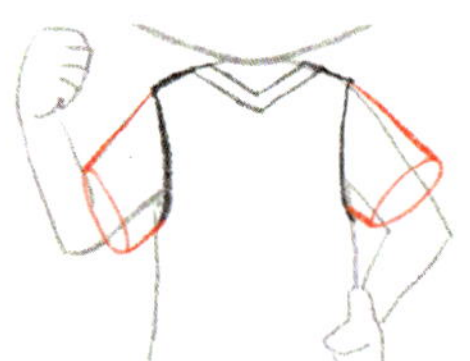

SHIRT OR BLOUSE

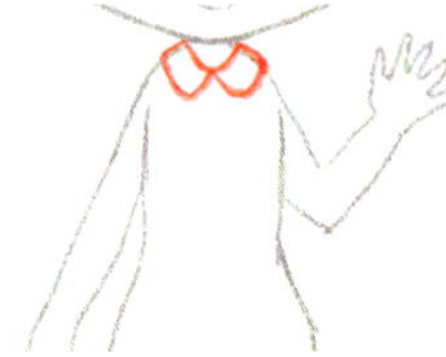

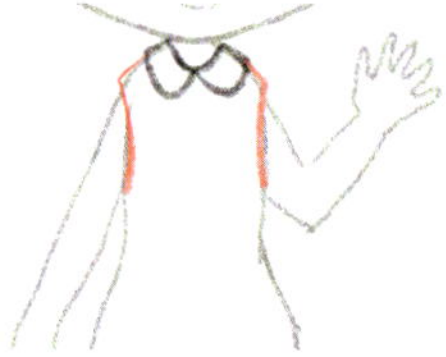

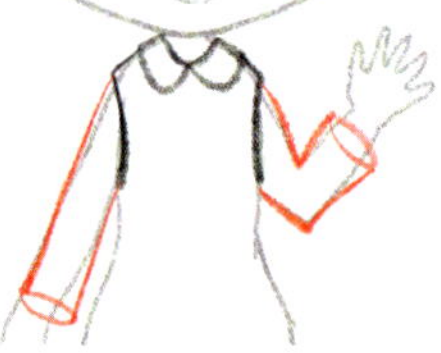

1 Choose a neckline. Add a collar if you wish.

2 Draw shoulder and armhole lines for your clothing. Loose clothing such as a T-shirt will have lines that drop a little from the shoulder.

3 To add sleeves, draw the cuff shape first: make a narrow oval shape that is wider than the arms. Next, draw the sides of the sleeves from the cuffs to the armholes.

T-SHIRT

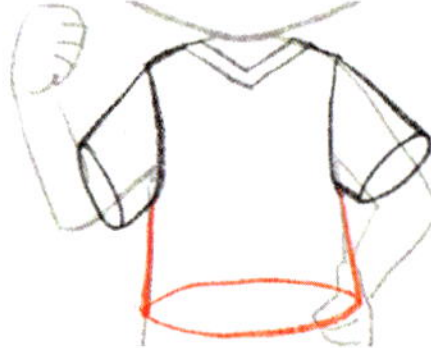

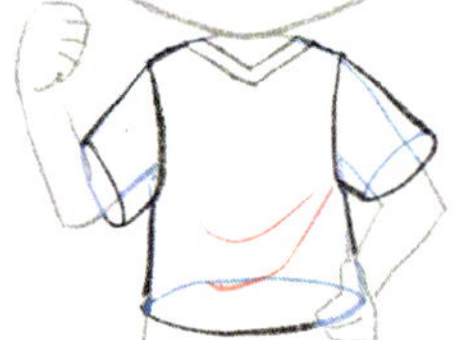

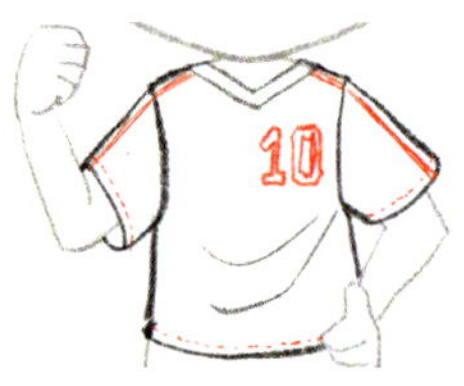

SHIRT OR BLOUSE

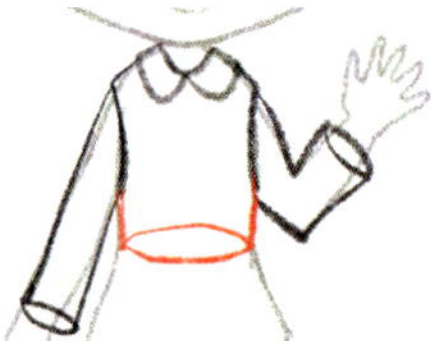

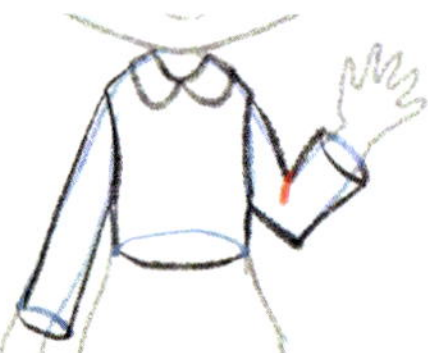

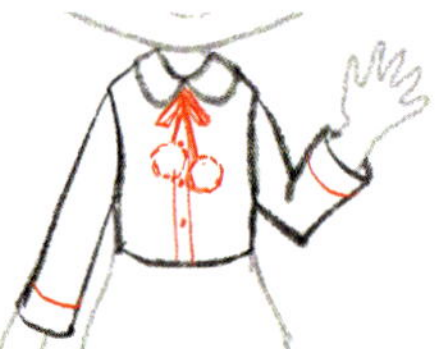

4 Draw another oval for the base of the shirt, then draw the sides of the shirt to connect the base to the armholes.

5 Erase the parts that should no longer be visible, then draw in some creases.

6 Add any details such as a pattern, buttons, turned-over cuffs, ribbons or patches.

SHORTS OR TROUSERS

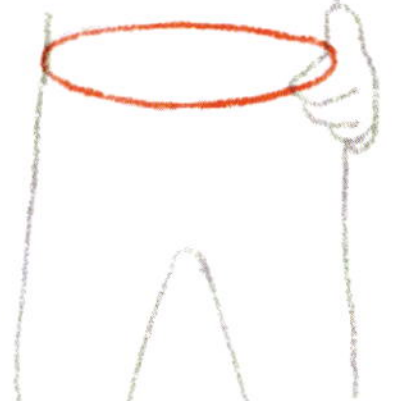
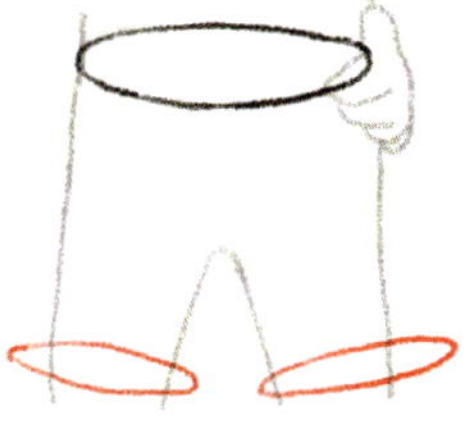
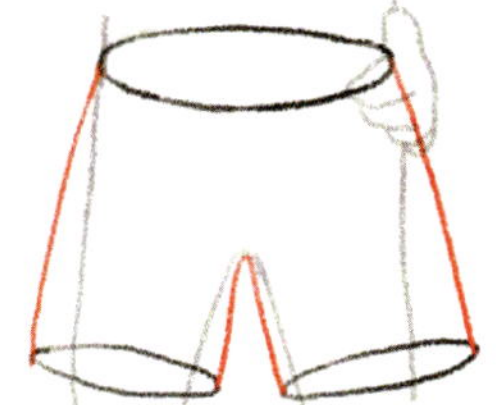
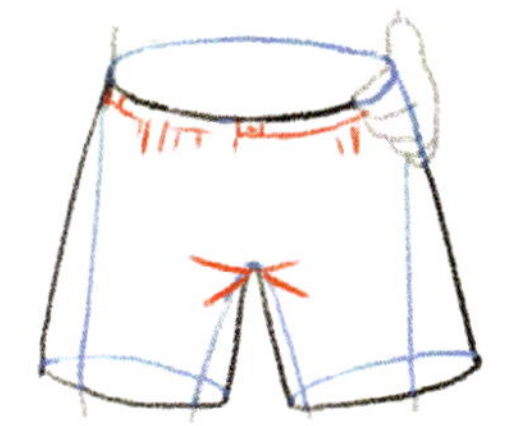
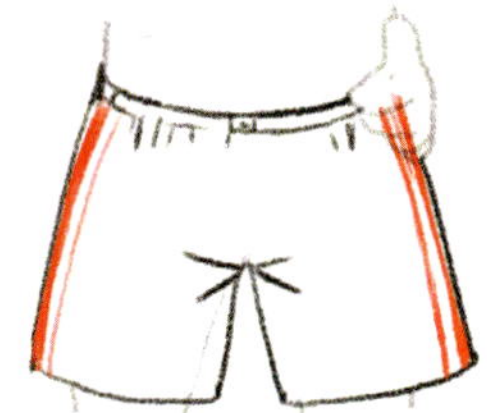

1 Draw an oval for the waist.

2 Draw ovals for the bottom of the shorts or trousers. Make sure they are wider than the character's legs.

3 Connect the ovals to make the sides of the shorts or trousers.

4 Erase the lines that should no longer be visible. Draw a waistband and add creases.

5 Add any other details, such as a pattern or seams.

SKIRT

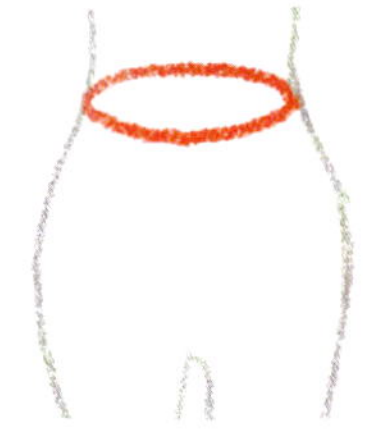
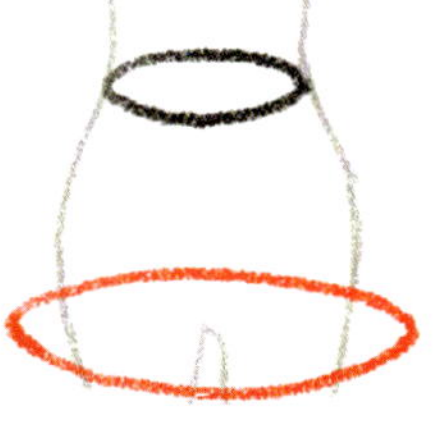
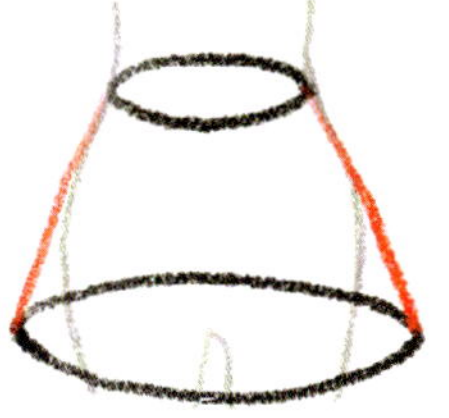
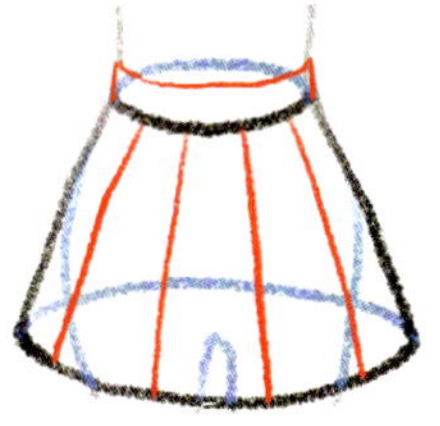
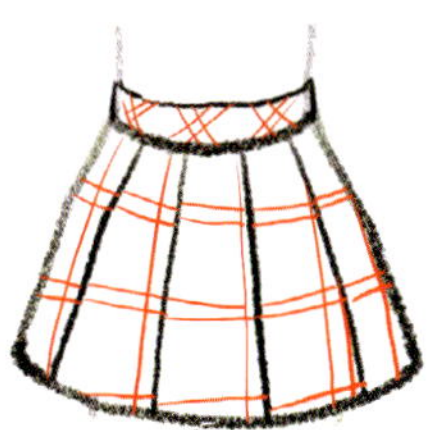

1 Draw an oval for the waist.

2 Draw an oval for the hem; it should be wider than the waist.

3 Connect the ovals to make a shape like a lampshade.

4 Erase the lines that should no longer be visible. Draw a waistband and add some pleats.

5 Add any other details, such as a pattern, pockets or seams.

SHOES AND BOOTS

SHOES

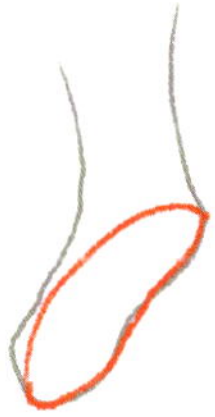
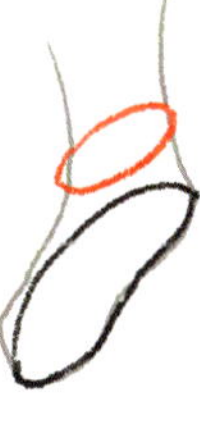
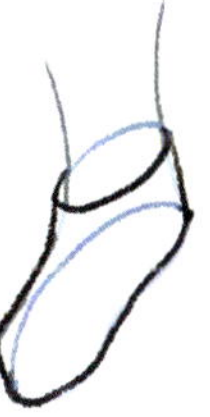
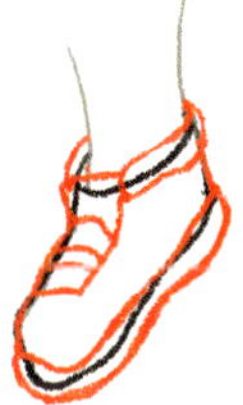

BOOTS

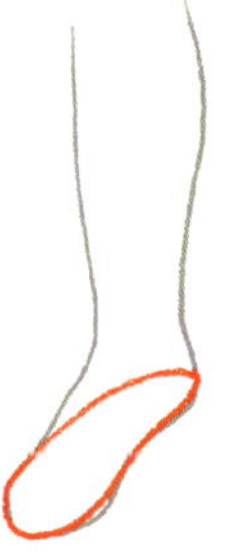
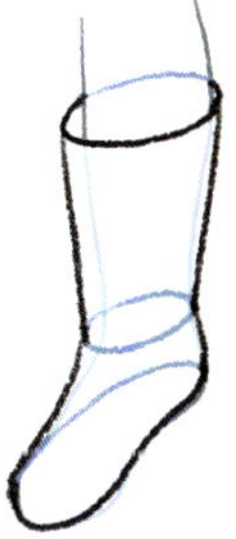
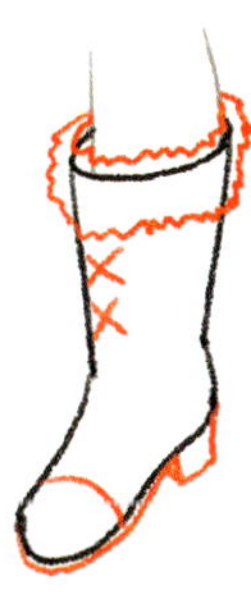

1 Draw the sole – it should be the shape of a footprint.

2 Draw the ankle holes of the shoes. They should be wider than the legs.

3 Draw the sides of the shoes or boots, joining the soles to the ankle holes.

4 Erase the lines that should no longer be visible and add any details.

STAGE 4

CLEANING UP YOUR SKETCH

Remove all the guide lines and marks that will not be part of your final drawing. Check all your lines for clean strokes and ensure they are fully connected where they meet. Make sure the lines aren't overlapping, and that there are no unnecessary gaps. Make a final check for any errors in your drawing – for example, checking the positions of the thumbs, eyebrows, ears and so on.

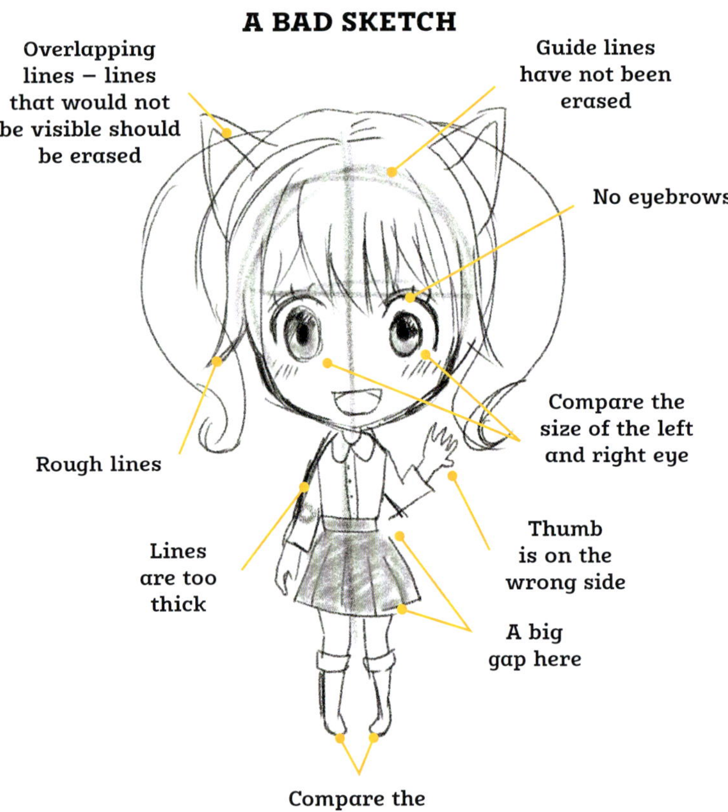

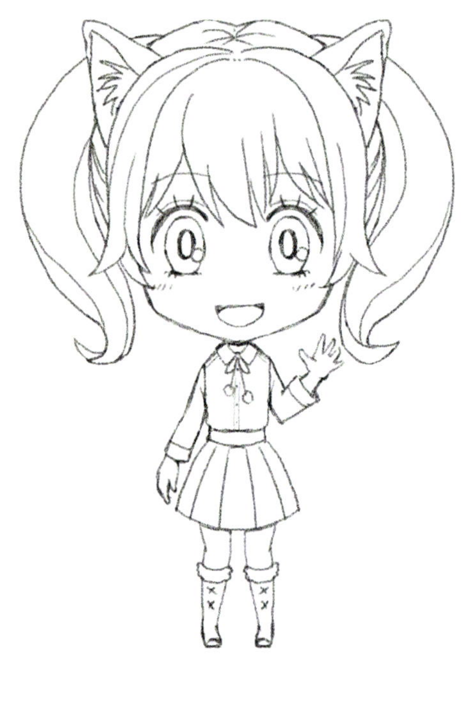

TIP

It may be a good idea to completely erase your pencil lines if your drawing has a lot of rough lines. You will still be able to see faded lines (these are called ghost lines) on the paper, and you can trace them for a cleaner finish.

CHECKLIST

- Ensure the sketch lines are not too thick and that the guide lines and marks have all been cleanly removed.
- Check there are no overlapping lines or any unnecessary gaps between them.
- Look out for and correct any other common errors – especially the positions of the thumbs and the facial details.

STAGE 5

FINISHING OFF

The final stages are simplifying the lines and tidying up your art, then planning on where to add the details.

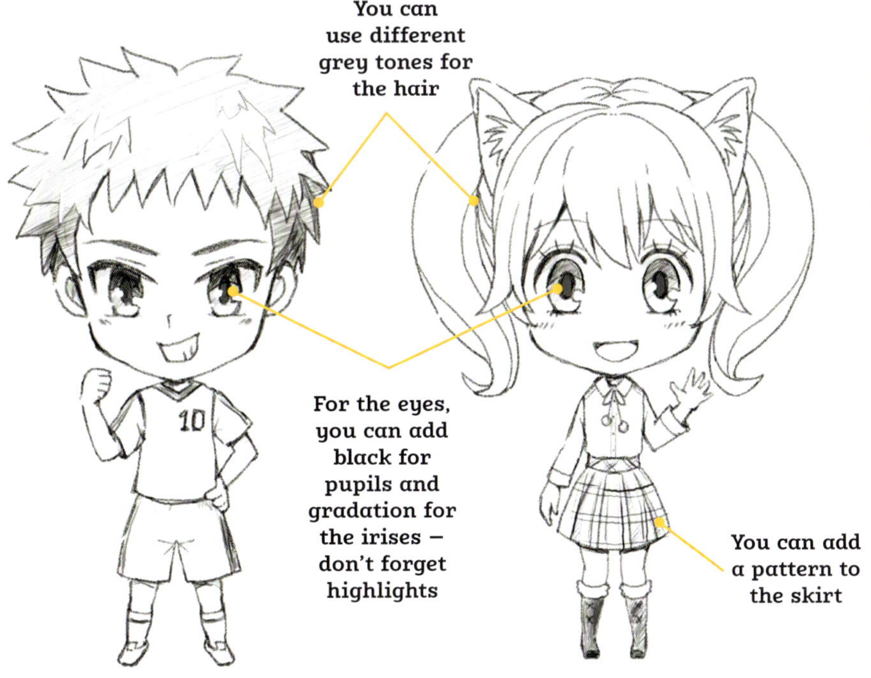

ADDING TONE, TEXTURE AND FINAL DETAILS

At this stage, you have a clean drawing but one that is lacking in detail. The final stage is to add some simple pencil shading and any details you wish to include.

COLOUR FINISH

Ink and markers are popular tools for colouring in manga art. You can find the details for how to use them in projects 8 and 9 (see pages 98–123).

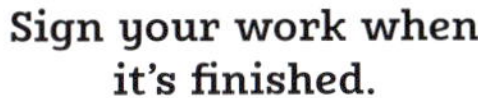

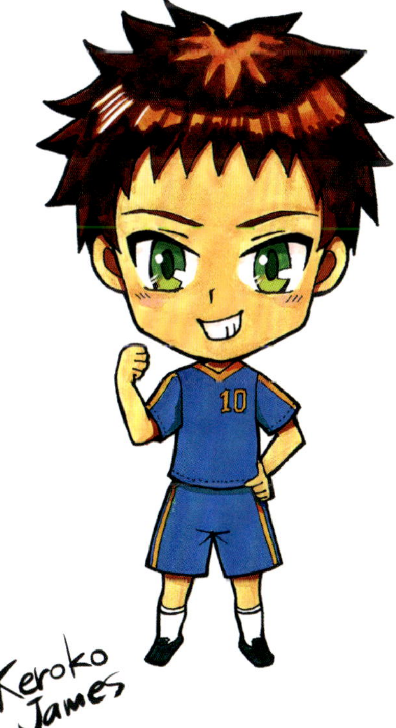

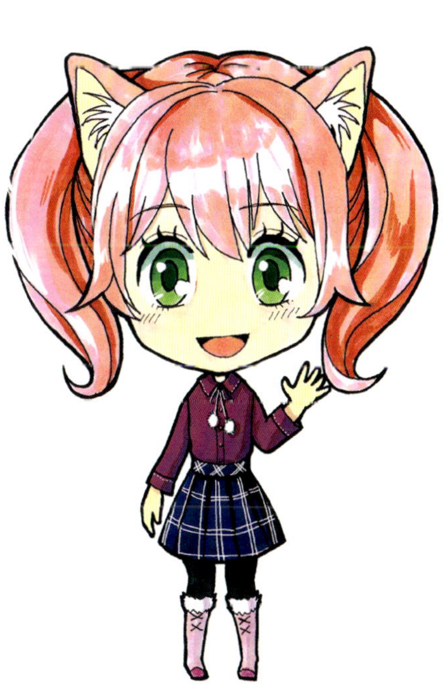

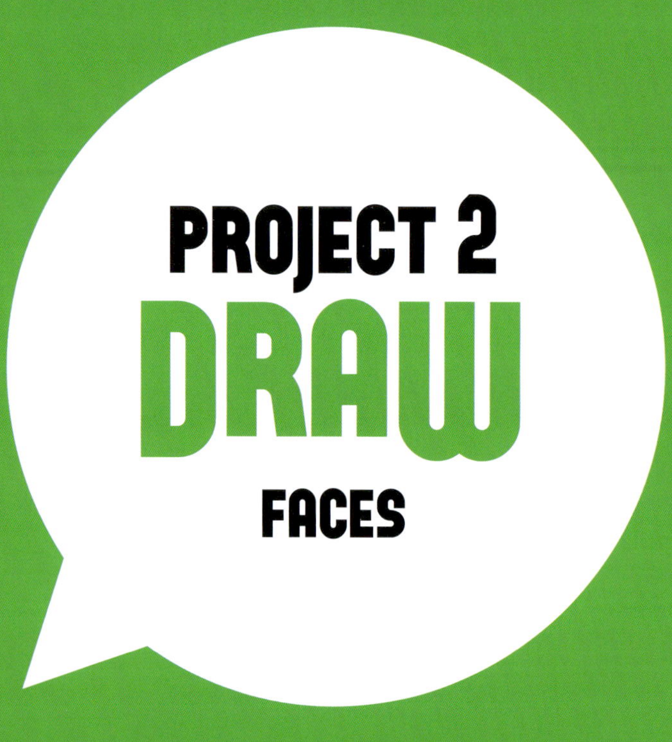
PROJECT 2
DRAW
FACES

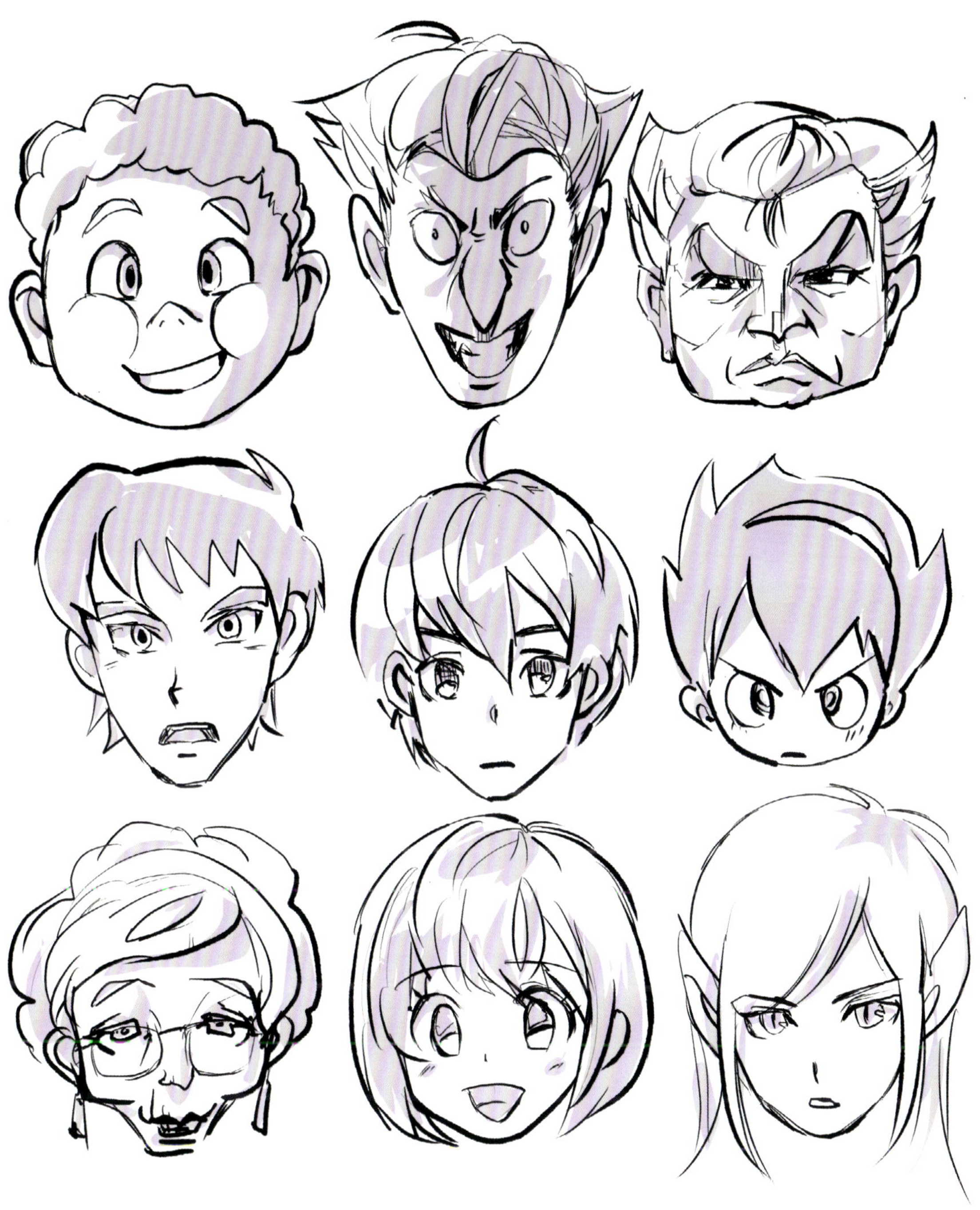

In this project, you'll discover everything you need to know to draw manga faces, from young to old. Follow the step-by-step tutorial first, then use the tips and techniques in the rest of the project to learn how to draw different features and emotions. At the end of this section, there is an exercise for drawing nine different faces – use it to test out everything you've learned!

Facial proportions

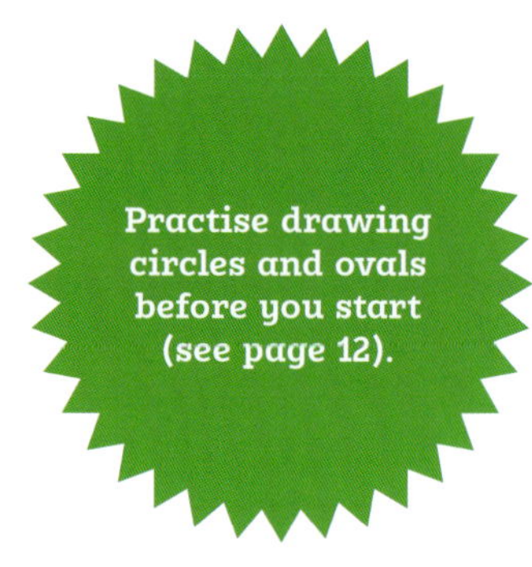

Before starting, examine these different styles of manga faces. Note the height of the eyes – I recommend drawing them lower than the central line on the face. In manga-style art, it is more appropriate to draw most of the facial features in the bottom half of the face and to make the forehead larger. All the faces start with a circle, but teen and realistic manga have a more oval shape.

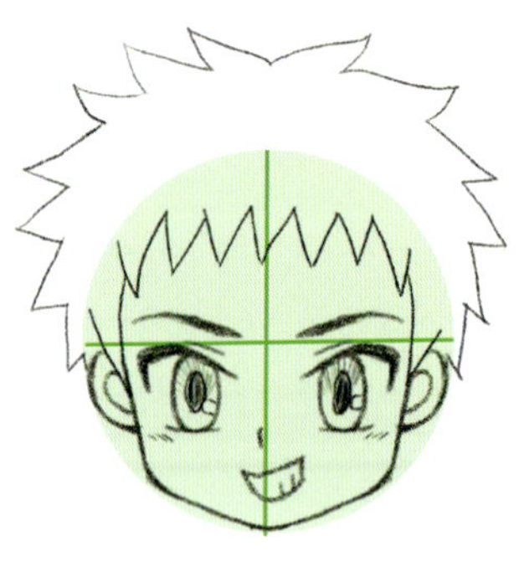

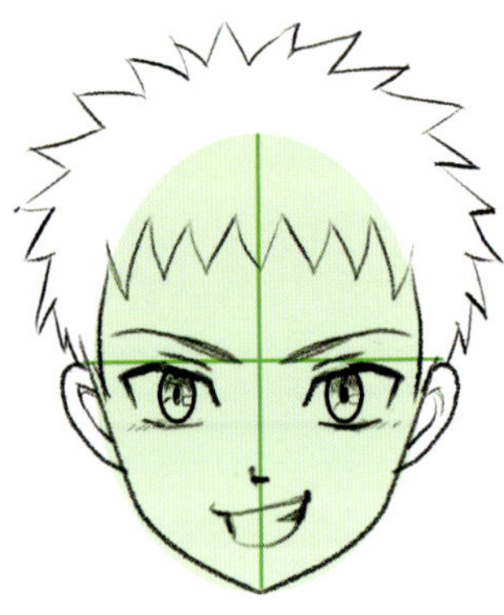

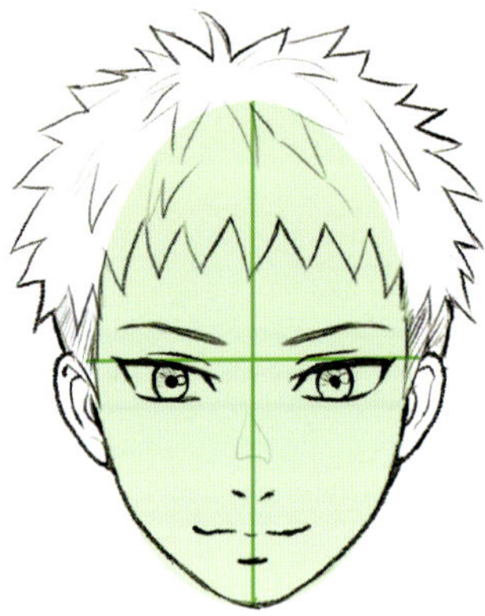

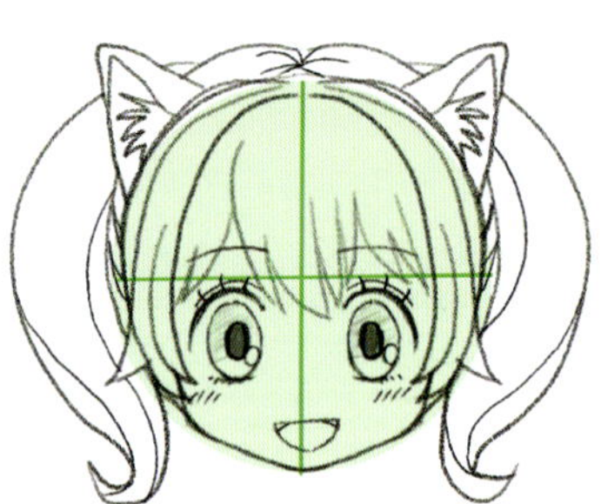

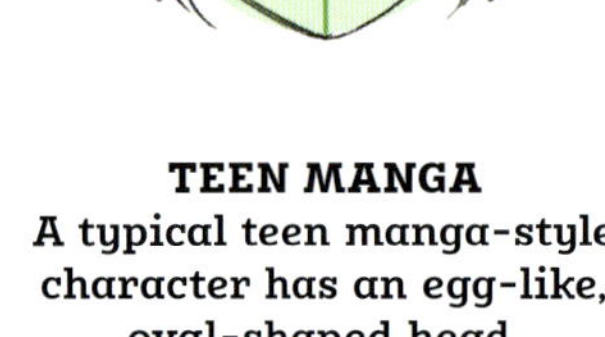

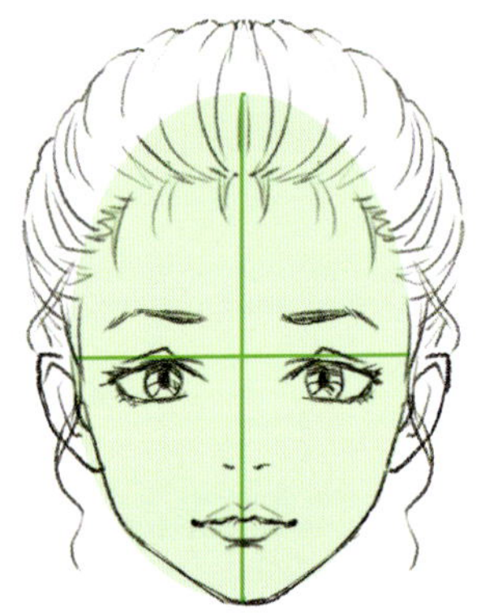

CHIBI
Chibi and cute characters have circular faces.

TEEN MANGA
A typical teen manga-style character has an egg-like, oval-shaped head.

REALISTIC MANGA
Characters in a more realistic style require longer ovals for their head.

PROPORTIONS ARE FLEXIBLE
Just as every person has a different face, every artist has a different way of drawing faces. Be flexible when deciding on the shape of the head and features (even the eye height), and experiment with different facial looks.

AGE AND FACIAL PROPORTIONS
Facial proportions also change by age. Here are the different stages and their changing features for drawing them. Note how the shape of the head gets longer with age.

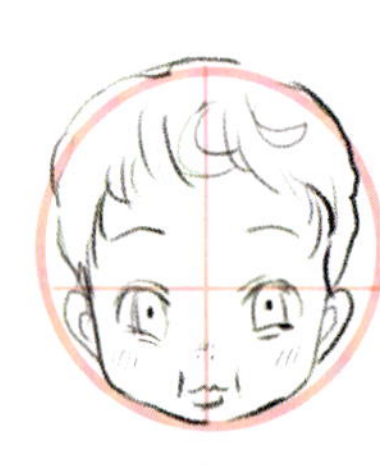

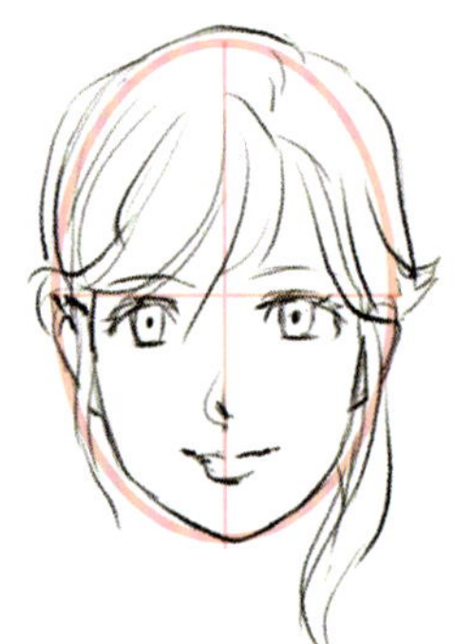

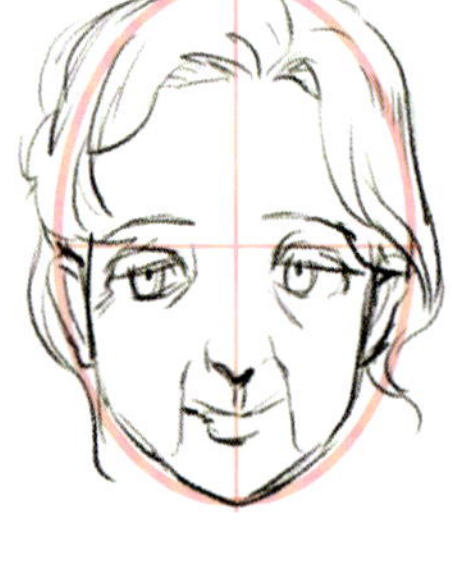

BABY **CHILD** **ADULT** **ELDERLY**

DRAWING THE HEAD

You can draw different types of faces by starting with a circle and and extending it to different heights along the vertical line. Here, I will demonstrate a typical teen manga character's face, starting from a circle with guide lines and marks, then creating the facial shape, adding features and finishing with the details. See pages 30 to 35 for more details on how to draw each of the facial features.

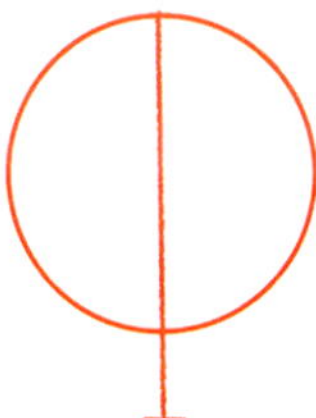

1 Using a pencil, draw a neat circle. Add a vertical midline, extending it a little below the head, then mark the end. The length will depend on the manga style and your character's age (see opposite).

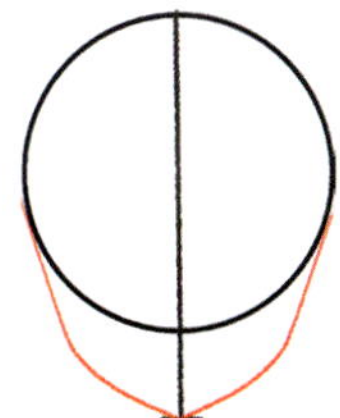

2 Draw in the shape of the jaw and chin. Bring the lines down from both sides, changing direction in the middle towards the chin point. The angles of the jaw and the chin should be slightly rounded.

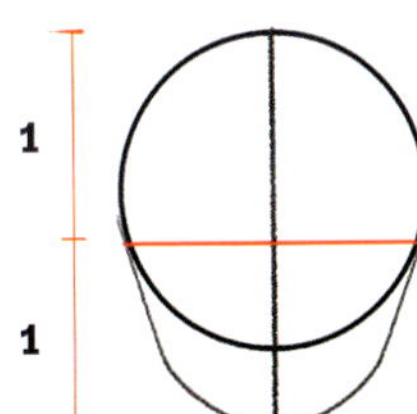

3 Measure the middle of the new shape and draw a horizontal line across it. It should be lower than the middle of the original circle. The eyes will be just below it.

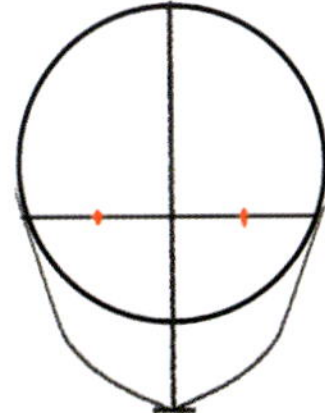

4 Find the right spot to draw the two eyes on the horizontal line. On each side, measure halfway between the vertical line and the edge of the face, then make a mark for the eye.

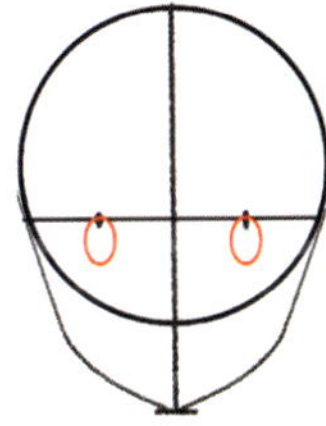

5 Draw ovals under the two marks for the eyes. They should be smaller than chibi eyes, but ensure you make them symmetrical.

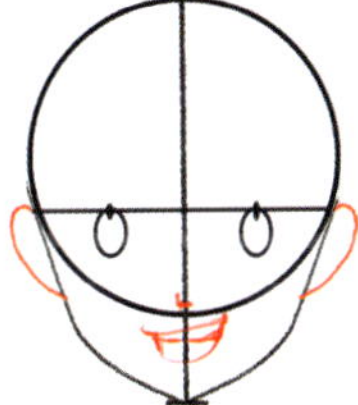

6 Draw the nose in about the middle of the lower half of the face, and draw the mouth underneath it. Add the ears; they should be positioned from the top of the eyes down to the nose.

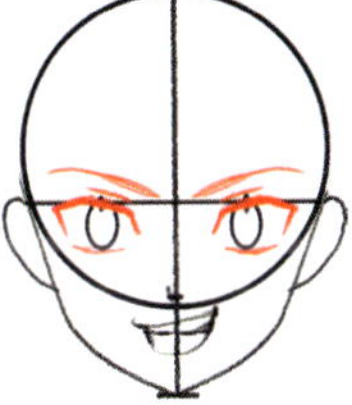

7 Add eyelids and eyebrows. (For eyelids and eyebrows on a chibi girl or boy, see page 18.)

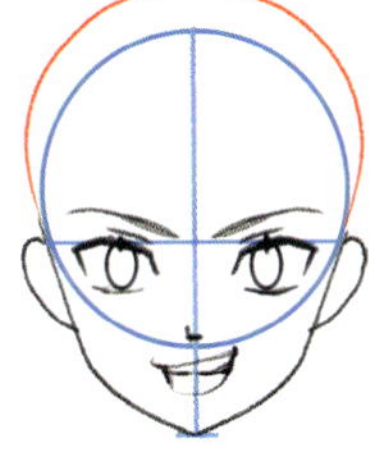

8 Draw a half-circle at the top of the existing circle, like a helmet. This will be the base for the hair shape, which is usually exaggerated in popular manga styles.

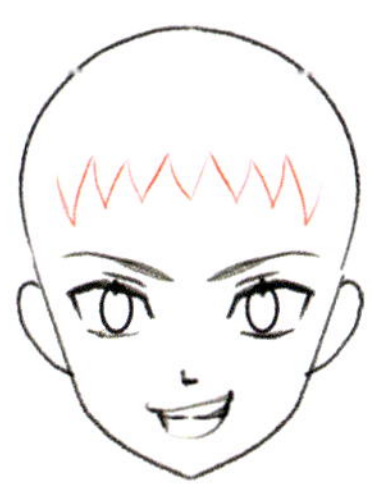

9 Erase all the guide lines and marks. Now begin to draw the hair, starting at the fringe.

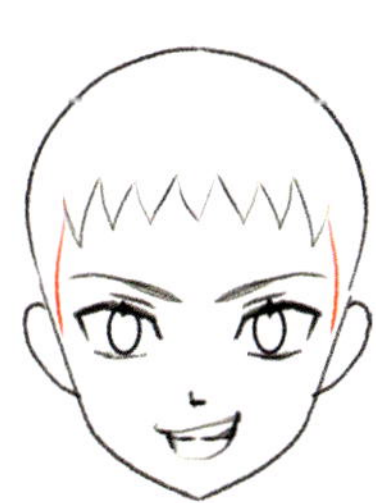

10 Draw hair along the sides of the head.

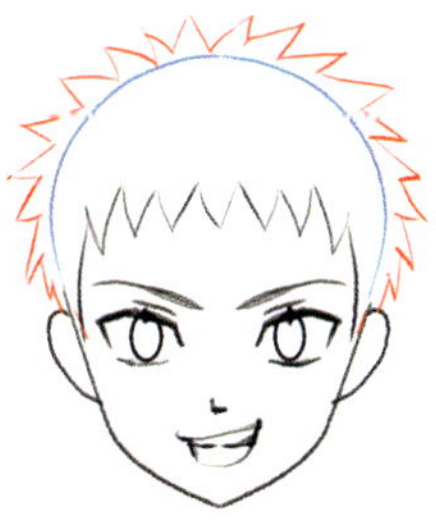

11 Draw the top of the hair, following the helmet shape you made in step 8.

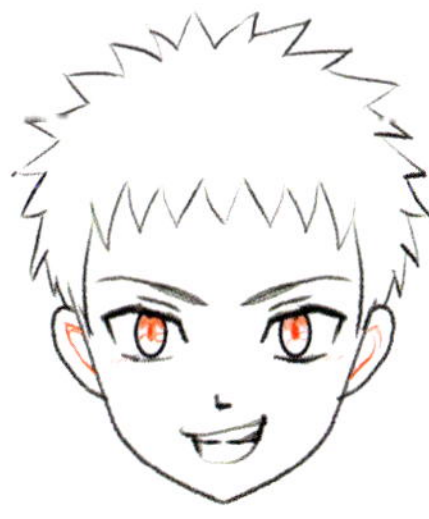

12 Erase the helmet line and clean up the other lines. Then add any final details such as those to the eyes and ears.

FOCUS ON:
DRAWING EYES

Manga eye types vary, and each artist draws them in a different way. Even the same character may have different styles of eyes to reflect their different emotions. Study range of styles of drawing eyes different artists use to build up your knowledge for future use.

EYES AND EYEBROWS

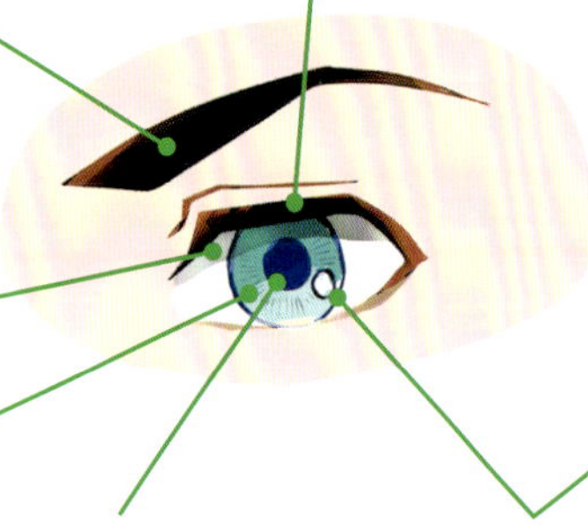
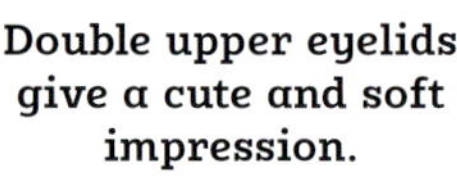

DRAWING EYES

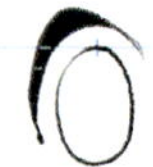
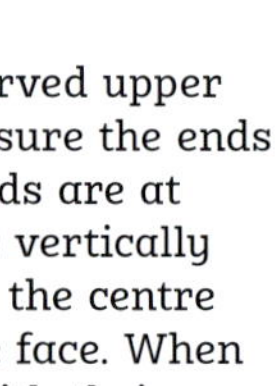
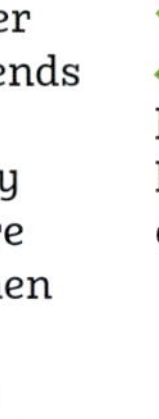
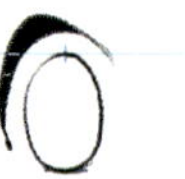
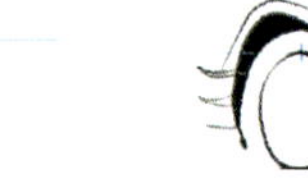

1 Decide the iris size and draw a pair of ovals or circles at the eye position. Check carefully they are the same height and the same distance from the central line and sides of the face.

2 Add the curved upper eyelids. Ensure the ends of the two eyelids are at the same points vertically as well as from the centre and sides of the face. When you're happy with their positions, make the lines thicker to give them weight.

3 Draw the bottom eyelids with thinner lines. Ensure the top and bottom eyelids form an almond eye shape.

4 Draw the eyelashes. You can also a second upper eyelid if you wish for a cuter look.

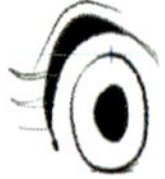
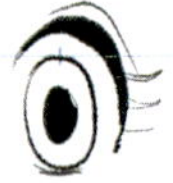
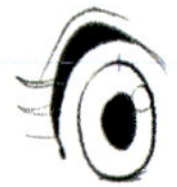
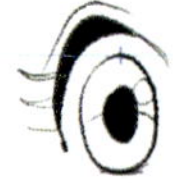
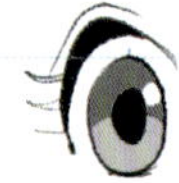

5 For the pupils, draw a smaller oval in the middle of each iris and fill them in with a dark shade or colour.

6 To create reflections of light in the eyes, draw one or more small circles on each eye, putting them on the same side of the eye.

7 If you wish to have a shadow from the eye sockets falling on the tops of the irises, draw a soft curved line across each iris.

8 Add the tones or gradations to the irises, leaving the reflections of light as white highlights.

EYE MOVEMENT

DRAWING SLEEPY EYES

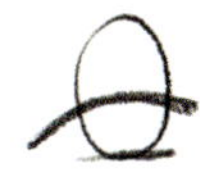
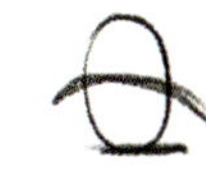
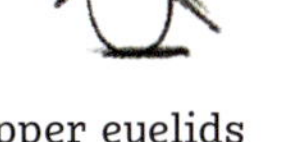
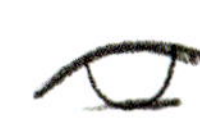
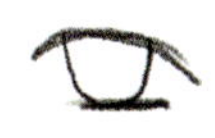
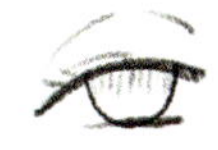
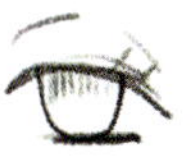
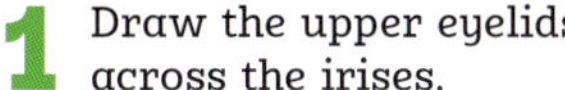

1 Draw the upper eyelids across the irises.

2 Remove the guide lines above the eyelids.

3 Add in details such as shading and eyelashes.

DRAWING SMILING EYES

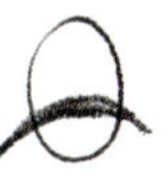
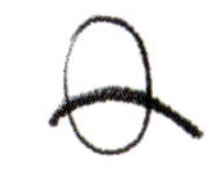
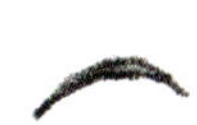
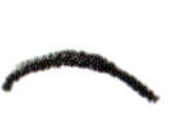
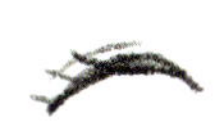
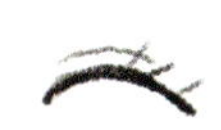

1 Add upper eyelids on the lower third of the irises.

2 Remove the lines above and below the eyelids.

3 Add in the details such as eyelashes.

IRIS POSITION

The irises can move in any direction, but usually together as a pair. Firstly, draw the eyelids, then draw the irises in the direction you want the character to look towards before adding in any details.

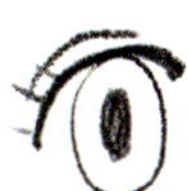
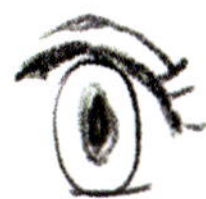

Look to the front

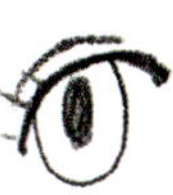
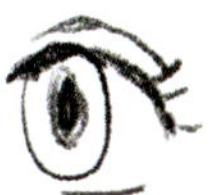

Look to the right

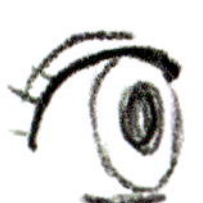
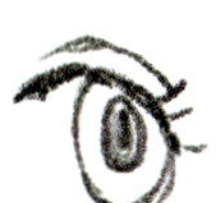

Look to the left

EYE AND EYEBROW POSITION

Be aware of the eye's vertical position. A manga face looks cuter when you draw a smaller face, so drawing eyes in the lower half of the head is my recommendation. The position and shape of the eyebrows will depend on the character's mood and emotions (see pages 36–37).

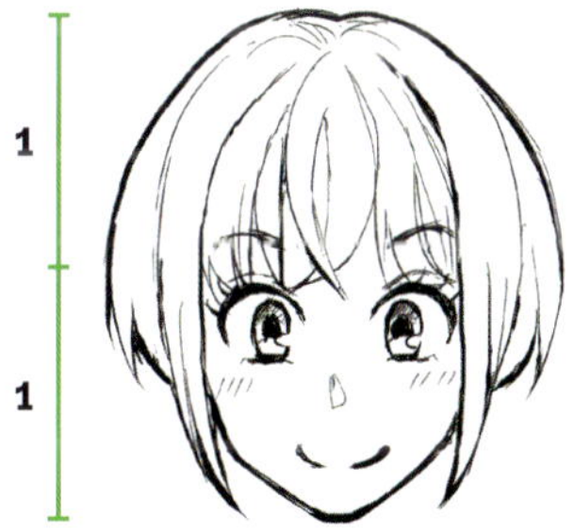

DRAWING EYEBROWS

Realistic eyebrows are often a little wider than the eyes. Keep the ends of the eyebrows the same height on both sides. The curve of the eyebrow rises up two-thirds of the way, starting from the end that's near the nose, then drops down towards the end that's closer to the ear.

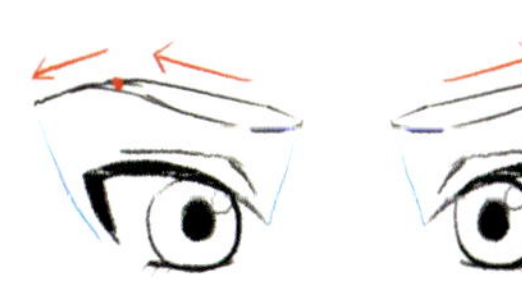
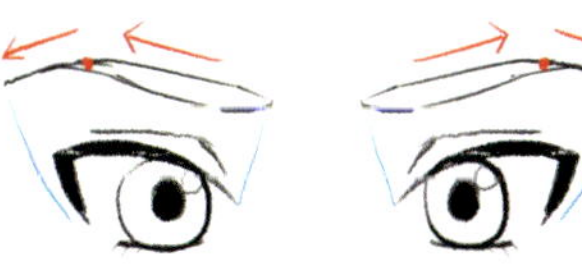

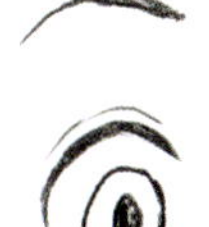
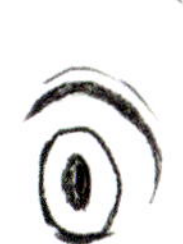

High

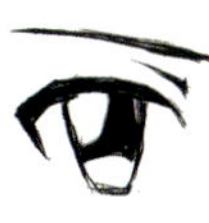
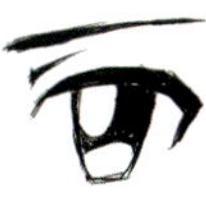

Middle

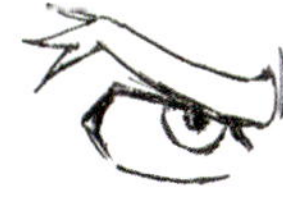
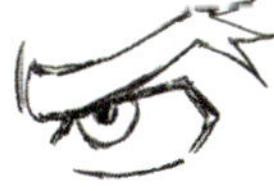

Low

EYE GALLERY

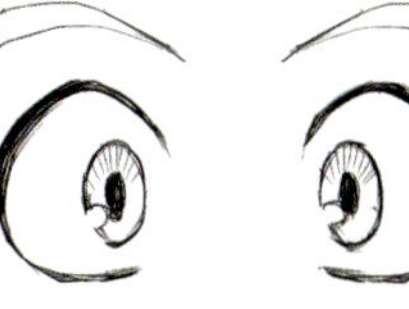
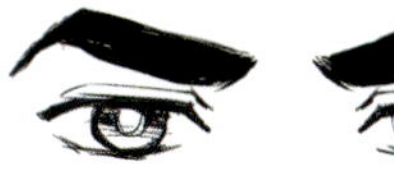
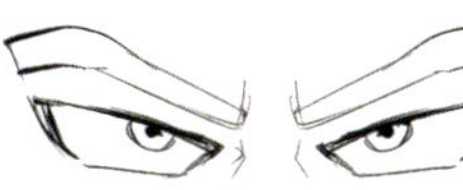
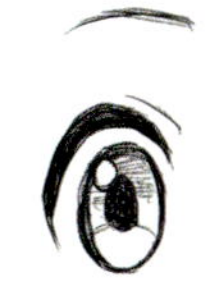
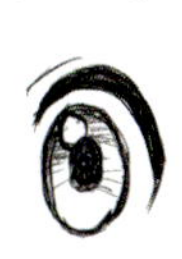
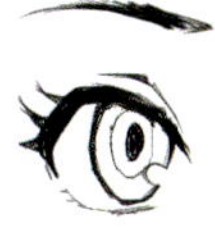
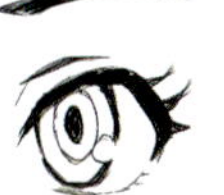
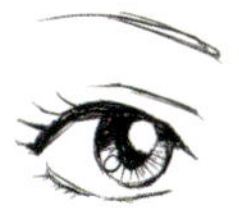
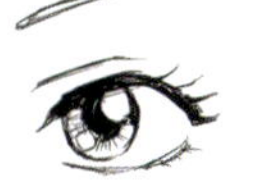
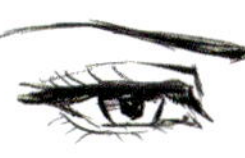
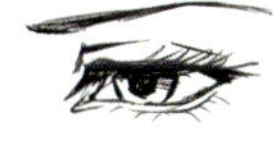
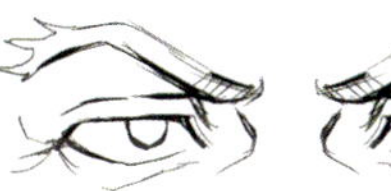
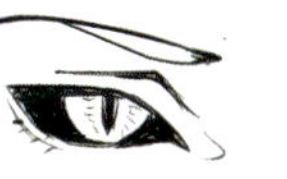
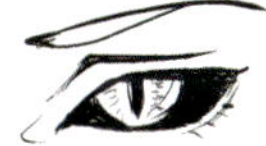
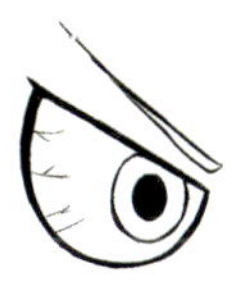
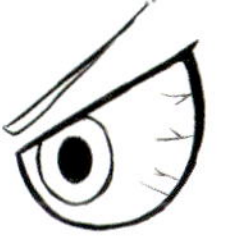

Focus on:
Drawing noses, ears and mouths

Noses

Manga noses are very different to actual noses, being just a hint of the real thing. To draw a manga-style nose, think about which parts of the nose you don't need to include and draw what remains.

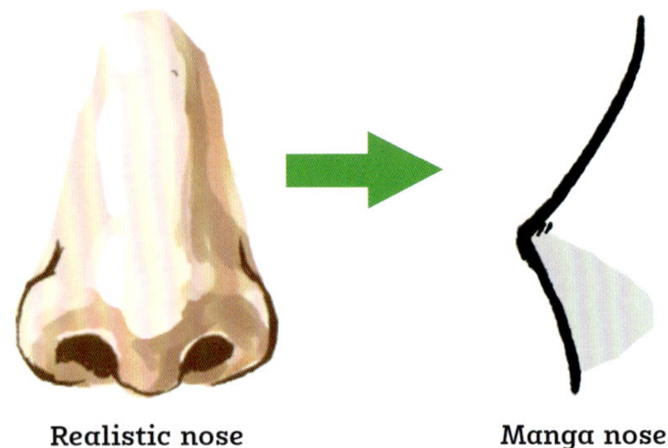

NOSE SHAPES

The basic nose shape is a three-dimensional triangle. Find the silhouette line (shown on the right in red) that contains the apex of the shape. Then add shading, if necessary, to express the height of the nose.

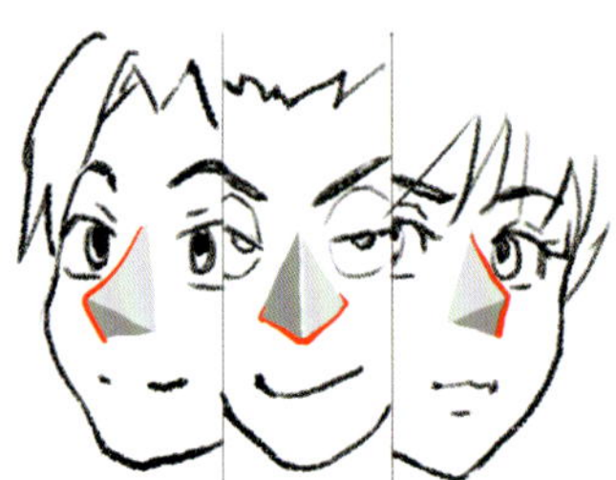

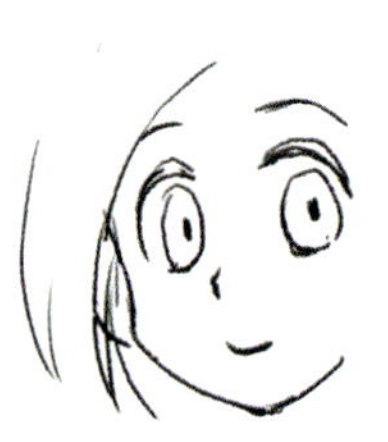

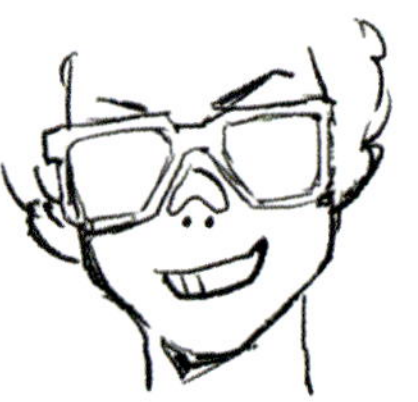

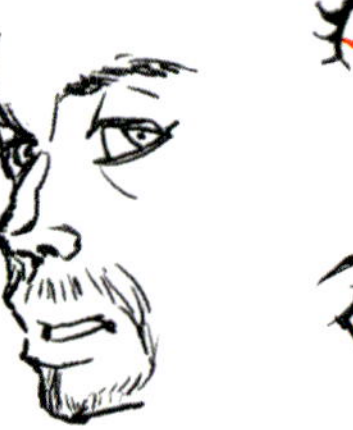

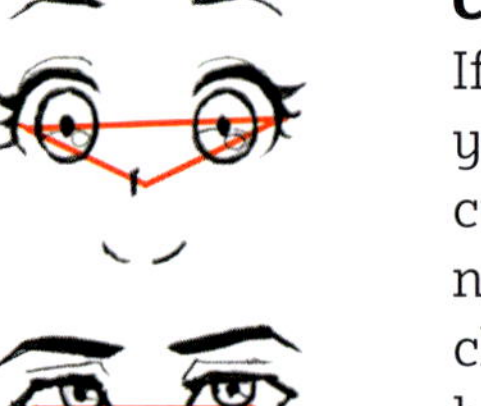

CHIBI NOSE

If you wish to make your character even cuter, leave out the nose. On mini animal characters, noses can be drawn between their eyes.

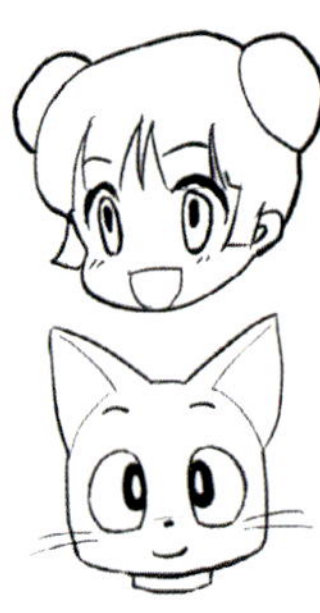

Ears

Ears have complex shapes, but they are rarely drawn realistically in comics. A good way to learn about different approaches is to look at drawings by professional artists, then experiment with simplifying them to use in your own drawings.

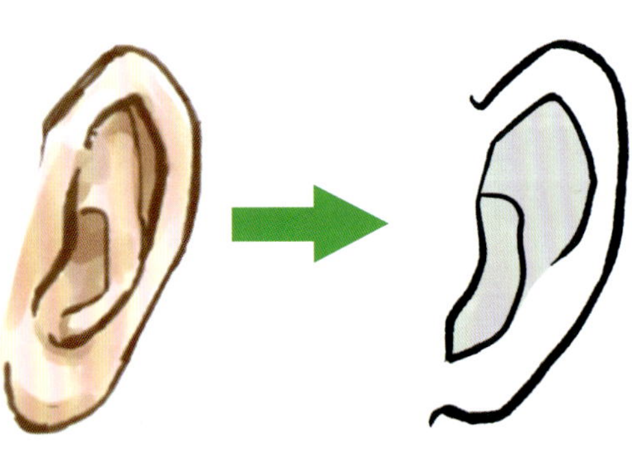

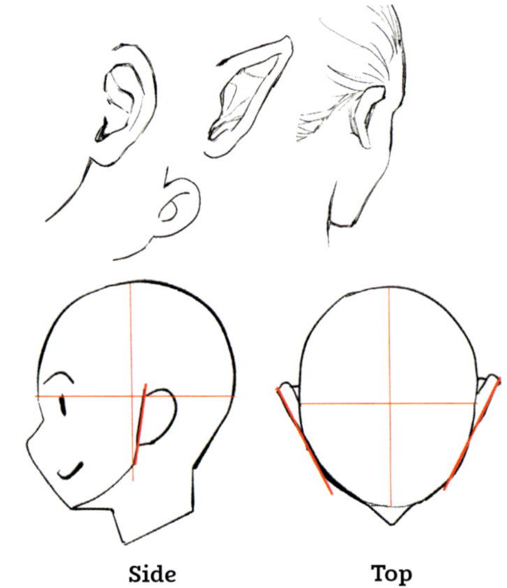

Mouths

While real mouths consist of many parts, mouths in manga are often represented by a simple curved line, sometimes with a line or shading to represent the bottom of the lower lip. When drawing mouths, think about what shape it should be and whether the teeth or inside of the mouth will be visible for a particular expression.

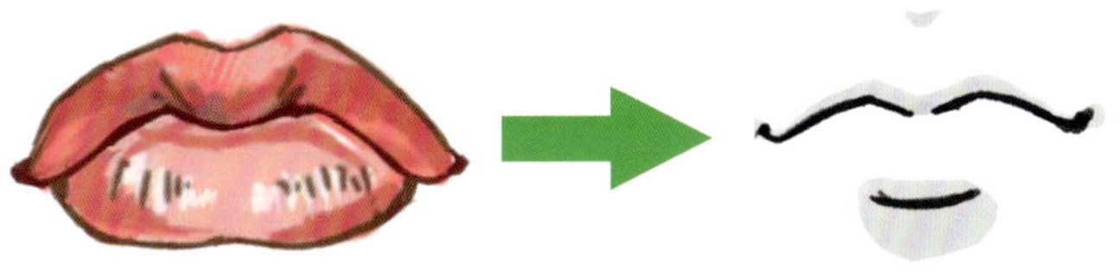

Realistic mouth **Manga mouth**

MOUTH GALLERY

TEETH

The teeth are arranged in a 'U'-shaped curve and, depending on the style of manga, they can be drawn realistically or omitted.

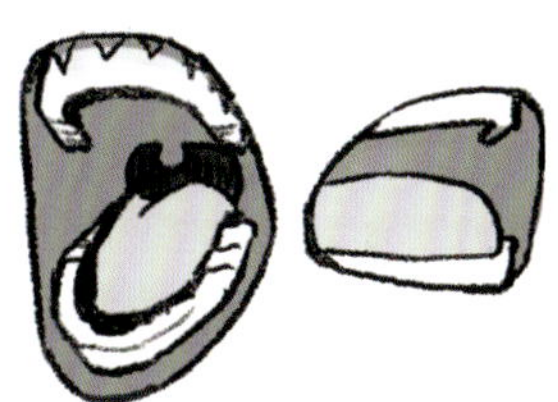

OPEN MOUTHS

When the mouth is opened wide, the jaw has to drop, which lengthens the shape of the face.

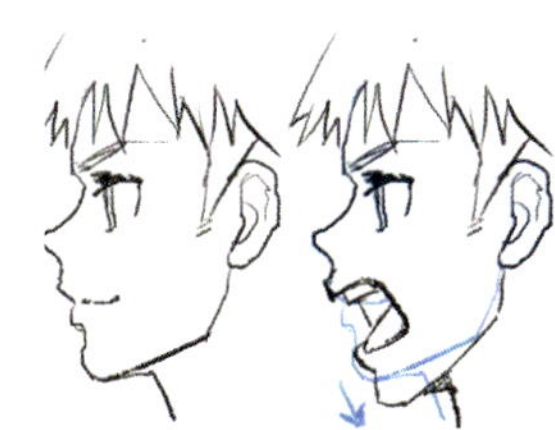

TYPICAL MOUTH SHAPES

You can show a range of different emotions by simply changing the shape of the mouth.

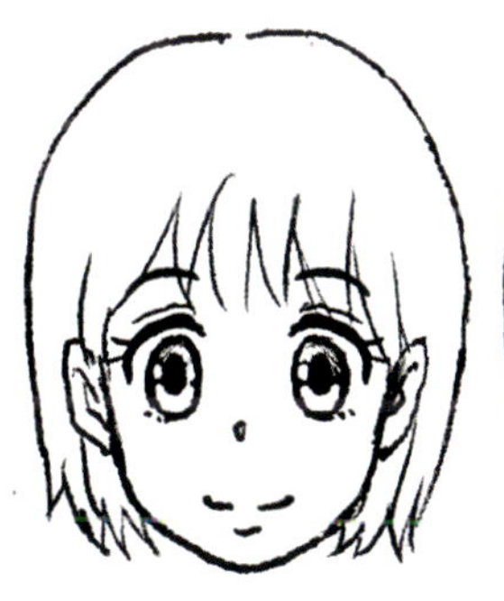

'A' line (content)

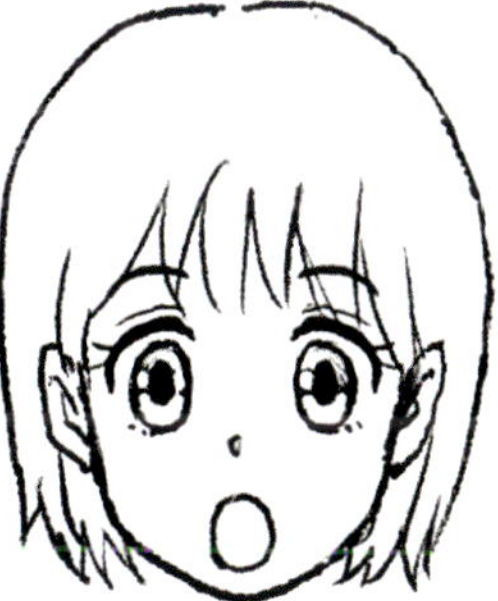

'O' shape (surprised)

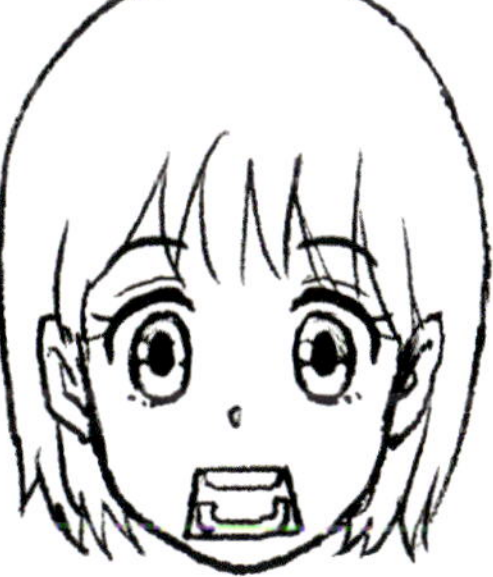

Trapezium (shocked)

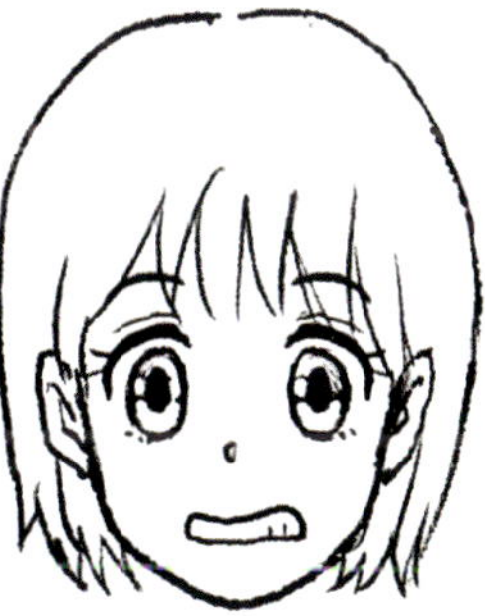

Wide rectangle (scared)

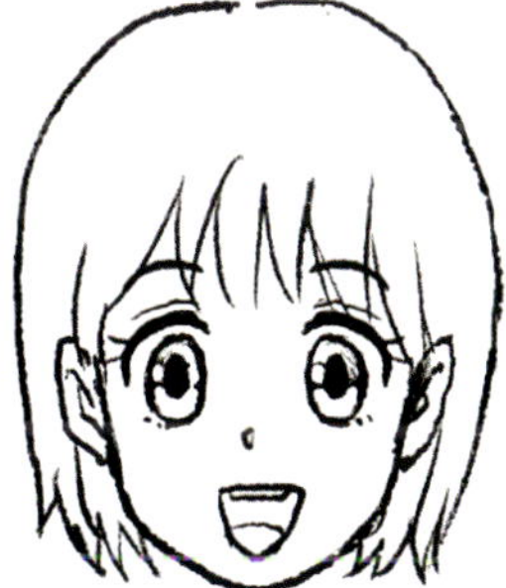

Triangle (happy)

DRAWING A GRIN

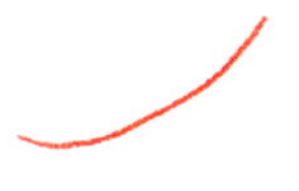

1 Draw a gently curved line for the top of the mouth.

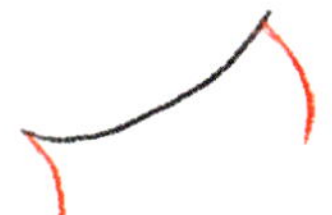

2 Draw lines going down from both ends. They should both be slightly curved in the same direction.

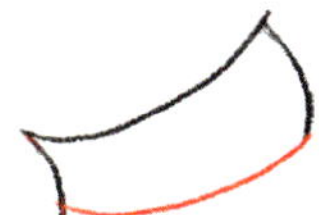

3 Add another gently curved line to form the bottom of the mouth.

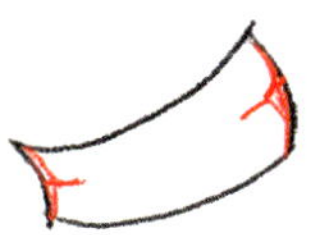

4 Add a small amount of shading at the edges.

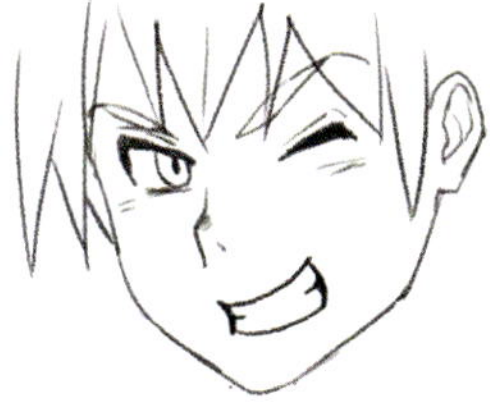

5 Add any details and adjust the shape if necessary.

Focus on:
Hair

A very helpful way to express characterization is through different hairstyles. By practising different types of hairstyles, you will soon be able to design them for your own characters. Some examples are shown here. Pay attention to the quality of the lines for the hair. This will make your drawing look even better.

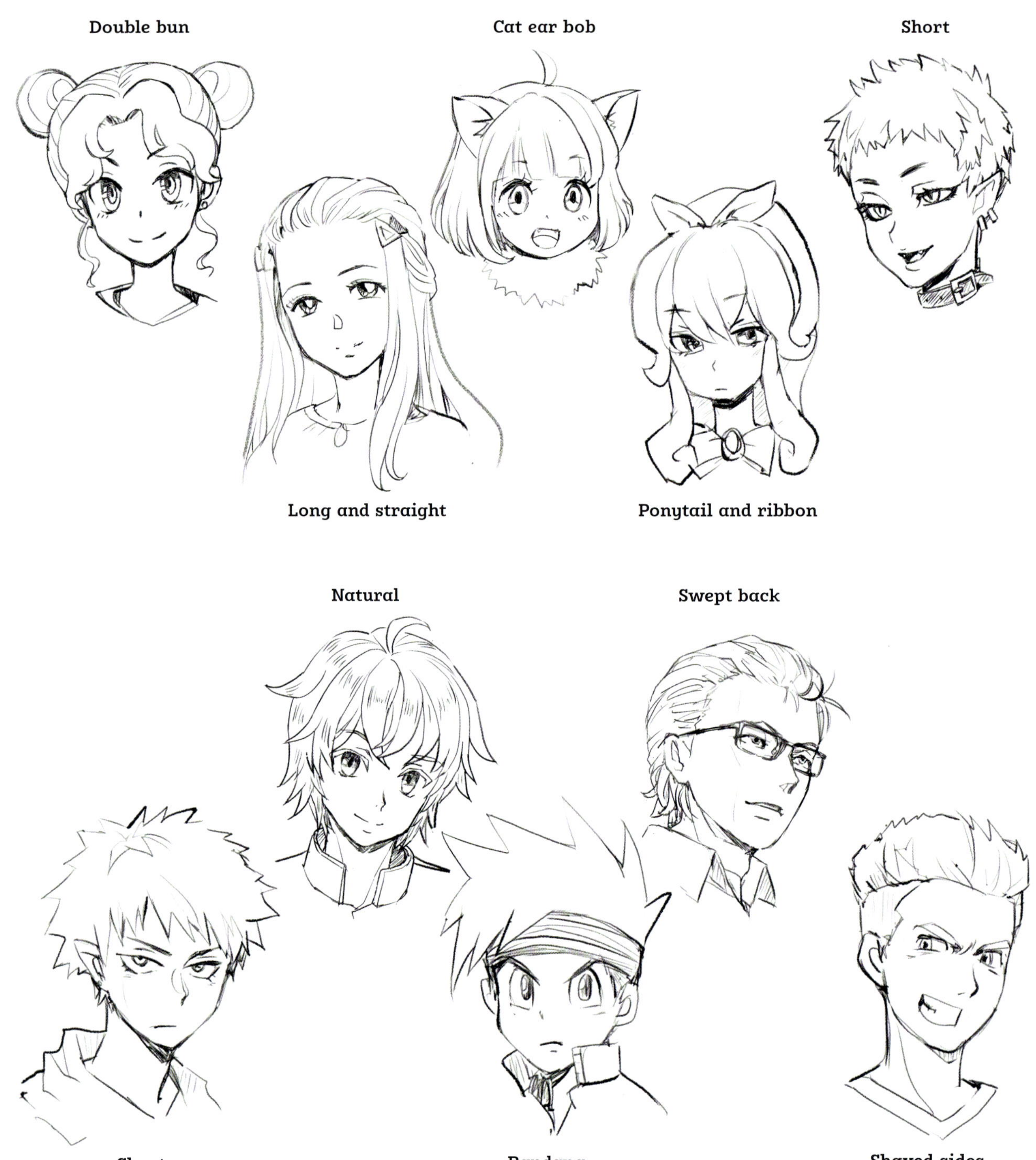

HAIR PARTS

You will find it easier to draw hair by dividing it into three parts: the fringe, the sides and the back. Think about which part is in front of or on top of the other parts.

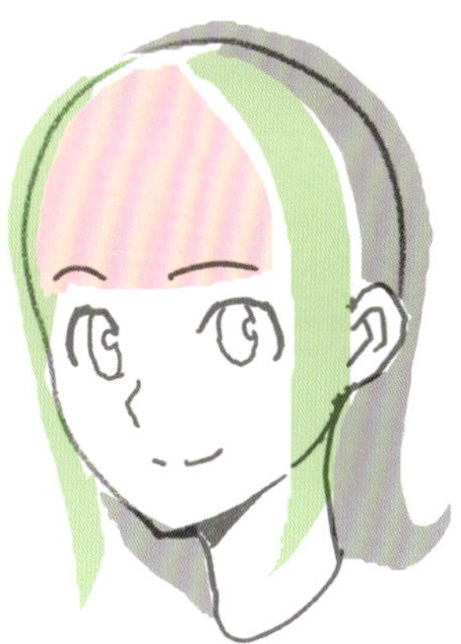

HAIR ROOTS

Think about where the lines of your hair start. This is usually the crown of the hair, a hair tie or a parting. Because the head is a sphere, the lines should curve gently from this point.

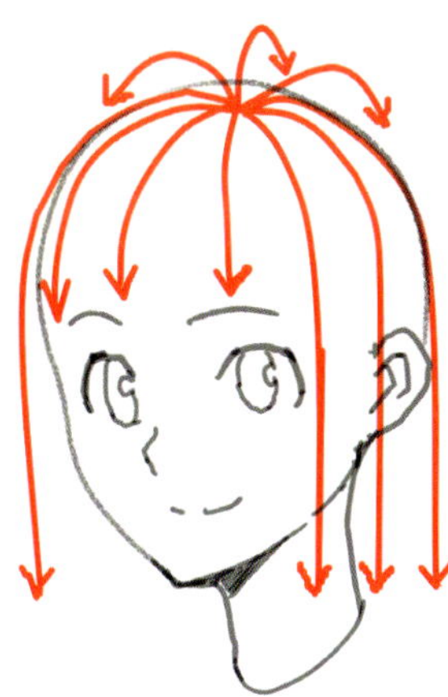

HAIRLINE

For short or shaved hairstyles, draw the fringe, then draw a line from it to the front of the ear. Draw a curve around and behind the ear, then continue around to the back of the neck.

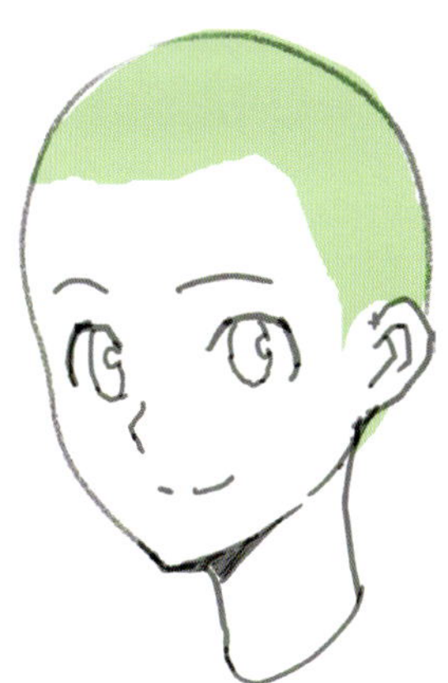

PAY ATTENTION TO LINES AND ENDS

The quality of your lines is very important, so ensure you're using the correct wrist stroke (see page 10). Drawing the curves individually will look much better than drawing a continual zigzag stroke. Compare the line quality below.

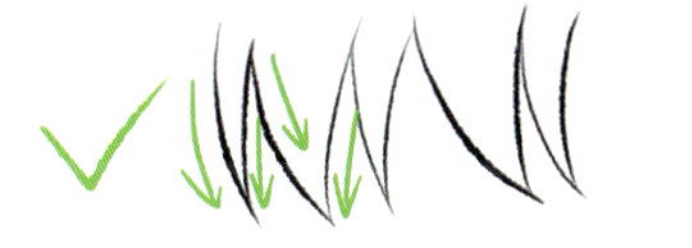

The hair looks soft overall while the ends look sharp.

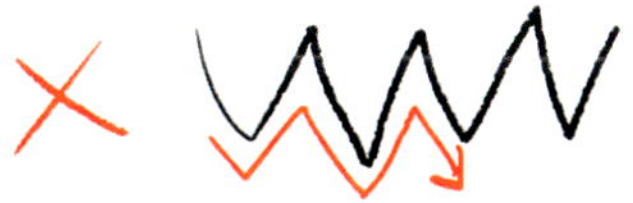

The ends are slightly rounded, and the hair looks like the teeth of a saw.

OVERLAPPING HAIR

You can give your character a clean, elegant haircut by tidying up where the tufts or strands of hair overlap each other.

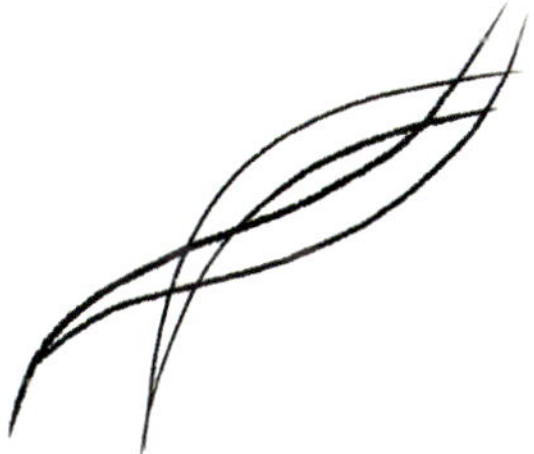

1 Draw all the strands of hair and plan which will be in front.

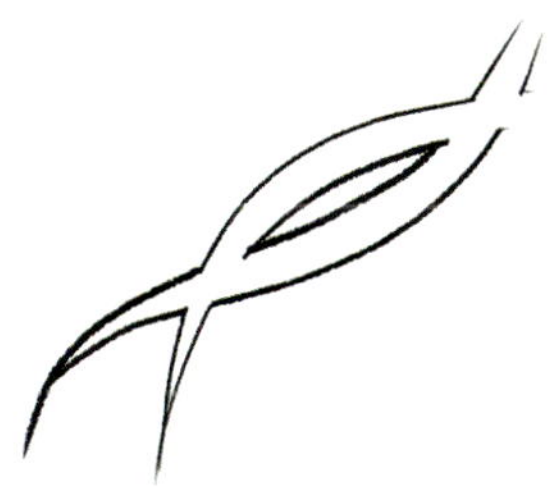

2 Clean up the lines where a strand of hair overlaps another one.

TWISTED HAIR AND RIBBONS SHAPES

Long curly hair can look pretty when it is twisted. You can also use this technique to draw ribbons.

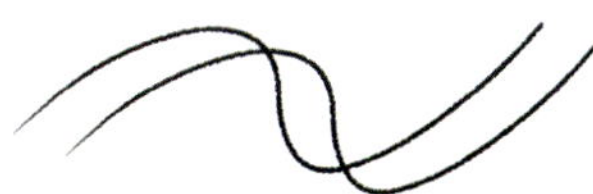

1 Draw two identical twisted, curved lines for the edges of the hair or ribbon.

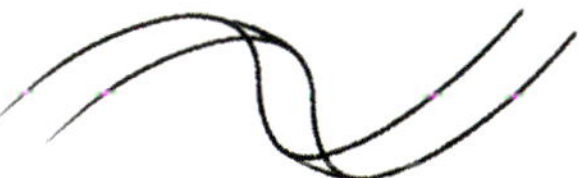

2 Connect the two lines where the lines cross.

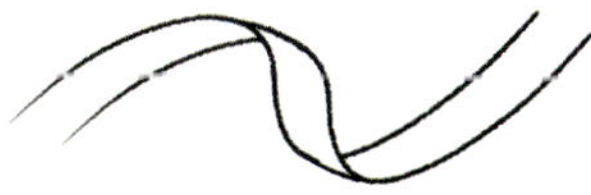

3 Erase the overlapping lines where they curve.

How to show emotions

To know how to draw different emotions effectively, study the expressions of people around you as well as how manga artists portray their characters' emotions.

The key parts of the face are the eyebrows, eyelids, mouth and cheek muscles. Pay attention to the angle of the eyebrows, the size of the eyes and irises, the shape of the mouth, and any lines or creases formed by the cheek muscles. You can try making these faces yourself and use a mirror to see how they look.

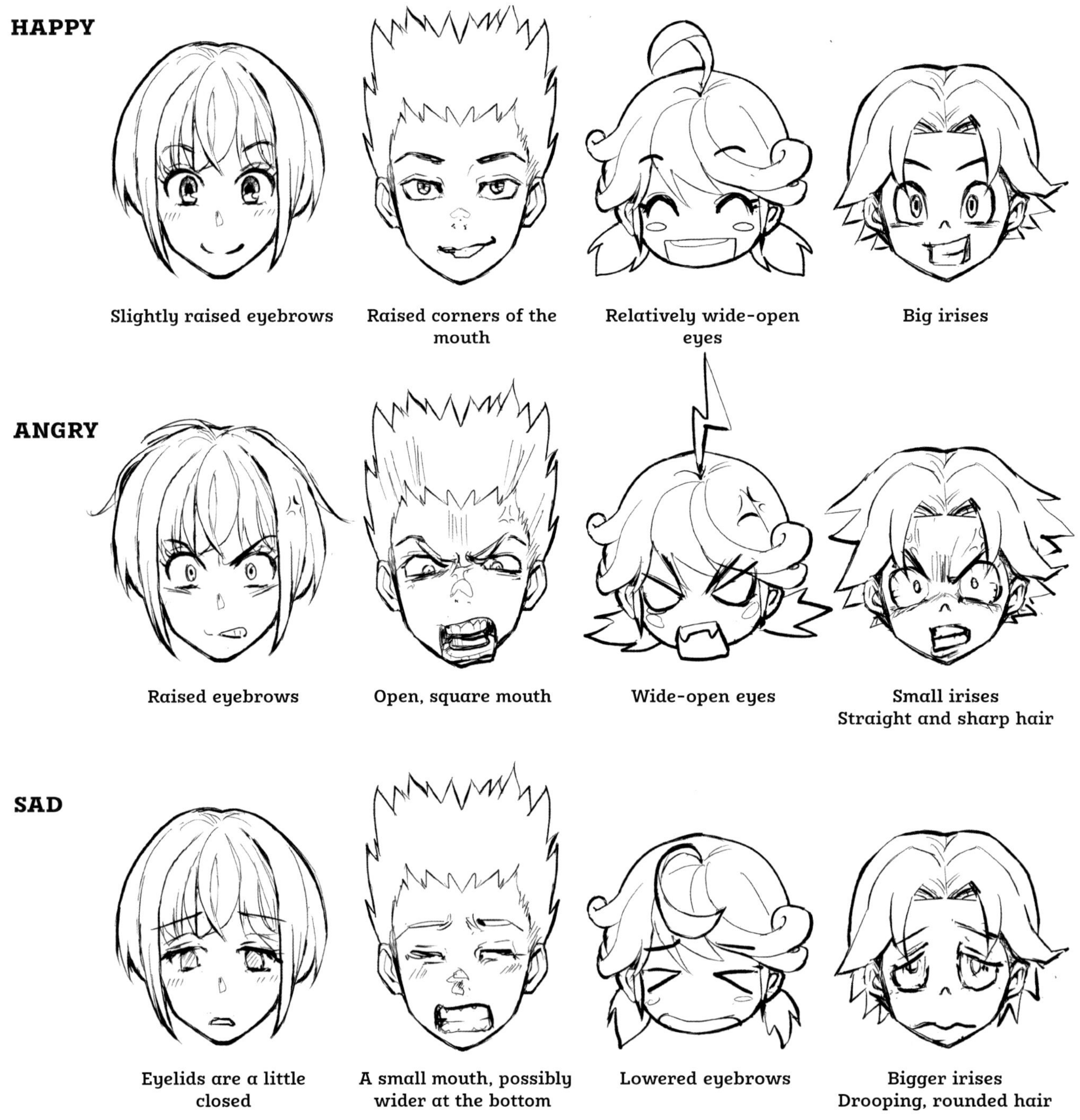

SURPRISE

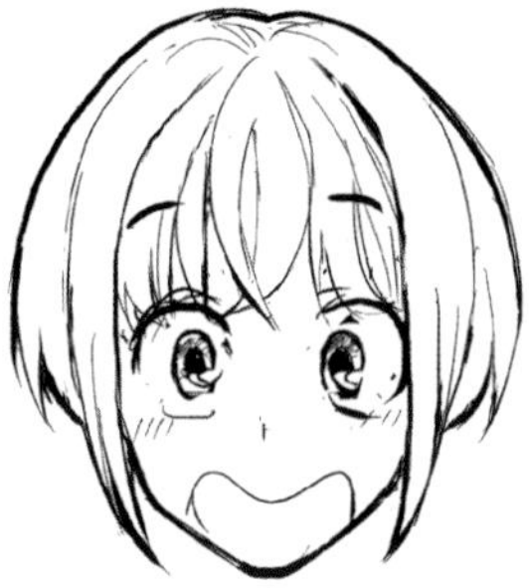

Arched eyebrows

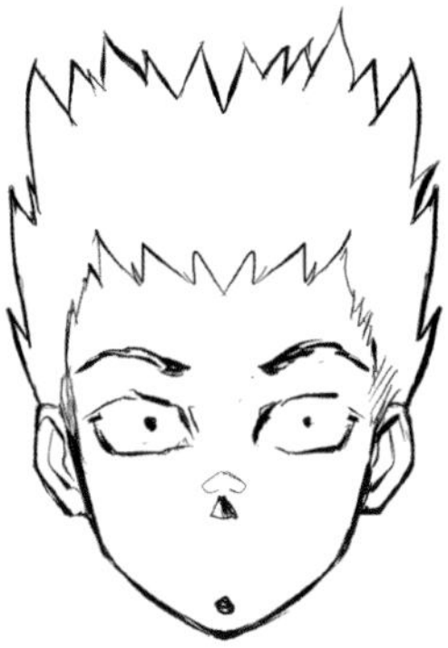

'O'-shaped mouth

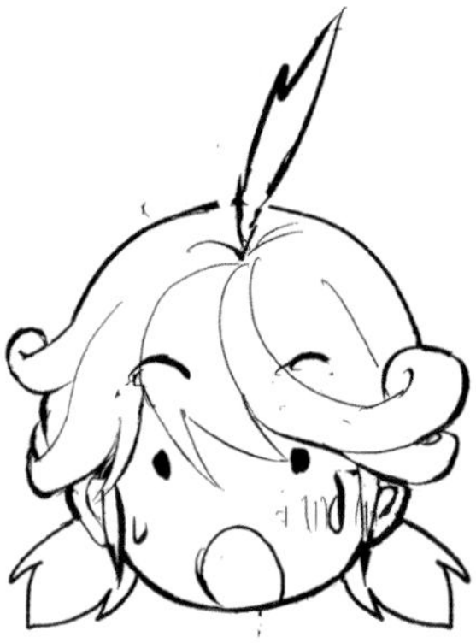

Raised eyebrows

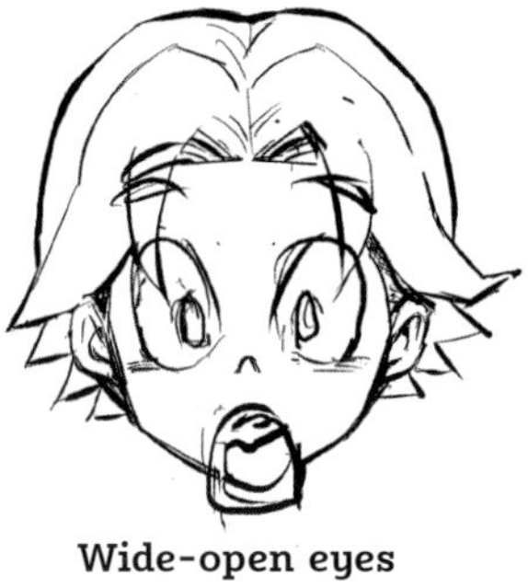

Wide-open eyes

DISGUST

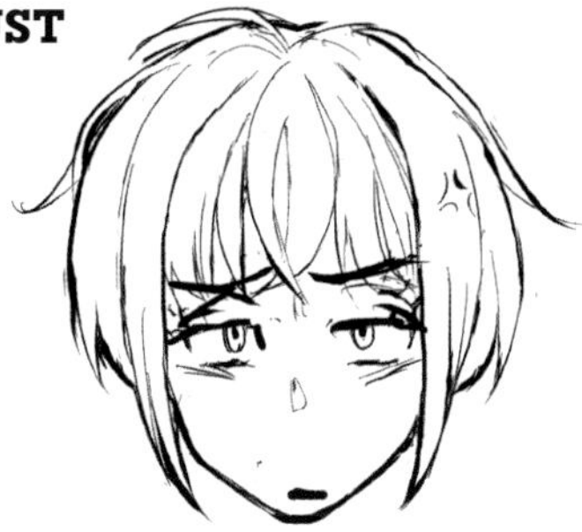

Twisted eyebrows

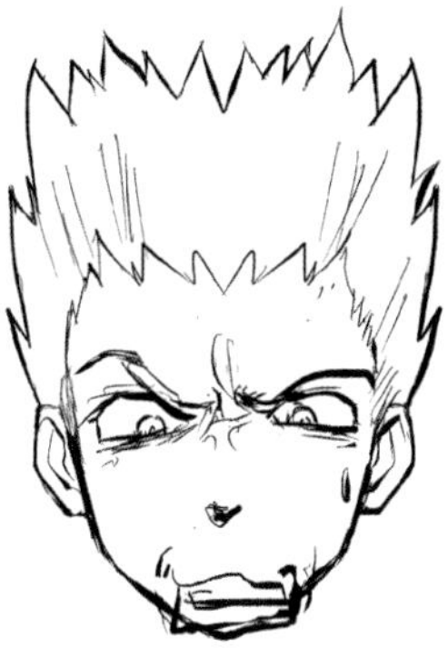

Low, shut mouth

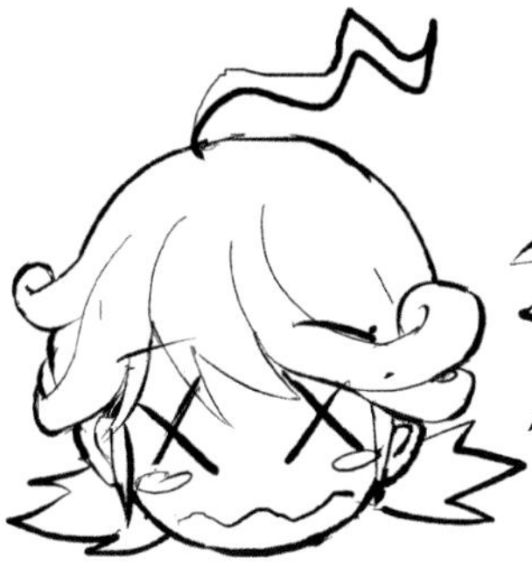

Eyelids are a little closed

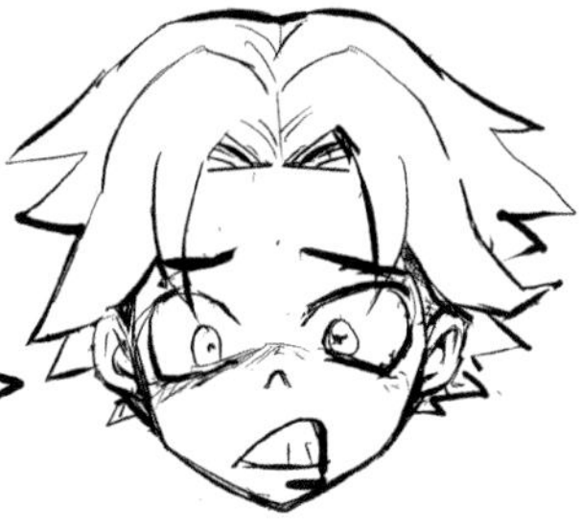

Smaller eyes with paler irises

CONFUSED

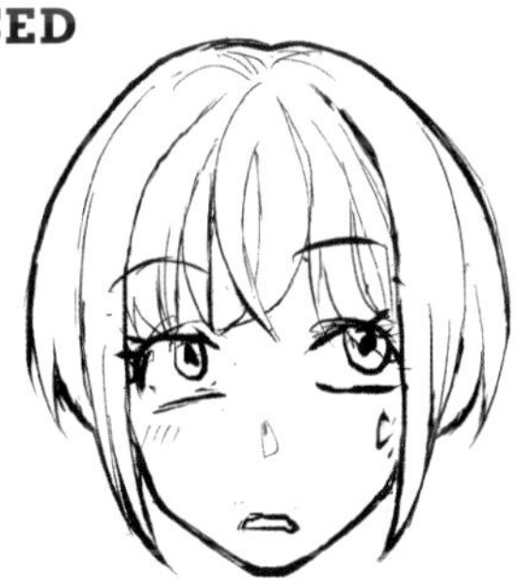

One eyebrow higher than the other

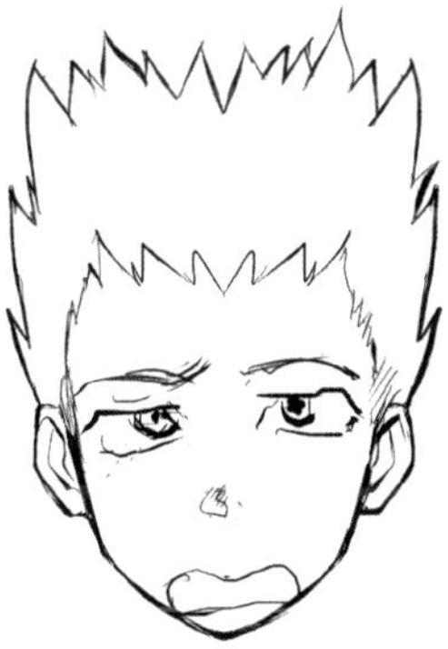

Small mouth

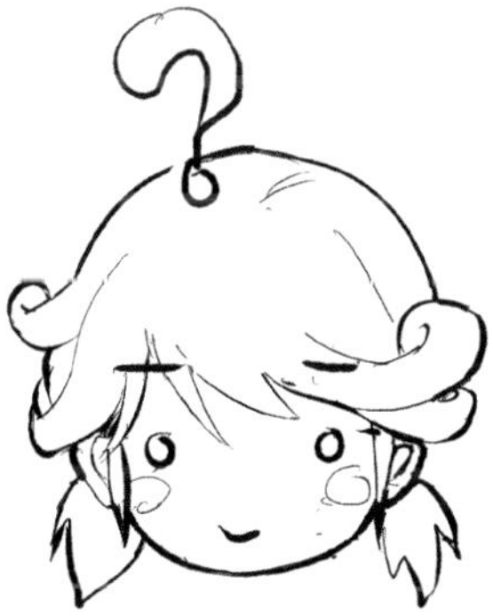

Eyes are looking to one side or crossed

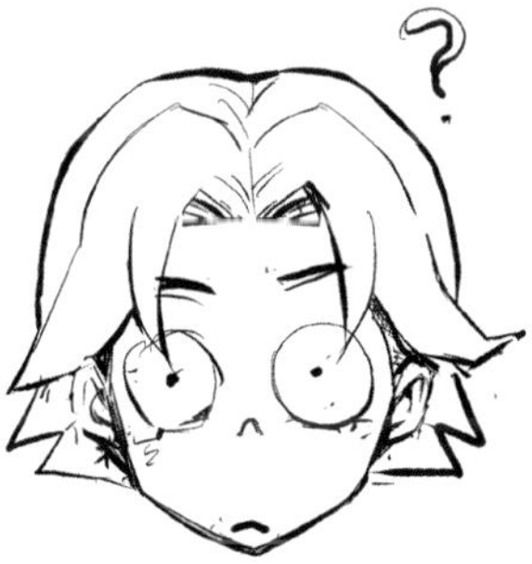

Very small irises

MIXED EMOTIONS

Human emotions aren't always simple – for example, you may have experienced times when you've smiled even though you are generally sad. You can show those feelings by using a mixture of features from more than one emotion.

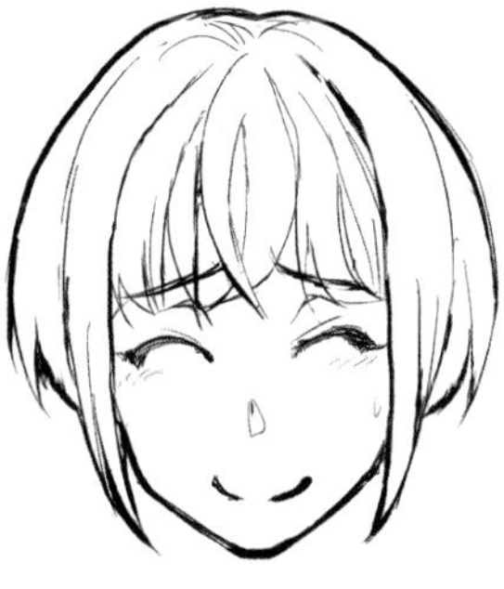

Happy but sad

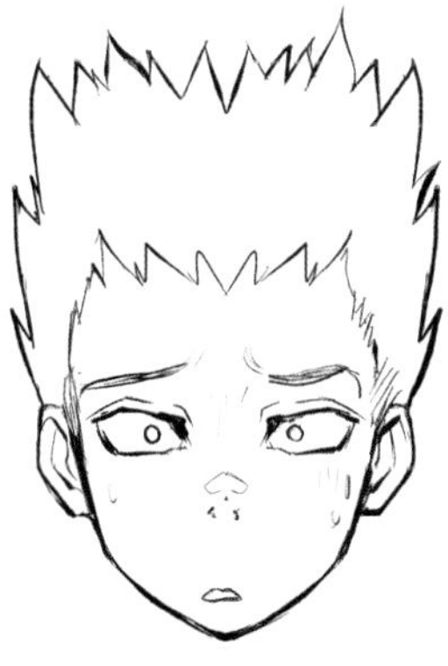

Disgusted and confused

PRACTICE:
DRAW NINE FACES

Developing different characters – each with their own unique features and range of expressions – is key to creating manga stories. Use the techniques provided in this section to try creating nine completely distinct faces. Create different type of characters of various ages, or even create humanoids such as fantasy creatures or robots. Force yourself to draw characters that you wouldn't normally draw, which will help you to expand your skills.

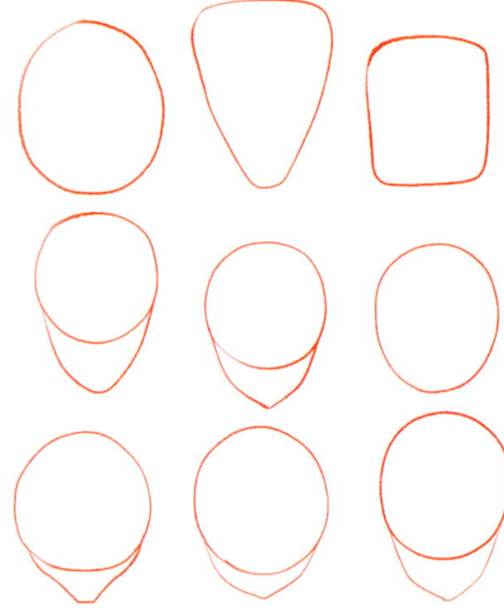

1 Draw nine simple face shapes. Include different shapes, proportions and sizes.

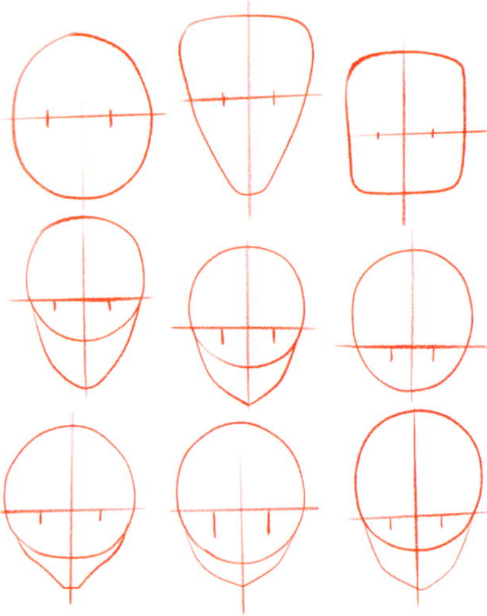

2 Add the central lines. Plan where and what size the eyes will be, then add the position marks.

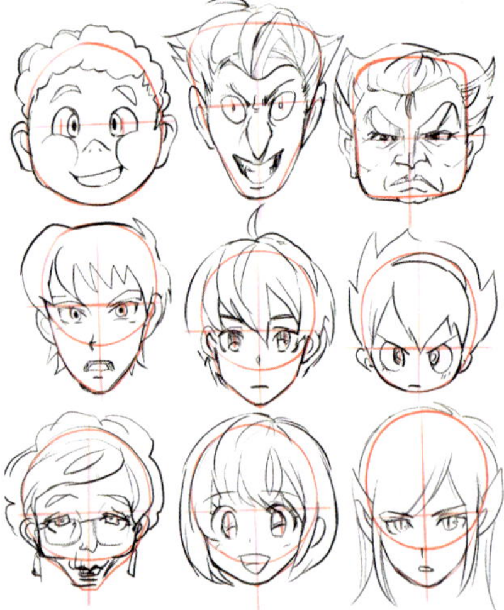

3 Add facial features, hair and details. Try to mix up different parts like a montage. Add details and clean up the lines.

TIP

Draw as regularly as you can. Always write a date on your drawings so that you can see your progress. The drawings will also provide a good stock of characters for your future art!

COLOUR FINISH

You can colour in your gallery of faces. For details on colouring techniques, go to projects 8 and 9 (see pages 98–123).

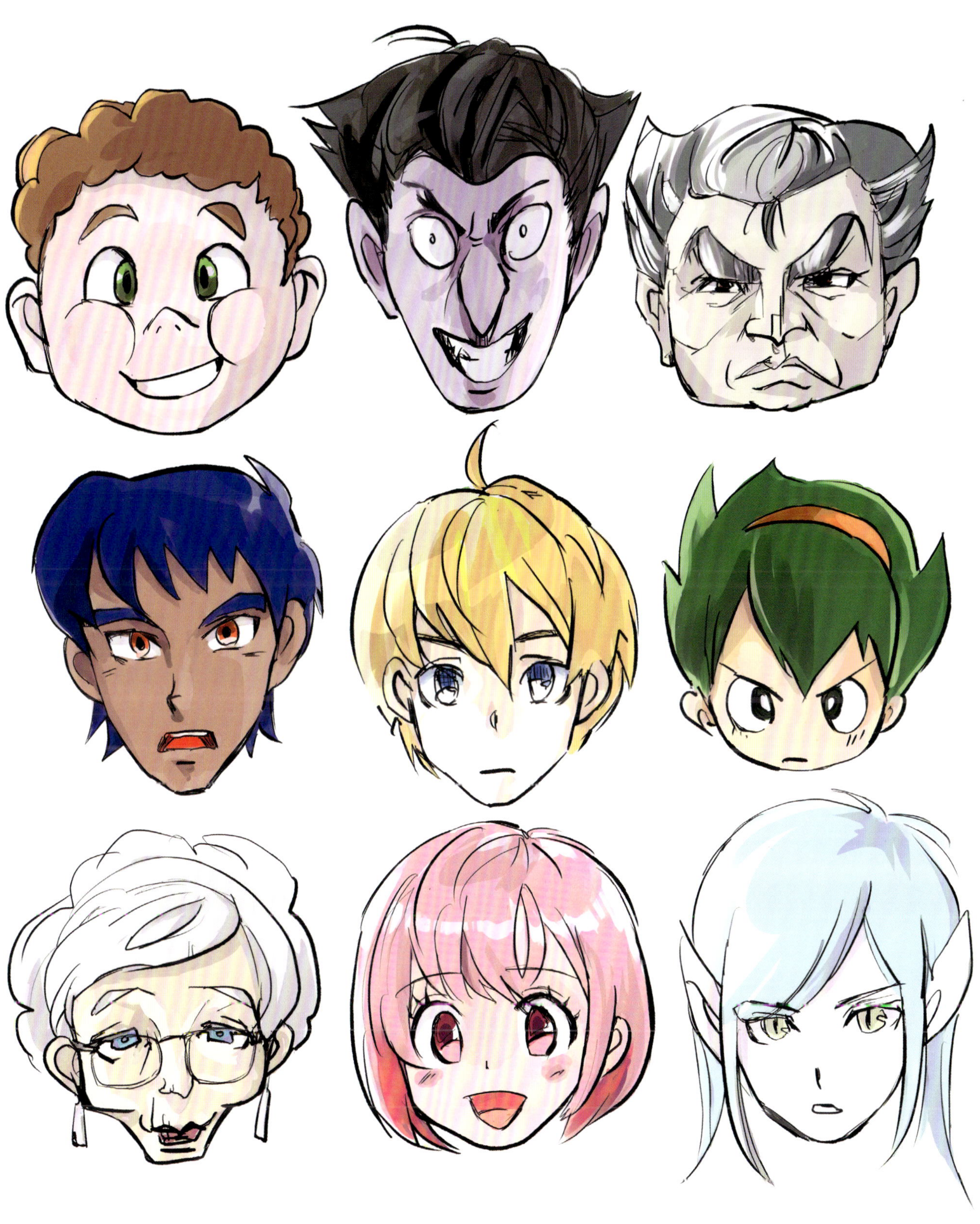

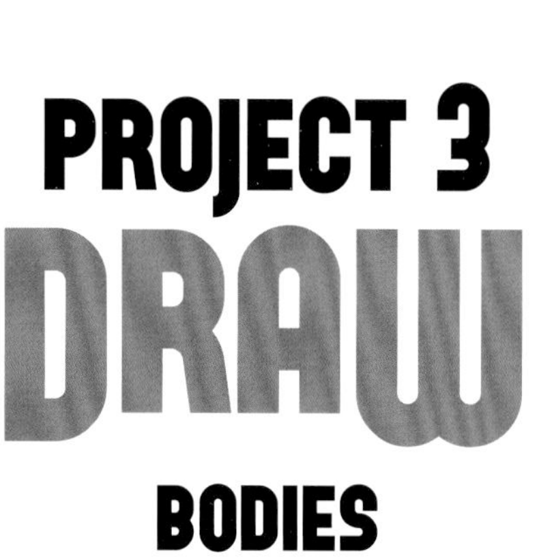

PROJECT 3 DRAW BODIES

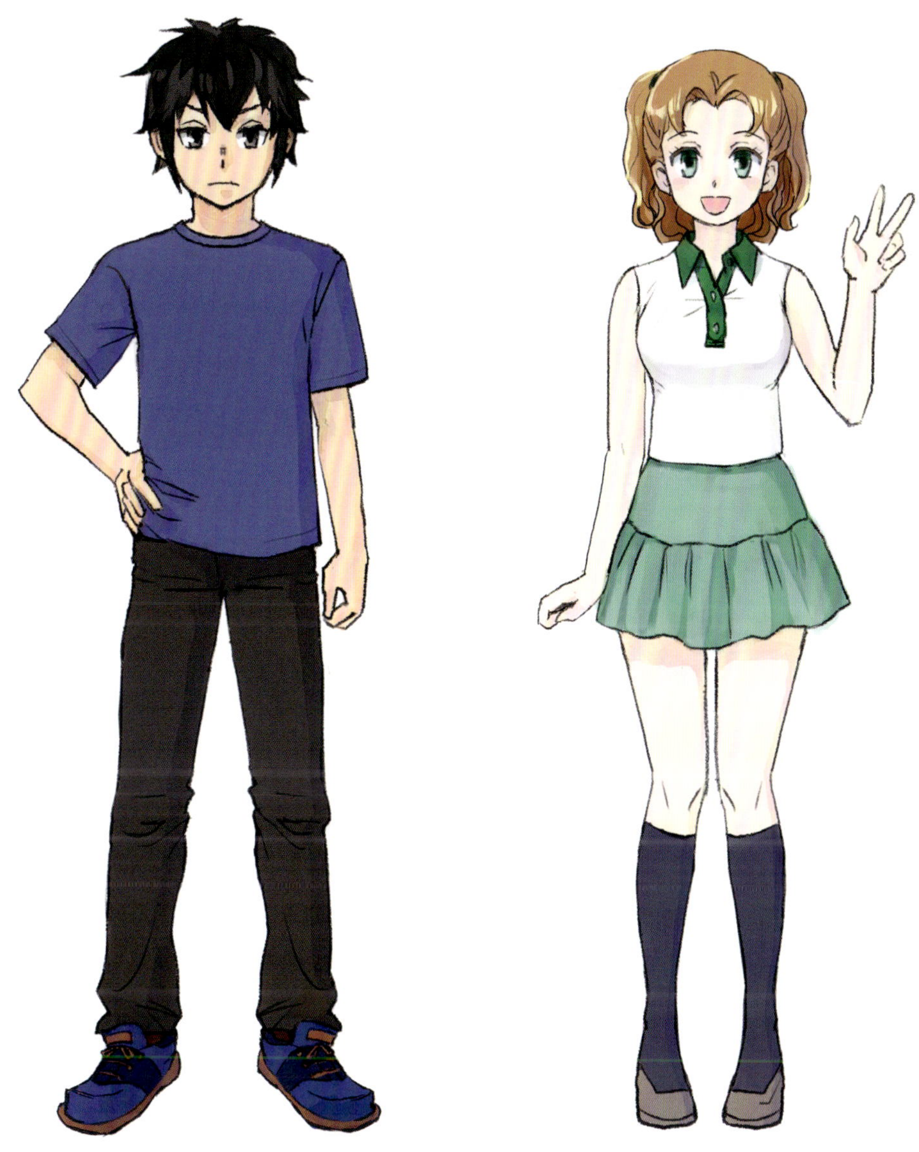

In this project, you will learn how to draw different body types in a manga style with confidence. You will start off with a basic stick figure, give it a three-dimensional shape and then fill in the details and add clothes. By the end of this section, you will be able to draw your choice of characters, ranging from young to old and slim to muscular or chubby.

Body proportions

Having an understanding of the relative sizes between the head, body, legs, arms, feet and hands will help you to confidently draw any character with balanced proportions and at the correct size.

In figure drawing, artists use a special unit for deciding body proportions, which is how many 'heads tall' something is. A figure's head is one head tall, and you can use it to tell the scale of a full figure by observing how many more heads can fit in its body. If a chibi figure has a body that is the same size as their head, the chibi is two heads tall (see page 20).

Let's start by observing your own proportions in a mirror. How many heads tall are you? How about your favourite characters? Measure them and make notes to find your favourite proportions. Body proportions vary considerably in different manga styles, so you will have a lot of flexibility to draw the figures you prefer. The most popular scale for manga is five to seven heads tall.

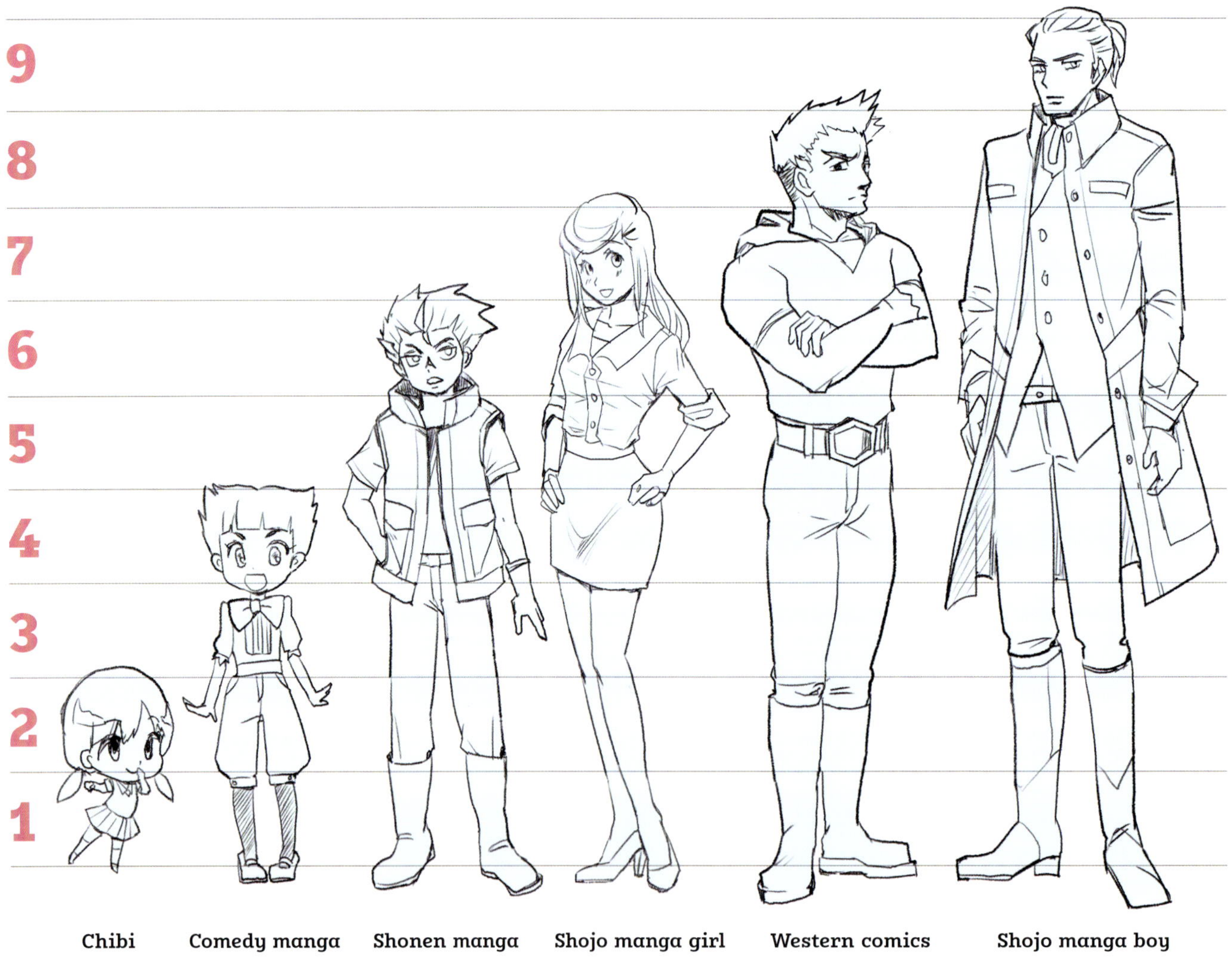

Chibi | Comedy manga | Shonen manga | Shojo manga girl | Western comics | Shojo manga boy

Age and body proportions

Body proportions change with age. A newborn baby is about three heads tall, but the child's head and body will continue to grow until around aged ten, when they will be about four heads tall. Then the head and torso will stay the same, but their limbs will continue to grow as the child moves through their teenage years. By the time someone is an adult, they will be seven to eight heads tall.

Proportions when drawing a figure

It is important you know what your character's proportions are so you can draw it consistently to the right size. Once you choose proportions for a character, check them as you draw a stick figure, where it will be easy to make changes until you get the proportions right. You will then be able to give your character shape and add the details in the following stages of drawing a body.

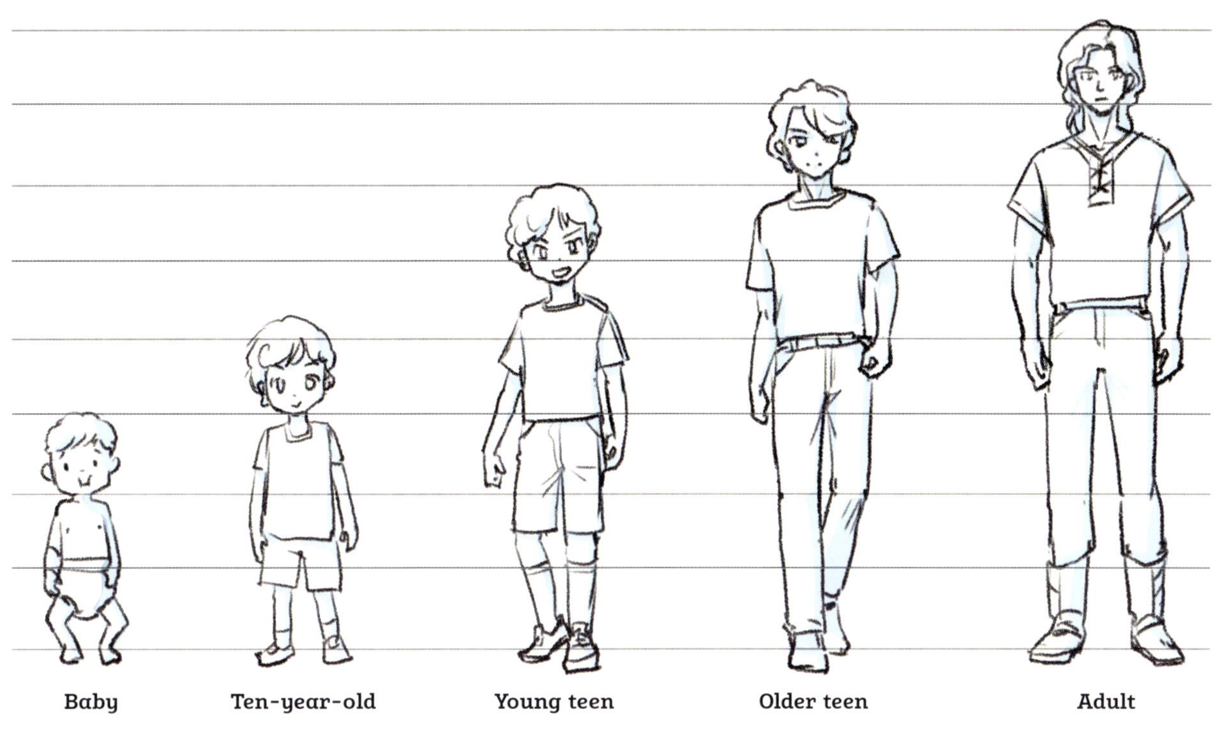

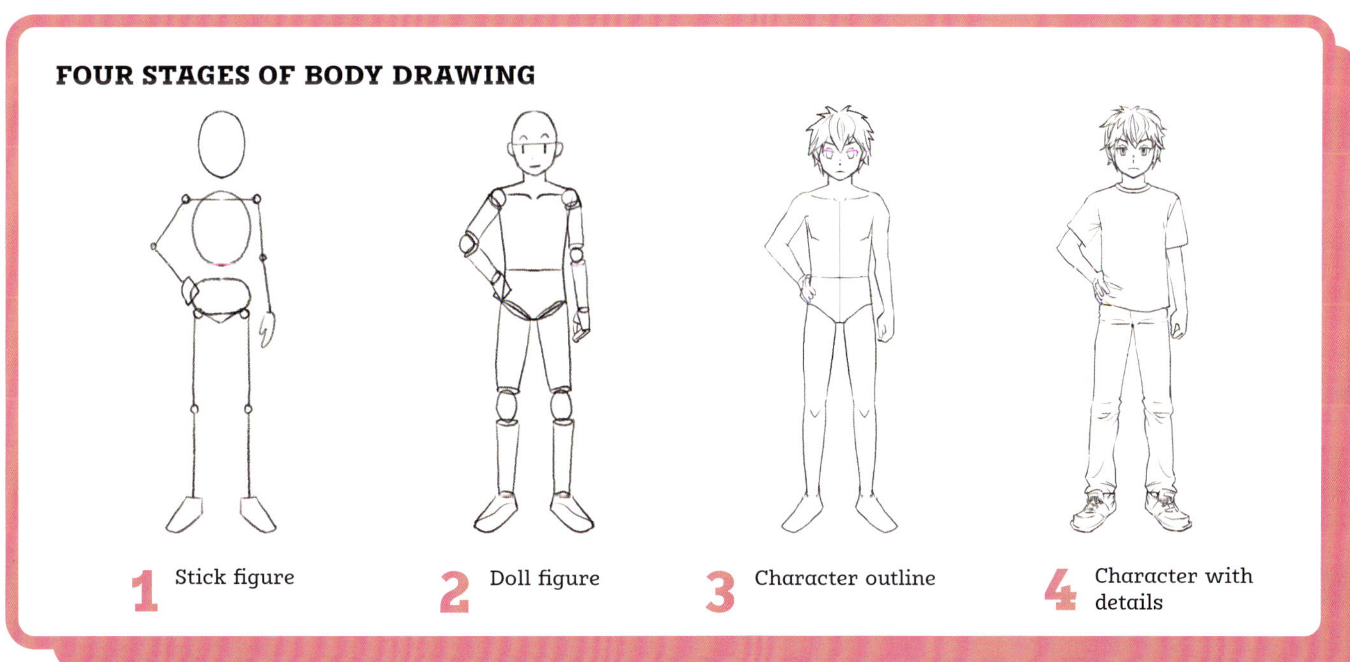

STAGE 1

DRAWING A STICK FIGURE

The first step in drawing a manga character is to start with a stick figure. It needs to have good body proportions with the joints at the correct places, so that the limbs look realistic when they are in a pose. For this project we will draw a model that is six heads tall, as it is one of the most popular character proportions in manga (for other proportions, see pages 20 and 53). The stick figure is just the framework for the final figure, so draw it using faint strokes that you can easily erase and change.

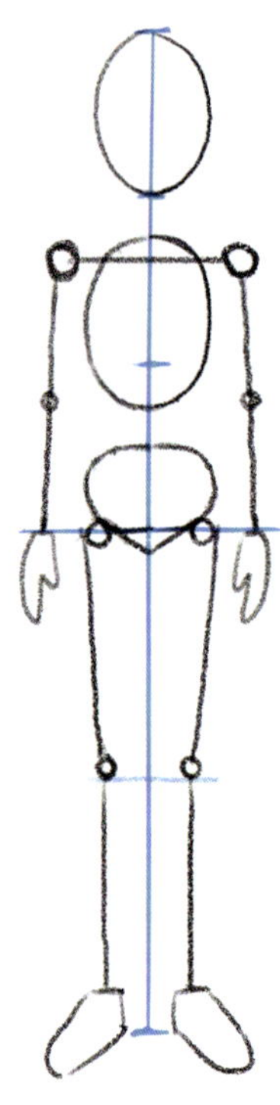

The major parts of a stick figure are the head, torso (the body between the neck and legs, including the ribs and hips) and limbs. The head and torso are three heads tall on the top half of the vertical line and the legs are the bottom three. The arms are shorter than the legs and about the length of the torso. The ball-shaped markings are joints. It is important to know where the joints are so that you can bend from them when posing your figure.

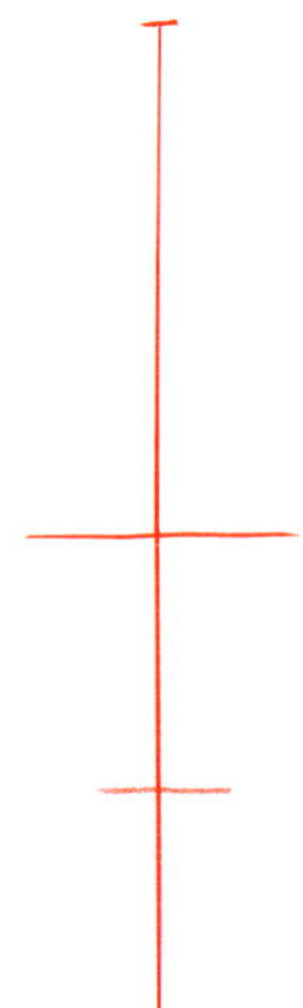

1 Leaving some space at the top and bottom of the paper, draw a vertical line that's almost the full height of the page. This is the height of your character. Divide the line into two equal halves with a horizontal line, then divide the bottom half into two equal halves with another horizontal line.

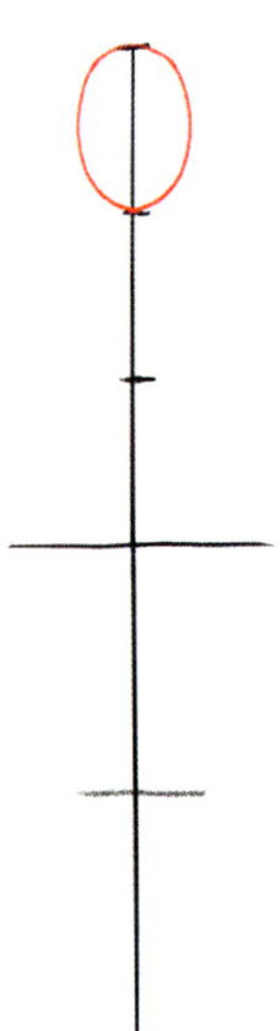

2 Divide the top half into three equal parts and mark these points. Draw a vertical oval for the head using the whole space between the top two points.

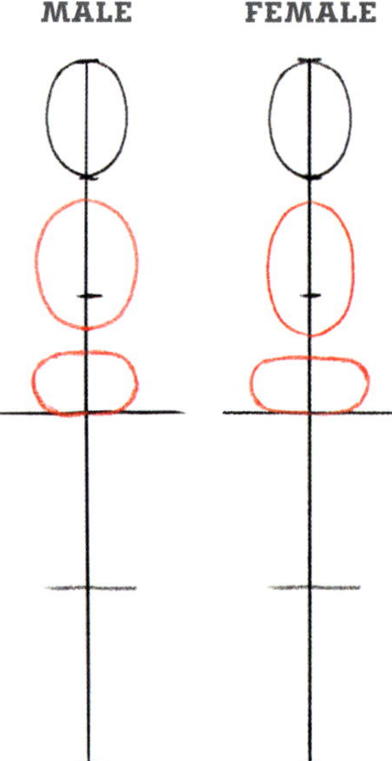

3 Draw a horizontal oval for the pelvis (the hips) on the horizontal line. The oval should be slightly wider for a female than a male. Draw another oval for the ribcage, slightly wider than the head, and wider still for a male character. Ensure there is some space both above and below the ribcage for the neck and waist.

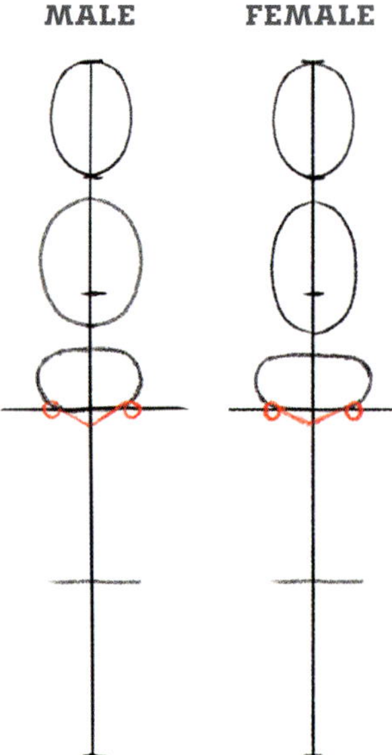

4 Add a wide 'V' shape below the hips, with the point meeting on the vertical midline, and draw the hip joints on the two ends of the 'V', which should be on the horizontal line.

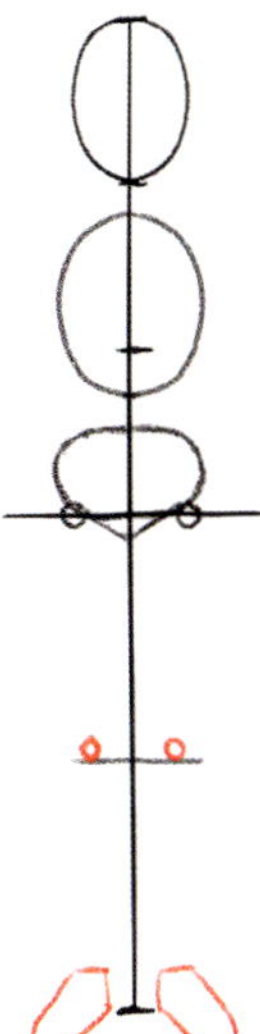

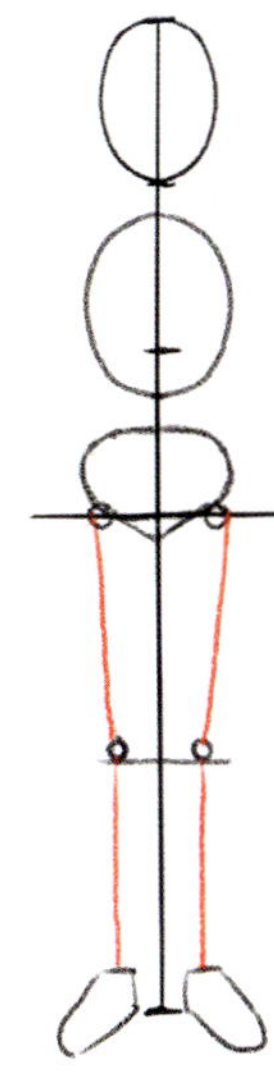

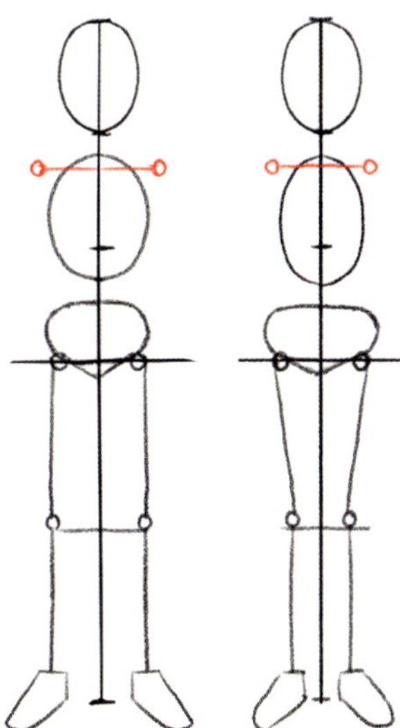

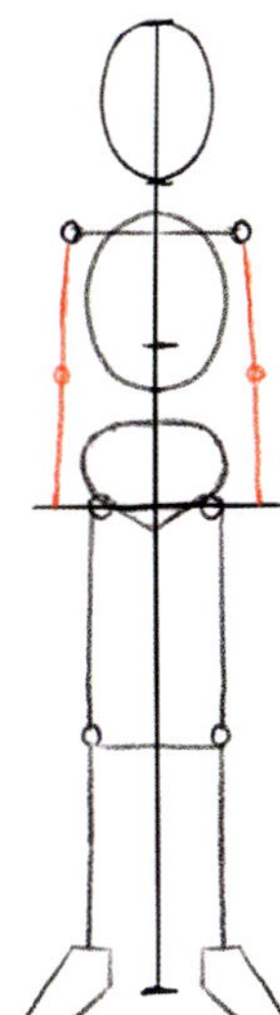

5 Draw the feet. They are quite big: the heels should be at the bottom mark. The ankle joints will be a little higher than the heels, and the toes should either come forward or point diagonally. Draw the knee joints halfway between the hip joints and the ankles.

6 Connect the leg joints with straight lines to create the leg bones. Check that the top and bottom lengths are same. If not, move the knees but keep the bones straight.

7 Draw a shoulder line, allowing it to overlap a little with the ribcage. Draw the shoulder joints at each end, keeping them symmetrical. The shoulder width will be different depending on the character – usually, males have wider shoulders than females.

8 Draw the arms, starting at the shoulder joints and ending at the central horizontal line, which is the wrist position. Draw an elbow joint halfway down each arm line.

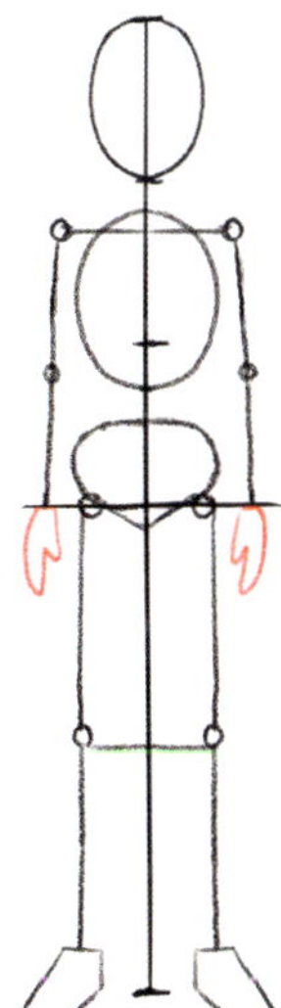

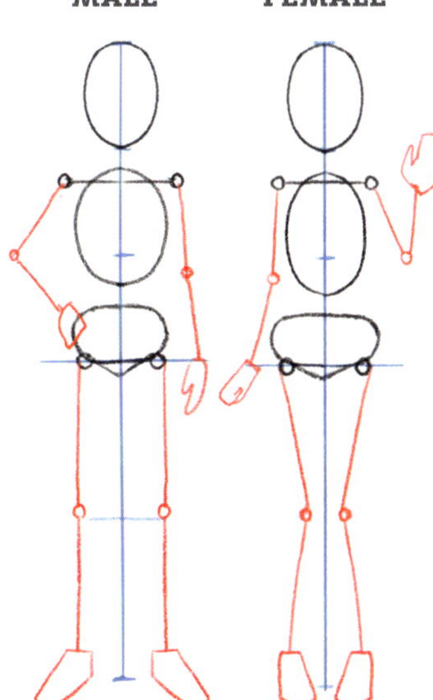

9 Add hands below the wrists. Simple mitten shapes are fine at this point. They should be about two-thirds the length of the arm section between the wrist and elbow.

10 This is the best time to change the pose. Ensure that you change the angle of the limbs only at the joints and keep the bone lines the same length.

Checklist

- The length of the head and torso combined should be equal to the length of the legs.
- The thighs and the lower legs should be the same length.
- Check that the arms connect to the wrists at the central horizontal line.
- Ensure the shoulders and hips are the right shape for a male or female character.

STAGE 2

DRAWING A DOLL FIGURE

A doll figure forms the core foundation for a manga figure drawing. In this process, you will turn your two-dimensional stick figure into a three-dimensional doll figure. I will break this down into simple three-dimensional shapes, which combined will create the figure.

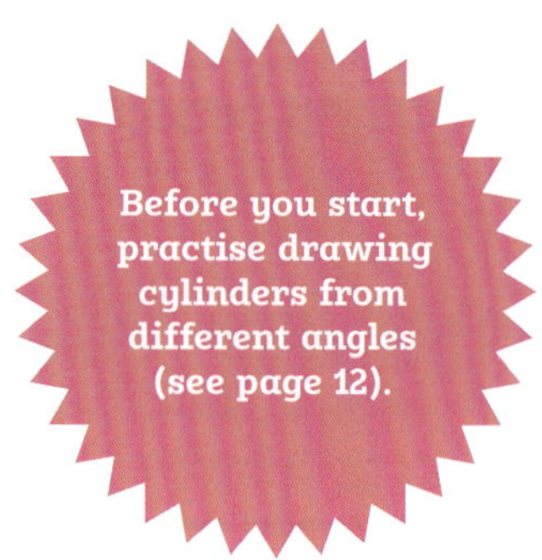

Before you start, practise drawing cylinders from different angles (see page 12).

Check that you are happy with the proportions of the stick figure before you start making it three dimensional.

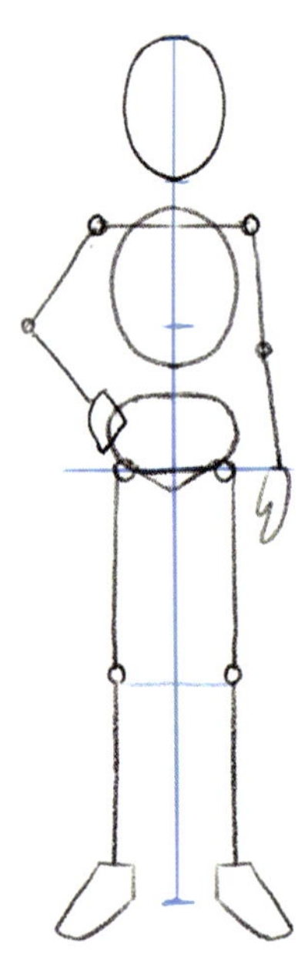

ARMS

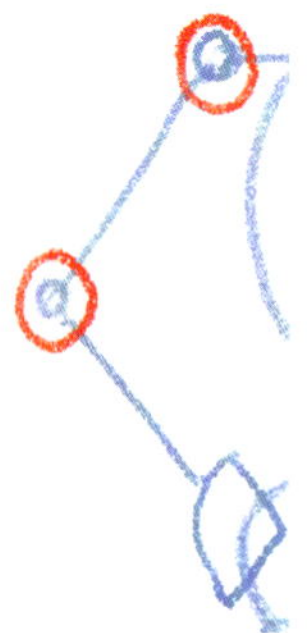

1 Let's start with arms. Increase the shoulder and elbow joints to look like larger ball shapes.

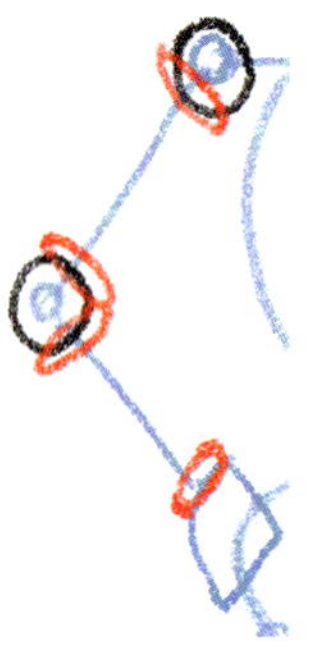

2 Fill the gap between the three arm joints using cylinders. Draw the cylinder's top and bottom disc shapes first. The wrist is a little thin, so draw a smaller disc.

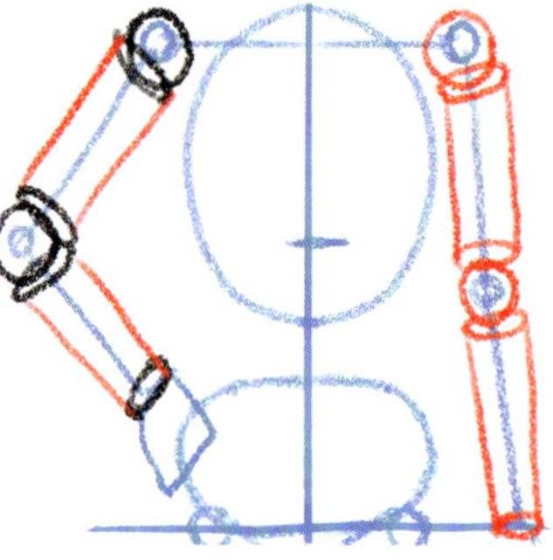

3 Draw two lines to connect the top two discs, forming the sides of the upper arm. Draw more cylinders for the forearm. Now draw the sides for the other arm.

LEGS

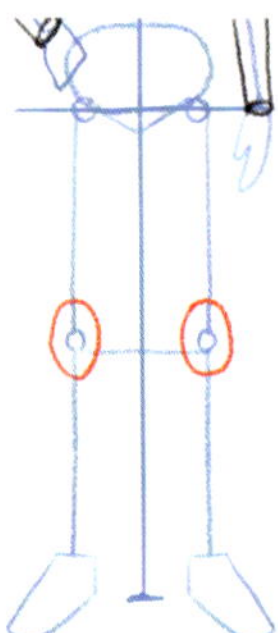

4 Make the knee joints larger, and at the same time change them into vertical oval ball shapes.

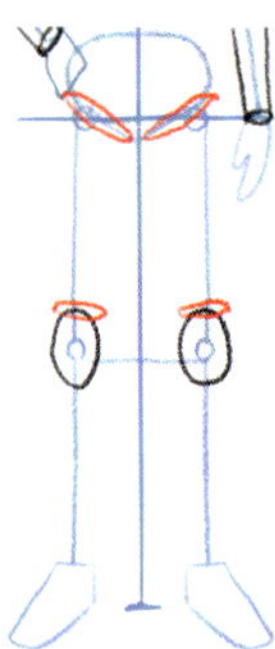

5 Draw disc shapes for the top and bottom of the thighs. Make larger discs at the top, following the 'V' shape of the hips.

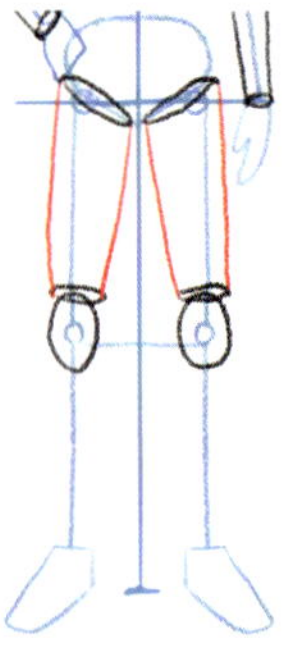

6 Connect the discs to form the sides of the thighs. Ensure that the lines at the top are adjacent to the discs and that the lower width of the thighs are about the same as the knee balls.

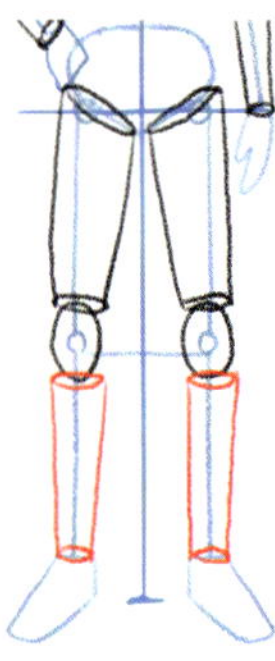

7 Draw two more pairs of cylinders for the lower legs. The ankles are a smaller diameter.

HEAD AND SHOULDERS

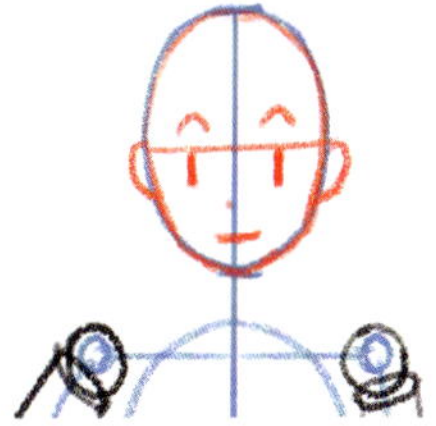

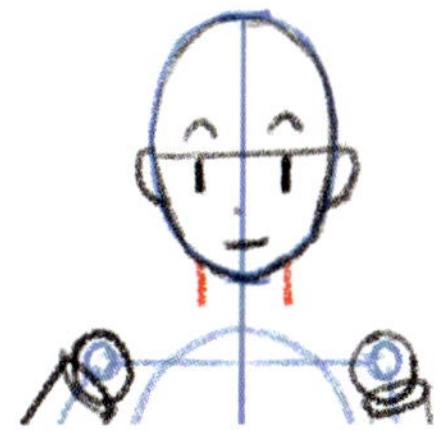

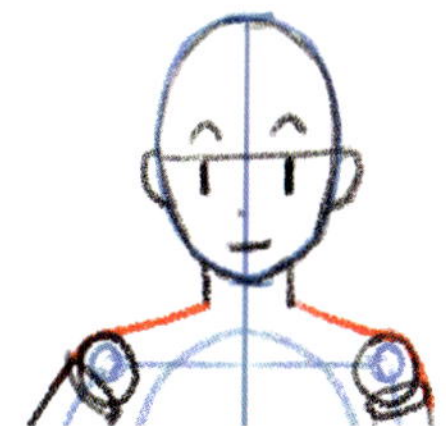

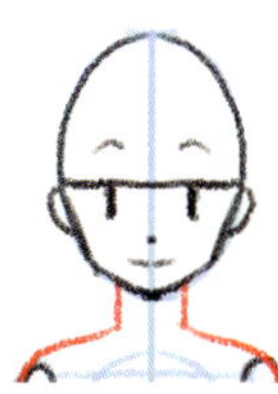

8 Draw guide lines and a rough sketch for the face (see page 29). The eyes and ears should drop from the horizontal central line.

9 From the lower jaw, drop the lines for the sides of the neck and stop them in the middle of the neck area.

10 Connect the neck lines to the shoulder balls, making sure the lines slope slightly downwards as the approach the shoulder joints. A slightly narrower neck makes the figure more feminine.

TORSO

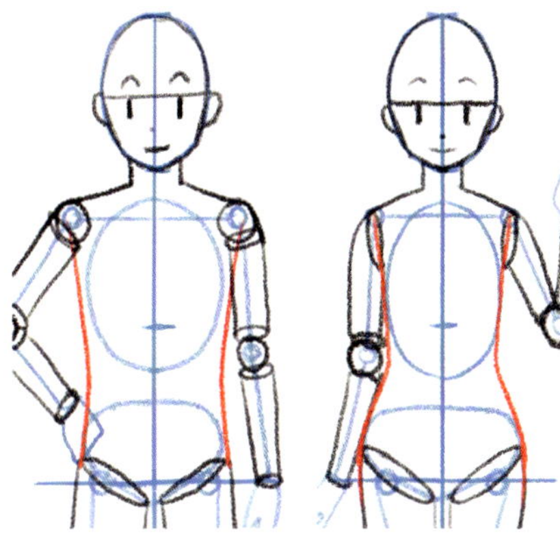

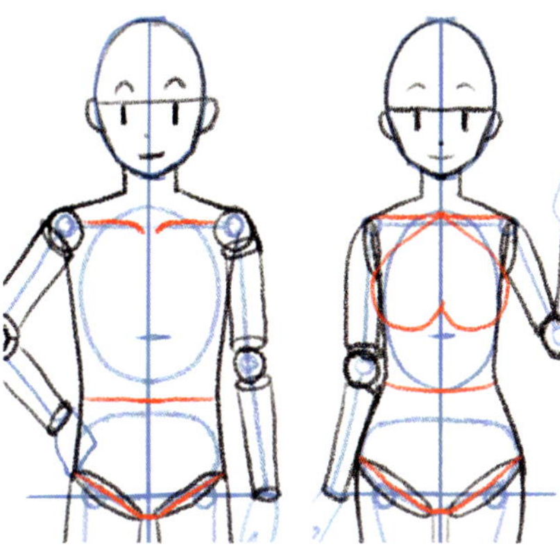

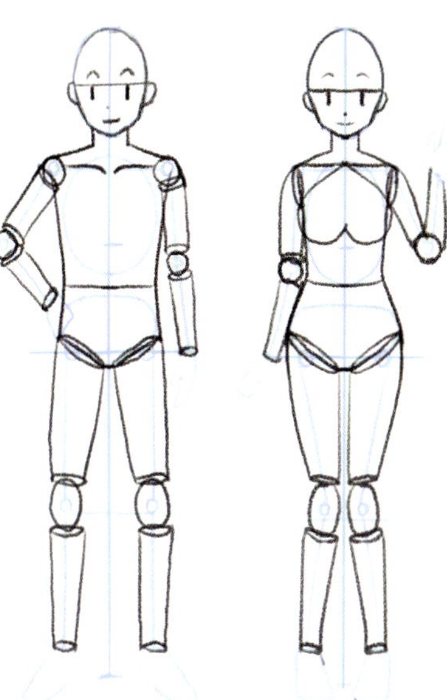

11 Connect the torso to the rest of the body. The waist comes between the ribcage and hips, and it is usually the thinnest part of the torso. Curve the lines to give your figure a good waist. The female body usually has a waist that curves in more than a male's waist.

12 Draw the collarbones below the shoulder lines and add the waistline; also add curves where the torso meets the legs. Adding these lines will make it easier to think about clothing. Add breasts to females by drawing an upside-down heart shape from the centre of the shoulder line.

HANDS

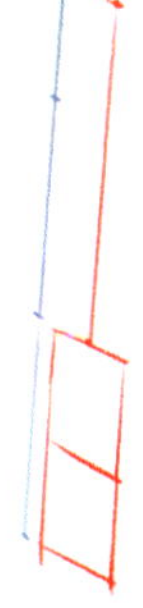

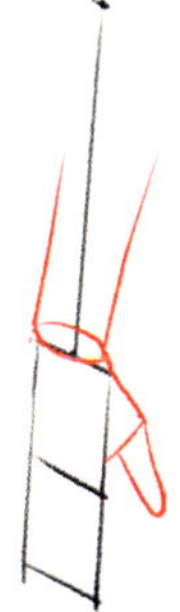

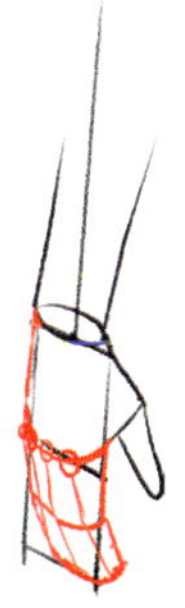

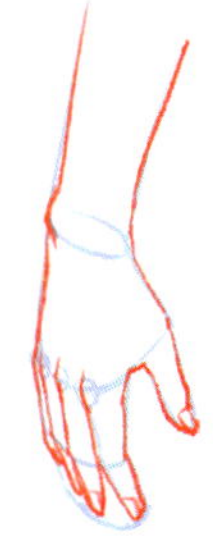

13 Refine the hand. Draw a rectangle and then halve it: one half is for the palm, the other is for the fingers (see page 49). Create a little angle so it is seen from a side view.

14 Adjust the palm to align the little finger with the wrist and arm. Add the fleshy base of the thumb and the thumb itself on the opposite side of the palm.

15 Add the joints for fingers and draw the sides to connect them, making them straight, bent or spread apart.

16 Erase the guide marks and clean up the lines.

FEET

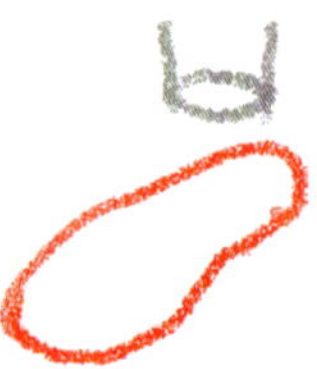

18 Draw the sole of the foot, leaving a gap between it and the leg.

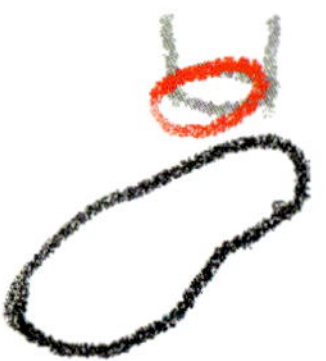

19 Draw an oval shape at the bottom of the leg, following the direction of the sole.

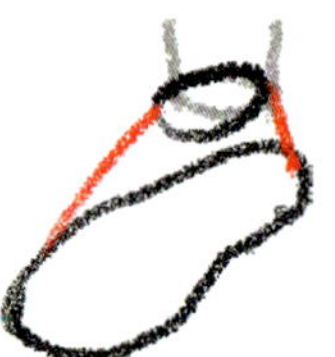

20 Connect the front of the sole to the front of the oval to shape the foot, then connect the back to form the heel.

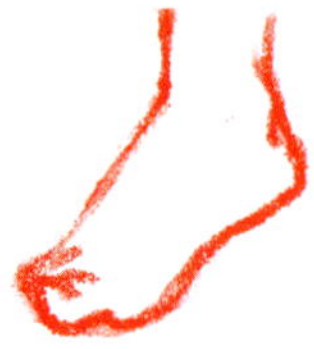

21 Remove the lines that should no longer be visible and add details such as toes if the figure is barefoot, or shoes if not.

BODY OUTLINE

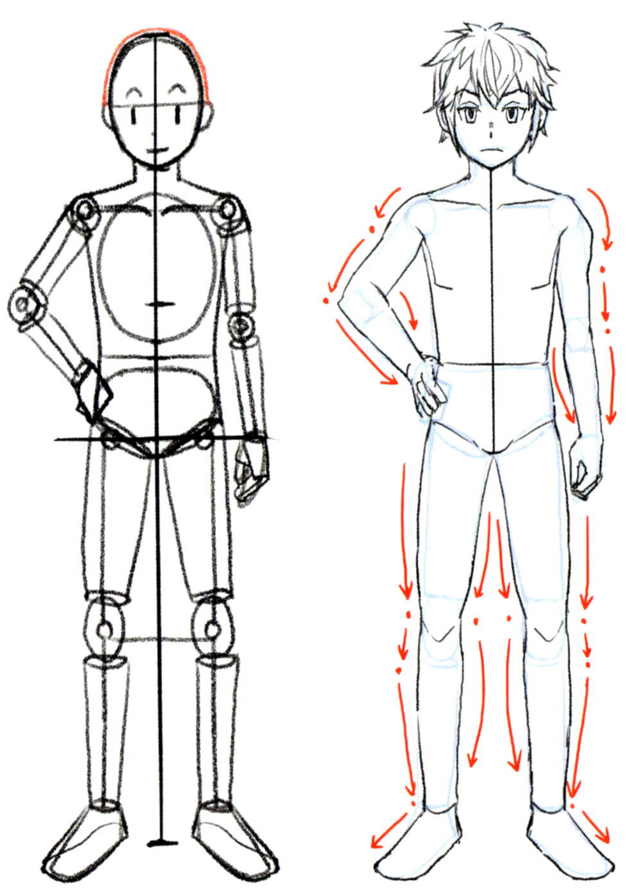

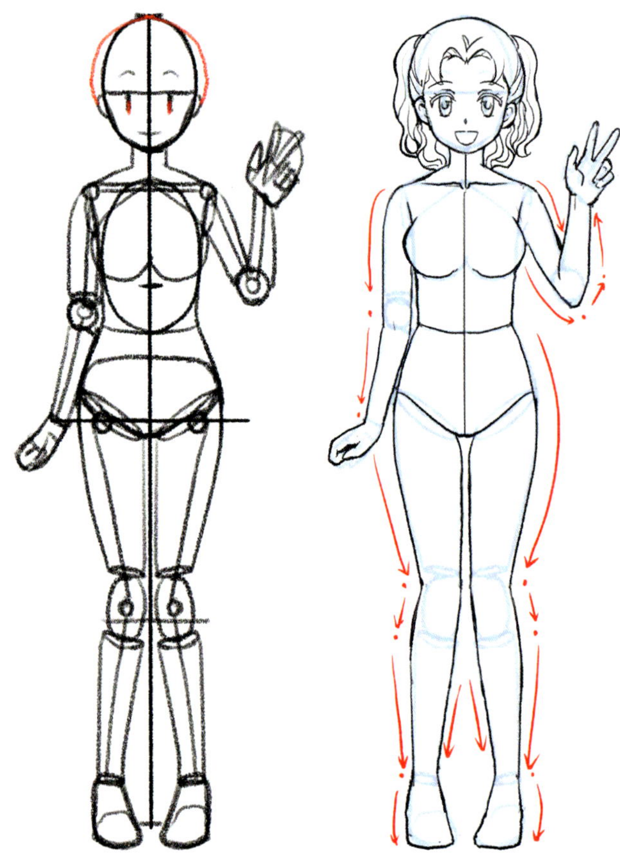

22 Your three-dimensional doll figure is now ready to be outlined. Draw over the main lines to create a solid pencil line. Draw in the character's face and hairstyle. Erase all the guide lines and clean up the body lines – your body is now ready to add clothing (see pages 51–52). You may wish to keep the vertical line down the torso and the line for the waist to help position the clothes.

FOCUS ON:

HANDS

Hands are the most difficult part of the body to draw, so don't be upset if you dislike drawing hands – most people do. However, humans have hands and we can't avoid drawing them. The tip is to break them down into simpler shapes and to practise. Avoid drawing a pose that hides the hands, as you will miss a chance to improve by practising!

HAND SIZE

Use a mirror to compare the size of your head with your hand – your hand will cover almost your whole face. Next, compare the length of your hand with your lower arm – the hand is about two-thirds of the lower arm's size.

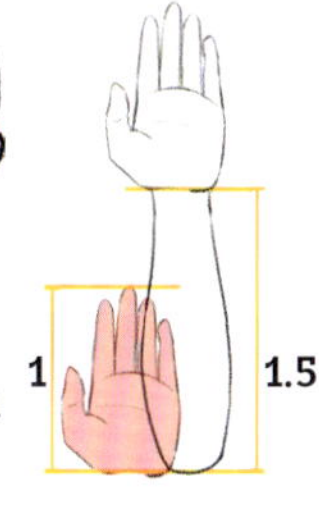

DRAWING HANDS

1 The palm and the fingers are the same length. Draw a rectangle that is twice as tall as it is wide and with rounded corners, then divide it in half vertically to form two squares.

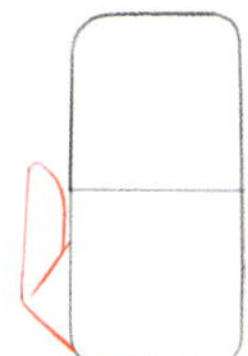

2 To add a thumb, draw a triangle at the bottom of the palm. Add a sausage shape to the triangle.

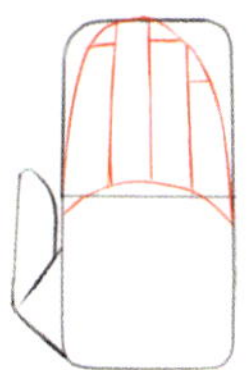

3 Change the top and middle horizontal lines into curves, and divide the top half into four finger shapes. Copy your own fingers to get the right proportions and shapes.

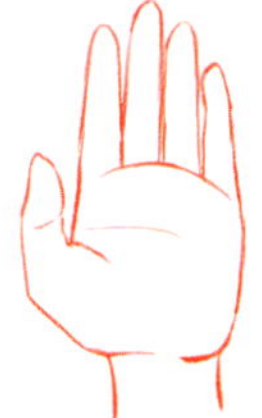

4 Clean up the lines and add the details such as shaping the fingers and creases in the palm and thumb.

SPREAD FINGERS

To draw spread fingers, start by drawing lines for the bones and adding the wrist and the knuckle joints. All the finger bones are joined together at the wrist and the knuckles are at the midpoint.

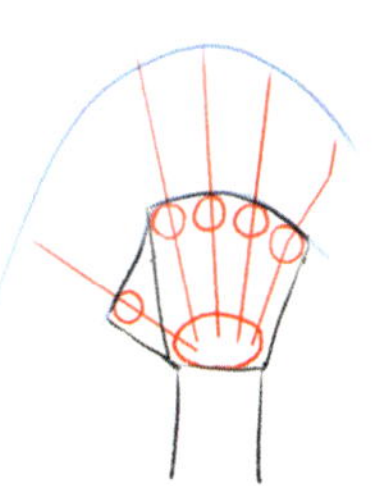

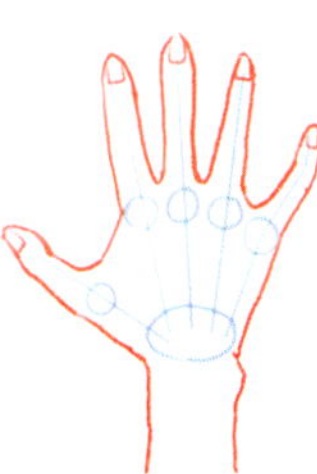

FEET

It's important for the proportions of your figure to look balanced, so when you start pay attention to the size and angle of the feet.

FOOT SIZE

Use a mirror to compare the size of your head and your shoe. The foot is quite big, almost head size. Does your figure have feet of a good size? The size of the feet are important so that your character appears to be steady on the ground.

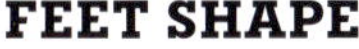

FEET SHAPE

The shape of a foot can be simplified as a trapezoid with one side longer than the other. The big toe is much larger than the other toes. Remember when creating a pose that the foot has joints at both the ankle and the toes. When drawing shoes, remember to allow for the space between the shoe and the foot.

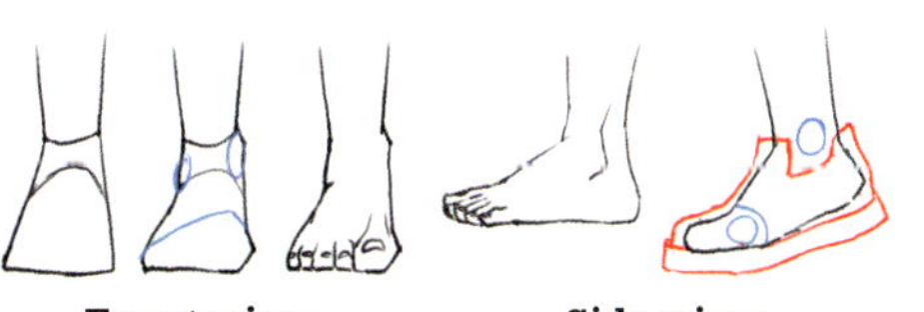

Front view

Side view

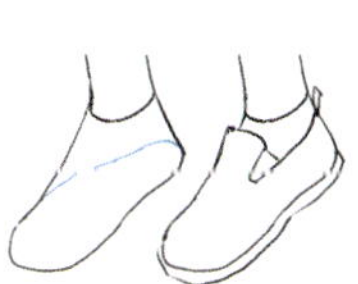

Top three-quarter view

Focus on:
Clothing

DRAWING CREASES

Use a piece of cloth to observe when and how fabric creases. Try pulling at one point: you will see creases going straight down with gravity. If you pull at two points, you will also see loose stretch curves between the points. When drawing clothes, find the points in the fabric that are being pulled, then draw gravity and stretch lines.

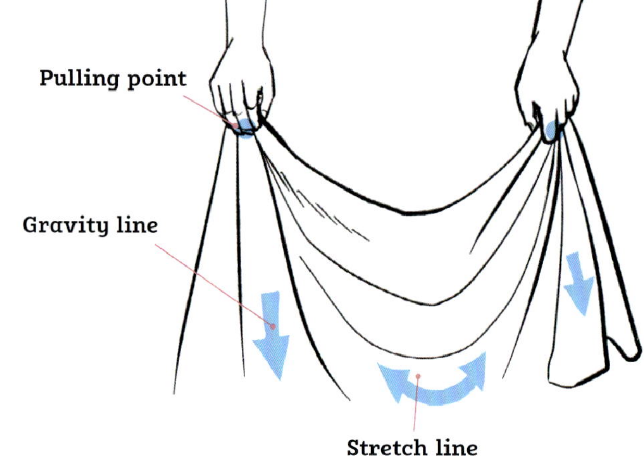

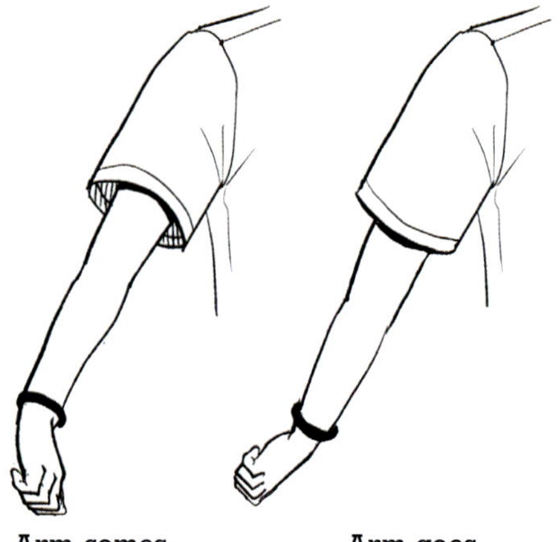

Arm comes forwards

Arm goes backwards

CURVES AT THE END OF THE FABRIC

Be aware of the shape at the edges of clothes. They do not sit straight on the body. The edges of sleeves, trousers and belts are curved lines because they are the top or bottom of a cylindrical shape. Depending on whether the inside of the sleeve is visible or not, you can draw the way in which it is angled.

MATERIAL AND FIT

Pay attention to type of material and clothing sizes. In tight clothes, you can see more straight creases than loose ones, and you can usually almost see the original body outline. Loose clothes will have fabric overhanging at the bottom, curvy relaxed creases and will be a bigger shape than the body line.

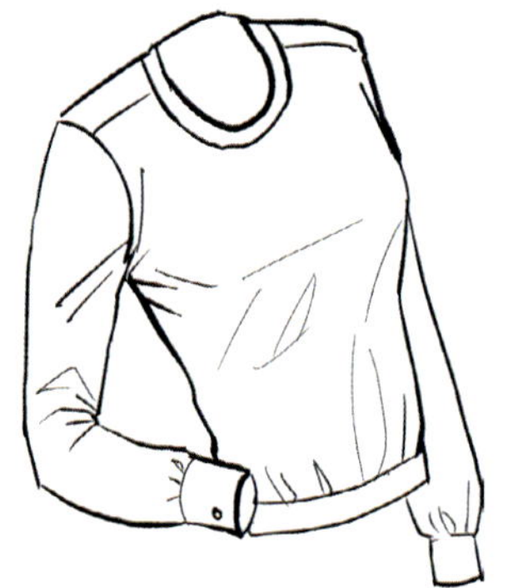
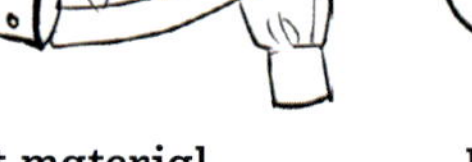

Tight material

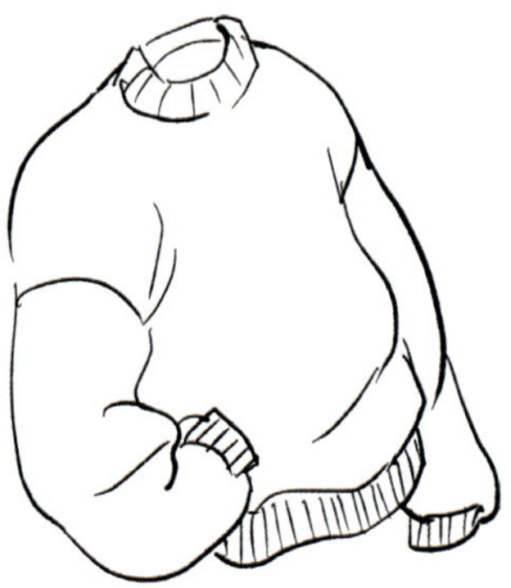

Loose and soft material

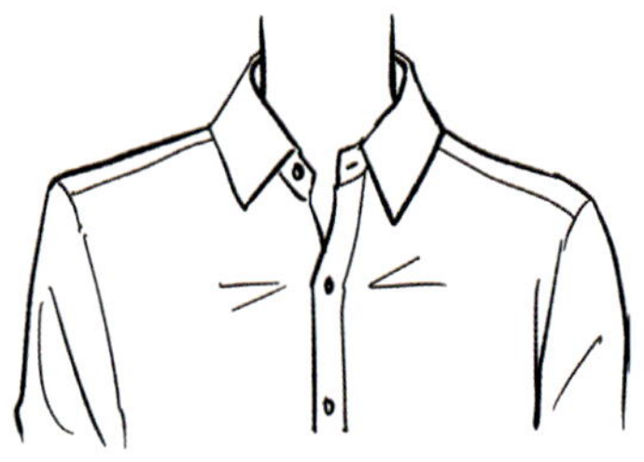

Men's

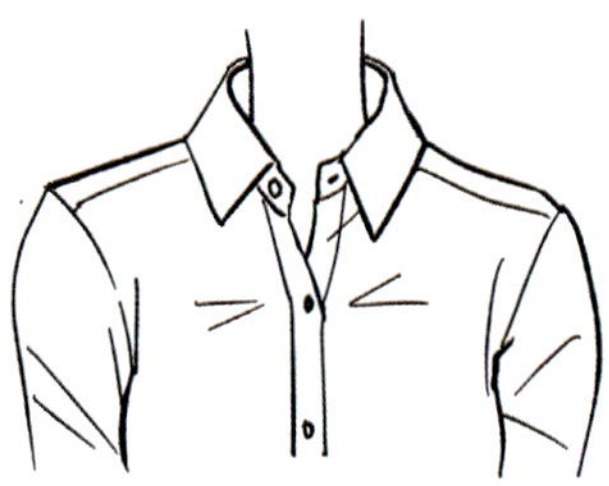

Women's

FASTEN ON THE CORRECT SIDE

Men's and women's clothes are fastened on different sides. For shirts and belts, women's clothes fasten on the left side, while men's fasten on the right.

STAGE 3

DRESSING YOUR CHARACTER

You are now ready to add your clothing to your character. Follow the steps below to draw clothes, but for the girl's shoes and socks and the boy's T-shirt, follow the steps on pages 22–23.

TIGHT BLOUSE

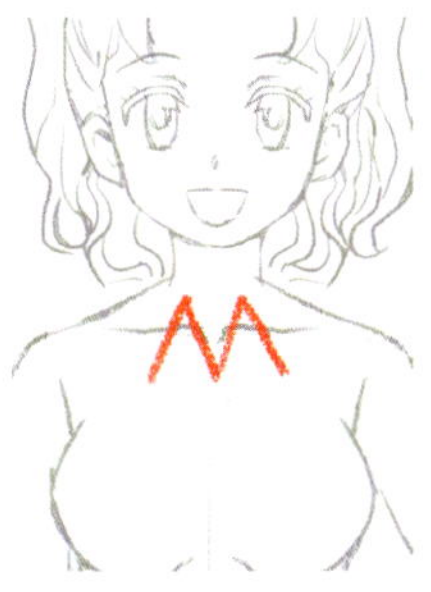

1 Draw an 'M' shape at the base of the throat to make the shape for the front of the collar.

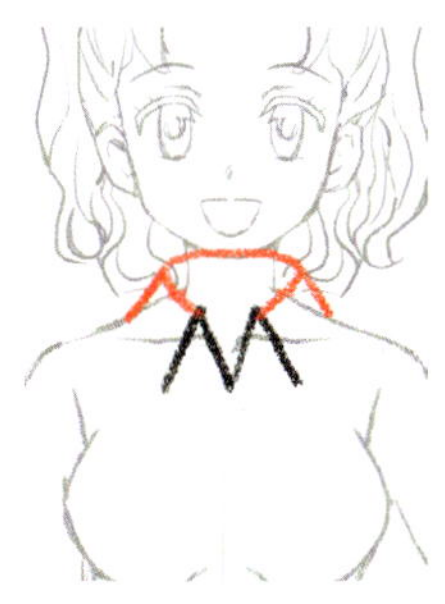

2 Draw a ring at the top of the collar that loosely circles the back of the neck, connecting it to the two top points of the 'M'. Add lines from the top of the collar to the shoulders.

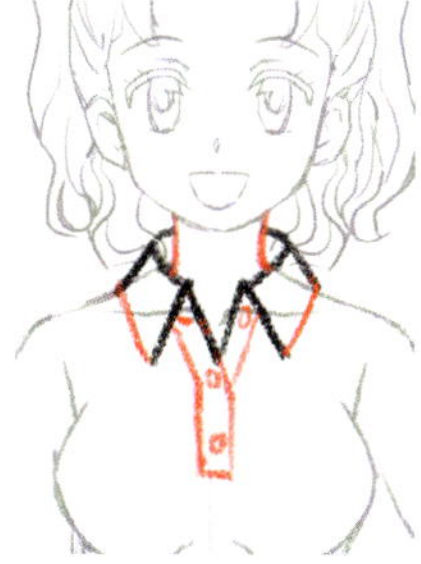

3 Draw lines to form the bottom edge of the collar. Erase the lines that won't be visible, so that the neck is in the middle of the collar. Add the details such as buttons.

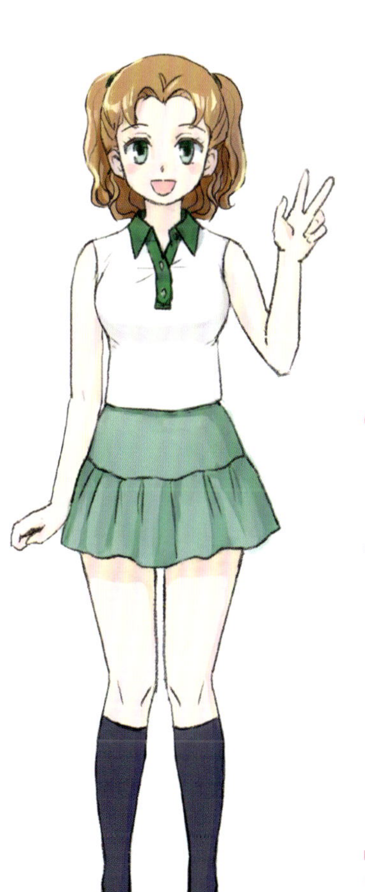

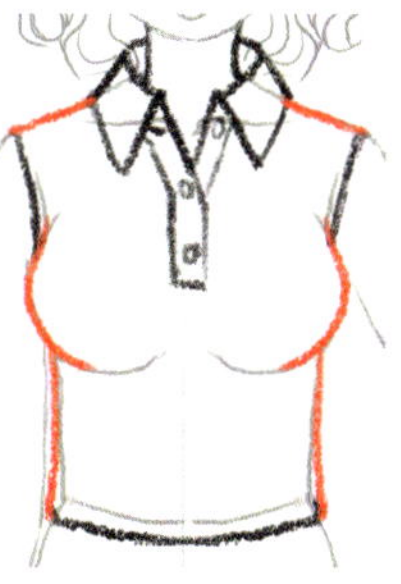

4 Draw curves for the armholes and the hem.

5 Draw the sides of the blouse, following the shape of the body.

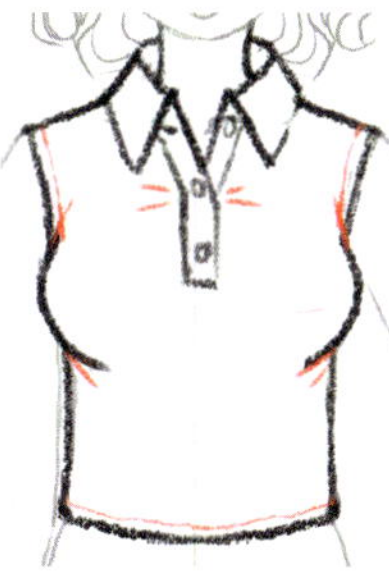

6 Add details such as creases. The fabric should stretch at the top of and below the breasts.

TIERED SKIRT

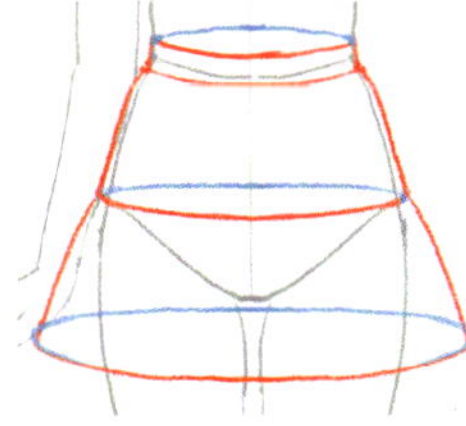

1 Draw three ovals: at the waist, in the middle and at the bottom of the skirt, then connect them, making a lampshade shape.

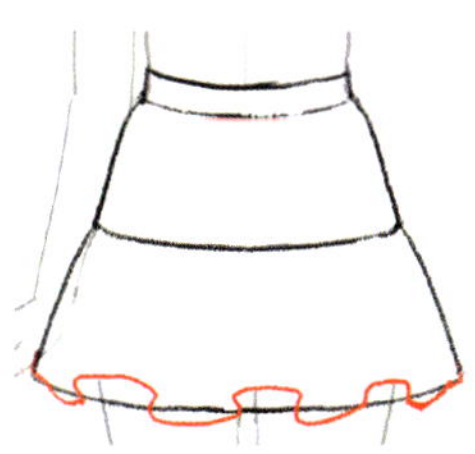

2 Change the hemline to create a wavy shape.

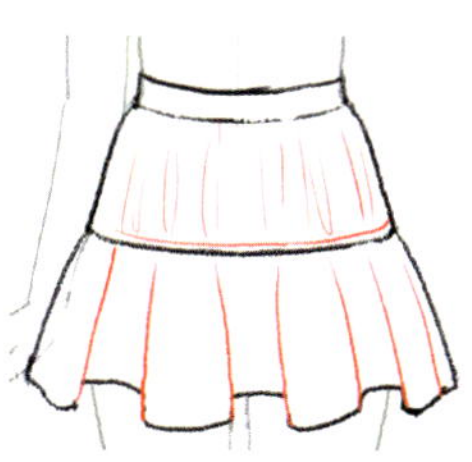

3 Draw vertical lines of gathered fabric. Where fabric overlaps, think about the front-back relationship and erase the lines that should not be visible.

DENIM TROUSERS

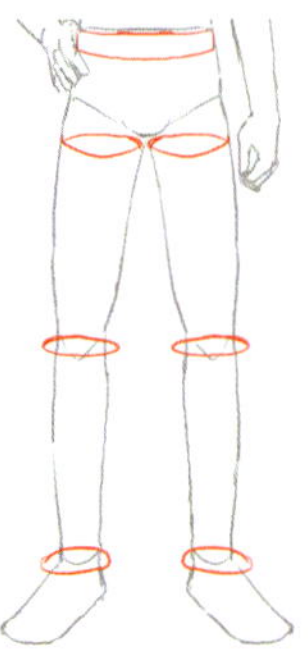

1 Draw an oval at the waist, then at the top of the legs, the knees and the ankles.

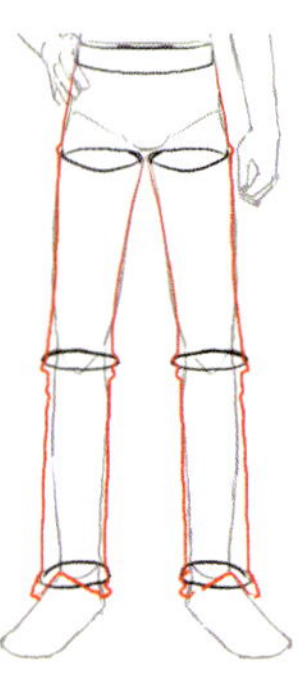

2 Draw an outline for the trousers by connecting the ovals. When near the ovals, use fine wavy lines to represent the sagging of the fabric.

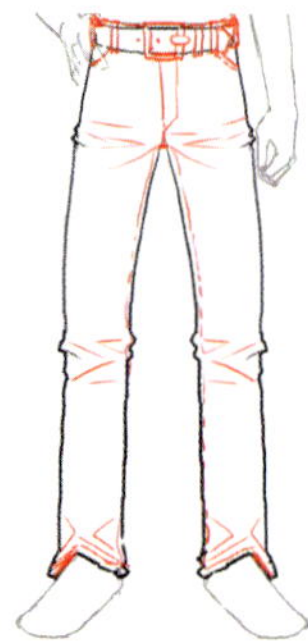

3 Erase body and guide lines that should not be visible, then add details. Draw triangular creases near the wavy lines, then draw belts, pockets, stitch lines, and so on.

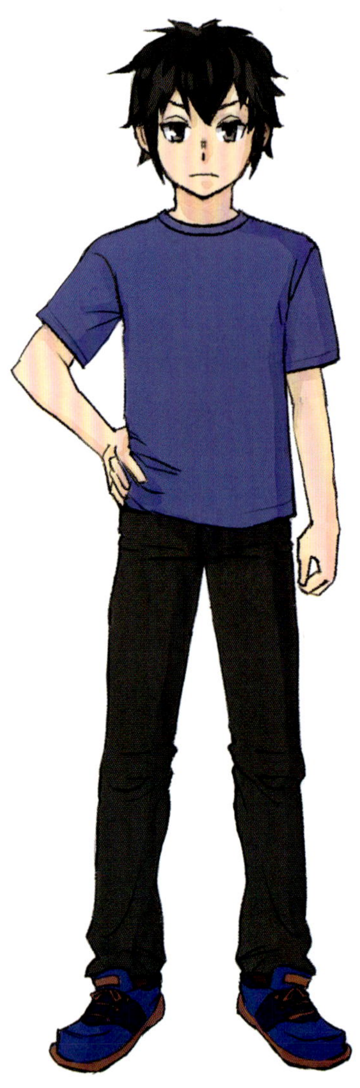

SPORTS SHOES

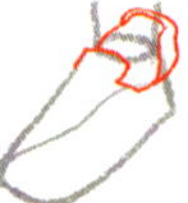
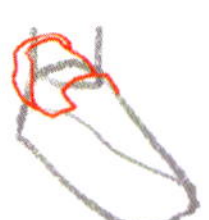

1 Draw the opening holes in the trainers (aka 'sneakers'). Be sure to look at the real thing or a photograph to draw them, as they are padded and complex.

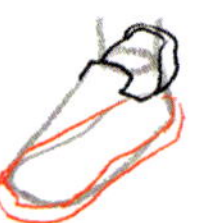
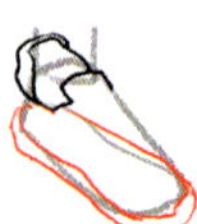

2 Draw the soles of the shoes. Shoes are one size larger than the foot, and the soles of trainers are even larger and thicker than that.

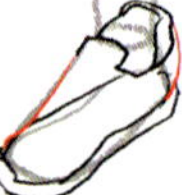
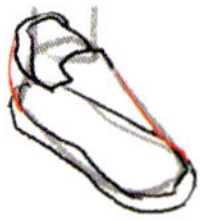

3 Draw the side lines for the shoes. The shape will vary according to the shoe's design, so observe carefully and connect the lines.

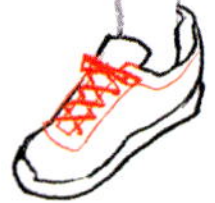
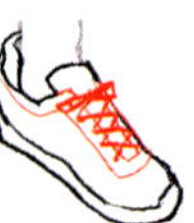

4 Erase any lines that should not be visible and draw in the details such as shoelaces.

FINISHING OFF

It is important as an artist that you polish up the final drawing.

CLEANING UP YOUR SKETCH

Erase any unnecessary lines and tidy up your drawing. Check that all the lines are clean and fully connect where they meet.

COLOUR FINISH

When you're happy with your final figure, you could give it a colour finish – you will find the details in projects 8 and 9 (see pages 98–123).

PRACTICE:
BODY TYPES

DIFFERENT BODY SHAPES

You might wish to draw a muscular or large character. Here are some tips to add extra muscles or bulk to your figure.

MUSCULAR FIGURES

Thick neck

Shoulder muscles hide the base of the neck

Wide shoulders

Pecs

Biceps inside the upper arm

Triangular forearm muscles

Abdominal muscles

Thigh muscles bulge on the outside

Calf muscles are thick at the top and taper down

LARGER FIGURES

Soft, curved underside to the chin

Broad, rounded shoulders curve down to the arms

A large oval shape for the stomach

Thick arms and legs

DIFFERENT PROPORTIONS

FOUR HEADS

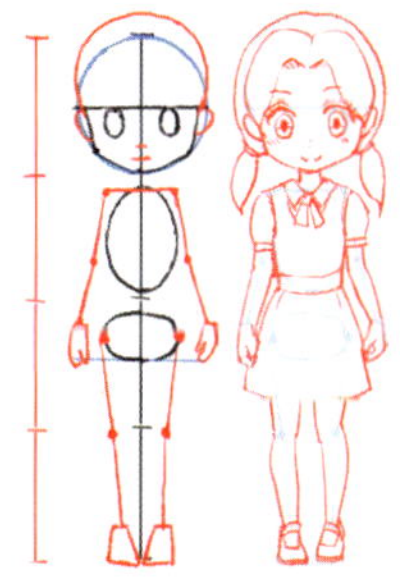

For figures two to five heads tall, draw the vertical line and then mark the head divisions. Draw the head in the top section, then add the horizontal central line halfway between the bottom of the head and the base of the vertical line. Follow the rest of the steps of the six-head-tall figure, but with the elbows halfway between the bottom of the head and central line.

EIGHT HEADS

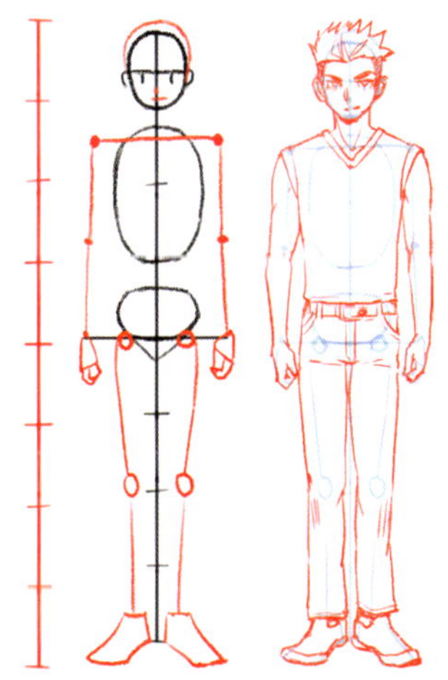

For figures seven heads or more tall, simply draw the vertical line and mark on it the head heights, then follow the instructions for the six-head-tall figure.

Practice:
Draw more figures

The method of starting a drawing from a stick figure introduced in this project is the basis for drawing three-dimensional bodies in any pose. Practise creating lots of characters using the four stages of body drawing, and you will soon gain confidence in drawing a variety of three-dimensional bodies in different shapes and poses.

1 Practise drawing of stick figures (see pages 44–45) until you can draw one figure in a minute. Draw some with different genders and heads, and some with different poses.

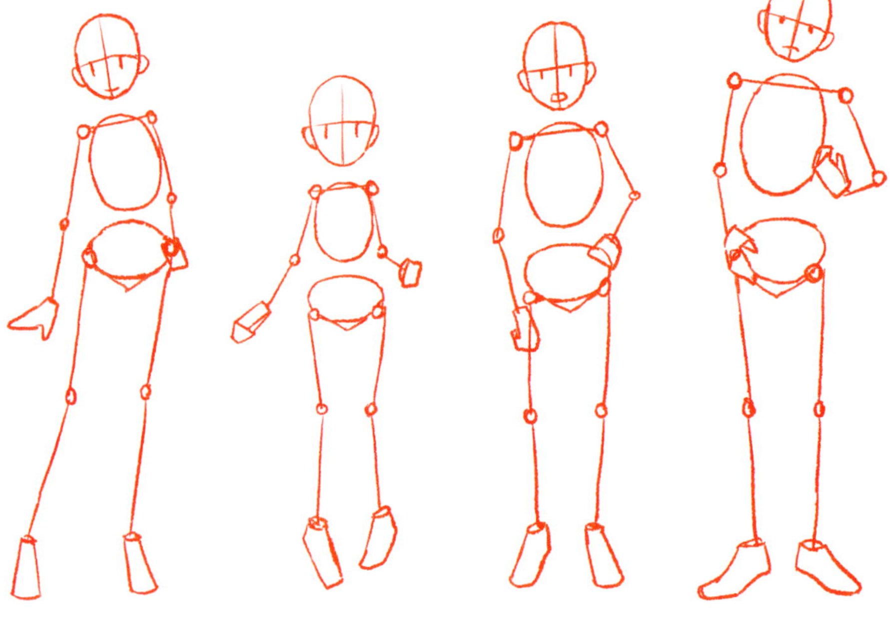

2 Once you can confidently draw a stick figure, practise the following stages. First, add shape to your character to turn it into a doll figure (see pages 46–48).

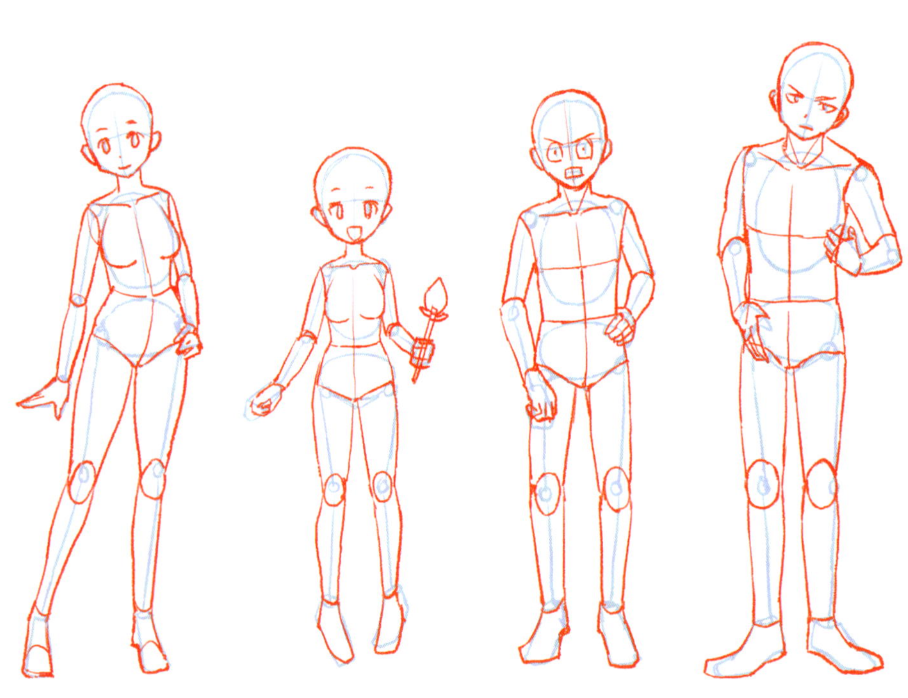

3 Add the outline (see page 48) and then add other details such as faces (see page 29), hairstyles (see pages 34–35) and clothing (see pages 51–52). If you wish to colour your final figures, follow the details in projects 8 and 9 (see pages 98–123).

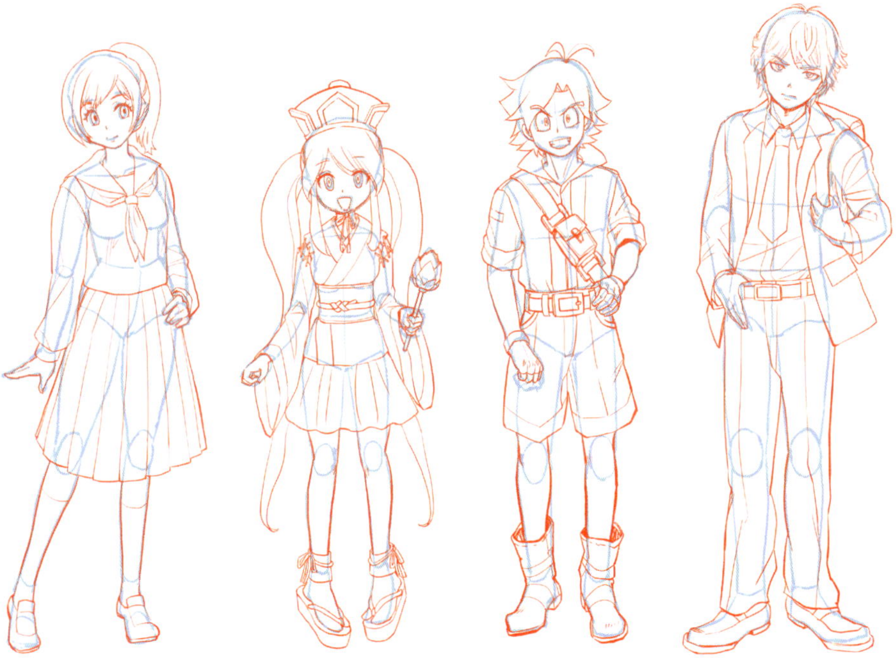

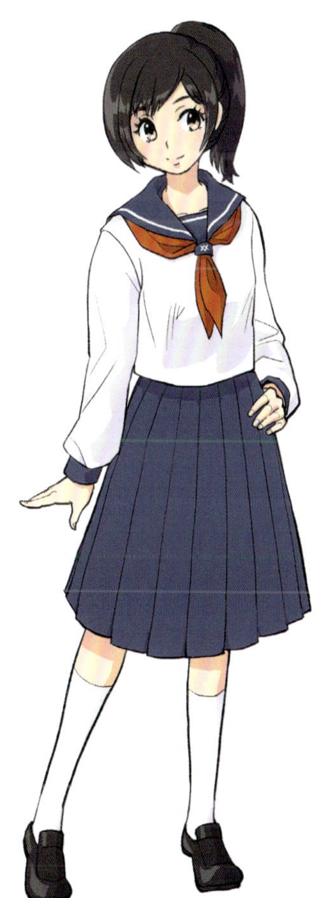

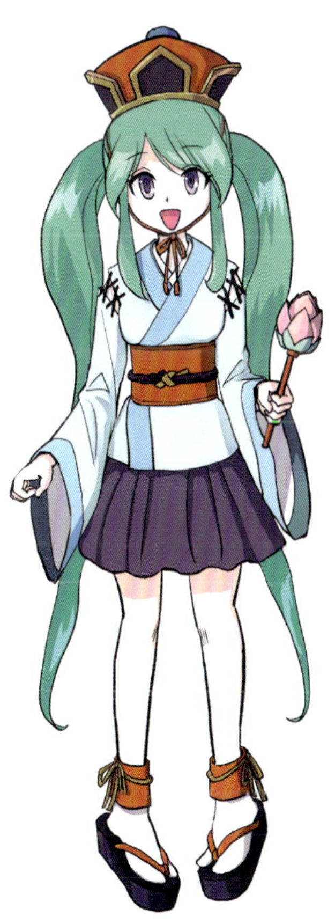

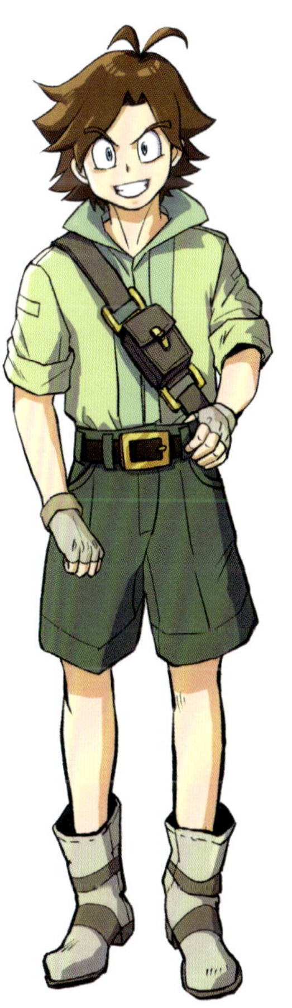

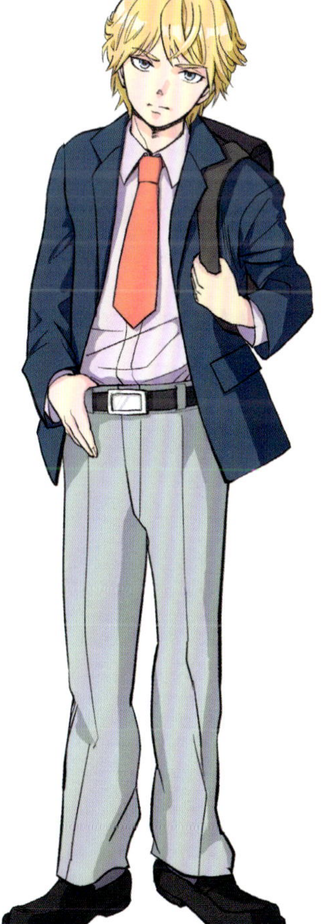

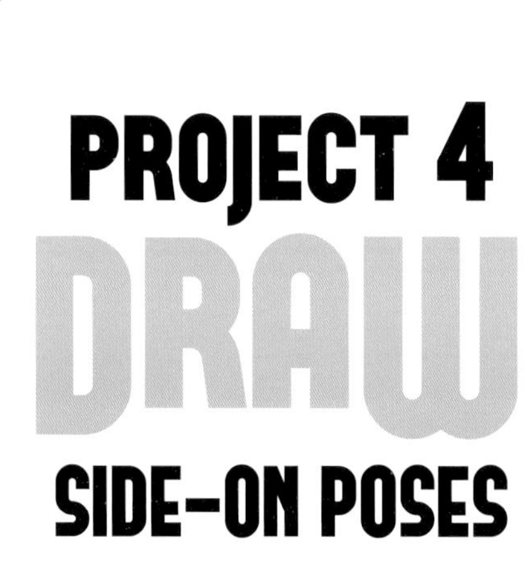
PROJECT 4
DRAW
SIDE-ON POSES

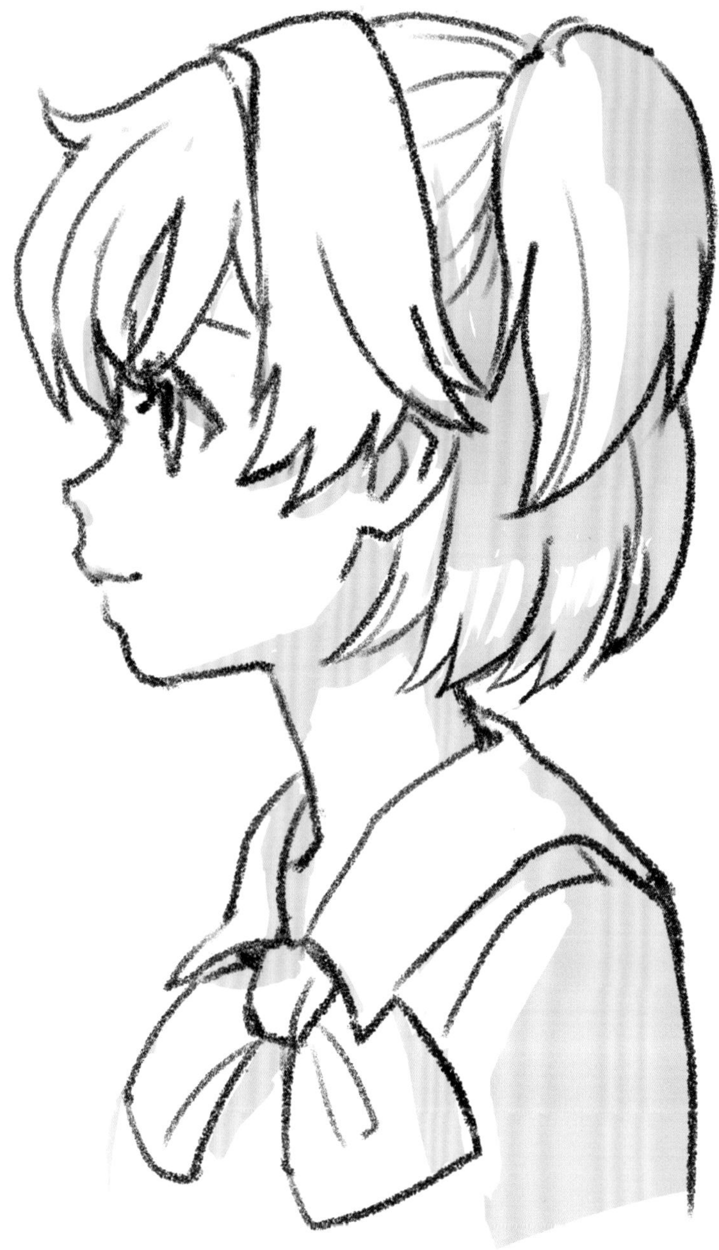

The previous projects have concentrated on drawing figures as they are seen from the front, but we often also see people from other angles. In this project, you will learn the different drawing skills used by manga artists to create faces and bodies that are seen from a side view.

Drawing the Head

Have you ever tried to draw faces from a side view? It isn't difficult if you know a little about facial proportions, especially since you don't have to worry about symmetry! Let's draw one.

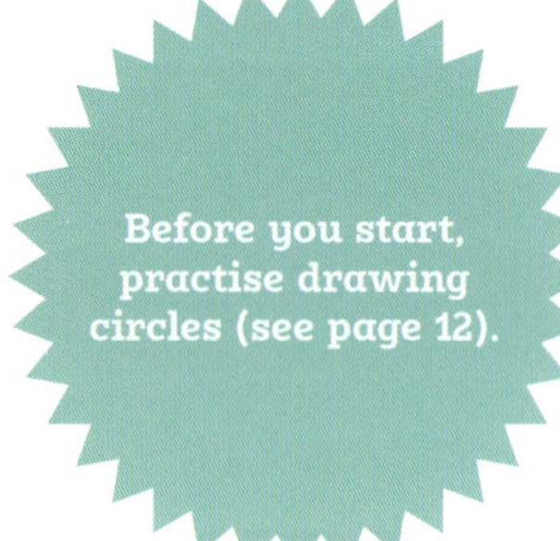

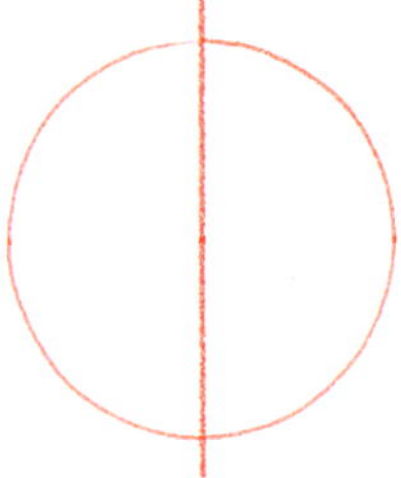

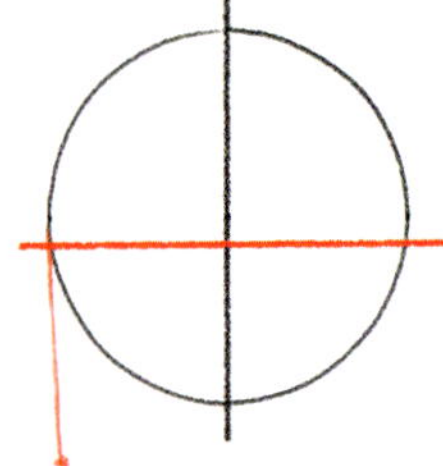

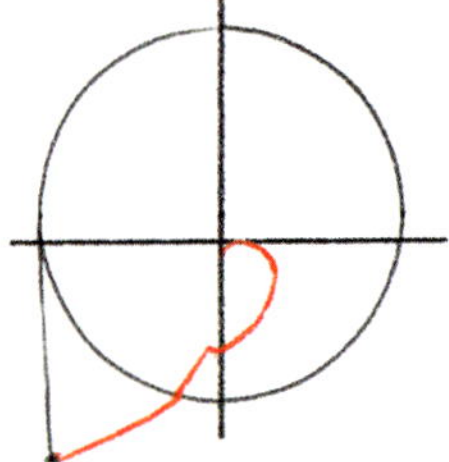

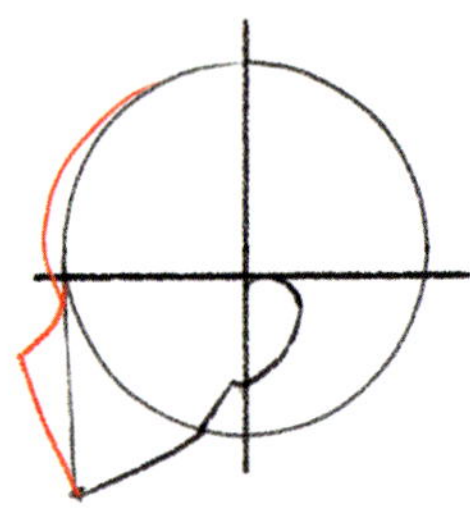

1 Draw a circle and divide it exactly in half with a vertical line.

2 Draw a horizontal line across the centre of the head. From where it meets the left edge of the circle, draw another line a little past the base of the circle. Mark the bottom of this line for the tip of the jaw.

3 For the ear, draw a line starting from the centre of the head and create an outline of an ear, then continue it to the mark at the bottom on the vertical line, making a jaw shape.

4 The top of the nose sits just below the horizontal line. Start at the top of the circle, drawing a curve for the forehead and sloping it down towards the top of the nose. Continue the curve outwards to the tip of the nose, then join it to the tip of the jaw.

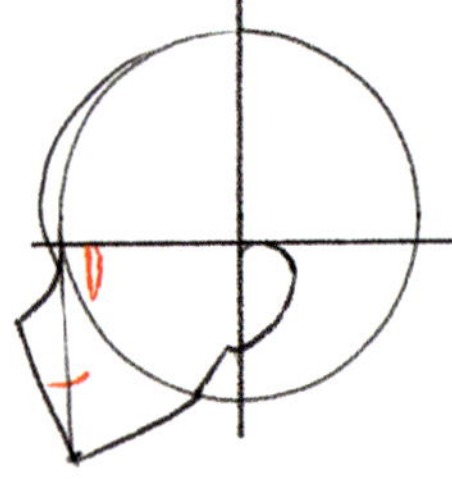

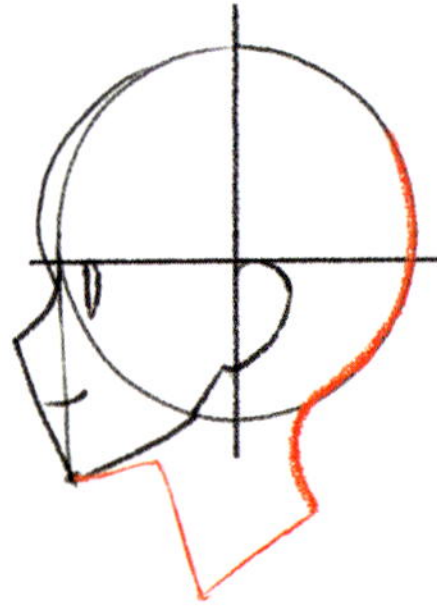

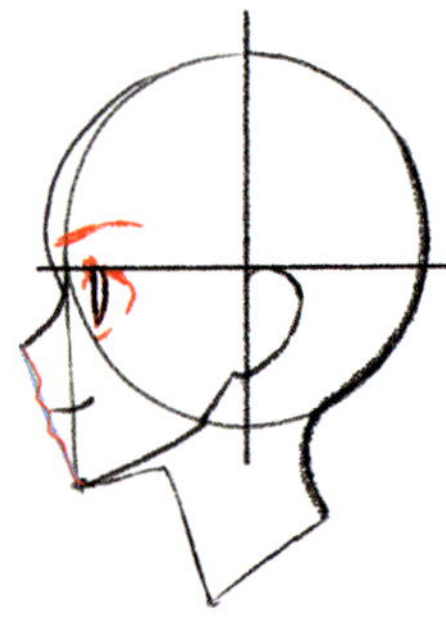

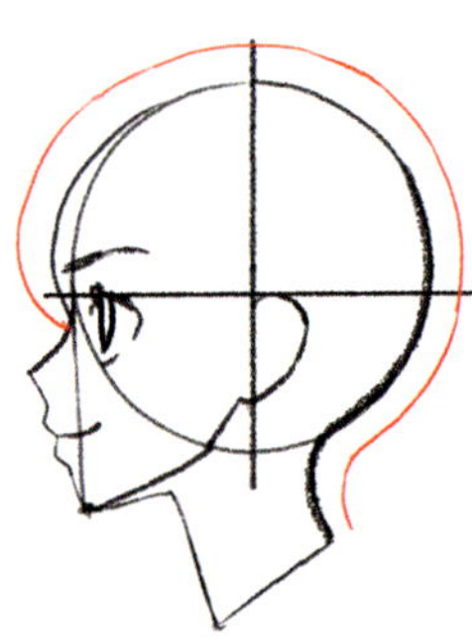

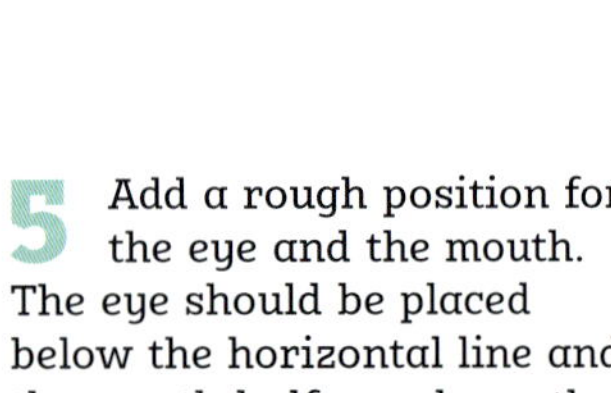

5 Add a rough position for the eye and the mouth. The eye should be placed below the horizontal line and the mouth halfway down the line between the top of the nose and the tip of the jaw.

6 Add the neck. Draw a horizontal line from the tip of the jaw to make the base of the chin, then draw the front of the neck at an angle so the head is tilted slightly forward. For the back of the neck, draw a line that curves and naturally joins the shape of the circle.

7 Draw in the details of the eye and the mouth (see page 60), then add the eyebrow – it should start a little in front of the eyelid.

8 Draw a helmet shape over the head; this will be the guide line for the hair.

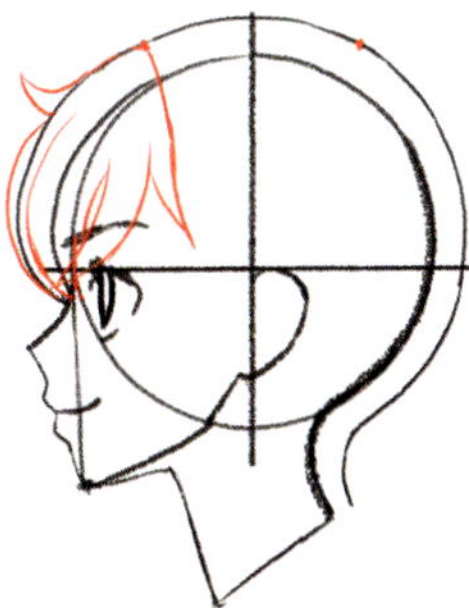

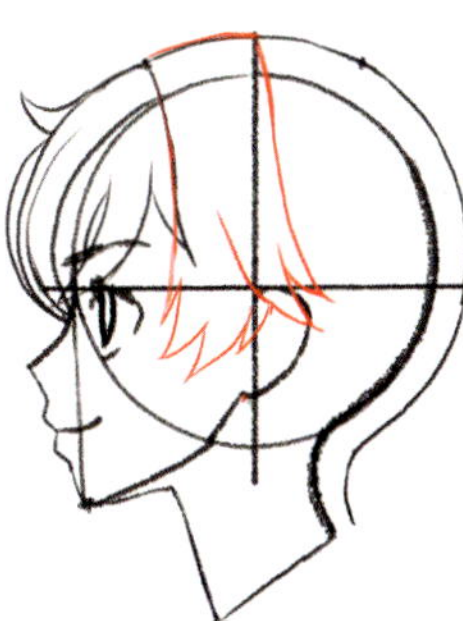

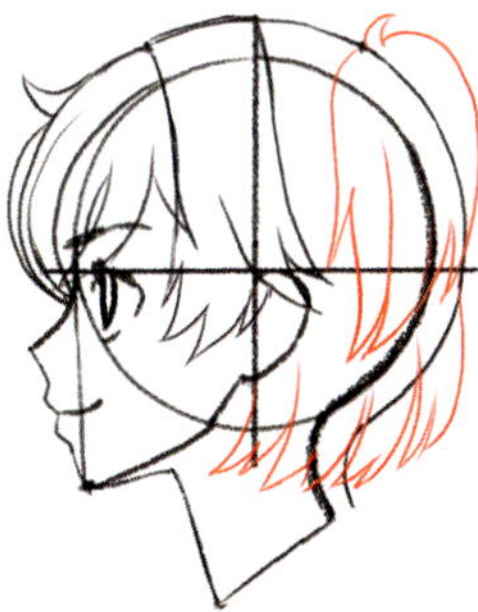

9 Mark the crown on the top of the head, then draw tufts of hair (see pages 34–35) to make the fringe. Use a curving line from the crown.

10 Draw the hair that falls down the side of the head. It will look best if you use a long curve from the crown.

11 Now draw the hair that falls down from the back of the head. If drawing a girl, you can add a pigtail on the side or a ponytail at the back.

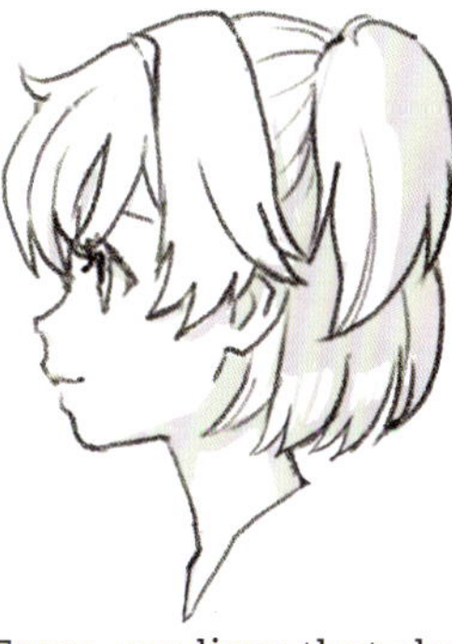

12 Erase any lines that should not be visible and tidy up your drawing. Check that all the lines are clean and they fully connect where they meet. If you wish to colour your drawing, you will find the details in projects 8 and 9 (see pages 98–123).

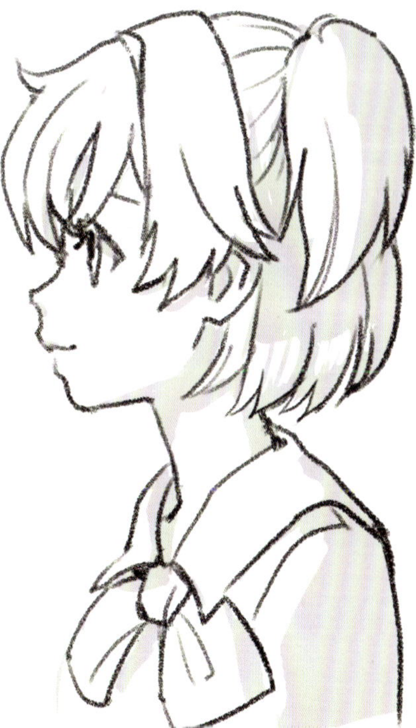

Focus on:
Eyes and mouths from the side

EYES

Because eyes are spherical, you can see only half the iris and pupil when viewed from the side. Make the iris and eyelids narrower than how they look from the front. The eyebrow should start a little further forward than the eyeball.

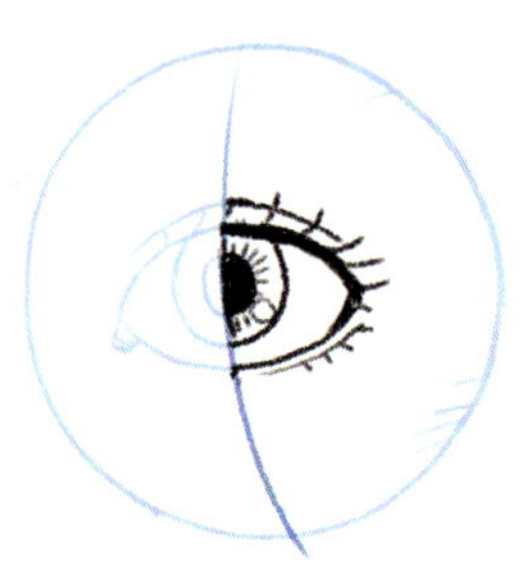

The side view (right) compared to the full eye

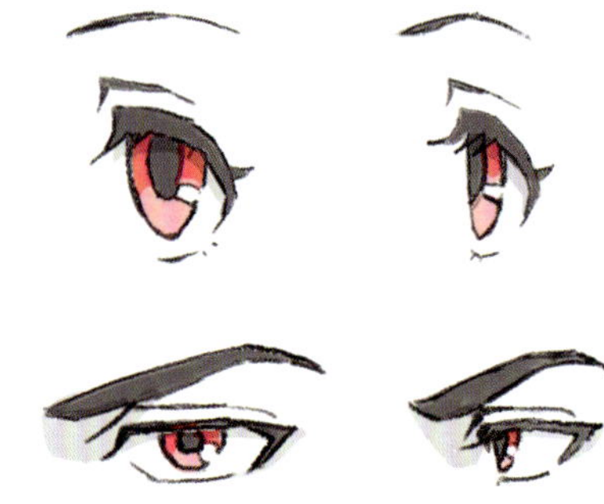

Front view **Side view**

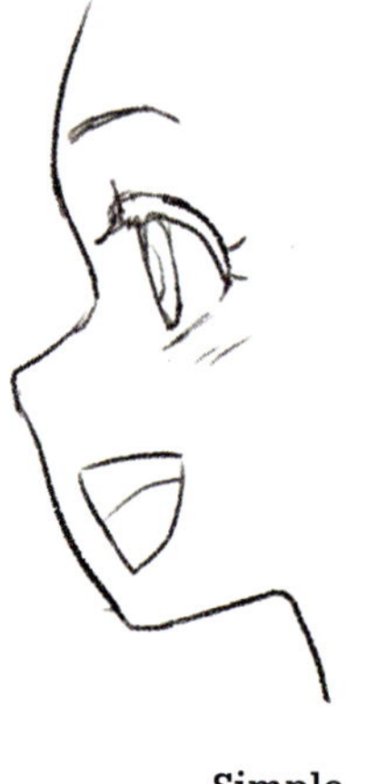

Simple

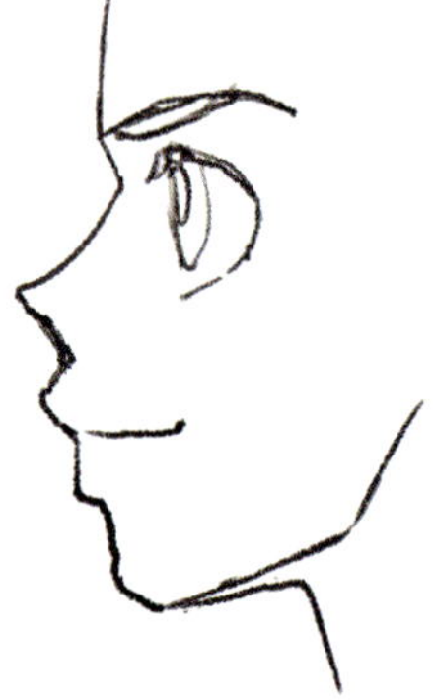

Realistic

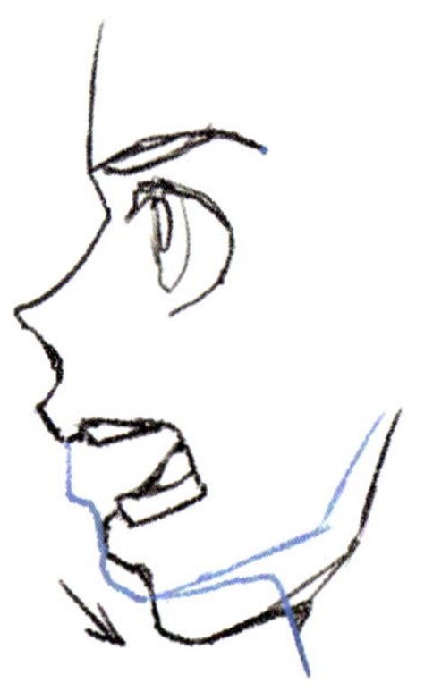

Open mouth

MOUTHS

For a simple mouth, just draw the same mouth as you would when viewed from the front. For a more realistic mouth, add lip shapes above and below the mouth's line. Remember the jaw will drop down with the mouth is open.

EARS

The ears should be drawn from the centre of head to the top of the jaw. Once you have the outside shape of the ear, draw just a few lines to suggest the more complex parts that can be seen inside the ear (see page 32).

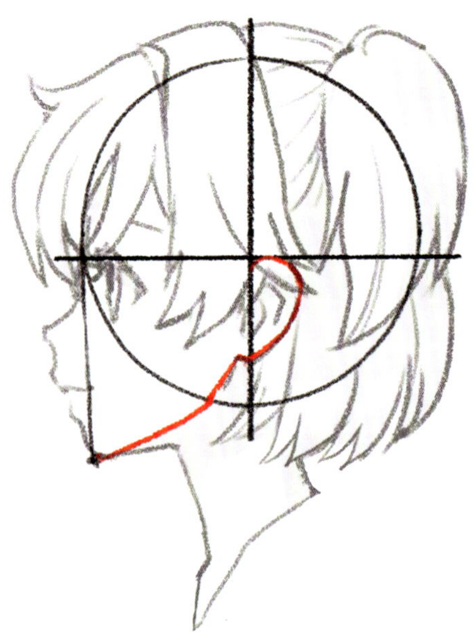

DRAWING THE BODY

A human body is quite curvy, especially when you look at it the from the side. This figure is six heads tall.

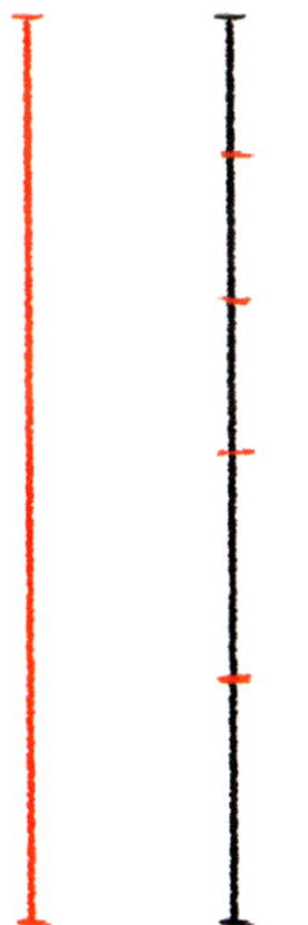

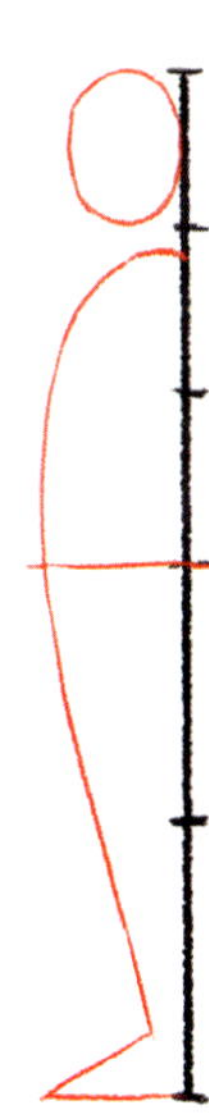

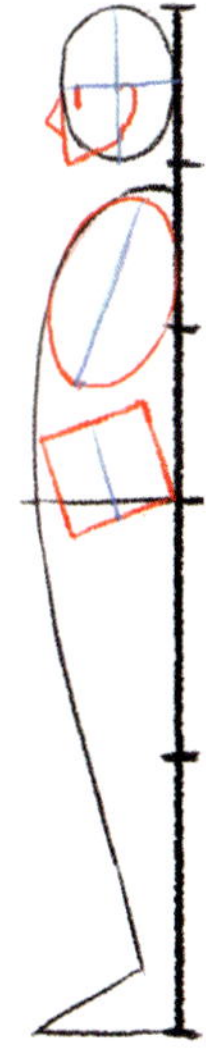

1 Draw a vertical line, the same length as the full height of the figure you intend to draw. Draw a horizontal line across the centre of body, then divide the top half into three parts and the bottom half into two.

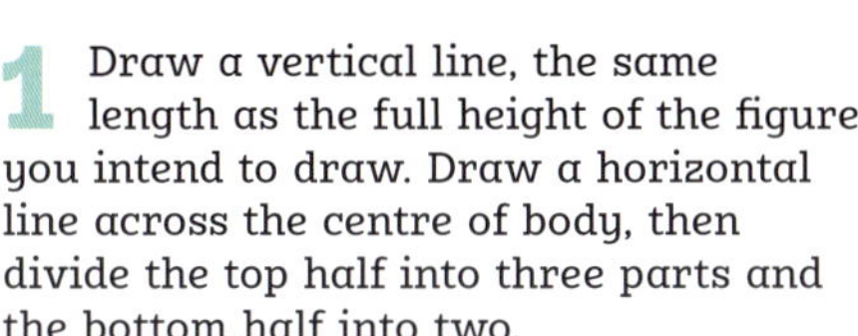

2 In the top section, draw an oval for the head on the side of the vertical line that you wish your character to face. Now draw a long 'C'-shaped curve from just below the neck space towards the base of the line, adding a triangle shape for the feet. Halve the body by drawing a horizontal central line.

3 Following the 'C'-shaped curve, draw the ribcage as an oval and then the pelvis as a rectangle above the horizontal central line. Take care that they are both tilting in opposite directions, like the picture above. Add a jaw and facial features to the head (see page 58).

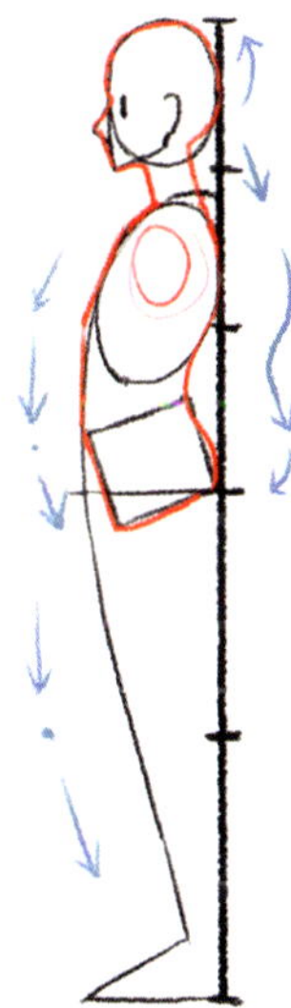

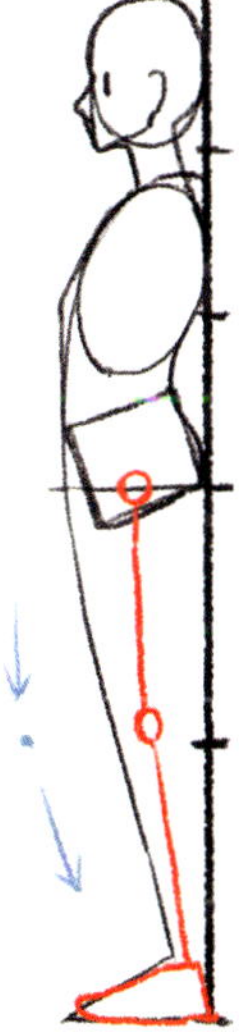

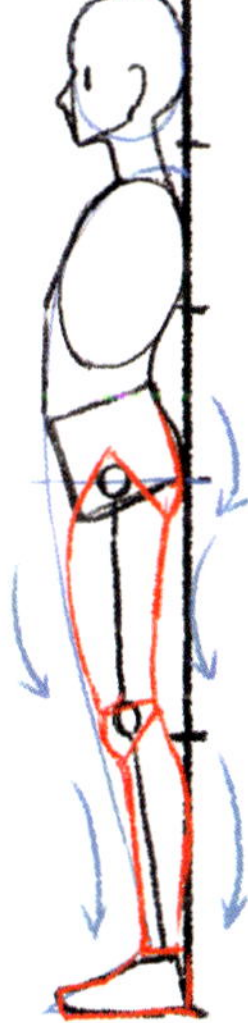

4 Draw the neck tilted slightly forward. Connect the body parts with strong curving lines (follow the waves in the guide arrows shown above). Adjust the shape of the head so that the top is more of a sphere.

5 Add the leg joints in the middle of the horizontal central line for the hip, on the lower quarter line for the knee. Also mark the ankle position, where the foot shape starts. Connect the joints to form two sticks for the leg.

6 Turn the sticks into a leg. Draw 'C' curves for the thigh, curving it forward, then curve the shin in the opposite direction, tapering it off at the ankle. Add a bulge to connect the leg to the hip.

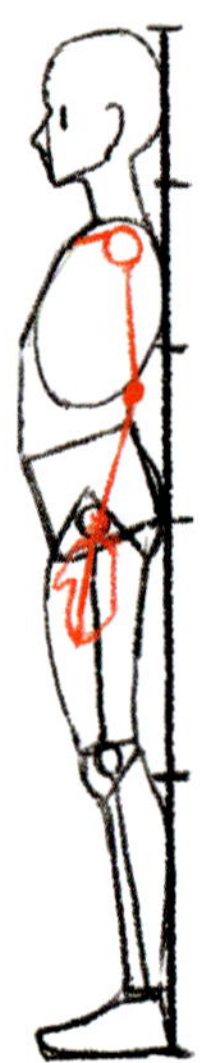

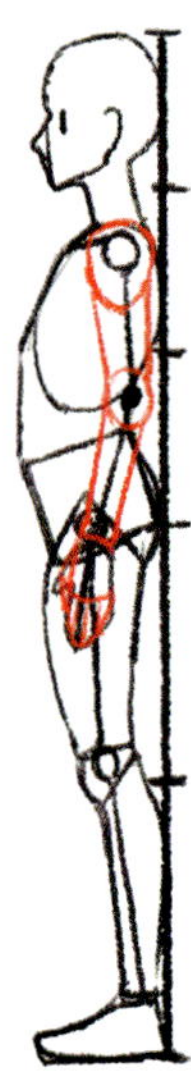

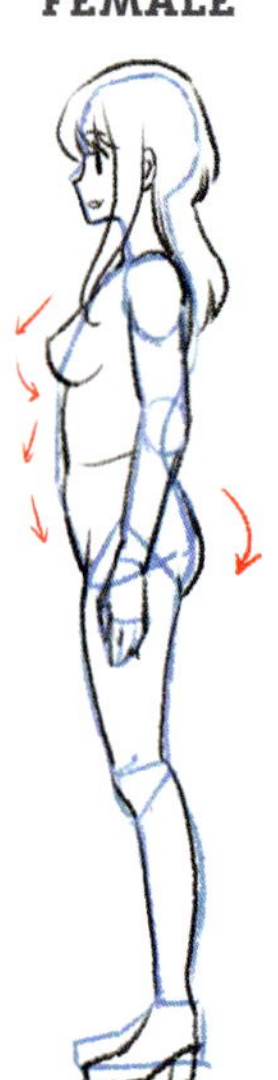

7 For an arm, draw a shoulder joint centred in the top of the ribs and connect it to the elbow at the bottom of the ribcage, in the middle of the torso. Connect it with another line to the wrist, which should be at the same level as the hip. The hand should be about two-thirds the length of the forearm.

8 Give the arm a fuller shape in the same way as for a front view (see page 46), making larger circles for the shoulder and elbow joints, then drawing lines to connect them. Halve the hand to divide it into the palm and fingers (see page 47).

9 Draw over the lines for the outline (see page 48) and add details. For women, add curves for breasts and the roundness of the hips. The overall effect should be more curvaceous and with slenderer limbs.

DRESSING YOUR CHARACTER

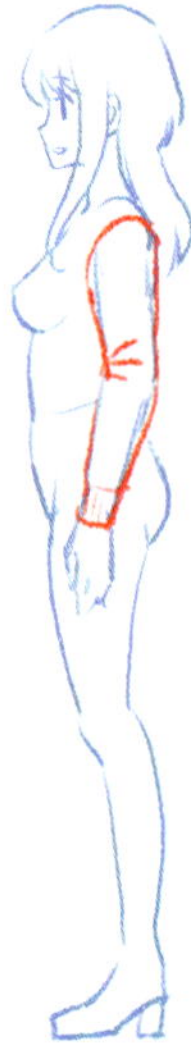

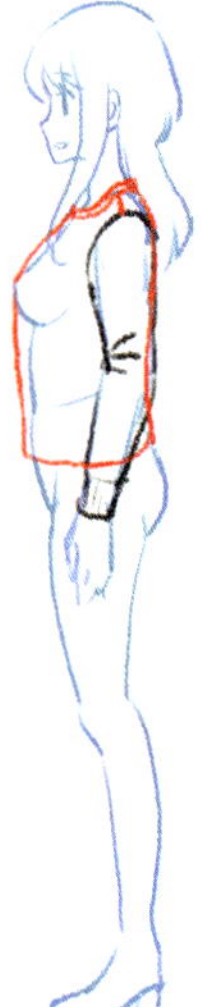

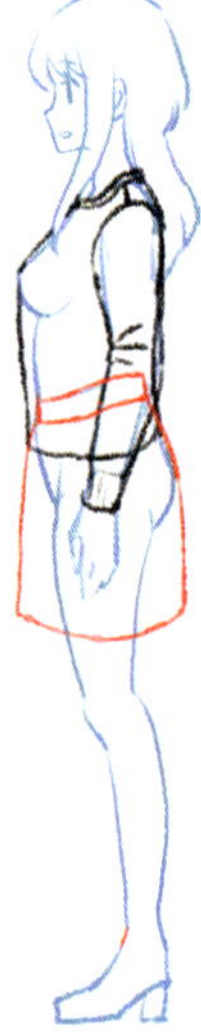

10 It is easier to draw the clothing items that are in the foreground first. Start by drawing the sleeve for the top from the shoulder seam.

11 Draw the rest of top. Add the collar shape and connect lines to it that drop over the widest parts of the torso. Note that the collar of a round neck will form an 'S' shape along the shoulders, and the hem will make a 'U' curve around the side of the body.

12 Draw the bottom layer such as a skirt. The waist should be tilted slightly higher in the back, so the belt is an 'S'-shaped curve with a lower front. From there, drop the fabric vertically, ensuring it will fall over any protruding parts of the body. The hem at the bottom should have a 'U'-shaped curve.

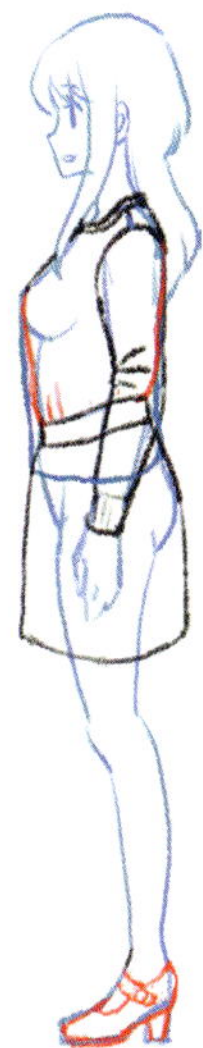

13 Tucking the hem of the top into the skirt will cause wrinkles around the waist area. For shoes with high heels, stand the foot on tiptoe and then draw the heel in the empty space. Add details such as straps and buckles.

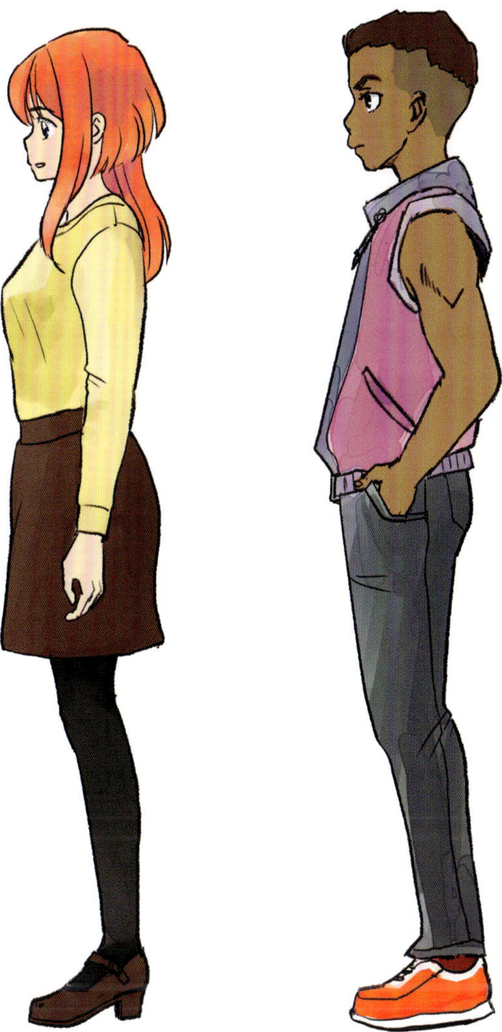

14 Erase any lines that should not be visible and tidy up your drawing. Check that all the lines fully connect where they meet. If you wish to colour your figure, you will find the details in projects 8 and 9 (see pages 98–123).

Checklist

- Check for the same issues as the front view (see page 24).
- Check that the back of the head, hip and heels align vertically.
- Are there any solid straight lines left in the body? Transform them into natural-looking, curved lines.

AVOID STRAIGHT LINES

Do not align the body so it will be standing too straight. This will make the figure look stiff and robot-like.

Build up the body parts so they form a zigzag and use curving lines instead.

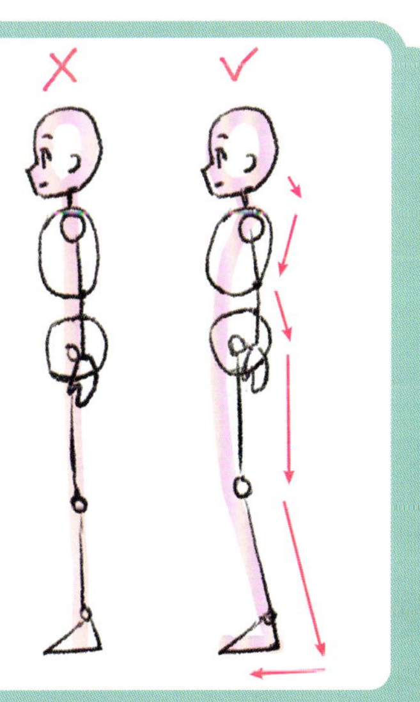

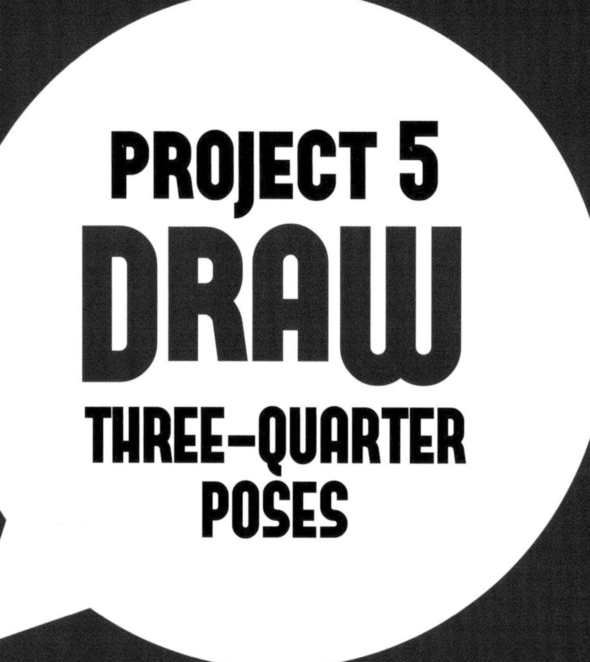

PROJECT 5 DRAW THREE-QUARTER POSES

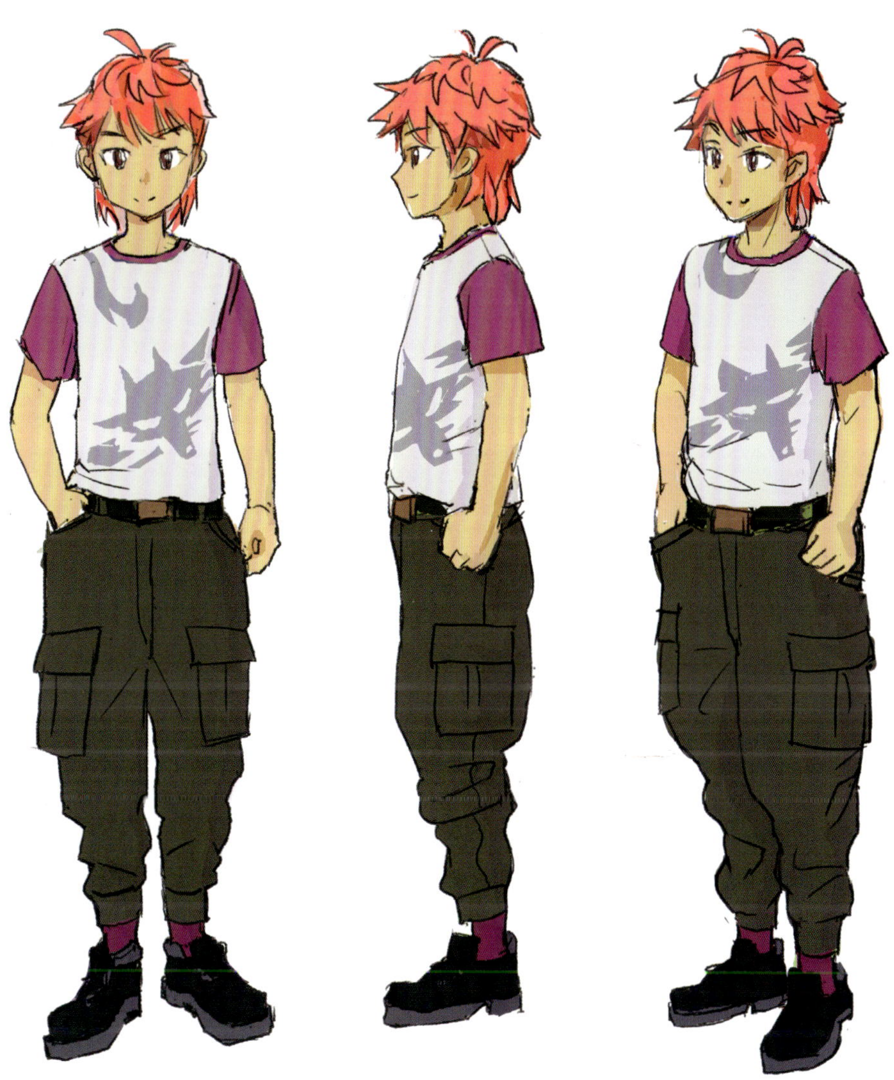

Let's now try drawing the head and body from a three-quarter view. Being able to draw figures that look three dimensional and have depth from different angles is a key skill to develop. Once you can draw a figure from a three-quarter view, you will be able to draw it from any angle – something you will need to master if you wish to draw comic strips or animation.

DRAWING THE HEAD

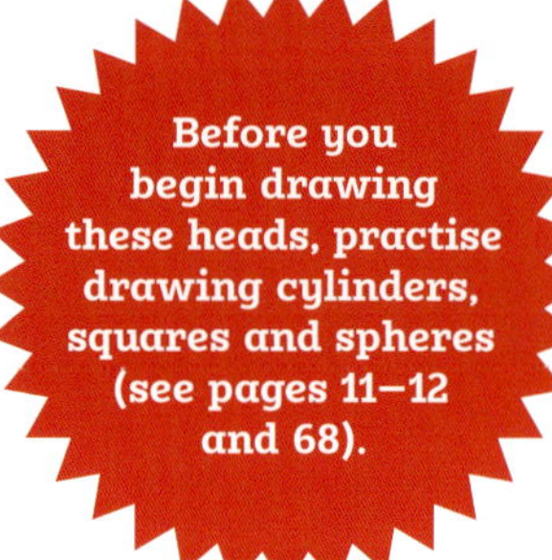

When you draw a head from a three-quarter view – or from any other angle – thinking in three dimensions is essential. You must learn to see two or three sides at the same time to be able to convincingly draw a head with a solid shape. The steps here are for a three-quarter view, but you can adjust the positions of the lines if you wish to draw a face from a different angle.

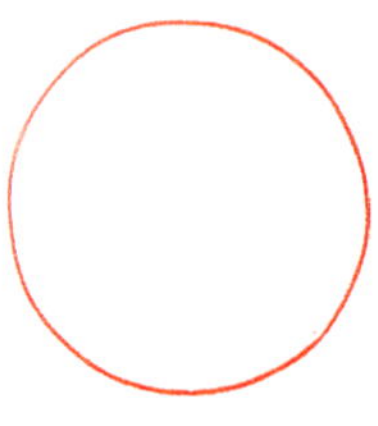

1 Draw a neat circle. (This is usually the starting point regardless of the angle you wish to draw the head.)

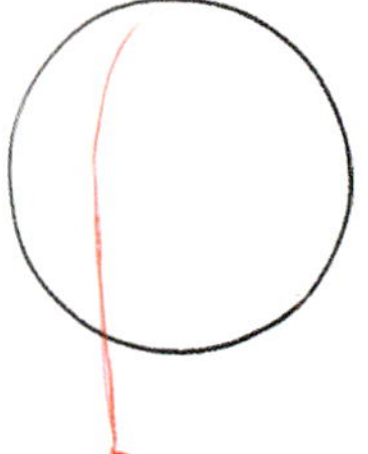

2 Draw the face's central line. For three-quarter view, draw the line about a quarter way around the sphere. This line should curve at the top of the head (see page 68), but make it straighter for the bottom half. Draw it a little longer than the circle, as it will mark the position for the chin.

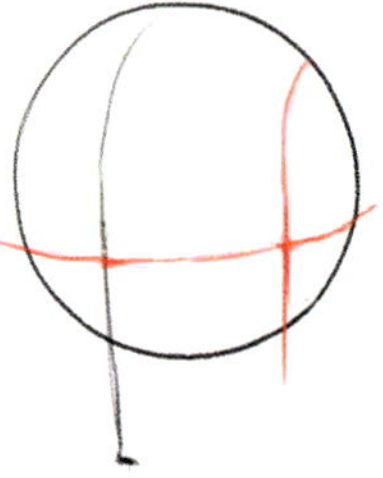

3 Draw another guide line on the other side. This forms the edge between the front of the face and the side of the head. Measure the height for the face from the top of the circle to the bottom of the central line. Divide it in half, then draw a horizontal line for the height of the eyes.

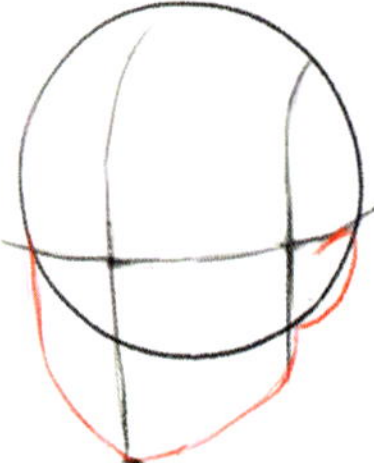

4 Draw the ear on the side of the head below the horizontal line, and continue the line to the base of the central line to form part of the jaw. Draw a line from the other side to finish the shape of the jaw and chin.

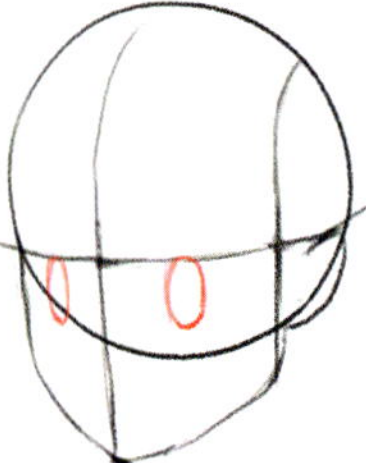

5 Draw eyes underneath the eye horizontal line, one each side of the central vertical line. The left part of the face space is narrower than the right, so make the eye on that side narrower.

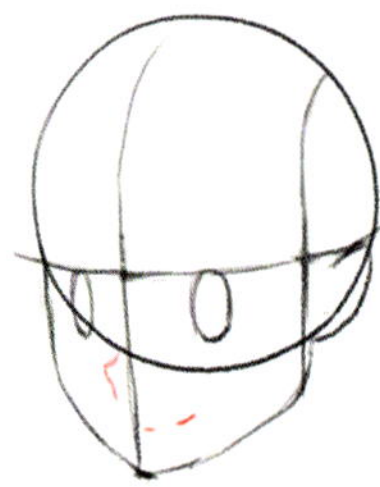

6 Draw the nose starting at the central line, with the depth of the nose on the left side of the face. Draw the mouth on the opposite side of the central line. It will look nicer than drawing it on the line.

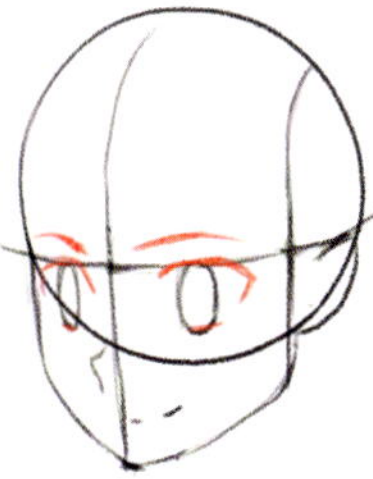

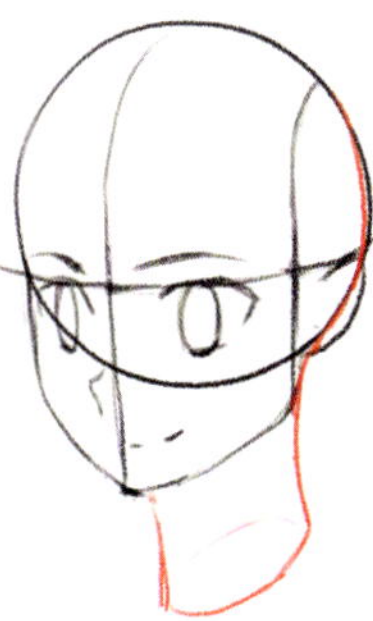

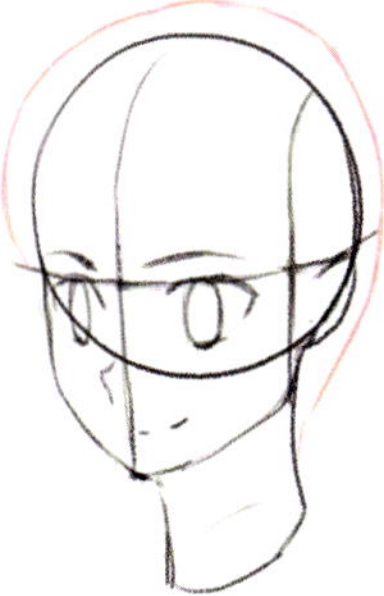

7 Add the eye details and eyebrows (see pages 30–31). For a three-quarter view, the one on the left should be narrower than the right side, and the right eyebrow should start further left than the eye, like a side-view eyebrow.

8 Draw the neck. The neck attaches to the head at the back rather than the centre of the head, so draw it further to the right (not from the face's central line). The line of the neck on the right should smoothly connect with the back of the head in an 'S' curve.

9 To add hair, enlarge the top of the head by drawing a helmet-like bigger circle over it.

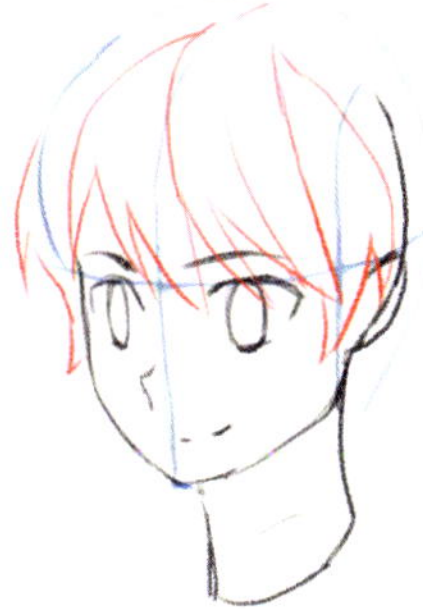

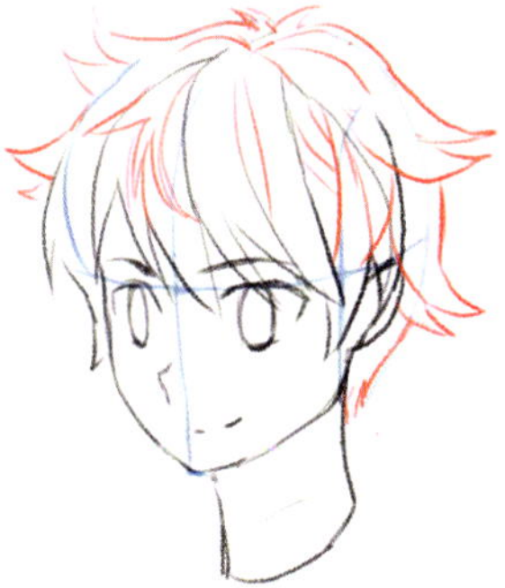

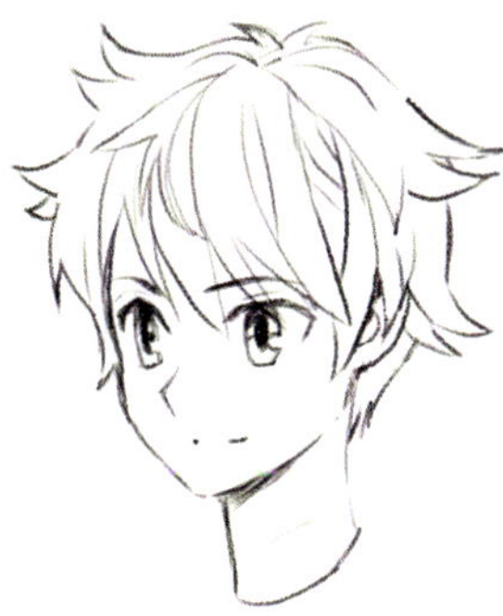

10 Add the fringe and sides of the hair (see pages 34–35). Make these shapes a mixture of those for a front view and side view (see page 59). Make the lines flow down from the crown of the head.

11 Draw the back of the hair. Think carefully: the hair will mostly be behind the head, so draw only what should be seen from this angle.

12 Add any details such as for the eyes and ears (see page 32). Erase any lines that should not be visible and tidy up your drawing. Check that all the lines fully connect where they meet. If you wish to colour your figure, you will find the details in projects 8 and 9 (see pages 98–123).

FOCUS ON:
TURNING CIRCLES INTO SPHERES

Up until now, we have been using circles for drawing heads, but since human heads are three dimensional, their heads are really spheres. So how do you draw a three-dimensional sphere on two-dimensional paper? There are two main methods: adding contour lines and using shading.

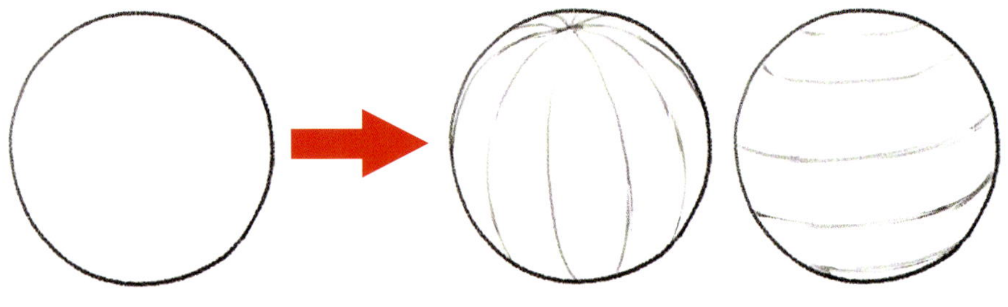

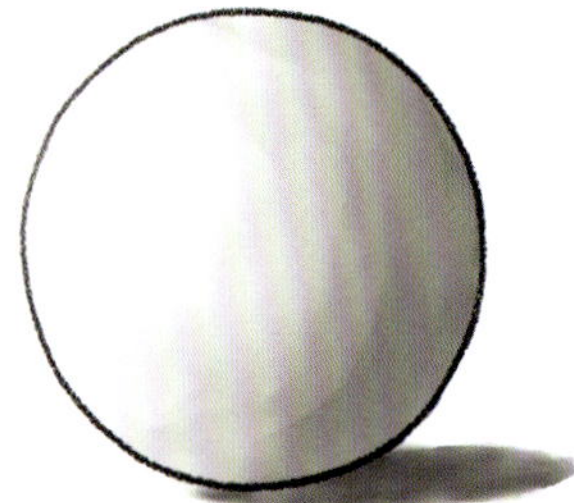

DRAW A FLAT CIRCLE

CONTOUR LINES
Contour lines give the impression of depth and roundness. They should bend around the sphere, becoming more curved at each end. Contour lines can be drawn horizontally or vertically.

SHADING
Adding shade and shadow is the other way to make a circle look like a sphere. This method will be important when you add tone and colour.

USING CUBOIDS TO UNDERSTAND SURFACES

Putting an object in a cuboid is a useful way to make it easier to understand three dimensions. In the example below, draw a head in a box so that you can clearly find the front, side and top surfaces. You can usually see two or three sides when you see the head from a diagonal viewpoint. Train yourself to be aware of where the surfaces change and of their boundaries.

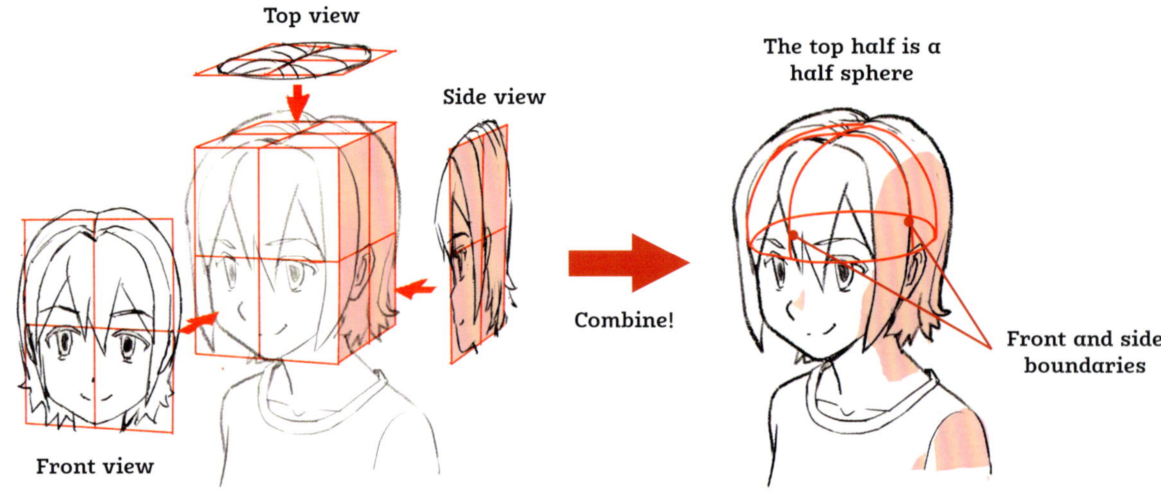

PRACTICE:
DRAWING HEADS FROM DIFFERENT ANGLES

Three quarters isn't the only view from an angle. You will eventually need to draw all 360 degrees if you wish to draw manga comic strips or animation, so it's a good idea to get used to thinking and drawing in three dimensions from any viewpoint. Here are some tips for drawing heads at an angle. Think about the box (see opposite) to understand the directions of the three surfaces of the head. Practise drawing boxes from all angles and try turning them into faces.

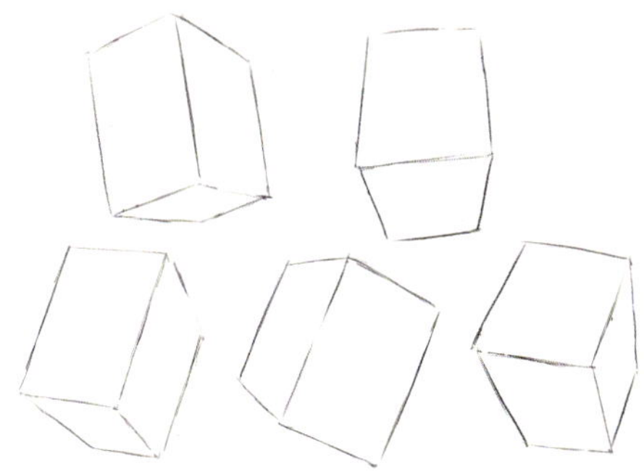

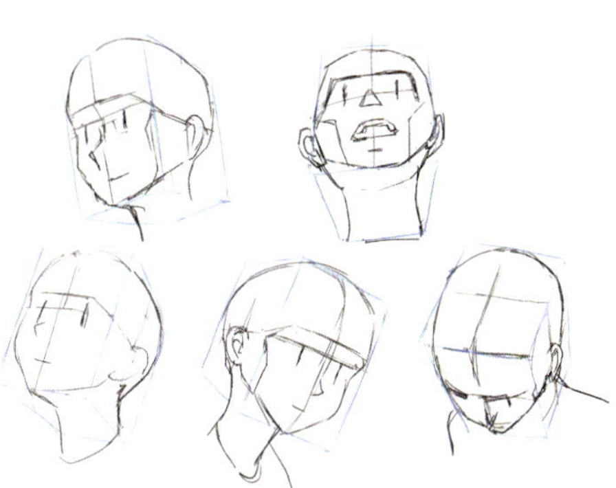

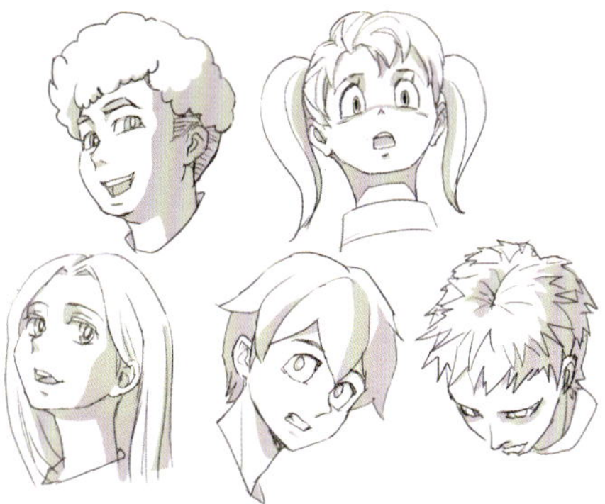

1 Draw a number of cuboids set at different angles.

2 Make the cuboids' corners round, then transform them into head shapes. Add central lines and marks for the eyes, ears, nose and mouth.

3 Add details and clean up your drawing.

DRAWING A CHARACTER FROM DIFFERENT ANGLES

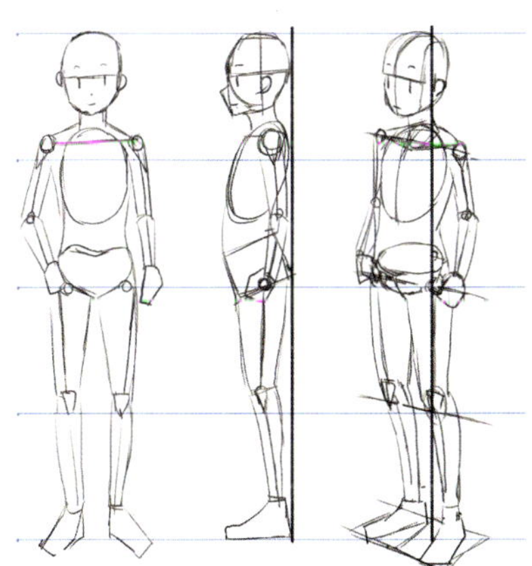

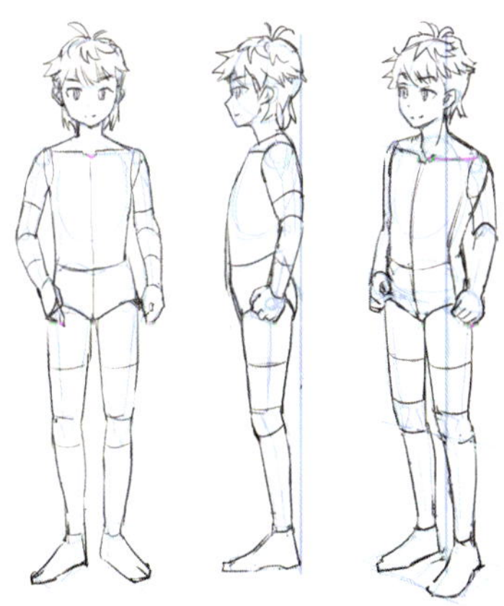

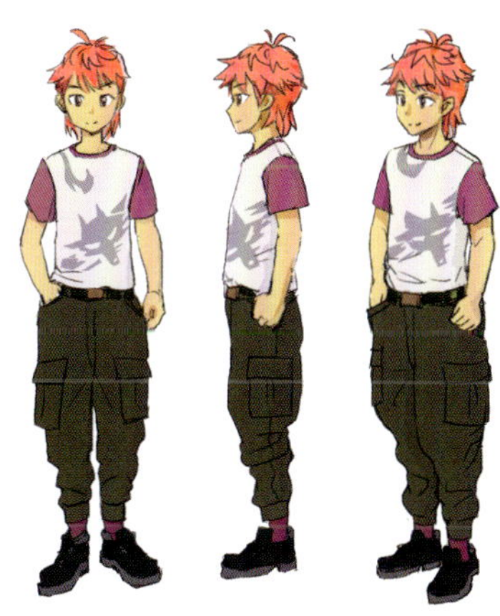

1 Draw a vertical rule. However, as you are just trying out different angles, only divide it into quarters. Draw a stick figure and flesh it out into a doll figure. Keep the body at the same level for views from all angles.

2 Turn the plain doll figures into outlined character bodies. Clean up the lines and then add the facial details and hairstyles.

3 Add the clothes, then clean up the lines. Add shading or colour as you wish, following the details in projects 8 and 9 (see pages 98–123).

Drawing the Body

Use the knowledge you have gained from drawing front and side views to draw a six-head-tall body from a three-quarter view. Remember to avoid a straight and stiff back (see page 63).

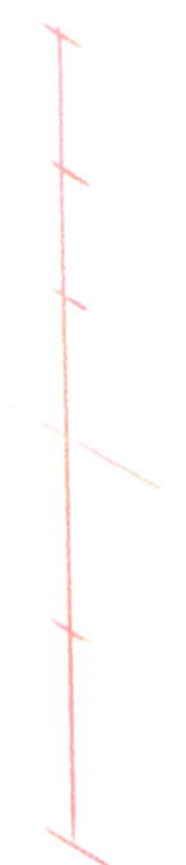

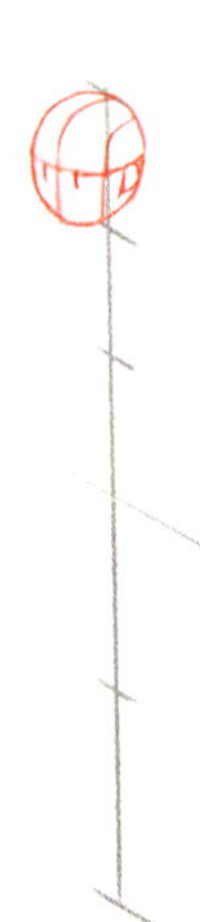

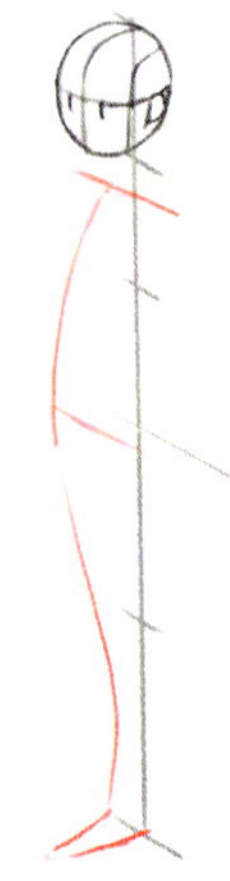

1 Draw a vertical line. Mark the line with an angled horizontal line halfway down, then divide the top half into three and the bottom half into two.

2 Draw the head in a three-quarter view in the top section. Align the back of the head with the vertical line, just like when drawing the side-view body (see page 61). Since the back of the head is also viewed at an angle, it should be drawn slightly overlapping.

3 Draw an 'S' curve and triangular foot line in the same way as for the side view.

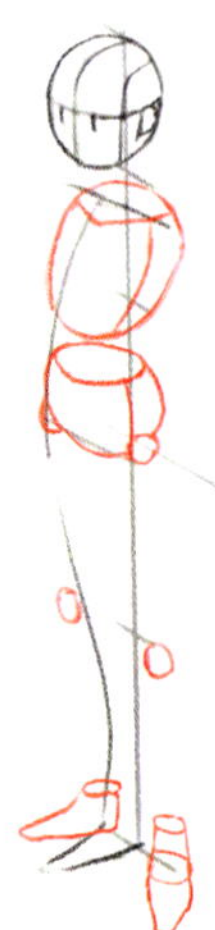

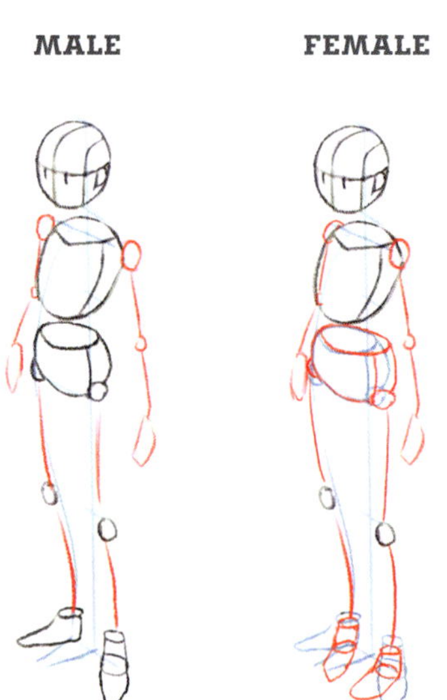

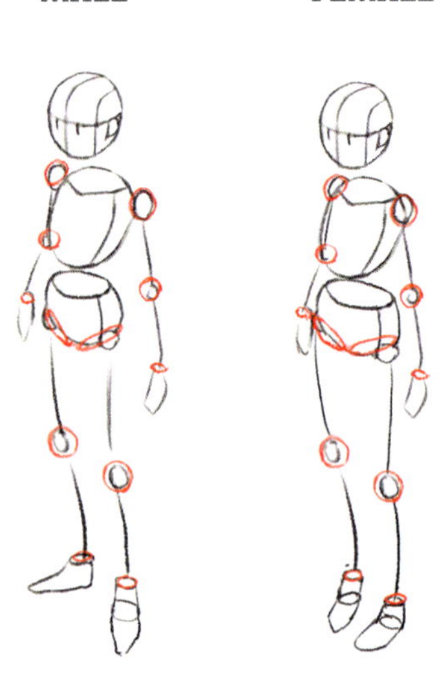

4 Add the ribcage and hips on the top half, following the 'S' curve. Then draw joints for the legs in the bottom half. Ensure the knee joints are at about the lower quarter height. Adjust the heels at the base of the line.

5 Draw the arm joints. Make the shoulder joints further apart for male figures, and draw wider hips for female figures. Connect all the limbs. Give your figure a pose if you wish.

6 Check the proportions of your stick figure and clean up the shapes. Make the joints bigger, ready to turn the stick figure into a doll (see pages 46–48).

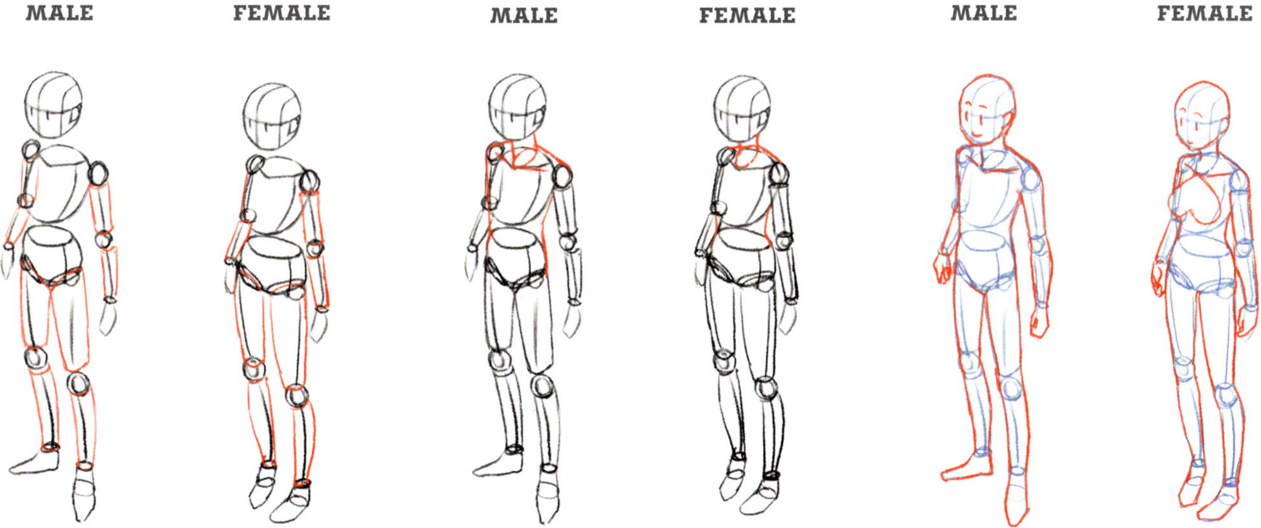

7 Add the arm and leg cylinders to give them shape. The cylinders should overlap at each joint.

8 Connect the neck and shoulder with a sloping curve. Connect the ribcage and hips with curving lines.

9 Erase the lines that will not be visible and outline the drawing to form a simple body shape (see page 48).

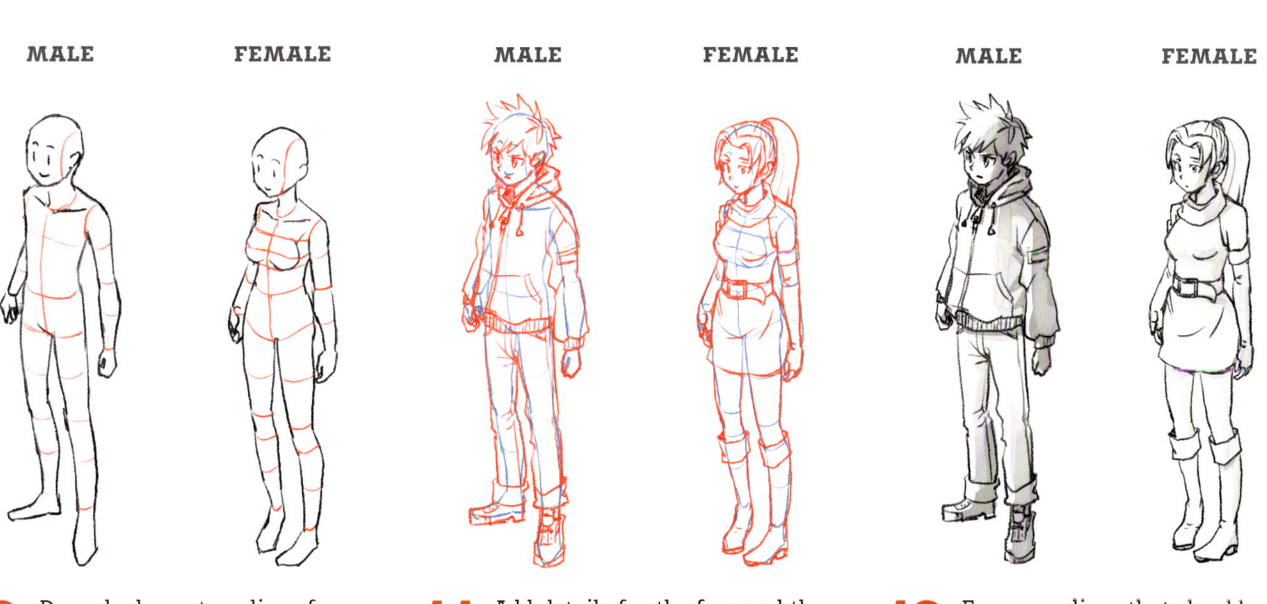

10 Draw body contour lines for arranging the figure's clothes.

11 Add details for the face and the hairstyle, as well as the clothes.

12 Erase any lines that should not be visible and tidy up your drawing. Check that all the lines fully connect where they meet. If you wish to colour your figure, turn to projects 8 and 9 (see pages 98–123).

PROJECT 6
DRAW
POSES

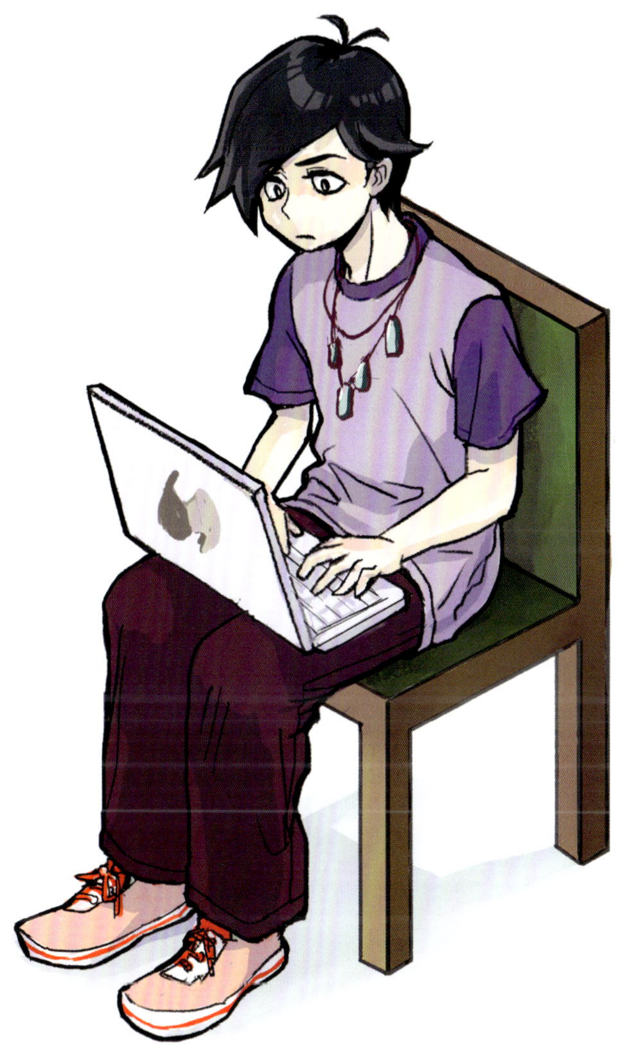

Now that you know how to draw characters from all angles with confidence, it's time to start putting your characters into different poses. We will start by looking at how the body's basic framework changes with movement – and practise drawing this in a classic pose – before moving on to learning how to position the arms and legs in dynamic poses.

Standing poses

Up until now, we've been drawing figures using a straight vertical line for a framework. This line follows the character's spinal column, and it also matches the character's centre of gravity. However, when we start moving, both the spine and the centre of gravity will shift, which means we can no longer use the basic straight line as a framework.

The basic framework

The key to drawing attractive, realistic poses is to understand the interaction between the spine, the shoulder line, the hip line and the centre of gravity.

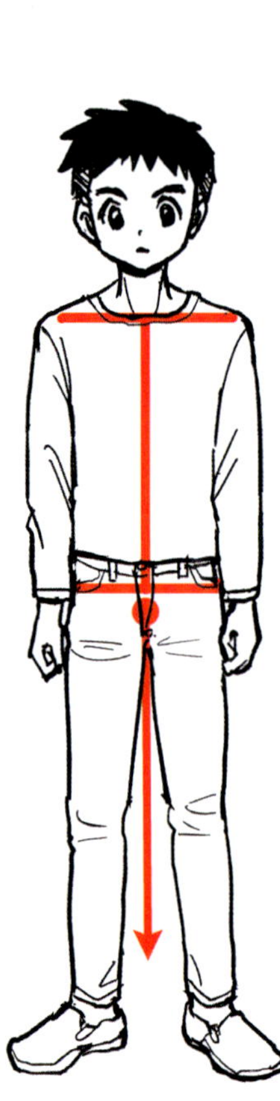

When the body is straight and stationary, the spine and centre of gravity follow the basic vertical line of the framework we've been using up until now, and the shoulder and hip lines are horizontal and straight.

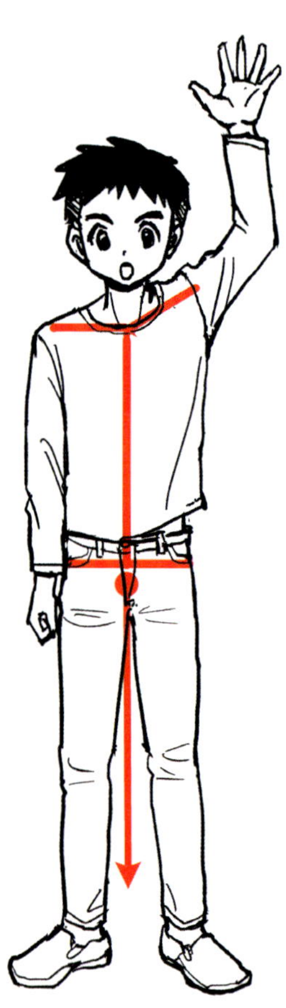

For small movements, some of these four elements will change while the others remain as they were. For example, if you raise one arm, the shoulder line changes as the shoulder is raised, but the spine, hip line and centre of gravity stay the same.

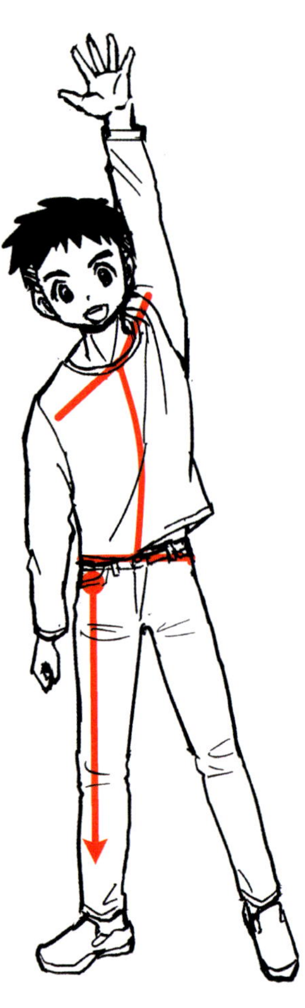

In large gestures, more of the elements and the extent of their movement changes. If you thrust your arm high into the air above your head, the shoulder moves up much higher, so the other shoulder needs to drop to compensate. This in turn twists the spine slightly and causes your weight to shift to the opposite leg.

Modelling the torso

The key part of drawing a pose is the torso because it dictates the positions of the head and limbs. The torso consists of the ribcage and hips (or pelvis). We have been treating them as oval and heart shapes when looked at from the front, but now we need to think of them as three-dimensional forms.

Looking at the basic doll figure, there is a gap between the ribcage and hips, which is where the stomach and organs can be found. Remember this as you think about how to bend and twist the doll's torso. As well as considering the shape of the torso, pay attention to the directions of the ribcage and hips.

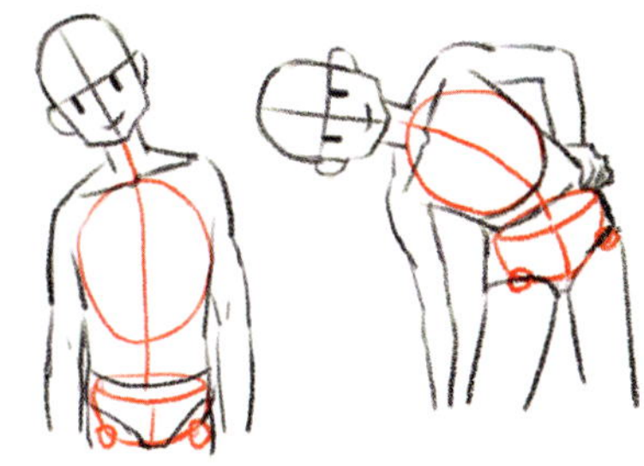

BEND TO THE SIDE
When the neck tilts, the head will tilt, too. An even greater tilt will also cause the upper body to tilt.

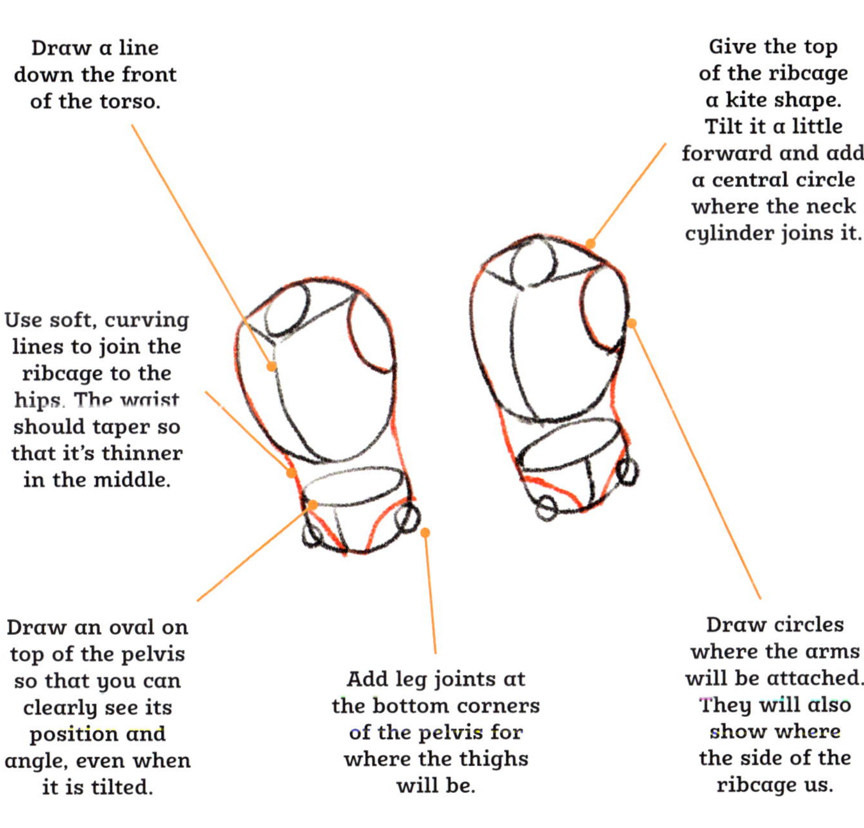

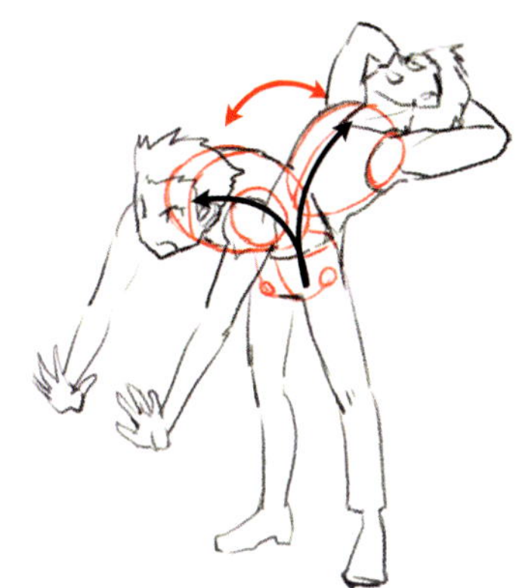

BEND BACKWARDS AND FORWARDS
The spine will have a smooth curve. The head will be the most angular while bending forwards.

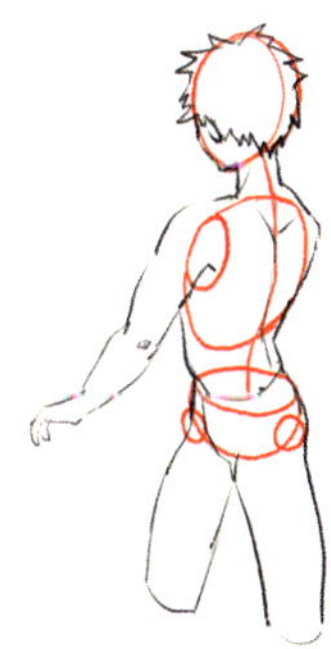

TWISTING MOVEMENT
The torso can also twist, so the ribcage and hips do not always face the same direction. Usually, if the head or arms move strongly to the left or right, the torso follows.

Drawing a contrapposto pose

Contrapposto is an art term that refers to a pose with the hips, legs and shoulders at different angles. It was first used in ancient Greek art and was revived during the Renaissance. If it was good enough for Leonardo and Michelangelo, it's probably worth using in your manga! In a contrapposto pose, a figure stands with most of its weight on one leg, which tilts the shoulder and hip lines. It is a relaxed look, with an elegant, curvy spine line. We will try it here with proportions for a six-heads-tall figure (see pages 42–43).

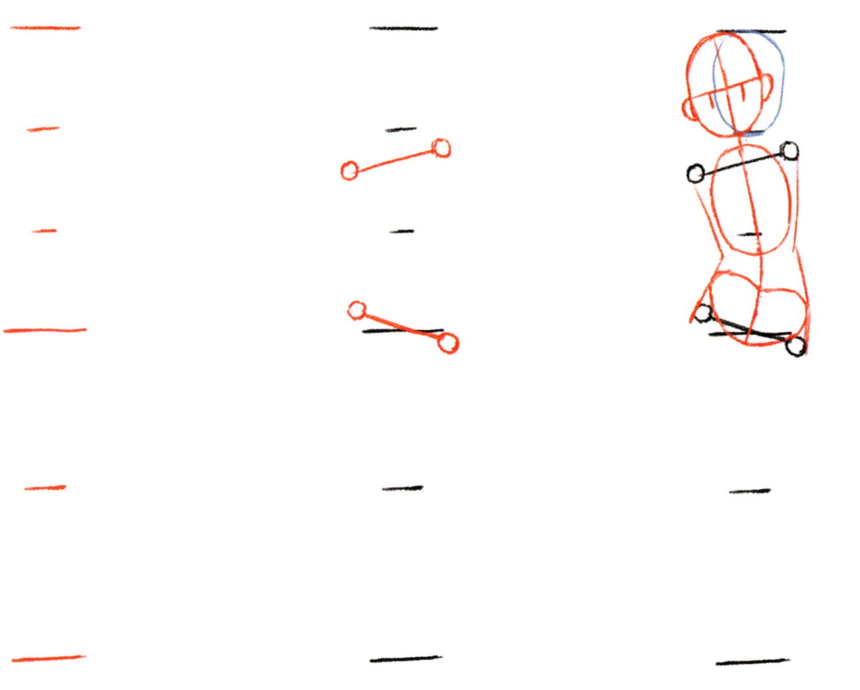

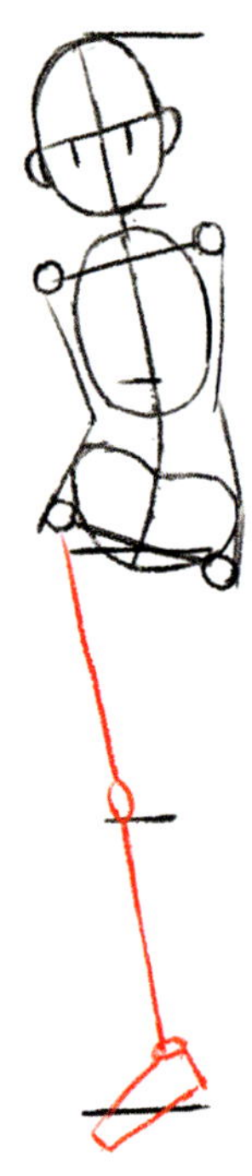

1 Draw the vertical guide line and add marks at the top, bottom and middle. Divide the top half into three and the bottom half into two with horizontal lines. Since the body won't be straight, erase the vertical line.

2 Draw the shoulder and hip lines slightly angled in opposite directions. The shoulder line is just below the second line from the top (leaving room for the neck), and the hip line falls on the line halfway down. Add the shoulder and hip joints.

3 Draw an oval head in the top section. Draw the ribcage and hips at an angle, following the shoulder and hip lines respectively. Connect them with lines along the sides, then adjust the position of the head so that it follows the shoulder line. Draw a central line across the head, then add marks where the eyes and ears will be.

4 Draw the leg supporting the body's weight with a straight, diagonal line from the hip to the ground. The foot should be at the centre of the bottom mark – the figure should look like it is balanced on one leg.

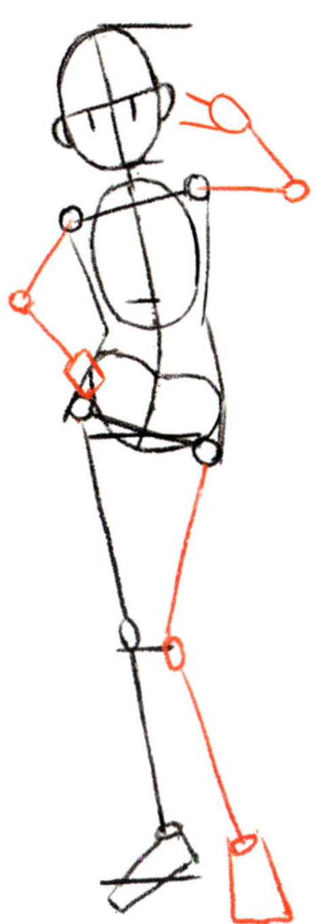

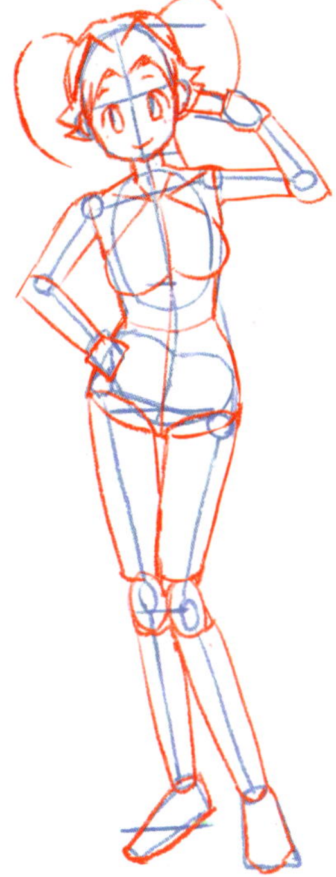

5 Since the other leg isn't carrying any of the body's weight, you can position it how you like. If the leg is pointing slightly forward, the hip will be slightly lower than the one for the other leg. Add the arms in whatever pose you like (see page 81 for more on arm positions).

6 Transform the stick figure into a doll figure by filling out the limbs (see pages 46–48) and giving the torso more shape. Add the facial features and hair (see page 29.) Now you can outline the body and clean up the lines, erasing any that should not be visible.

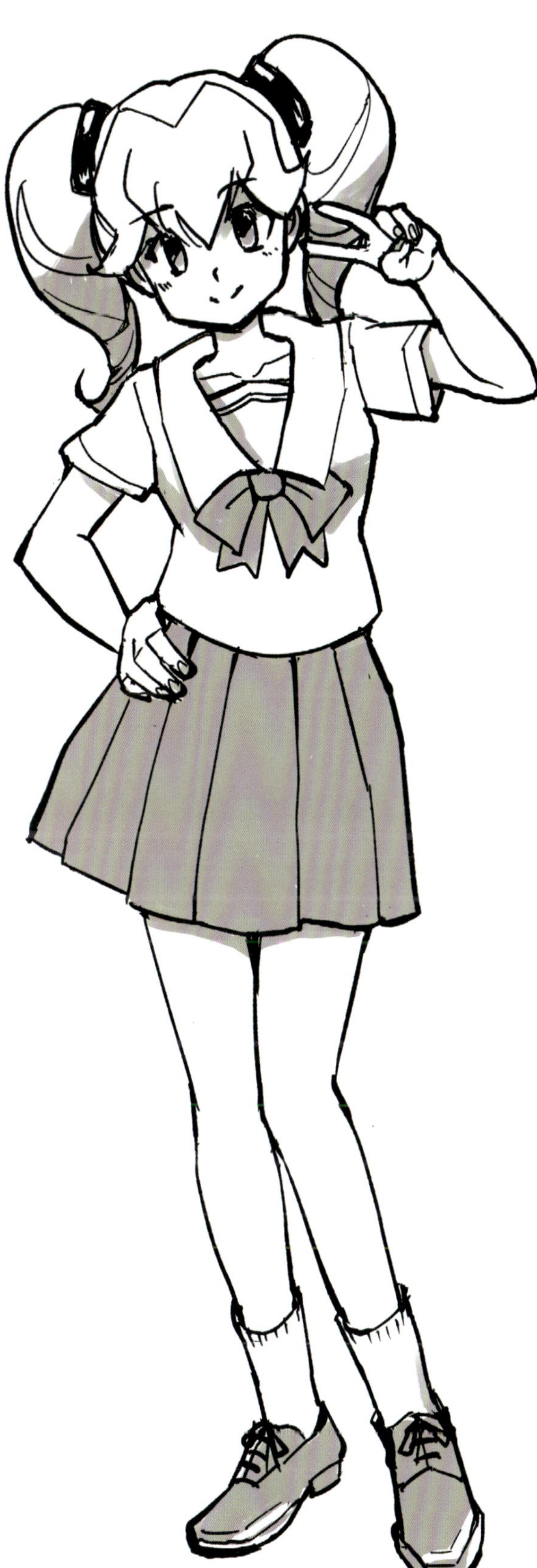

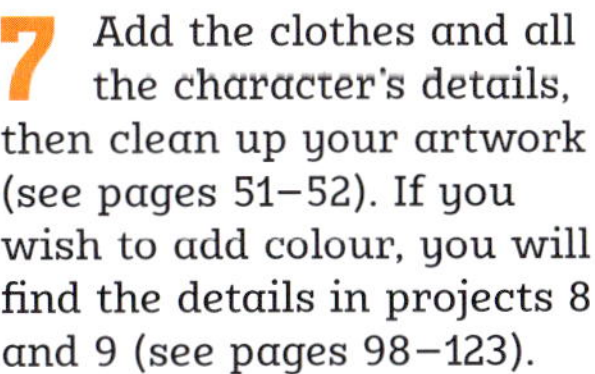

7 Add the clothes and all the character's details, then clean up your artwork (see pages 51–52). If you wish to add colour, you will find the details in projects 8 and 9 (see pages 98–123).

Drawing an anime-style standing pose

Drawing figures using perspective lines creates a sense of depth in this signature anime pose. When seen from behind, the neck curves away from the shoulders and the face recedes to the back. Note the 'S'-shaped curve of the spine and the fullness of the hips.

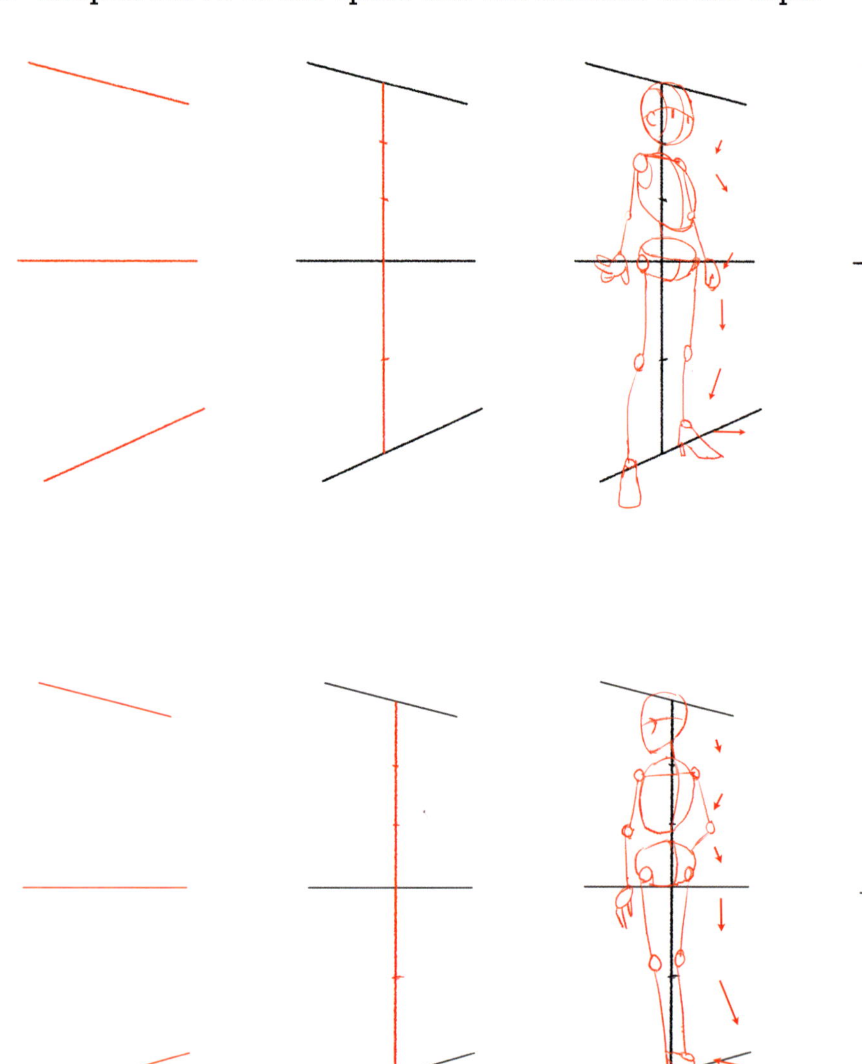

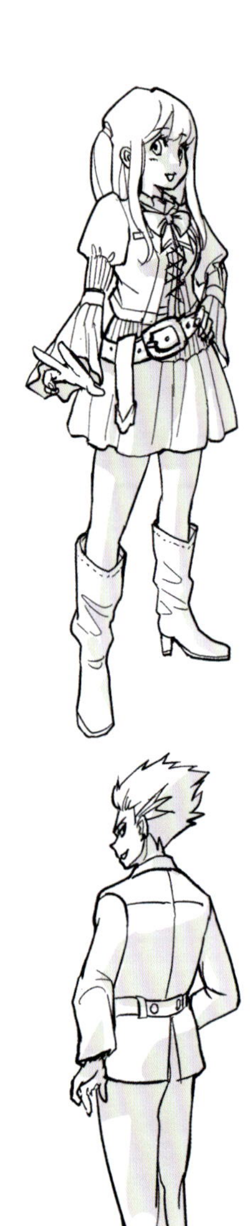

1 Draw a horizontal central line, then draw angled perspective lines (see pages 130–131) at an equal distance above and below it. These angles should be the same.

2 Add the vertical line and divide the top half into three and the bottom half into two to create proportions for a six-heads-tall figure (see pages 42–43).

3 Create a stick figure (see pages 44–45). Draw the head and torso from a worm's-eye view from below, and the legs and feet from a bird's-eye view above (see page 128). Add the arms and hands.

4 Transform the stick figure into a doll figure (see pages 46–48). Add the facial features and hair (see page 29.) Now outline the body and clean up the lines, erasing any that should not be visible.

5 Add the clothes and all the character's details, then clean up your artwork (see pages 51–52). If you wish to add colour, you will find the details in projects 8 and 9 (see pages 98–123).

Focus on:
Drawing emotions

Like mime artists, illustrators can show emotions by using only gestures. Try it yourself – stand in front of a full-length mirror and make a variety of poses to show different emotions. Memorize how you look, then sketch your pose. A single emotion can be shown through a variety of different poses; here are some of the most commonly used.

HAPPY
Create an open pose for happy emotions. Arms, hands and legs may be straight and stretched out as far as possible.

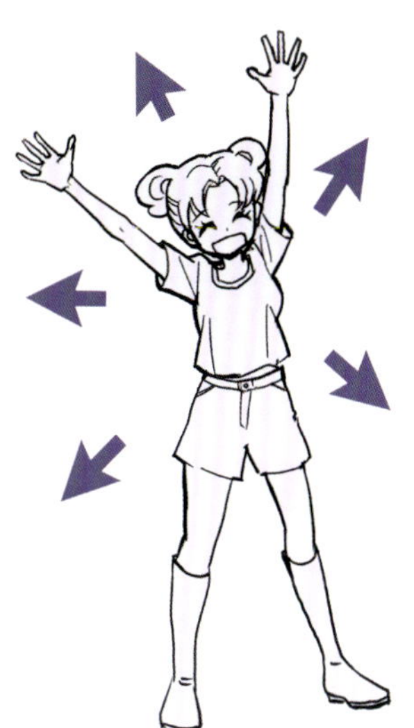

WORRY
A worried person needs a closed pose. For example, the character's arms may be in front of their body for protection or reassurance. The general direction of the pose should turn inwards. The same pose can also be used to show shyness.

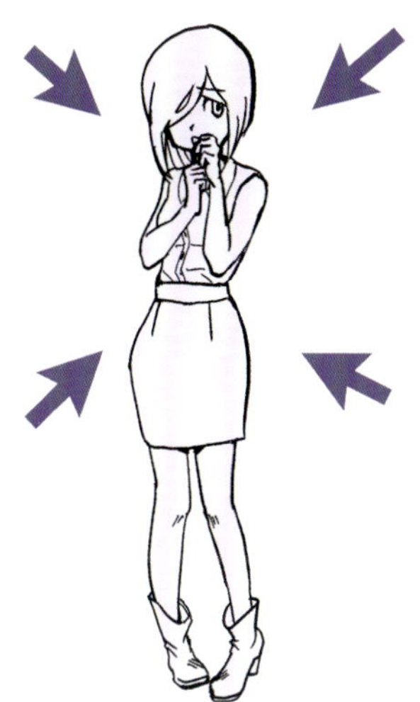

POWERFUL
One way to create a powerful pose is to thrust the chin out and draw a stretched spine. Use strong lines to make the pose look energetic. The hands are closed into fists for emphasis.

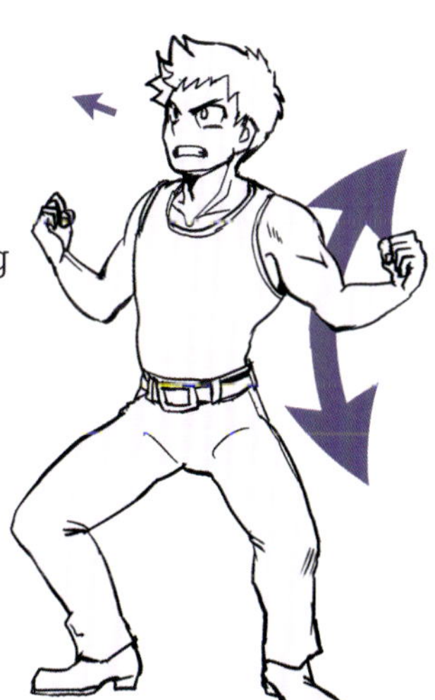

POWERLESS
This pose is the opposite to the powerful pose, with the chin dropping down, obscuring the neck, and the spine is slumped. The whole body tilts forward.

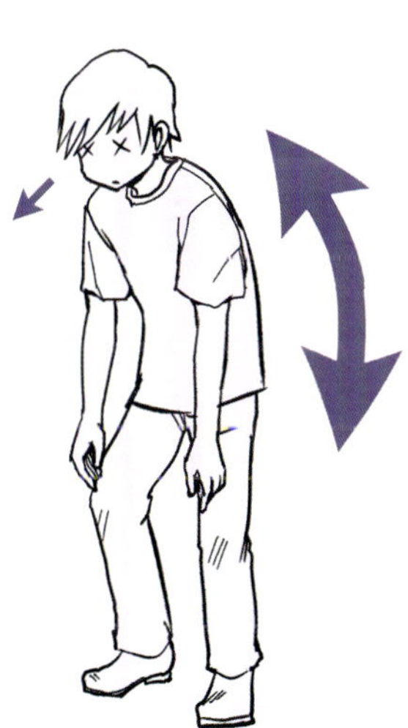

Foreshortening

To give a realistic sense of depth to your figure, you need to know about foreshortening. This is an illusion that occurs when we see an object from a front view – elements up close appear much larger and those in the back much smaller. In front of a mirror, try holding your arm straight in front of you with your hand bent up (see step 1 opposite) – you may not see your arm and your hand will look huge!

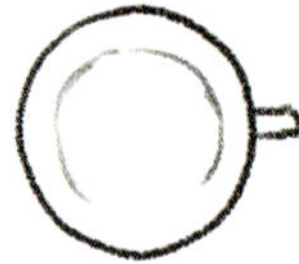
Top view

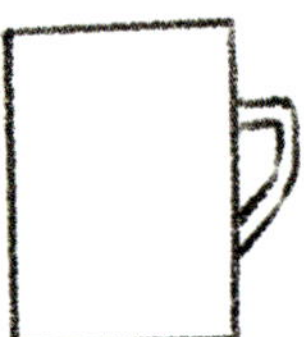
Side view

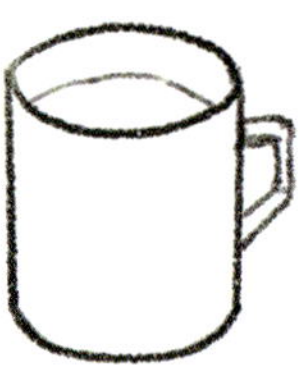
Angled view

The rules of foreshortening

When drawing an arm bent sideways or a leg angled out to the side, the only thing that changes about how the limb looks is the angle it is at. However, if you show a limb bent forwards or backwards, you need to use foreshortening.

A simple way of exploring the technique is to draw a mug from several angles. Sketch it from the top, the side and an angled position in between the two. You will see that you have a circle shape when drawing the mug from the top, a rectangle when drawing it from the side and a combination of the two when the mug is angled.

Next, focus on the height of the mug. Notice that as you move it from a side view to a top-down view, the height will seem shorter even though the object hasn't changed shape. This an important rule when you are drawing a three-dimensional object, and it is called foreshortening.

If you think of your limbs as being made up of two cylinders, you can see that just as a mug appears to change size and shape as it is moved upwards, so do your limbs such as in the arms on the right.

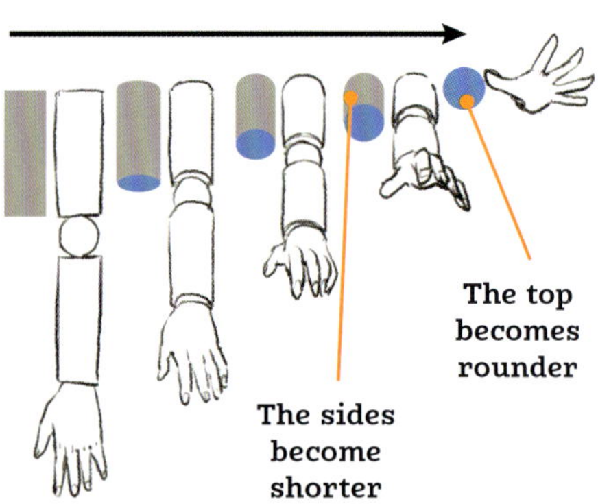

PRACTISE FORESHORTENING
Try drawing a bent leg to practise foreshortening. Start by drawing a cylinder for the thigh. Next, draw a second cylinder at an angle, then connect them to create the knee. Add the foot and flesh out the legs. Practise drawing legs this way in various angles from a side view to the front, observing how their appearances change, so that you can draw poses easier and quicker!

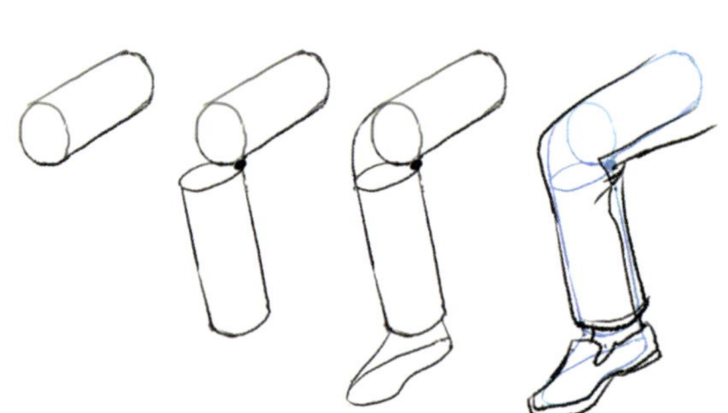

DRAW BENT ARMS
Depending on the angle of a bent arm, the upper arm appears shorter or nearly invisible when the forearm is in front of it. Draw the forearm first, then connect the lines from the elbow to the shoulder, which will make it easier to draw a foreshortened bent arm pose.

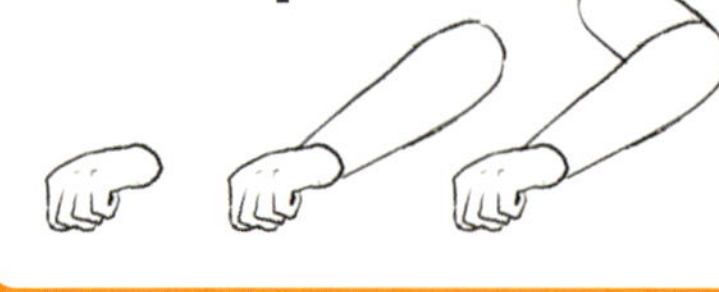

Drawing arms using foreshortening

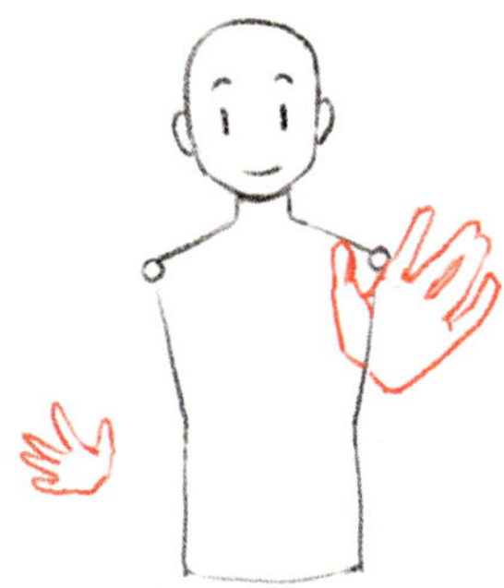

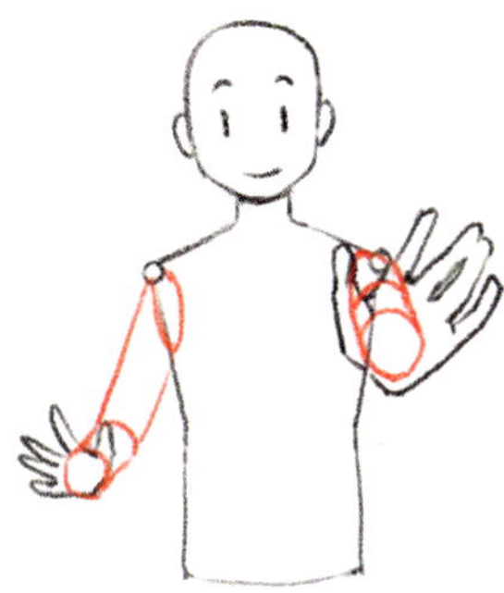

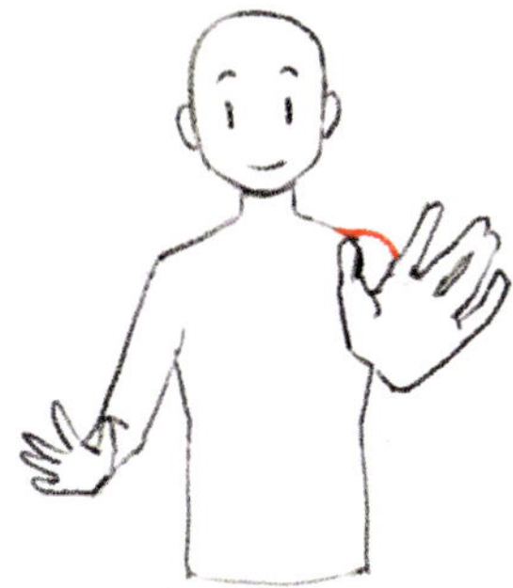

1 Draw the torso and head of a figure, then draw one hand held in front, overlapping the body, and the other hand held back. Draw the hand closer to the viewer bigger than it is normally and the hand further away smaller.

2 Connect each hand to the body using two cylinders. Think about the angle of the upper and lower arms and draw each cylinder at the appropriate size and shape, with a circle at the front.

3 Remove any lines that should no longer be visible and add the shoulder above the large hand.

Drawing dynamic arms

When drawing arms, rather than starting from the shoulder, draw them beginning at the hand. This way, you can place your character's hands where you want them to be. Since the arms and torso are about the same length, a good rule of thumb for positioning the hands is that they should each be within a circle centred on the shoulder joint that has a radius that matches the length of the torso.

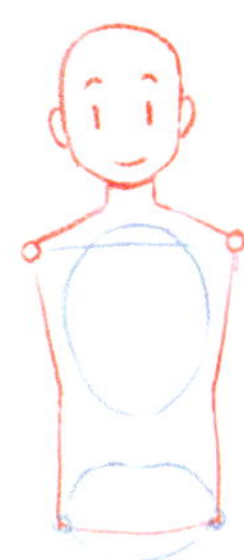

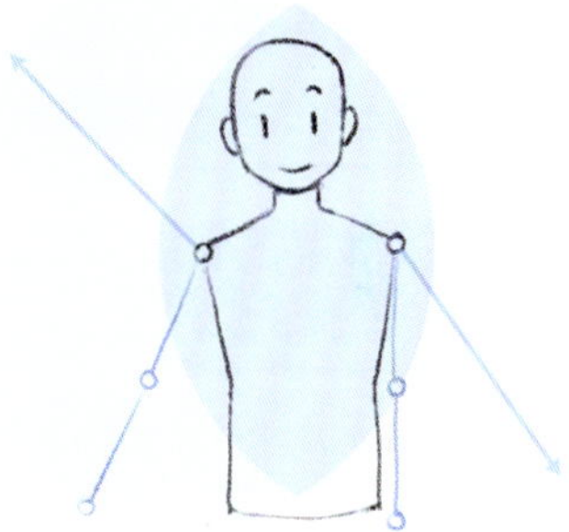

1 Draw the torso and head of a figure.

2 Draw two circles for the potential positions of the hands (see above). If you draw an arm held across the body, it can't be any further than the area where the circles overlap unless your character turns their whole torso.

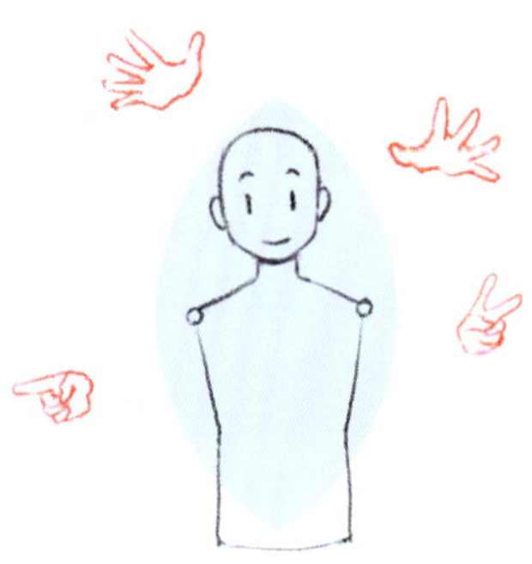

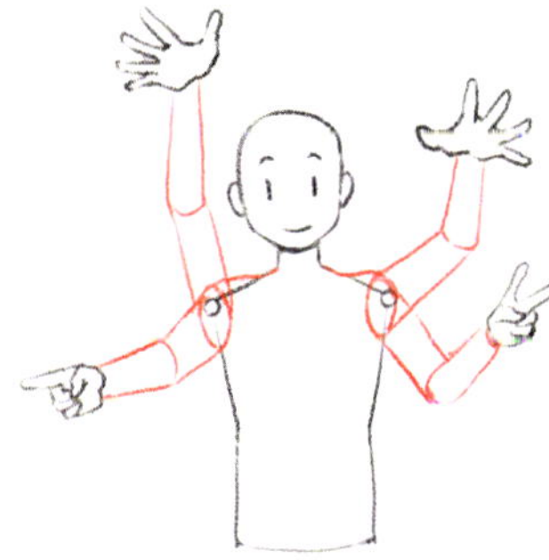

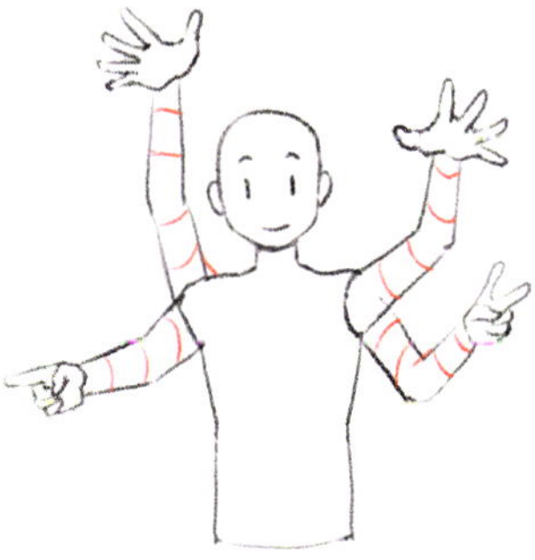

3 Draw the hands somewhere within the circles. Use the space not only on the left and right, but also in front and behind the body. Remember that because of foreshortening, if the arm is pointing to the front or backwards, it won't be able to reach the edge of the circle. The size of the hand is about the same as the face unless it is stretched out to the front or backwards.

4 Connect the hands to the shoulders with two cylinders, adjusting their size and shape and based on foreshortening (see opposite and above). If the arm is held above shoulder height, add the raised shoulder.

5 Drawing contour lines (see page 68) on the arms will help you to understand the direction of the arms and will be useful when you add clothing or shading.

Drawing a seated pose

Seated poses that include bent limbs are a good step up to the next level of drawing. Always start by drawing simple shapes and then adjusting them little by little. It's best to start with the chair and torso to keep the figure in proportion with the object. As you continue to practise drawing doll figures (see pages 46–48), you will gradually be able to draw seated figures with their head, body and limbs in other positions – and you will be able to draw them in other locations such as on a wall or in a car.

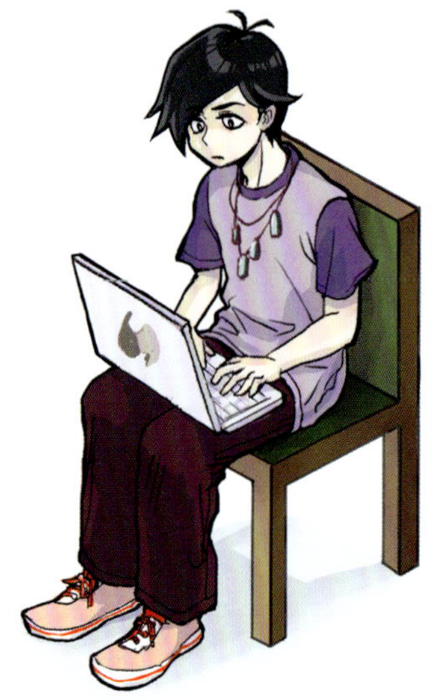

DRAWING A CHAIR

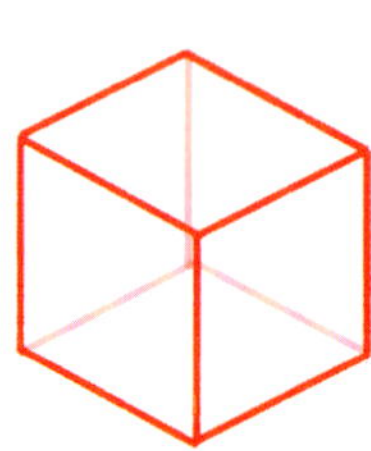

1 Draw a cube. Start with the bottom side and check that all the lines are parallel and the same length.

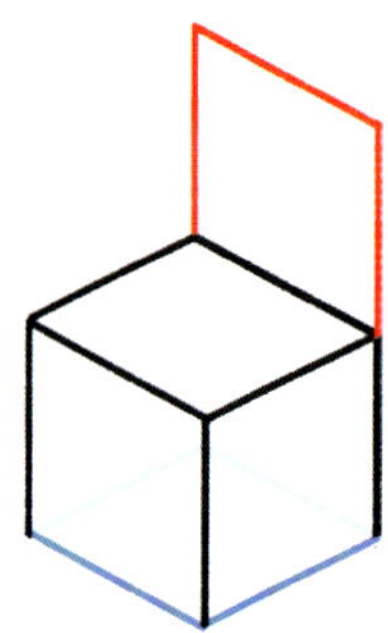

2 Extend one side of the upright and make the backrest. Ensure the backrest is the same height on both sides, and that the top is parallel with the other lines in the same plane such as the front and back of the seat.

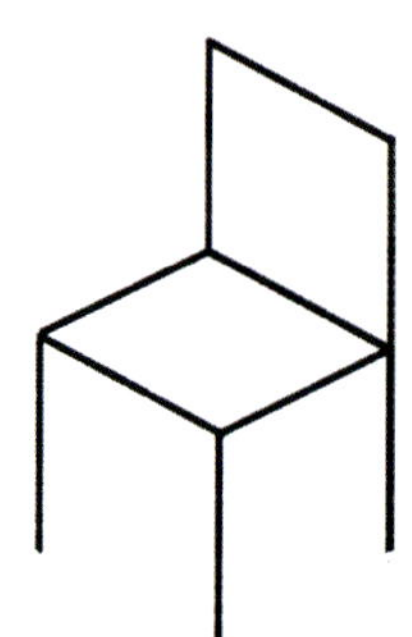

3 Erase the lines that form the bottom square on the floor.

ADDING A FIGURE

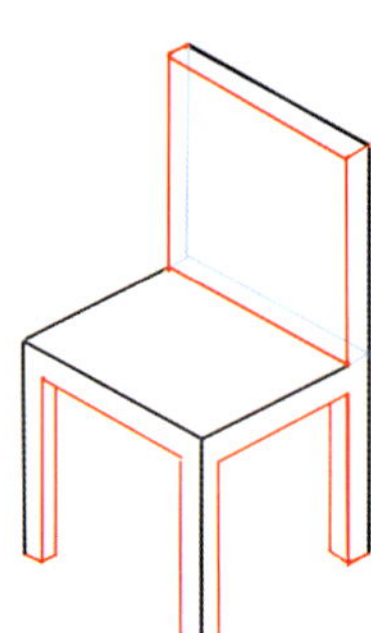

4 Add the details. Turn legs into cylinders or long cuboids. Give depth to the seat and backrest.

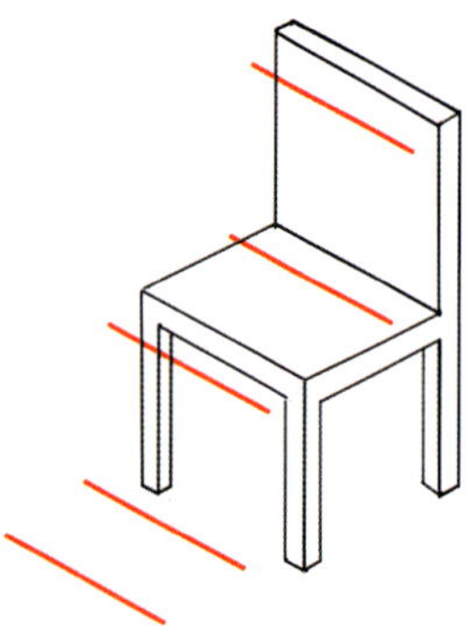

5 Draw guide lines for the feet, the top of the legs and the torso. They should be parallel with the chair.

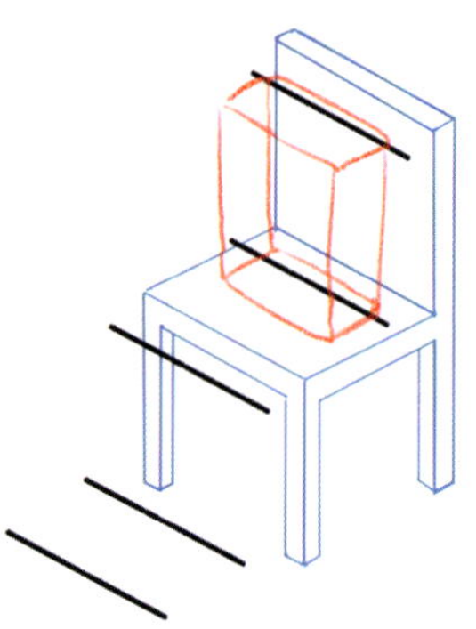

6 Position your torso on the chair. Draw a rectangle of an appropriate size on the seat and extend it upwards to draw a cuboid torso.

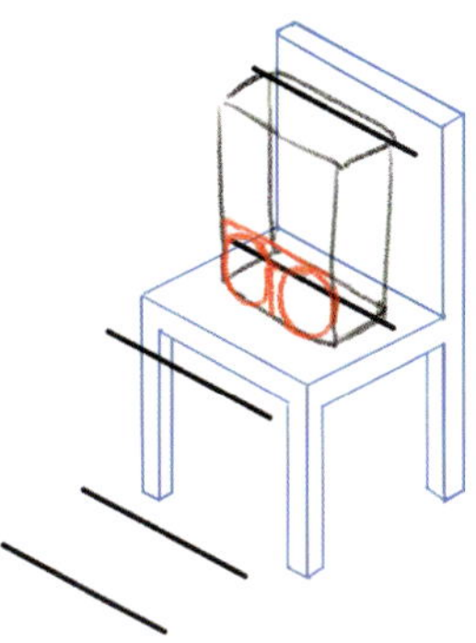

7 On the lower front surface of the cuboid, draw two circles to mark the position for the upper legs.

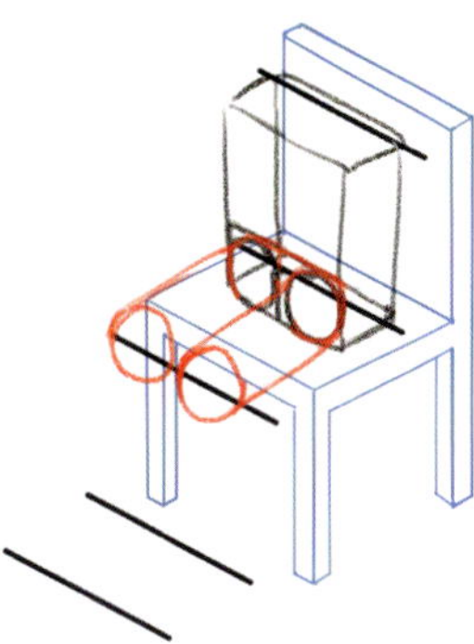

8 Attach cylinders to the circle marks for the upper legs. Draw knee joint circles at their ends and ensure they are a little further forward and higher than the seat. Use the guide lines and ensure the cylinders are the same length.

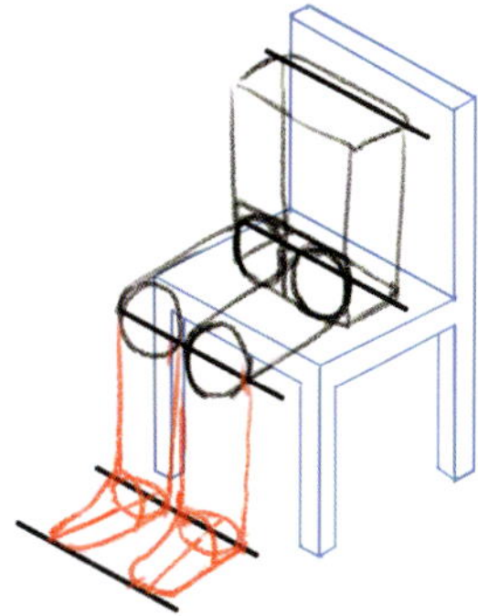

9 Draw heel circles just below the knees, at a position that appears to be flush with the ground level of the chair legs. Connect them with the knees to form cylinders to make the lower legs. Draw lines the same length from the heels and transform them into feet.

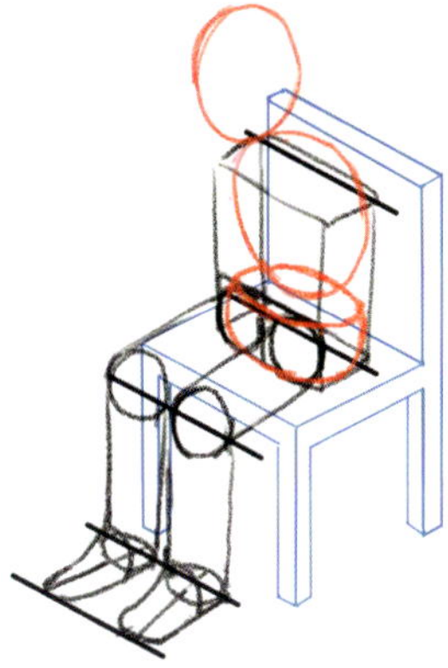

10 Draw an oval-shaped pelvis at the top of the thighs and add a ribcage and head roughly on top. Here, I posed the body to slightly tilt forward. Adjust the proportions so that the body above the chair is about twice the height of the lower legs.

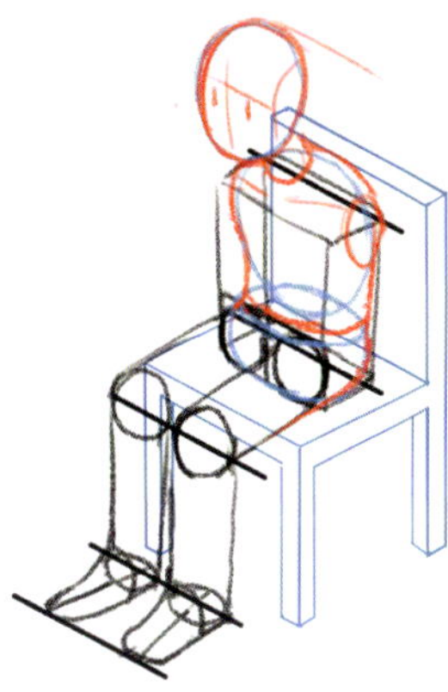

11 With these body parts in place, adjust each one into a three-dimensional doll figure. Note the diamond shape at the shoulders and the curve of the sides of the torso. Also add the circles for attaching the arms.

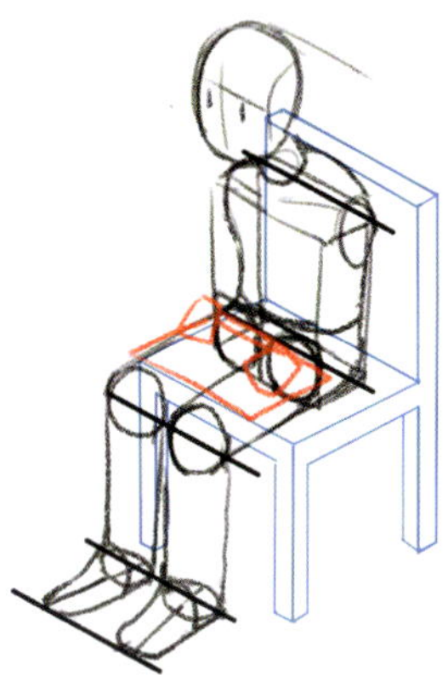

12 Put the laptop base (a parallelogram) on his lap and decide the hand positions.

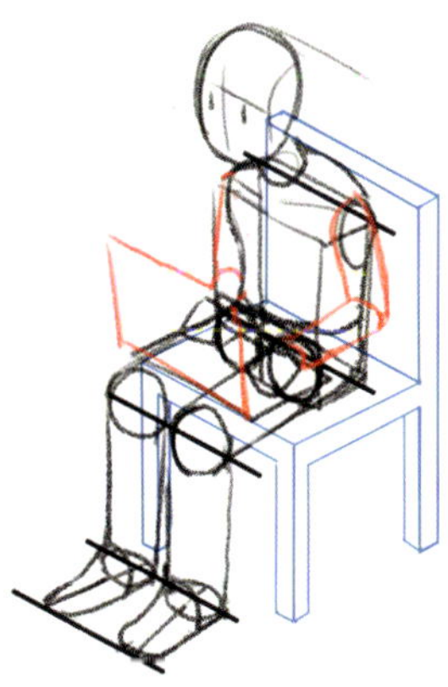

13 Connect the shoulders and hands with two cylinders for the arms. Add a laptop cover.

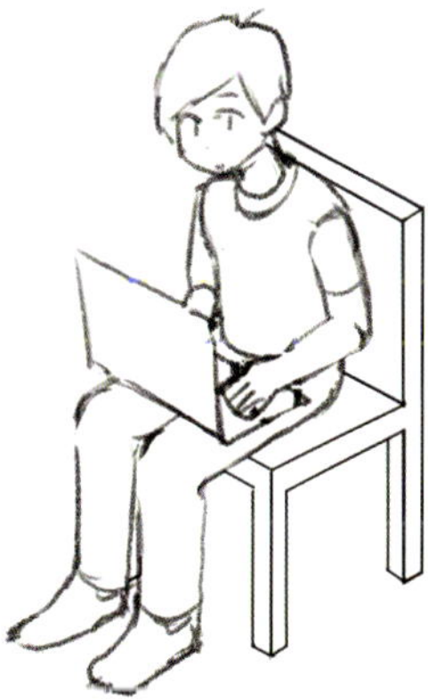

14 Adjust the pose and clean up the doll shape. Check the body is nicely sitting on the chair. Erase the guide lines and any lines that should not be visible. Add face and hair details.

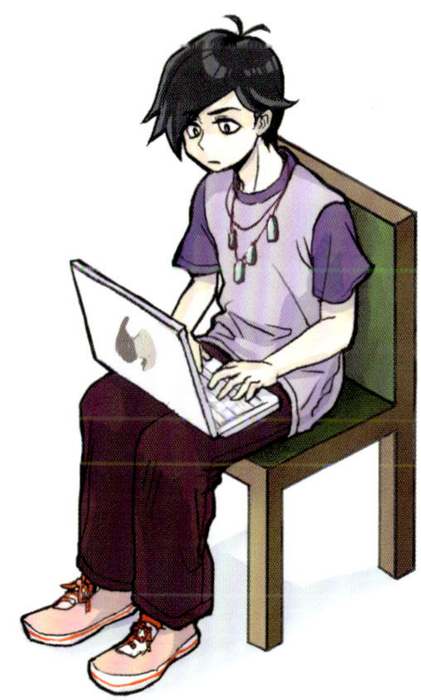

15 Add the clothes, then clean up the lines. Add shading or colour as you wish, following the details in projects 8 and 9 (see pages 98–123).

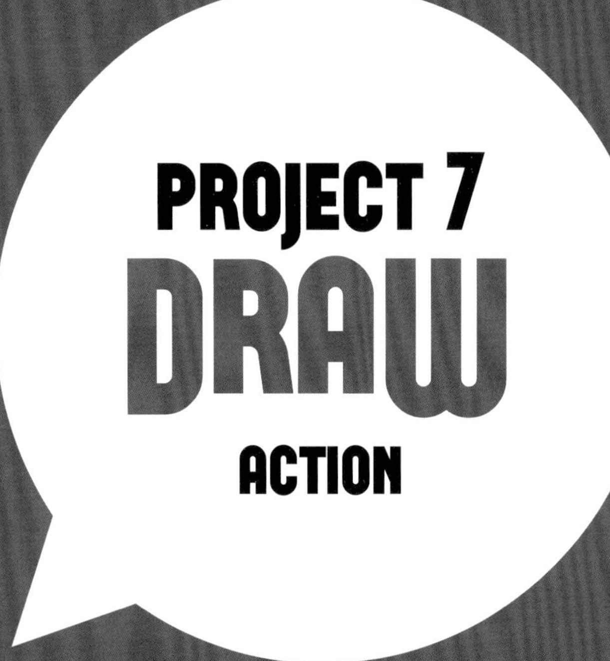
PROJECT 7
DRAW
ACTION

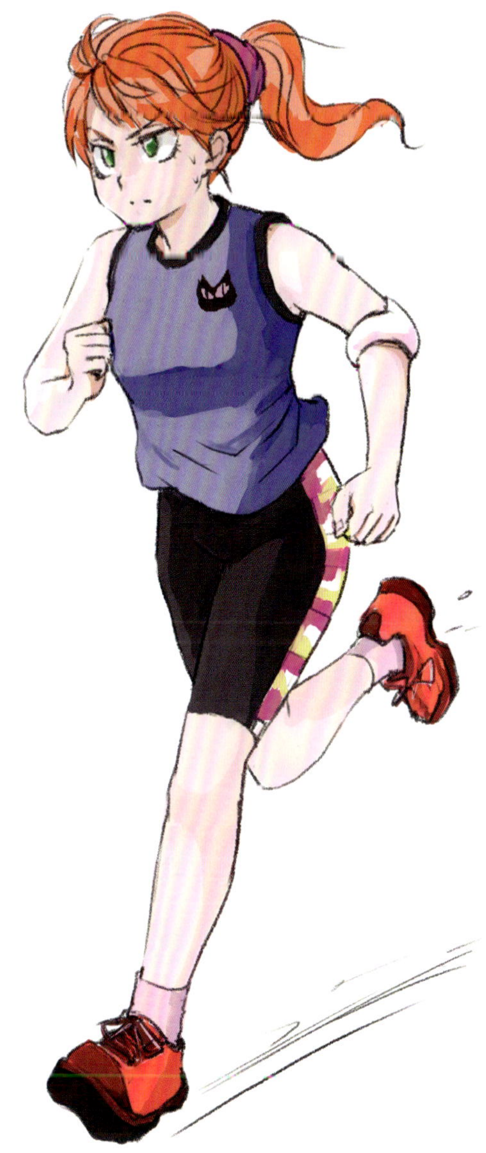

Dynamic action poses have to be one of the most exciting type of poses to learn. They can be difficult to draw at first, but once mastered you will be able to create any pose imaginable in a realistic and exciting way. Try to regularly practise quick sketching and gesture drawing to help improve your abilities in capturing action poses.

Observation

As an artist, you will need to develop a habit of observing almost everything you see, including how people move, because you can't draw something if you don't understand the nature of its movement.

One of the main reasons why drawing action can be difficult is that people don't consciously think about how they move their body – for example, a runner doesn't think about how a foot touches the ground or how far their arms swing as they run. However, to draw action poses realistically, animators and comic strip artists need to think about these movements to know how a particular movement will change from one frame to the next.

So, to draw a movement pose, you need to start by observing bodies in action. You can do this by actually posing yourself, by observing how people around you move or by sketching them from videos. To avoid adding too much detail to your manga drawings – which would make them confusing – practise as many poses as you can by drawing quick sketches and gesture drawings (see pages 96-97). These will help you to learn how to minimize your lines but still capture the gestures that suggest movement and action. Let's start by trying to draw action stick figures, following the details here, as quickly as you can.

Action stick figure

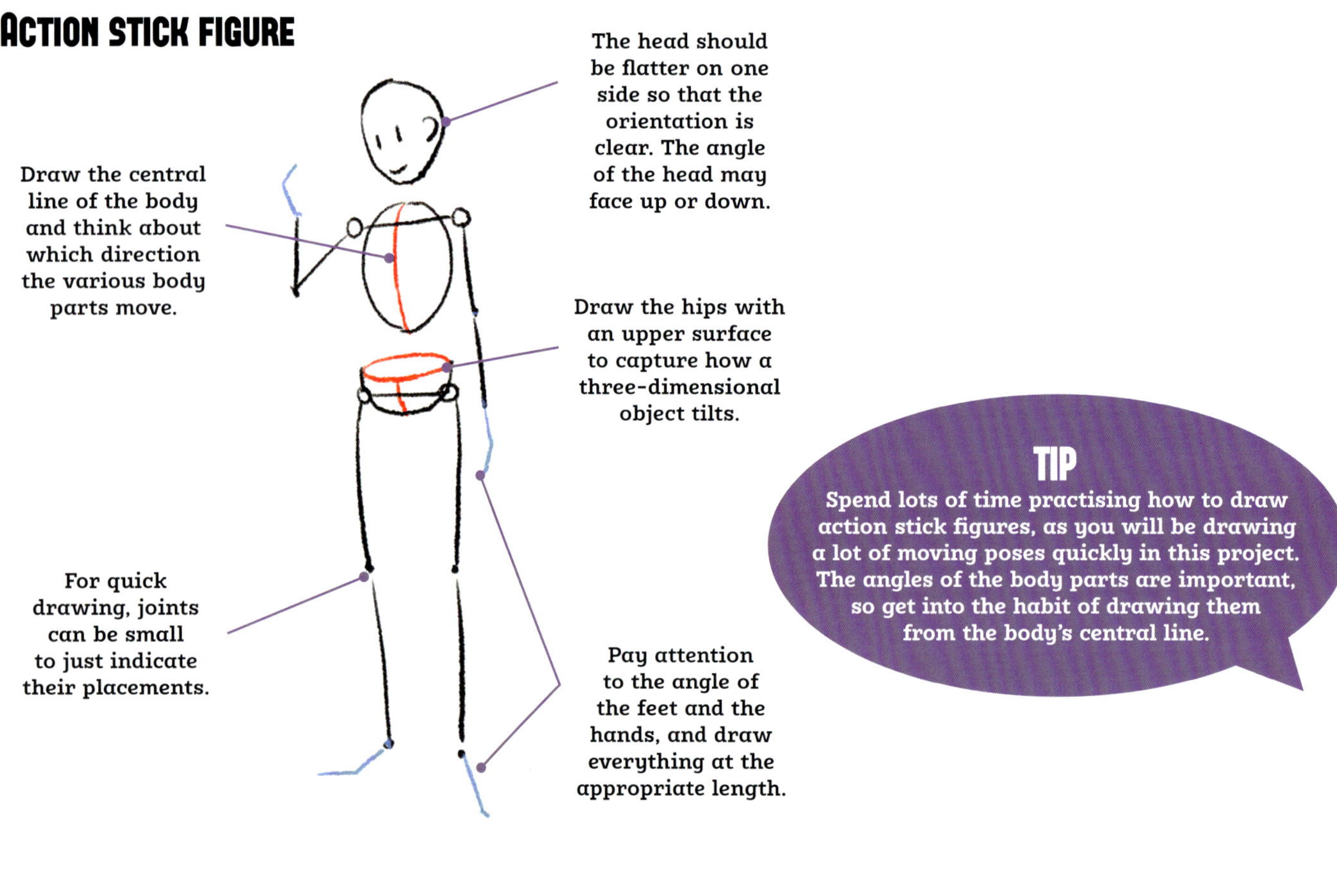

(SIX HEADS TALL)

Focus on:
Lines of Action

The key to creating strong dynamic poses is to use lines of action. These follow the movement of the body and flow of the pose, and they are far more important for bringing your pose to life than having lots of details in the drawing. The main line of action follows the body's spine. You can then add additional lines of action for the shoulders and arms, legs, hands and feet.

The method starts by looking at the movements of the whole body as a single, primary line of action. It could be a straight line, curve, 'C' curve or 'S' curve. There is no right or wrong – it depends on how you observe movements. On the following pages, you will learn how to use a line of action to draw a running figure.

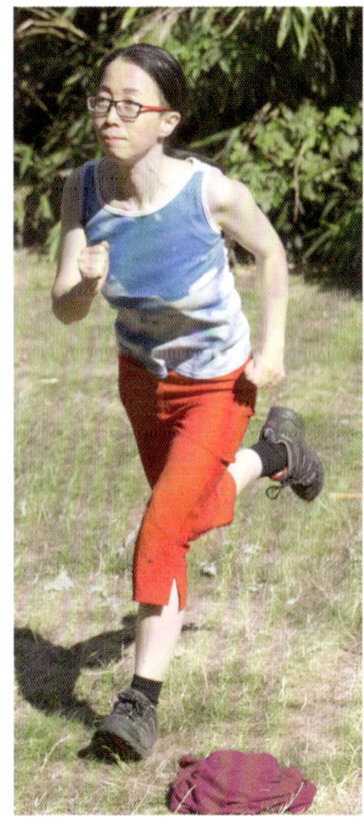

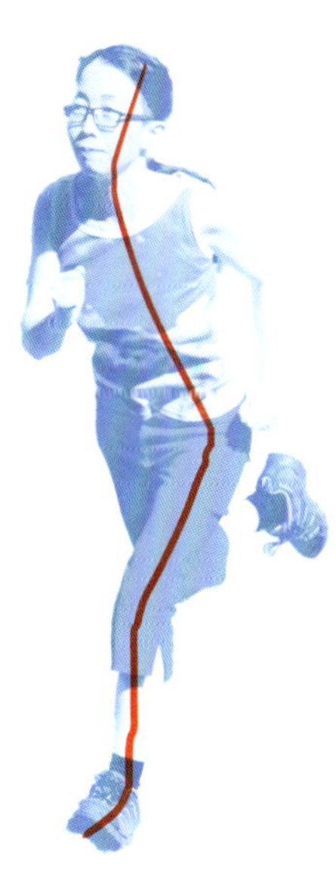

Silhouette and Negative Space

When drawing poses with movement, it is often difficult to capture the shape in a stick figure because of overlapping body parts. However, you can simplify the silhouette, or outline, of the body and draw it in two dimensions. You can then place a three-dimensional doll figure on top of it.

Negative space is the shape of the space created between the arms, legs and body. Shade in the negative space in the overall rough shape, and even with minimal lines, the body's shape will emerge.

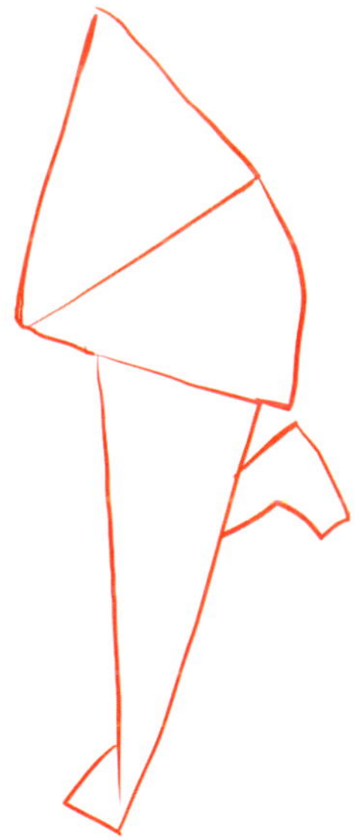

1 This is a simplified two-dimensional shape of the figure seen in the photograph above.

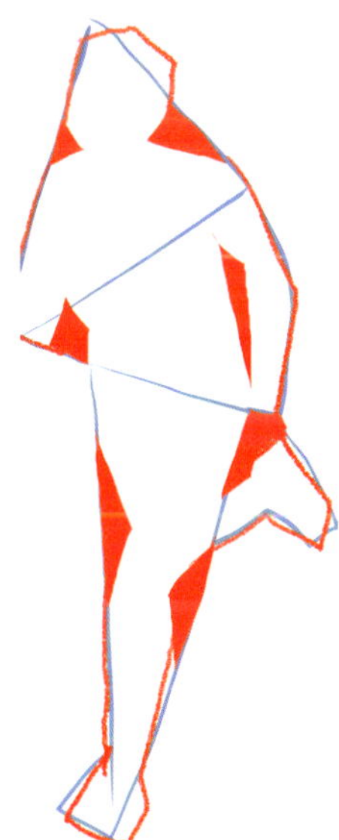

2 The red area is the negative space. By shading it in, a silhouette of the full body shape of the runner emerges.

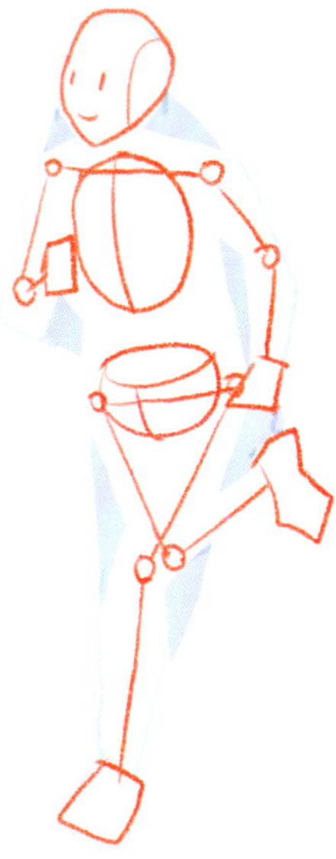

3 The silhouette of the runner creates an outline that makes it easier to position the body parts using stick and doll figures.

Drawing a running pose

You will need a model for this exercise. Take a series of photos of a friend or family member running, then choose the most dynamic pose.

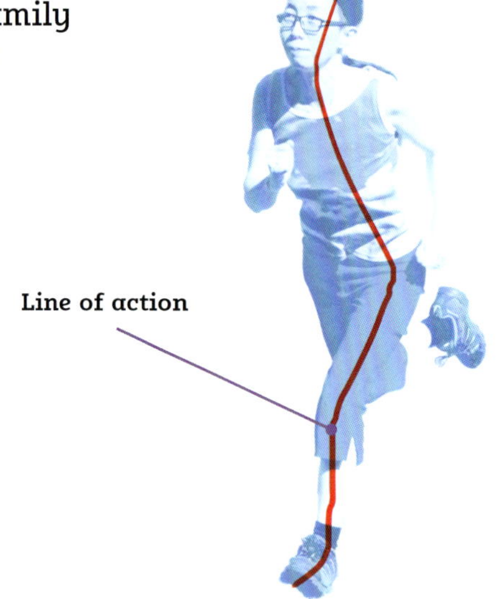

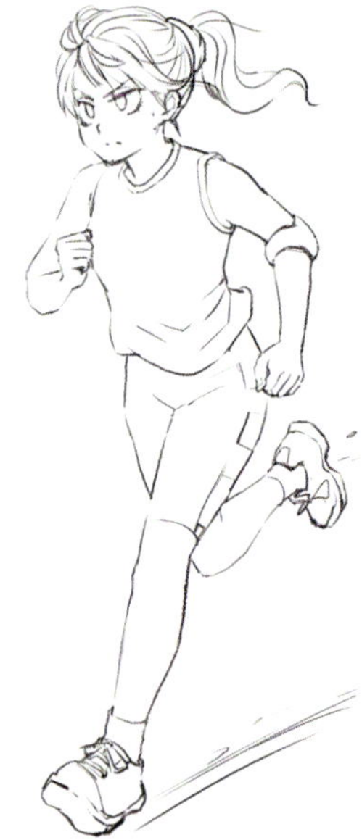

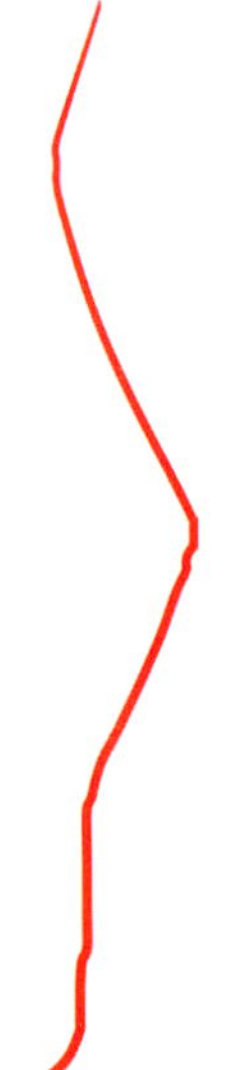

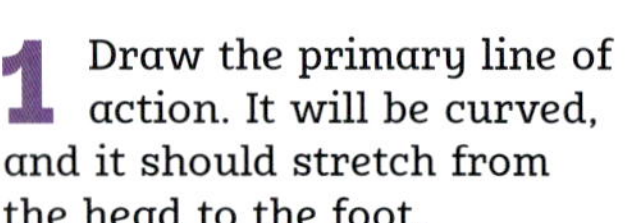

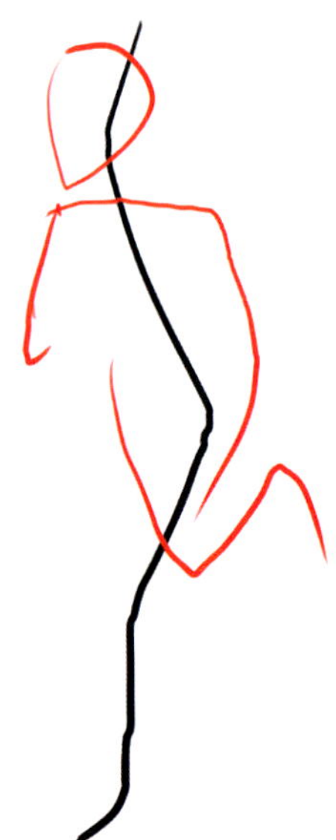

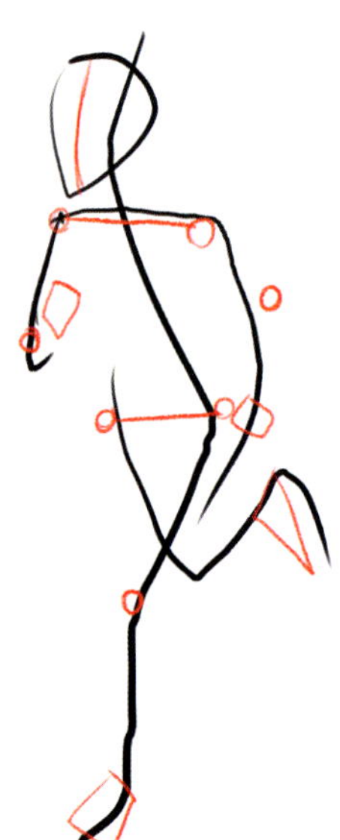

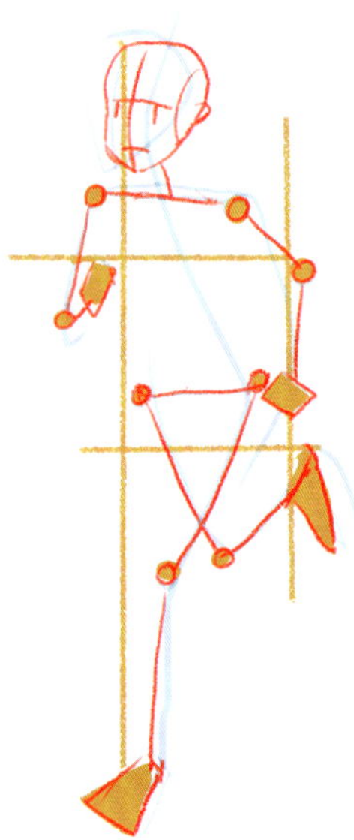

1 Draw the primary line of action. It will be curved, and it should stretch from the head to the foot.

2 Add one or more secondary lines to indicate the outline of the arms and legs, showing the flow of the whole body. Draw the head as a 'D' shape to show its angle and direction.

3 Add a six-head-tall stick figure (see pages 44–45) on the lines of action. Pay attention to the angles of the spine, shoulders, hips and feet.

4 Check the proportions. Are the legs half the length of the body? You don't need to consider the centre of gravity of poses in motion. However, compare the positions of the joints in the photo, both horizontally and vertically, and adjust the positional relationship as you need to.

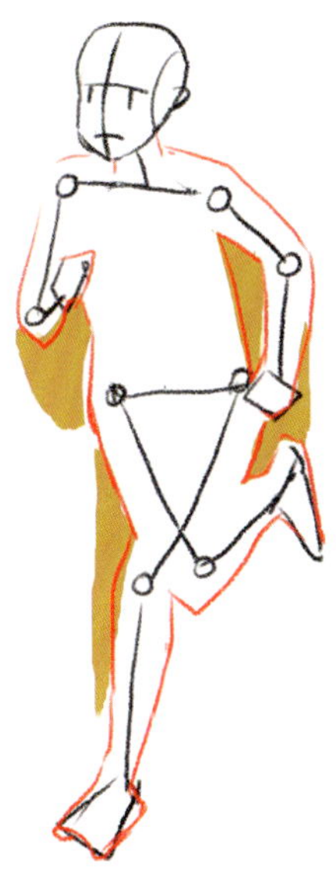

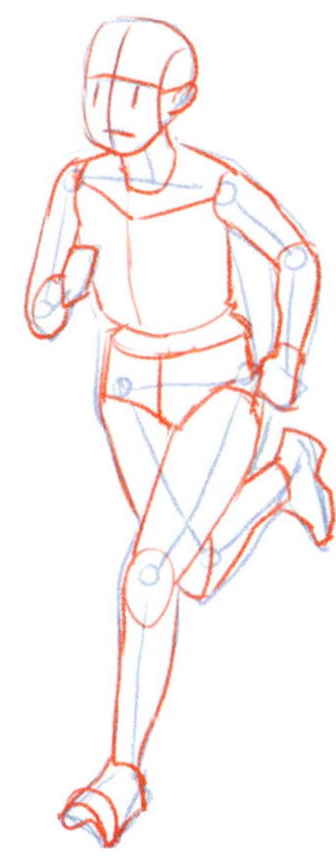

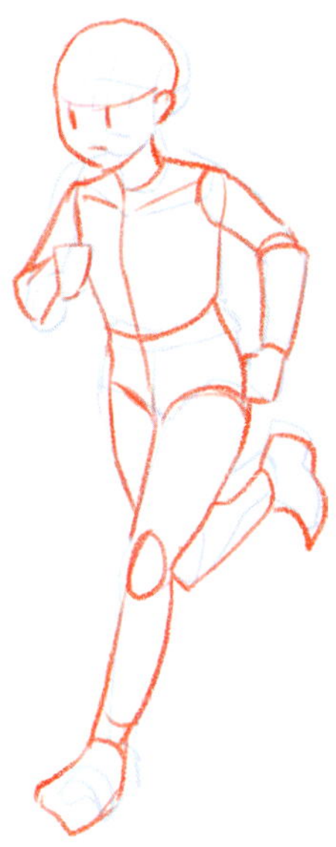

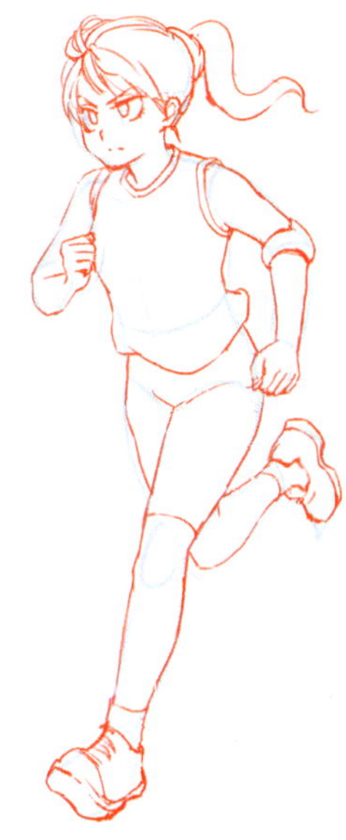

5 By drawing a rough silhouette (see page 87), you can further compare the overall impression. Drawing and comparing negative space shapes will help to copy the angles and positions of the body parts properly.

6 Use the silhouette to position the stick and doll figures.

7 From here, you can work on creating a character for the figure. Redraw the character in any desired angle, gender or body type until you are satisfied with the final pose.

8 Add any details such as the face, hair, hands, feet and clothing.

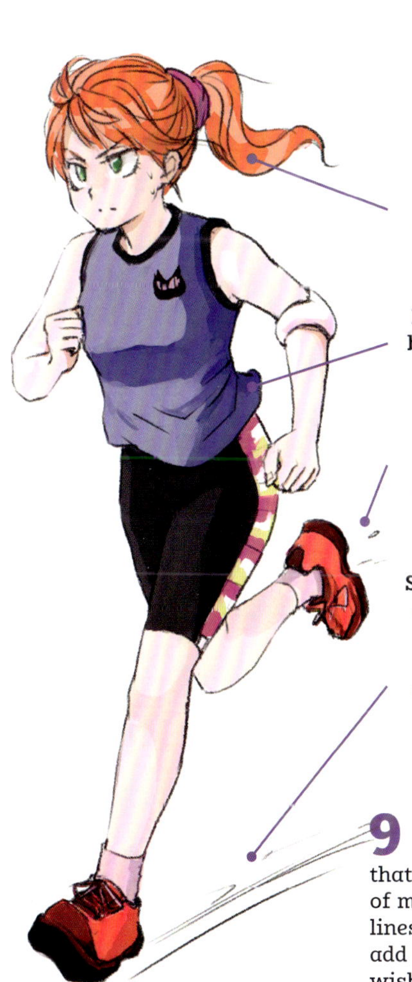

Her hair is swaying in the wind.

Her clothes will be flapping from her speed.

Add specks of dirt or mud coming off the shoes.

Speed lines are a great effect for giving a sense of speed and communicating the power of movement.

9 To make it more dynamic, draw details that accentuate the sense of movement such as speed lines. Clean up the lines and add shading or colour if you wish (see pages 98–123).

ARE YOU HAPPY WITH YOUR POSE?
Try drawing the same pose from different angles and practising different poses to increase the number of poses you can draw. Try more and more poses that you've never drawn before!

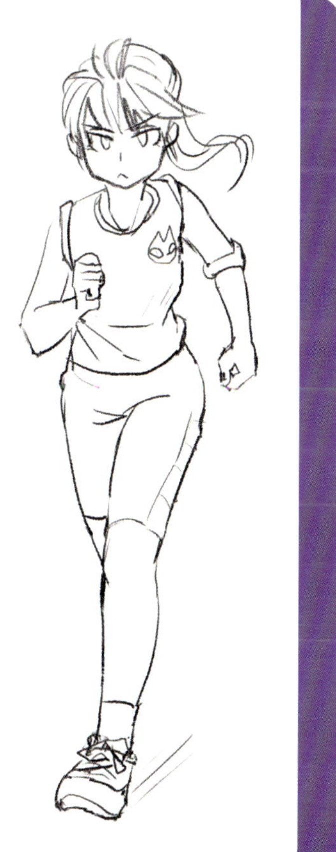

Focus on:
Action tips

When observing a real person, pay attention to the small details that add to the impression of action. Notice how the feet move as someone walks or runs and the movement of their neck and head, and include these details in your figures.

FEET ANGLES

Pay attention to the direction of the feet. In a moving pose, it is more likely that only one foot is on the ground. Take a couple of steps, and as you do so think about when your toes and your heels are touching the ground. Remember that the toes can be bent at a different angle to the feet because they are jointed. Think about how your ankles can bend at different angles and in different directions. Check your own feet to see where and at what angle they are bent during different movements.

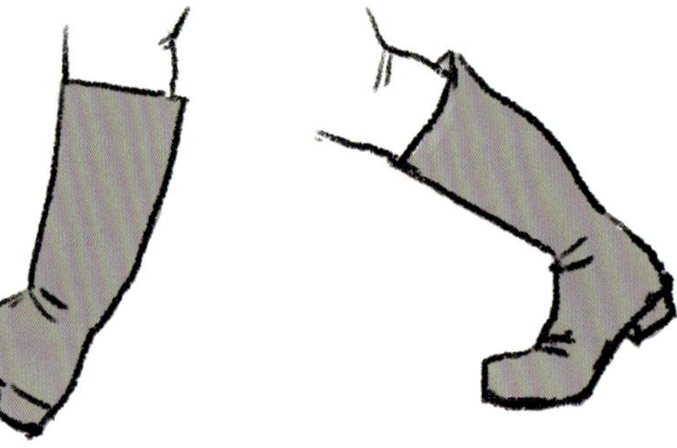

HIDDEN NECKS

It is important to observe and memorize the shape of the human body in different poses. For example, in many poses or movements, the body is often leaning forward or is hunched over. In such cases, the neck is often not visible when the body is viewed from the front. If you draw with the fixed idea that you must draw a neck as well as a head, it will be difficult to capture the pose accurately.

AVOID STATIC POSES

It is difficult to create a sense of movement in poses if the head and body are in a straight line. Use diagonals and extreme curves to find dynamic angles. If the centre of gravity is too far back, your figure would fall over, so it is better to have the body leaning forward as long as the next step would be supported by the leg currently in the air. Be aware of dynamic action lines and try to draw them.

Power up

Common action poses

Try drawing more dynamic poses using lines of action and the action stick figure. Here are some typical poses.

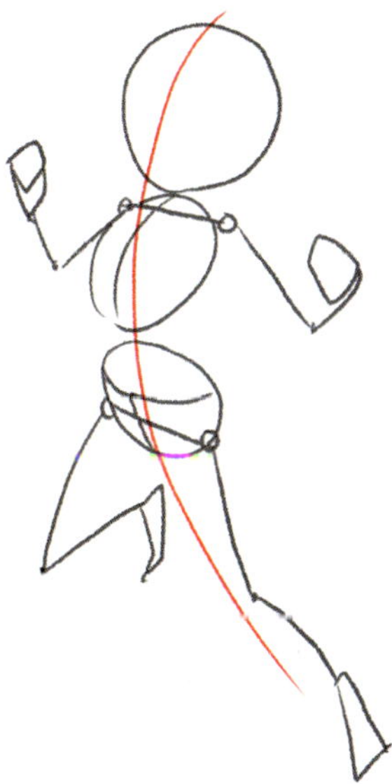

1 Start by drawing a shallow 'C' curve using an action line, then draw the other parts of a stick figure (see pages 44–45). Pose the figure dynamically, bearing in mind the proportions and angles.

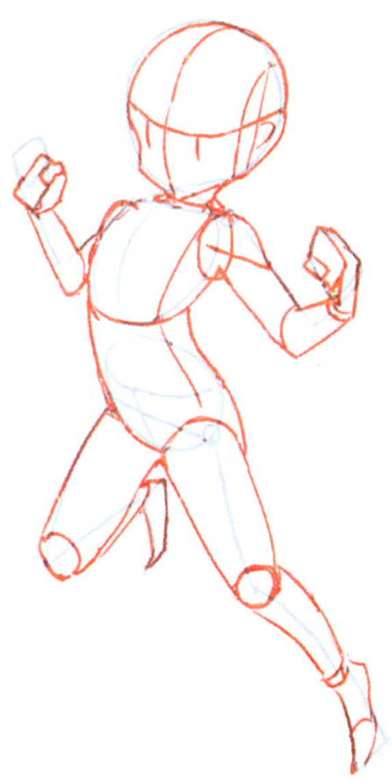

2 Turn the stick figure into a doll figure (see page 46–48). Adjust the pose to make the face, body tilt, position of arms and legs, etc. look cool.

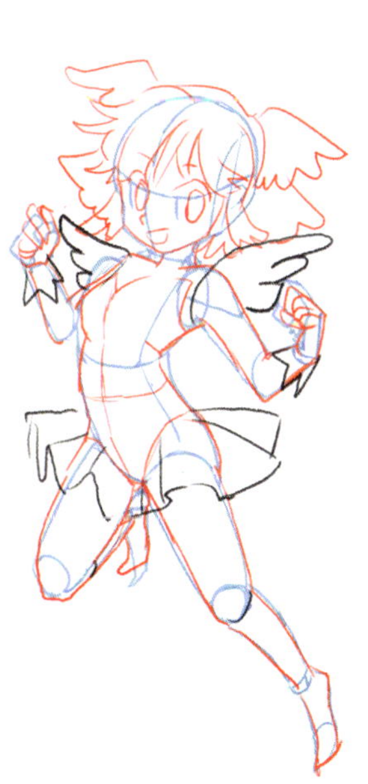

3 Add the face and body details, and add clothes to dress the figure.

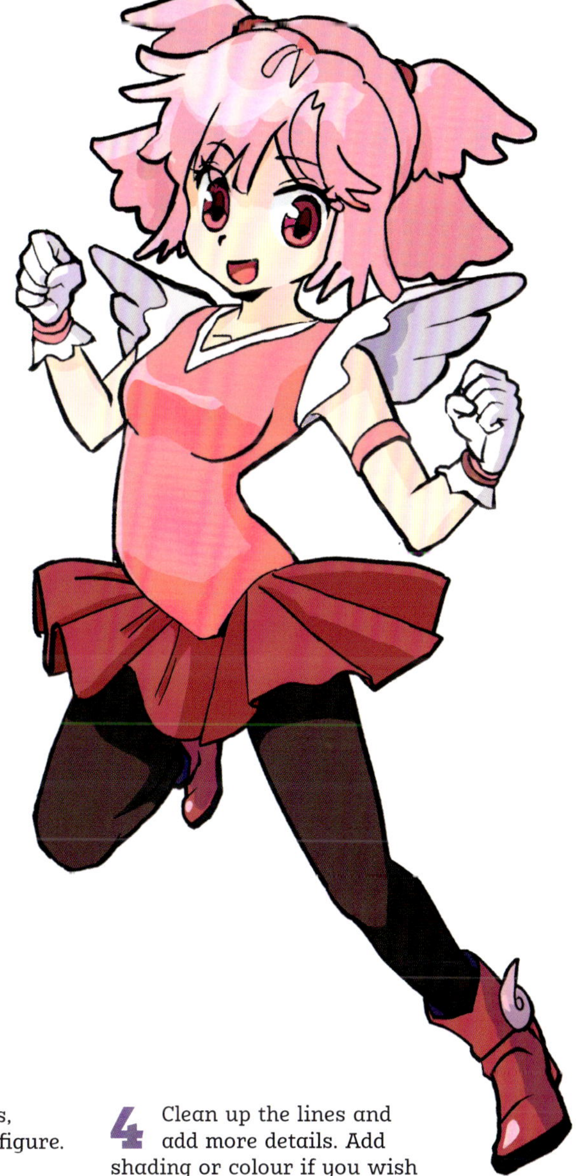

4 Clean up the lines and add more details. Add shading or colour if you wish (see pages 98–123).

Readying a sword

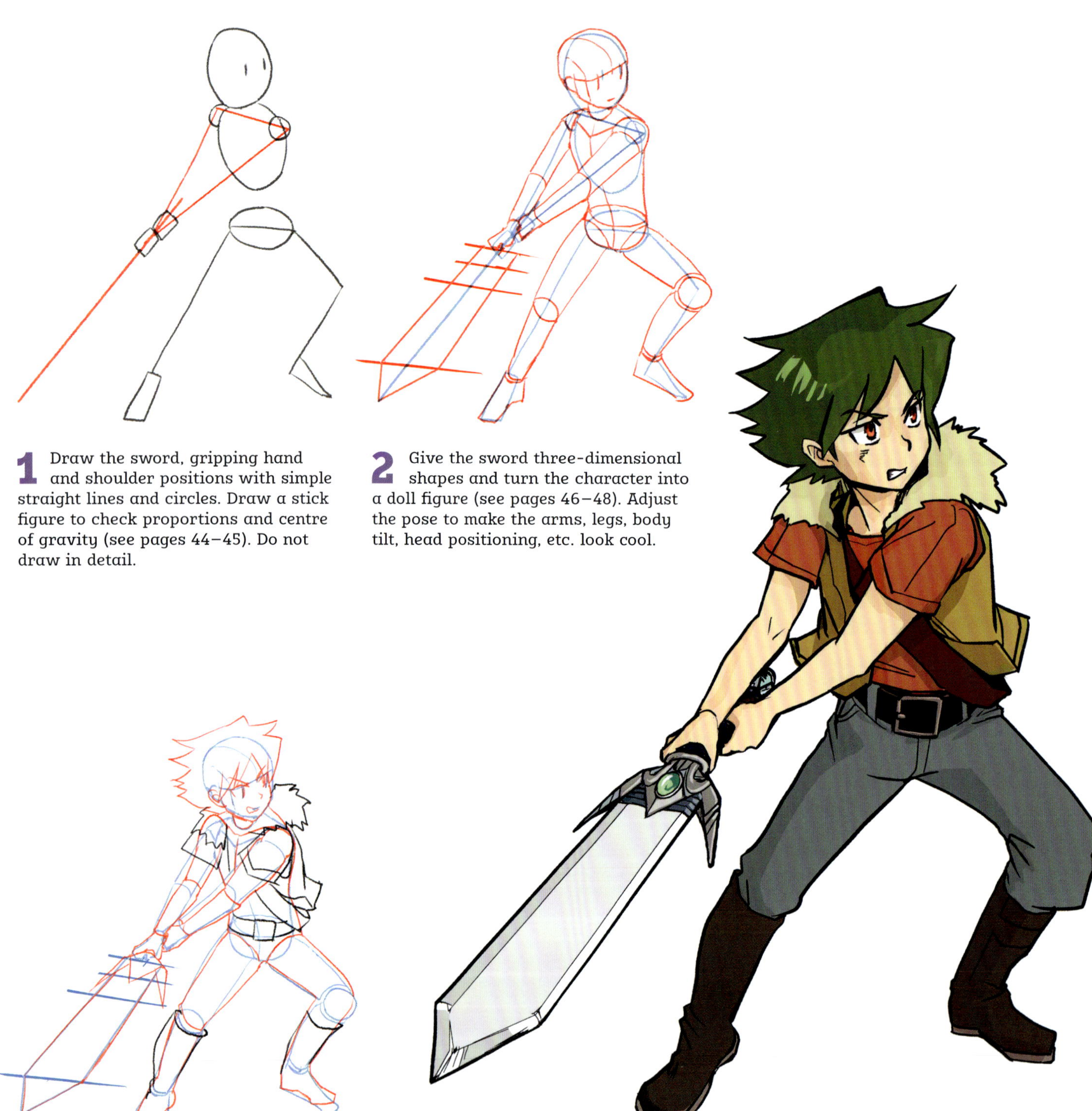

1 Draw the sword, gripping hand and shoulder positions with simple straight lines and circles. Draw a stick figure to check proportions and centre of gravity (see pages 44–45). Do not draw in detail.

2 Give the sword three-dimensional shapes and turn the character into a doll figure (see pages 46–48). Adjust the pose to make the arms, legs, body tilt, head positioning, etc. look cool.

3 Add the sword, face and body details, and add clothes to dress the figure.

4 Clean up the lines and add more details. Add shading or colour if you wish (see pages 98–123).

MONSTER ATTACK

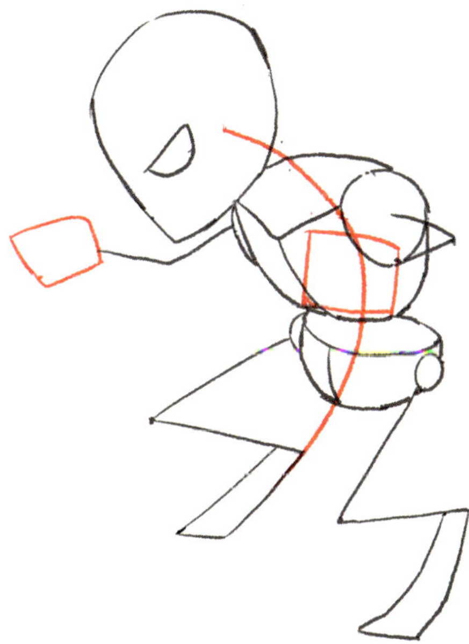

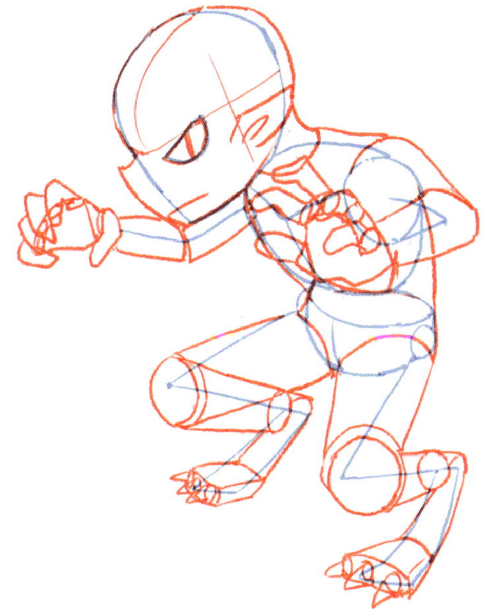

1 Draw a 'C' curve for the character's spine, and roughly draw the hands in front. Make the stick figure (see pages 44–45). Here, I've made the head much further forward than the torso and the feet larger.

2 Turn the stick figure into a doll figure (see page 46–48). Adjust the pose to make the face, body tilt, position of arms and legs, etc. look cool.

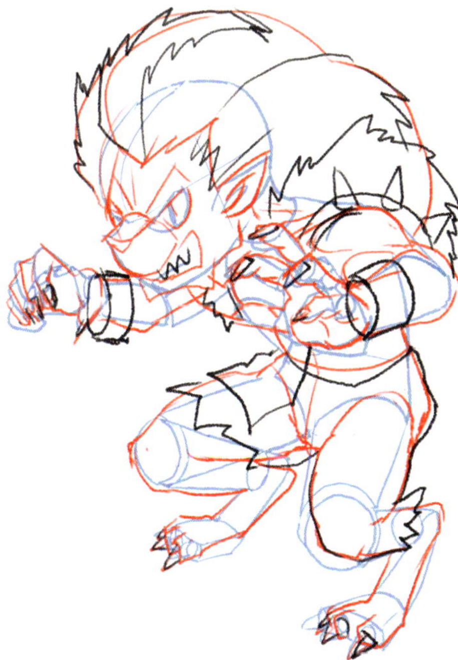

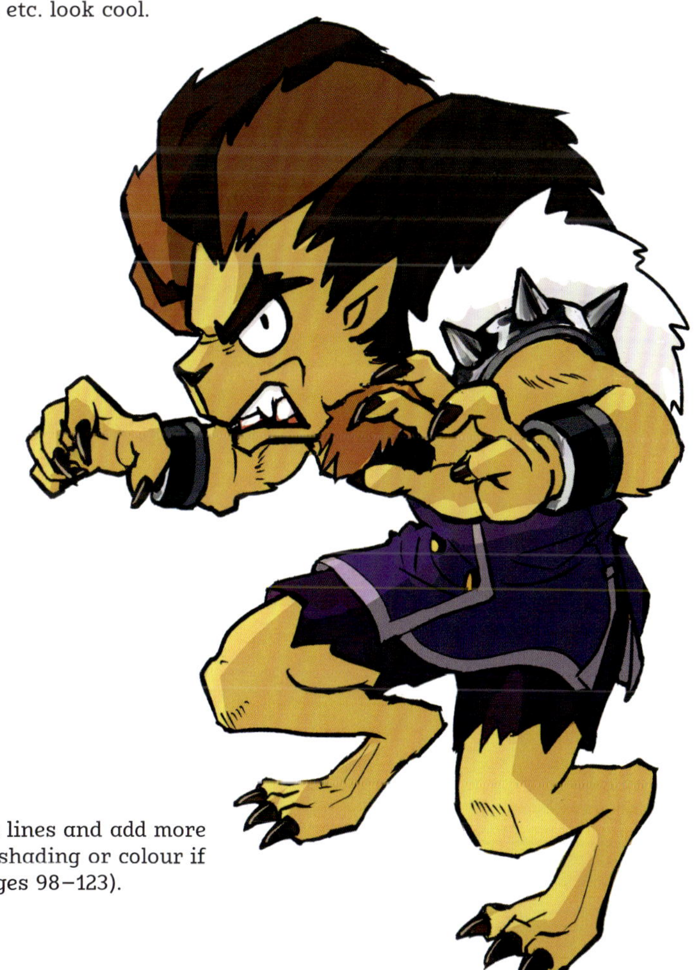

3 Add the face and body details, and add clothes to dress the figure.

4 Clean up the lines and add more details. Add shading or colour if you wish (see pages 98–123).

POWER BLAST

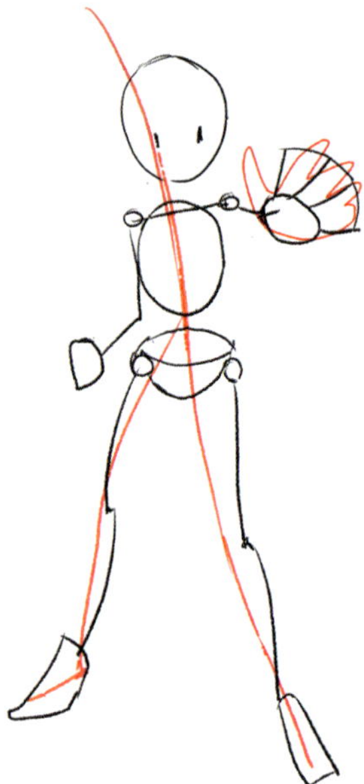

1 Draw action lines with a power hand position, then draw the stick figure (see pages 44–45). The outstretched palm in the foreground should be drawn a little larger (for foreshortening, see page 81).

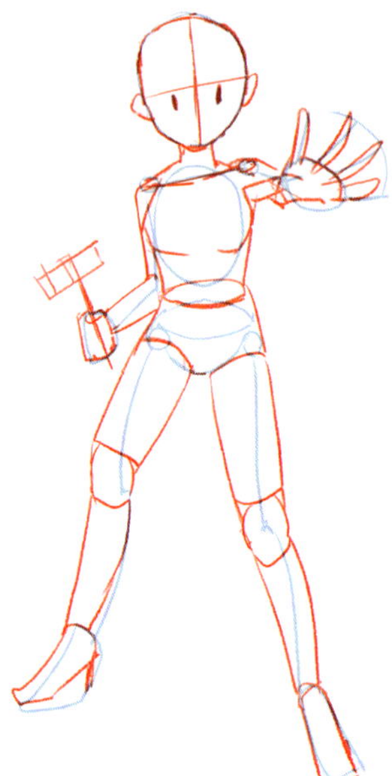

2 Turn the stick figure into a doll figure (see page 46–48). Adjust the pose to make the face, body tilt, position of arms and legs, etc. look cool.

3 Add the face and body details, and add clothes to dress the figure.

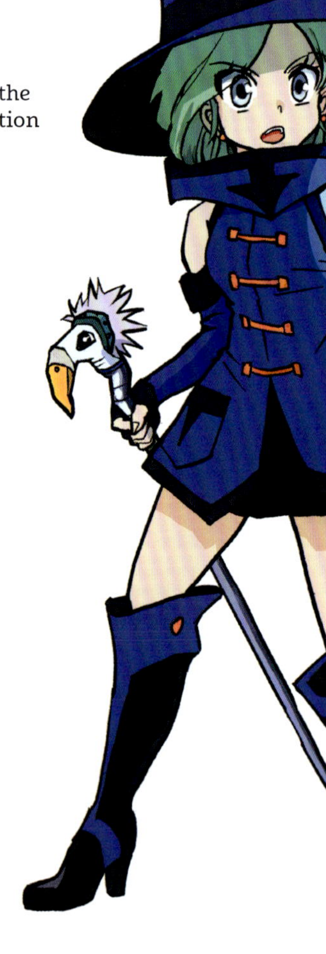

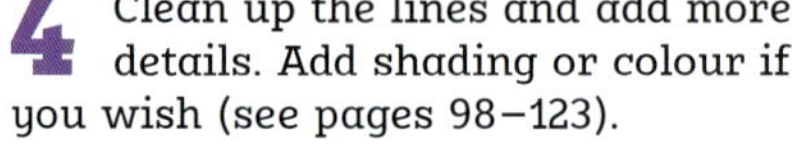

4 Clean up the lines and add more details. Add shading or colour if you wish (see pages 98–123).

Super punch

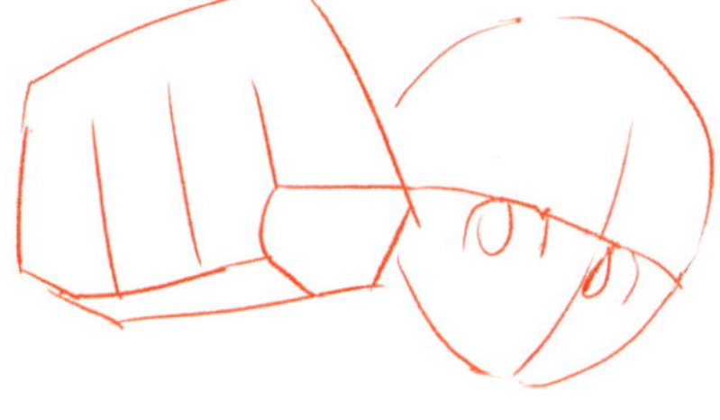

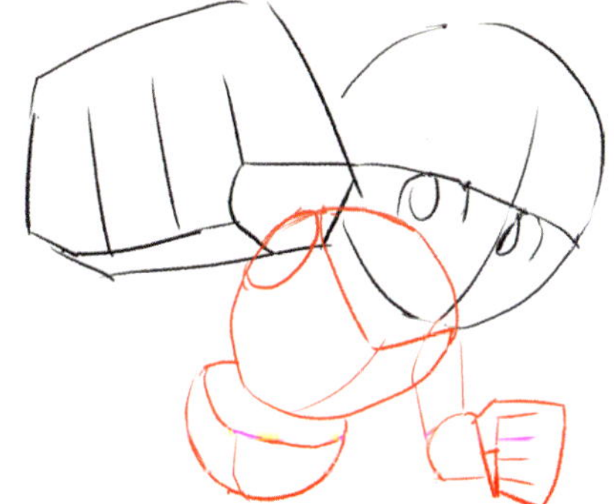

Extreme action poses

A good way to make a strong image is to draw a part of the body larger than the rest using foreshortening (see page 80). This technique is often used on comic covers and for manga action scenes.

1 Draw an ultra-large fist, then draw the head behind it at a similar size to the fist.

2 Add a top view of the body looking down. You won't see the neck from this angle. Add the other hand, drawing it small to show the distance.

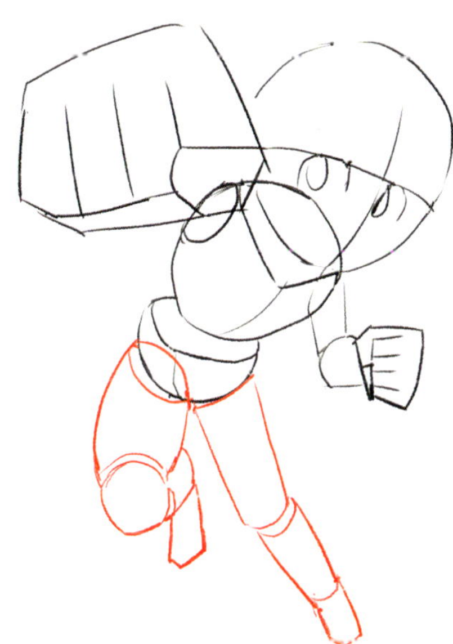

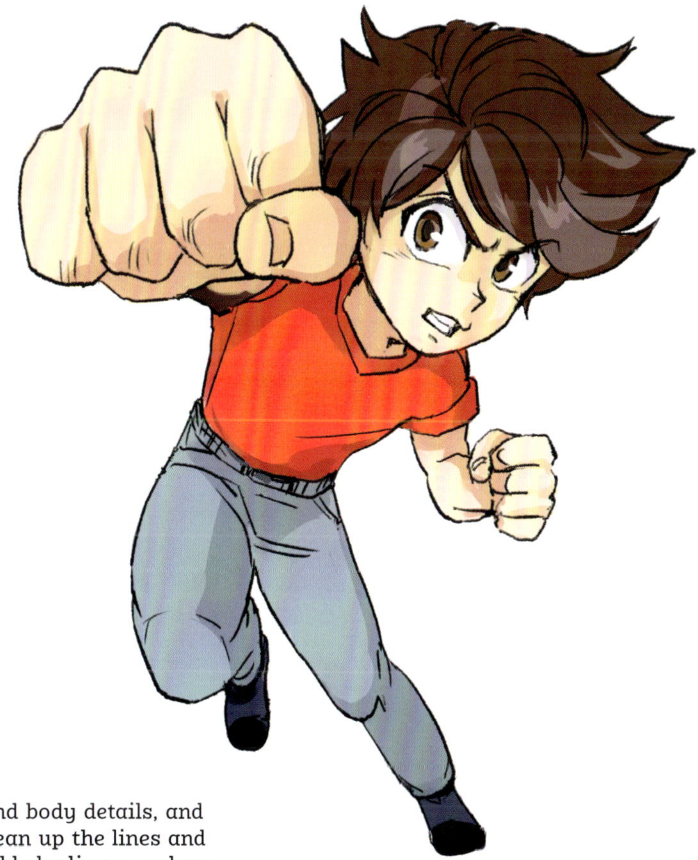

3 Draw the thighs proportionally small and draw the toes even smaller. You may not see the lower leg of the bent leg because of the top view.

4 Add the face and body details, and add clothes. Clean up the lines and add more details. Add shading or colour if you wish (see pages 98–123).

Next steps:
Quick sketching and gesture drawing

Manga stories and anime involve drawing many figures and poses, so rather than focusing on precision and detail while developing a story, manga and anime artists find it helpful to quickly draw the key features of the human body. They do this using two techniques: quick sketching (also called croquis) and gesture drawing.

The drawing methods differ in that the aim of a quick sketch is to copy the body shape, while the goal of a gesture drawing is to capture the figure's emotion or action. In both methods, the drawings are created quickly, starting from a line of action (see page 87), and use fewer lines and details than in a typical drawing. Try them – they will help to improve your drawing skills.

Ask a friend or member of your family to pose for you, or use a photograph or pause a video. These are just practice drawings, so use a cheap sketchbook with thin paper that you can easily carry with you to sketch in different surroundings. You don't have to fill the page, so you can draw several poses on the same sheet. Use a soft pencil, such as 2B, but don't use an eraser. Don't worry about erasing lines – just go over old lines. You can also use a pen.

It is important to use your observation skills when trying these exercises. As you draw, try to look mostly at the model and glance down briefly to your paper only occasionally. Let go of your assumptions and draw what you see. Take in the big picture, considering size, length, angles and curves, but don't get lost in the details.

Practice:
Quick sketches

Give priority to drawing the whole body in the time you have. You may run out of time if you stick to one part of the body for too long, so move on even if you're not happy with it. Add the individual shapes and details in any remaining time.

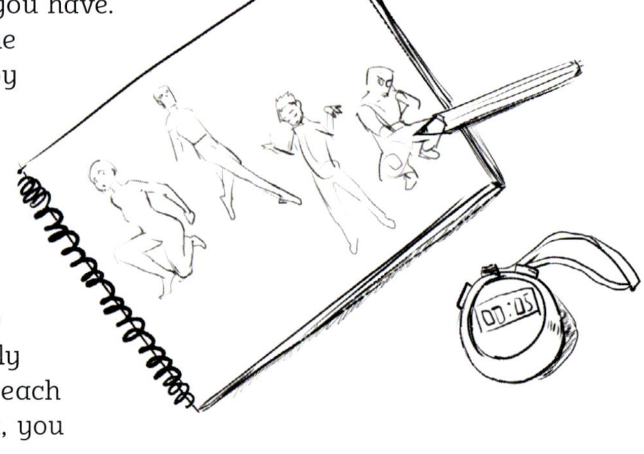

When first trying this exercise, set a timer for 10 minutes, then draw a pose. When you can draw a pose comfortably in 10 minutes, reduce the time to 5 minutes, then to 3 minutes, 1 minute and, finally, 30 seconds. Try to do this exercise every day, even if only for 10 minutes. Ideally, aim to draw five to ten poses each day. By the time you reach the end of the sketchbook, you should be confidently drawing body poses at a good pace.

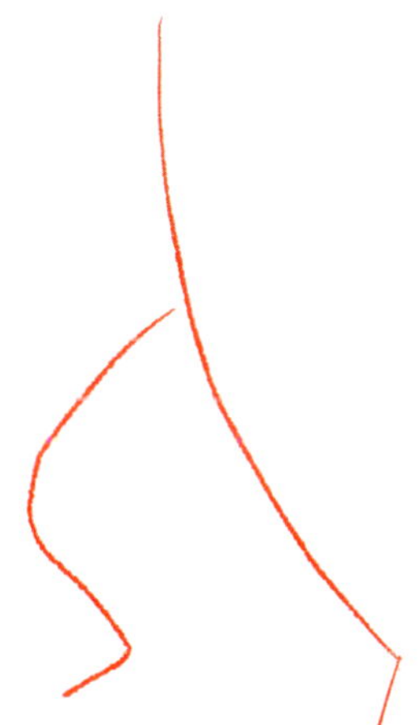

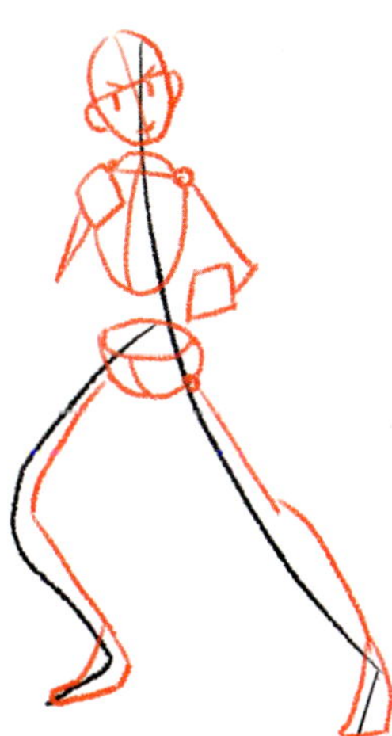

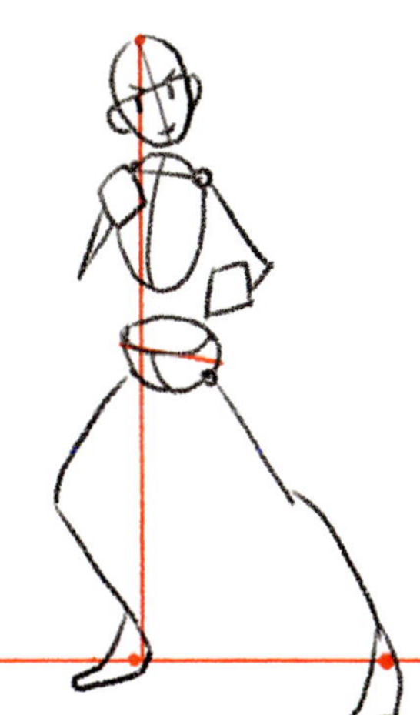

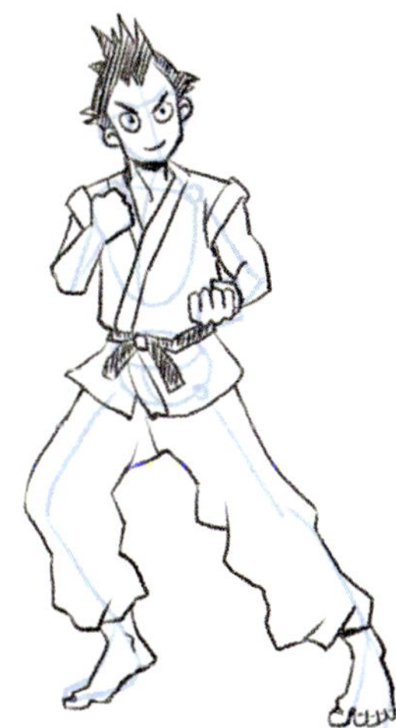

1 Start the drawing with a line of action.

2 Add the basic body shapes.

3 Check the proportions and the centre of gravity and adjust them if necessary.

4 If your subject hasn't moved, add in a few quick the details.

Practice:
Gesture drawing

Instead of copying the shapes, the focus in gesture drawing is on the movement and emotion. Draw your figures dynamically, using lines of action to express energy, feeling, rhythm and flow. Try to do this using as few lines as possible. Practise drawing your figures with different themes and emotions. Choose a different one each day, such as 'happiness' or 'running', and create a variety of poses using gesture drawings.

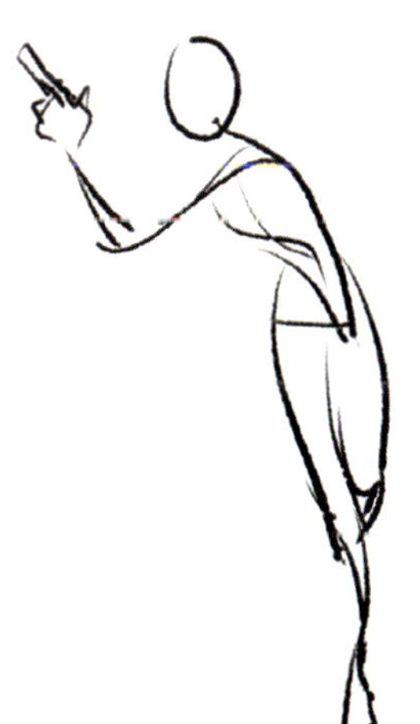

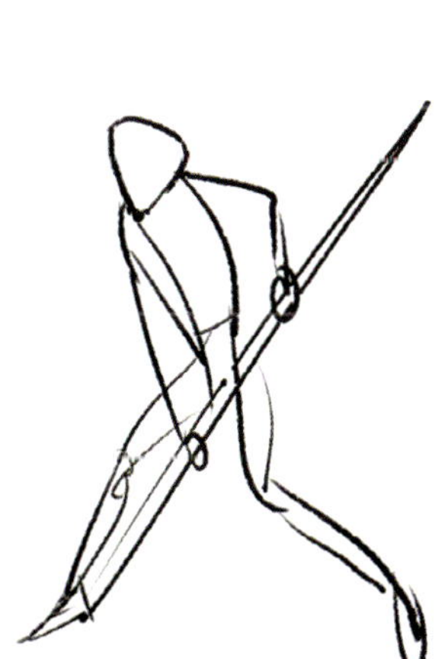

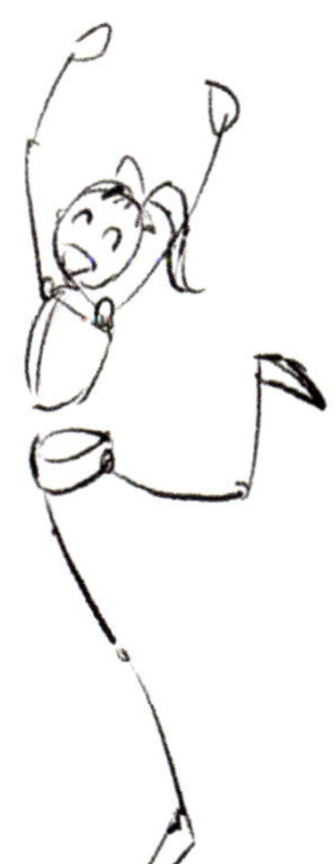

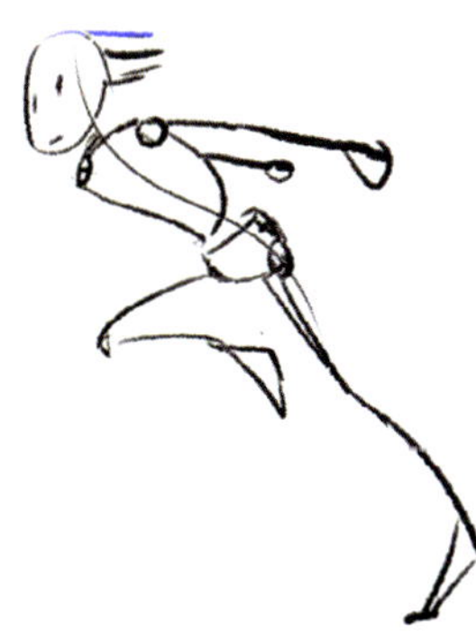

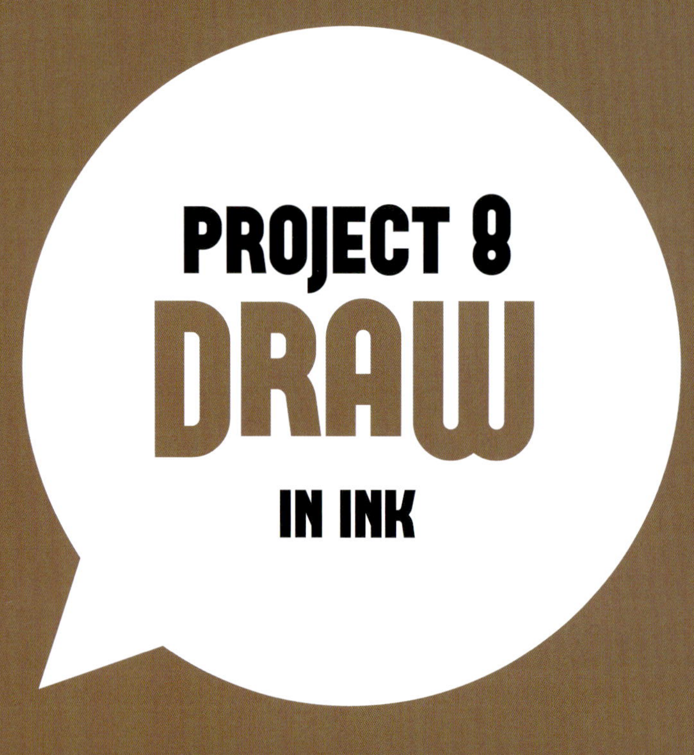
PROJECT 8
DRAW
IN INK

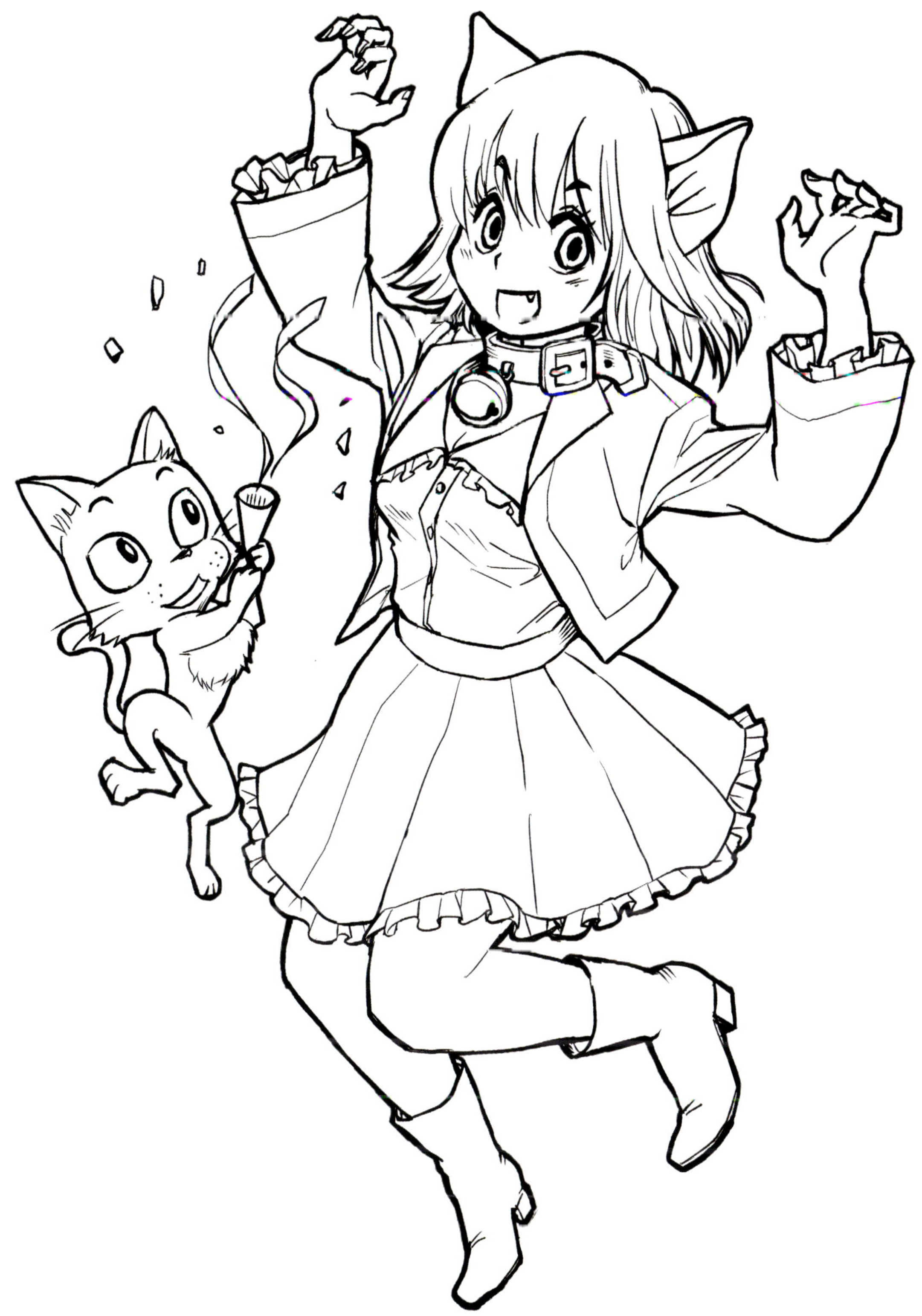

Black-and-white ink drawings are the traditional way to make manga comic strips. In this section, I'll introduce you to everything you need to know about drawing in ink, from what media to use, how to prepare your original sketch in readiness for inking and how to use ink. You will learn how to trace your drawings in ink as well as how to add tone, shading and special effects.

Black-and-white manga

Japanese manga is still predominantly drawn in black and white using ink. The pure black of the inked lines on white paper look striking, as they present greater contrast compared with pencil drawings. You can put energy and flow into your ink lines. You can also use small strokes to create different tones and patterns, allowing you to depict different materials and lighting conditions.

ANALOGUE AND DIGITAL INKING

Using a dip pen and bottle of ink was the traditional way to draw manga until the 20th century, and many artists still use them. However, they are difficult to master.

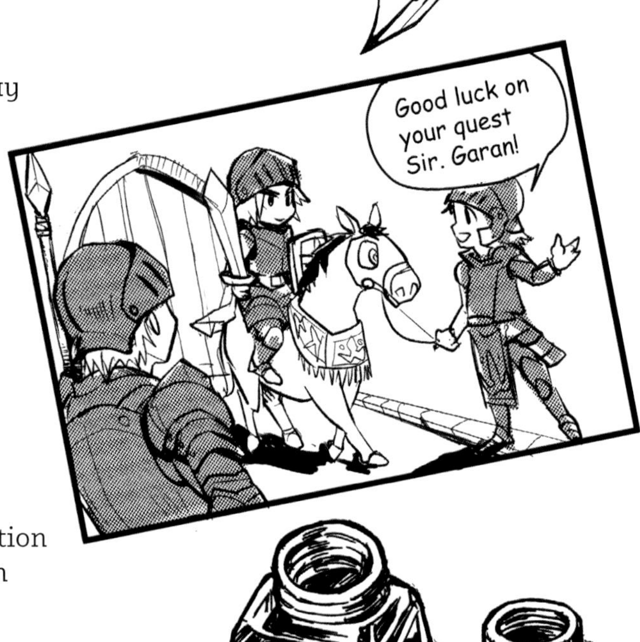

Many people draw digitally with a laptop or tablet and a stylus. However, they are expensive, and it can take some time to learn how to produce controlled lines. In contrast, paper and pens are comparatively cheap and much quicker to learn how to use.

I recommend buying three to five fineliners with different width tips, such as 0.1mm, 0.2mm, 0.3mm, 0.5mm and 0.8mm, and a brush pen set. You will also need 160–200gsm (60–110lb) card stock, a white correction pen and a light pad. See pages 6–7 for more information on different tools and materials.

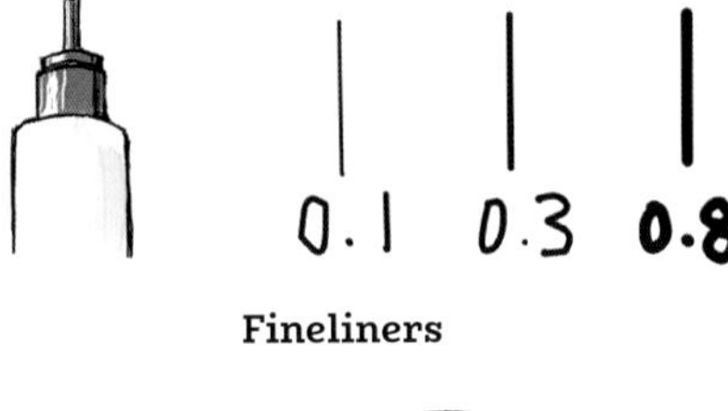

Fineliners

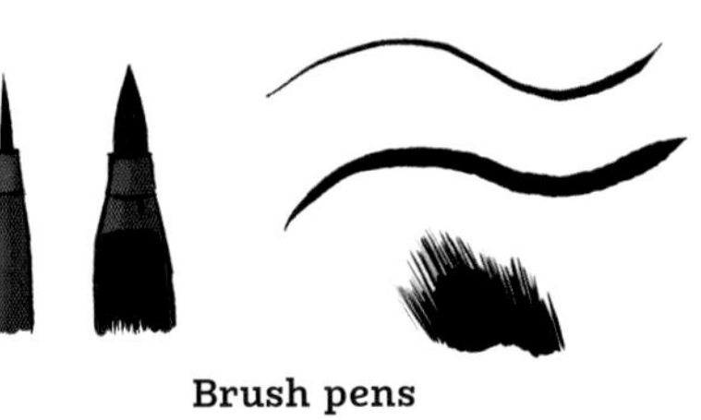

Brush pens

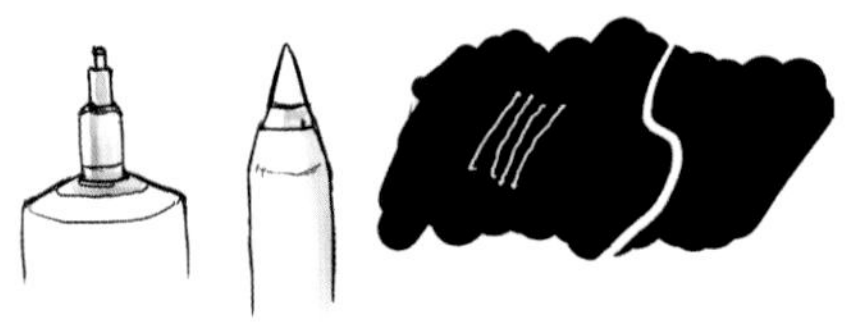

Correction pen and white pens

LEARNING TO USE YOUR PENS

Practise using your pens before you start adding ink to drawings. This is so you can learn how the fineliners and brush pens produce different line widths and how to draw clean lines in ink. You should also experiment to learn different ways to use them to add shading.

Test your pens on scrap paper and find the best weights for your drawing. Choose a different weight for the fine details, the main lines and the stronger outlines (for the project in this chapter I used 0.1mm, 0.3mm and 0.8mm, respectively). Try drawing straight lines, curved lines and shapes. When you're comfortable using the pen to draw good clean lines, practise different forms of hatching to draw shading. Finally, use the pen to create graduation.

When drawing with a fineliner, there is no need to apply pressure as you draw a line. Hold the pen slightly vertically and gently move your arm to draw. Practise until you can draw long lines with confidence.

DRAWING LINES

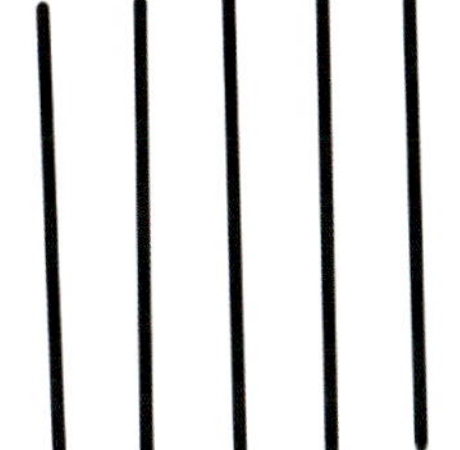

Straight vertical lines

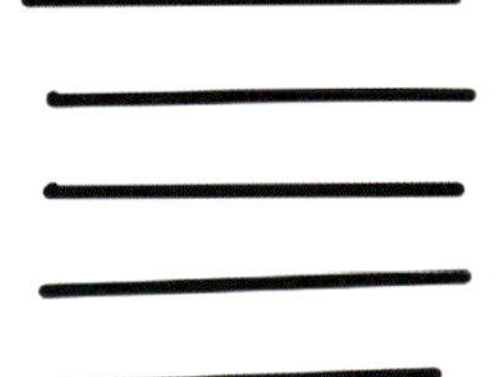

Parallel horizontal lines

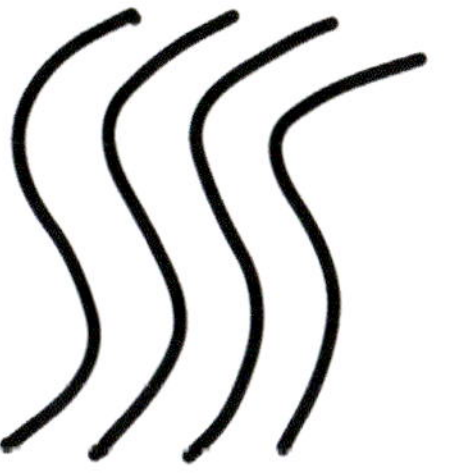

Curves

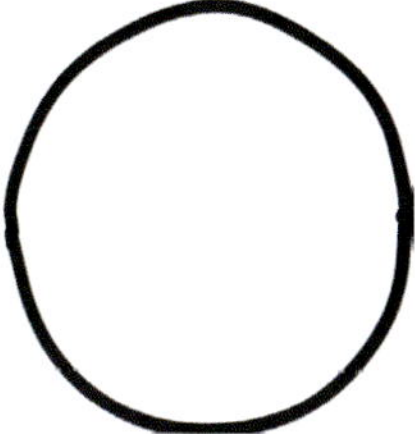

Shapes

DRAWING SHADING

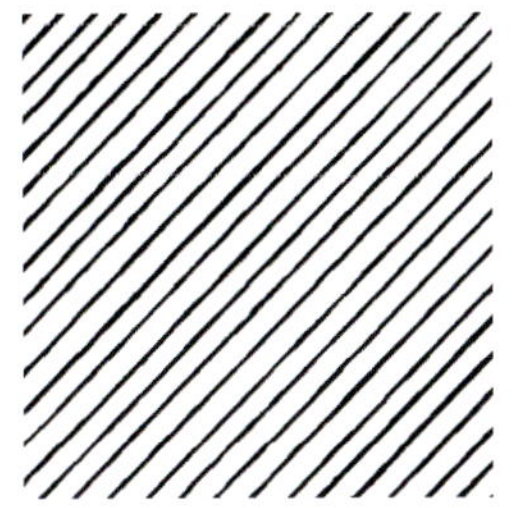

Single hatching

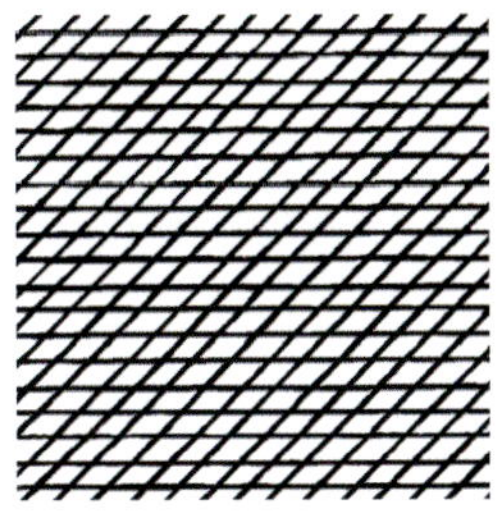

Cross-hatching

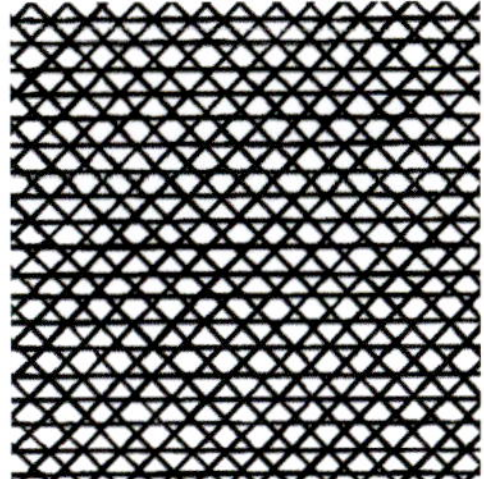

Triple hatching

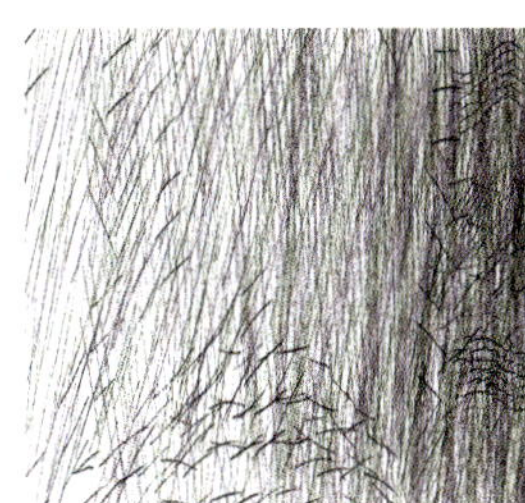

Graduation

DRAWING PATTERNS

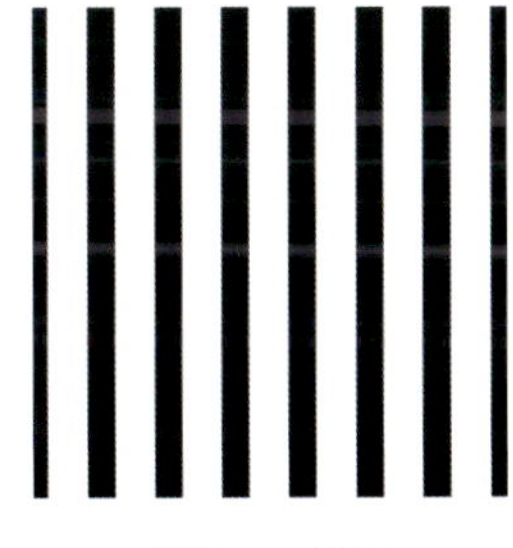

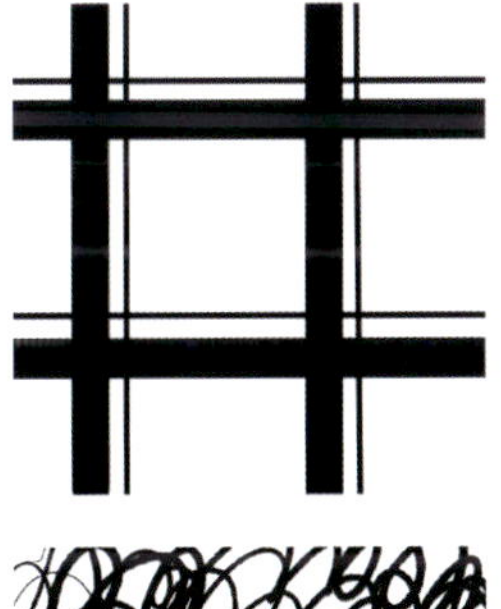

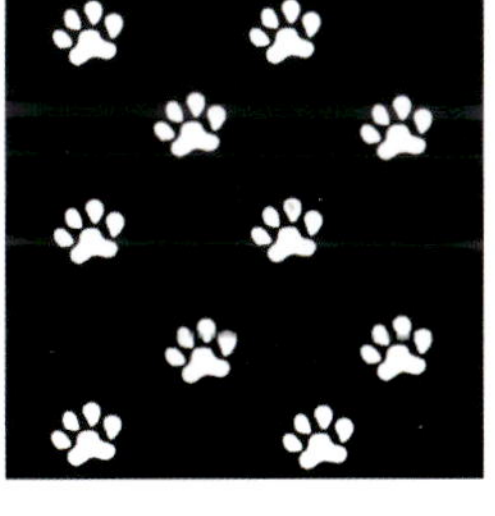

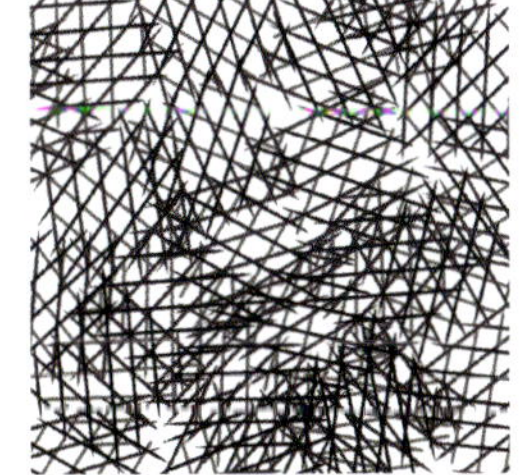

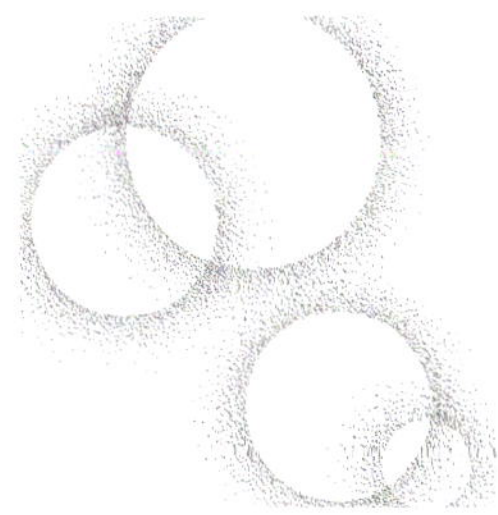

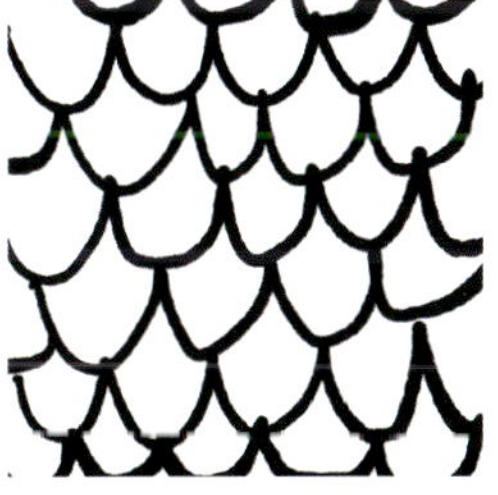

TIP

To avoid smudging your work, do not touch the lines immediately after drawing them. If you are right-handed, try to draw from the left-hand side of any line, and vice versa if you are left-handed. If you get any ink on your hands, wash it off so you don't accidentally wipe it on your work.

STAGE 1

COPY YOUR WORK

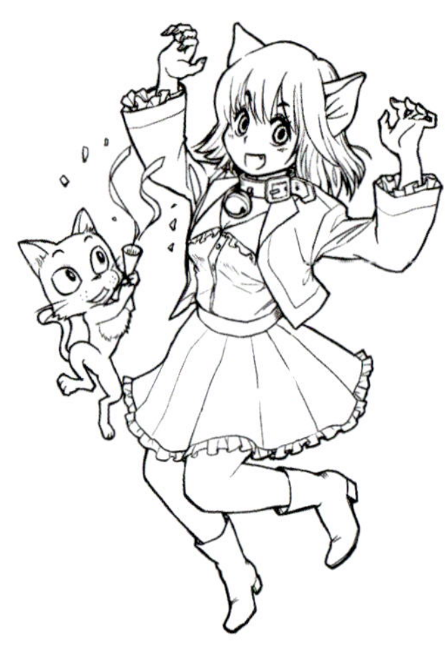

Once you are comfortable using your selection of pens, you can start inking your pencil sketches. While it is possible to ink your original sketch, it is better to copy the sketch onto a piece of card stock that won't bleed any ink. A light pad makes copying your sketch comparatively easy.

You can photocopy my drawing for this exercise, which I would suggest for practising, or use your own pencil sketch. Ink lines are not easy to erase, so starting with a good quality sketch is essential – ensure you clean up the pencil lines well (see page 24) before you begin tracing it.

For this project, you can photocopy the artwork on page 99.

PREPARING TO TRACE YOUR DRAWING

You can trace your drawing onto 160–200gsm (60–110lb) card stock by placing it over your sketch and providing a light source behind it. For the light source, use a light pad or one that is behind a glass surface.

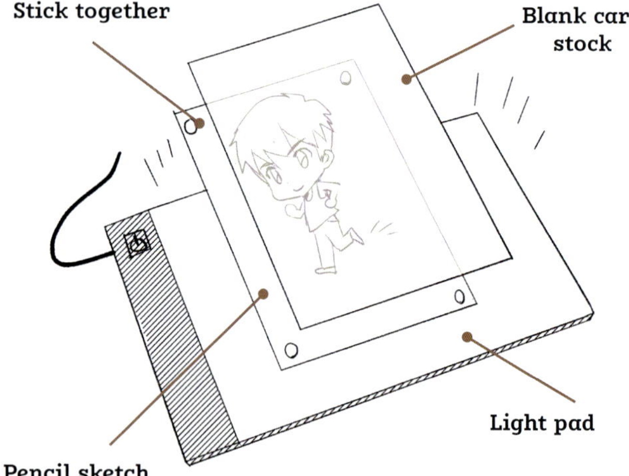

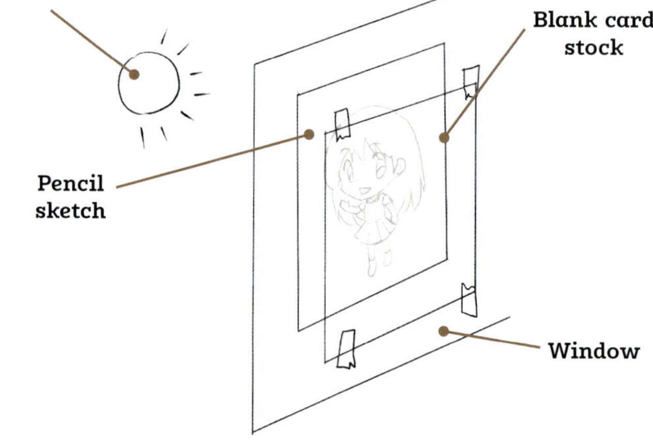

SETTING UP YOUR SKETCH ON A LIGHT PAD

Using adhesive putty or removable tape, stick your sketch to the back of a sheet of blank card stock to avoid the paper sliding and spoiling the image. Place them on the light pad.

USING ANOTHER LIGHT SOURCE

If you don't have a light pad, you can use a window on a sunny day, or try a clear glass table with a light underneath.

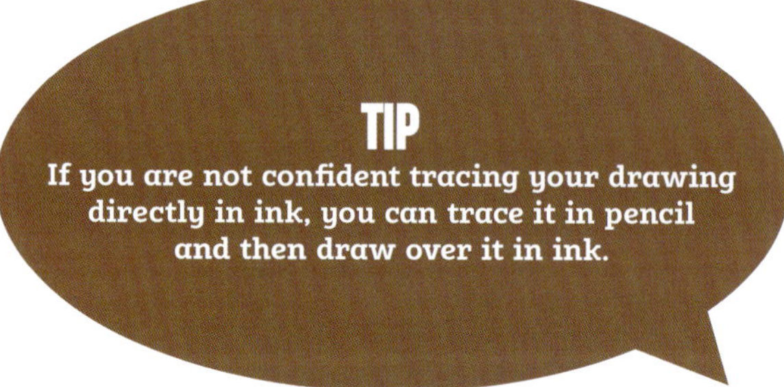

TIP

If you are not confident tracing your drawing directly in ink, you can trace it in pencil and then draw over it in ink.

Focus on:
Inking Tips

DRAW NEAT LINES

Avoid short broken lines and try to make a smooth, single line whenever you can. If you do need to stop a line in the middle of a shape, slightly overlap the continuation of the line over the previous one, so that it's as subtle as possible.

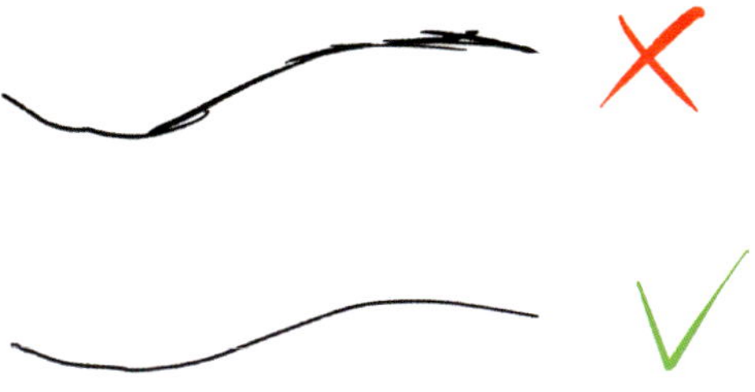

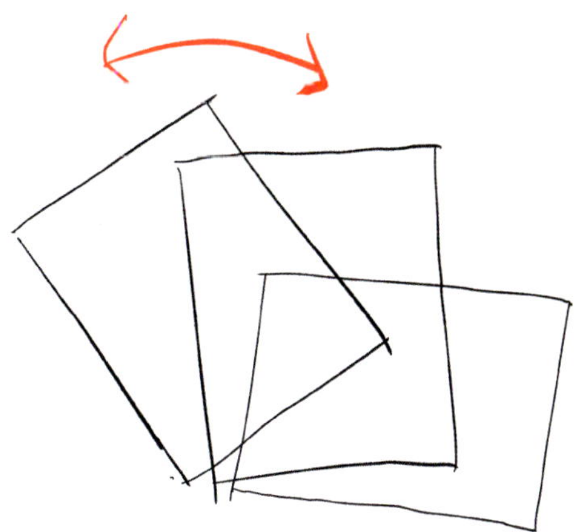

TURN YOUR PAPER

As you copy the drawing, turn the paper often so you can draw good lines. Arms are not designed to draw well at all angles, so this is the best way to maintain a steady line!

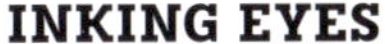

INKING EYES

Eyes are especially important. It's a good idea to practise some lines first before you trace them. Start with a thin fineliner and gradually use thicker ones to create bold upper eyelids and iris circles for a stronger impression.

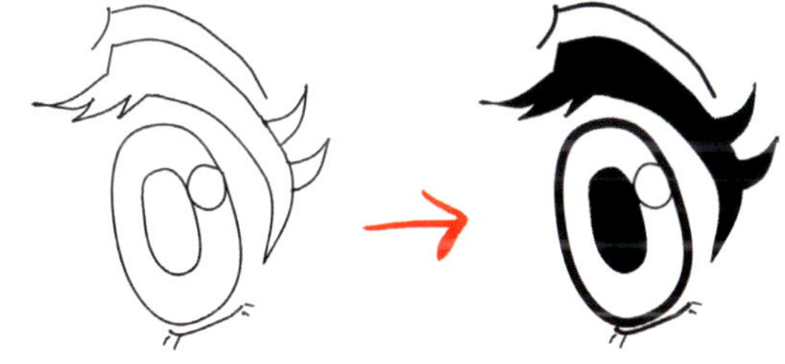

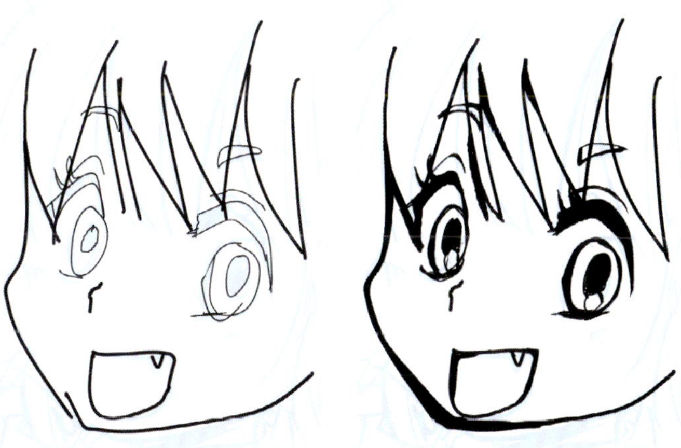

MAKING CORRECTIONS

Don't panic if you make a mistake. Ignore it for now and continue until all the inking is done. Using a correction pen on top of wet ink can cause smudging or smearing problems, so wait until the ink is fully dry, then make all your corrections.

To reduce the use of white correction pens and achieve a cleaner finish, try thinking of other ways to cover up mistakes such as adding lines or drawing extra scenery. For the drawing on the left, to cover up a mistake, I made part of a line thicker to look like a shadow under the chin.

STAGE 2

TRACING THE MAIN LINES

Pay extra attention when inking lines to avoid mistakes. Do not rush, and make sure all the lines are connected properly.

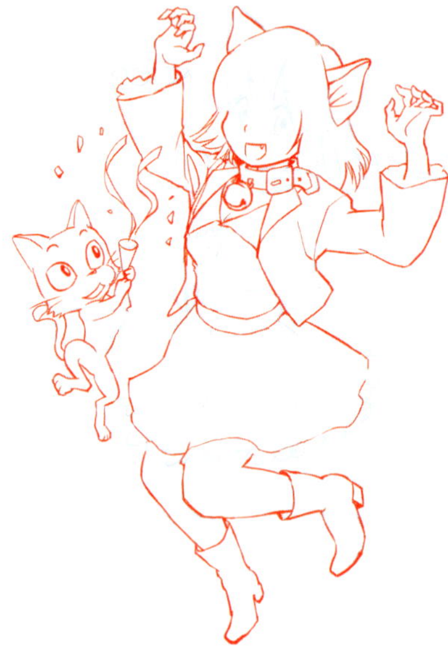

1 Start by inking the main lines. I suggest using a 0.2–0.4mm fineliner or a fine brush pen. Ignore the finer details such as the face, tufts of hair and clothing.

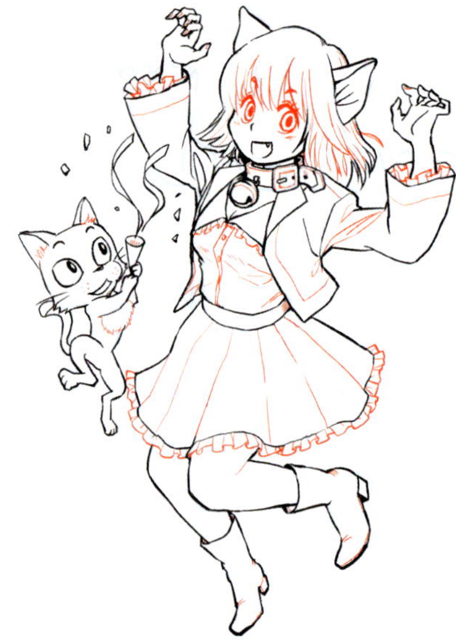

2 Add the details using a thin 0.1mm fineliner. Trace over the sketch lines that you skipped in the previous step and add extra details such as eyelashes, cheeks, and seams and creases in clothes.

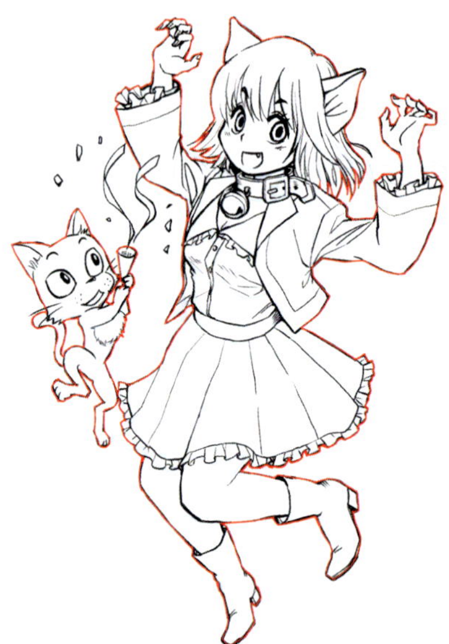

3 Outline the silhouette with a thicker line, using an 0.8-1.0mm fineliner. This is a technique to make your line art stand out. Be careful to stay outside of the character, and don't go over any of the lines inside!

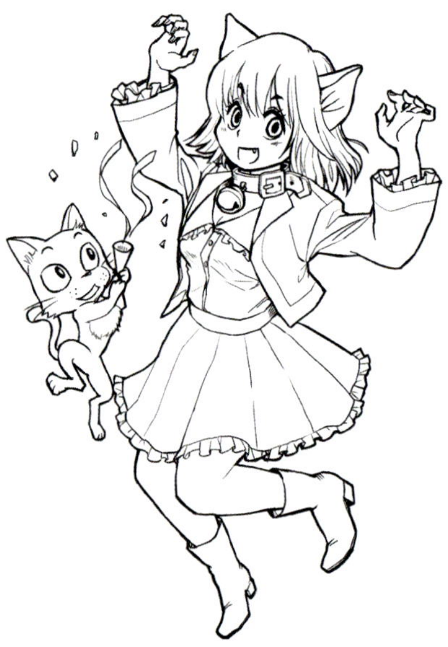

4 If you are inking an original pencil sketch, after the ink is fully dried, use an eraser to remove all the pencil lines, including those underneath the black lines. Brush all the eraser crumbs off the paper well.

STAGE 3

ADDING BLACK AND THEN WHITE

With the main lines inked, and dried, now it's time to think about areas that should be in black or could use white highlights.

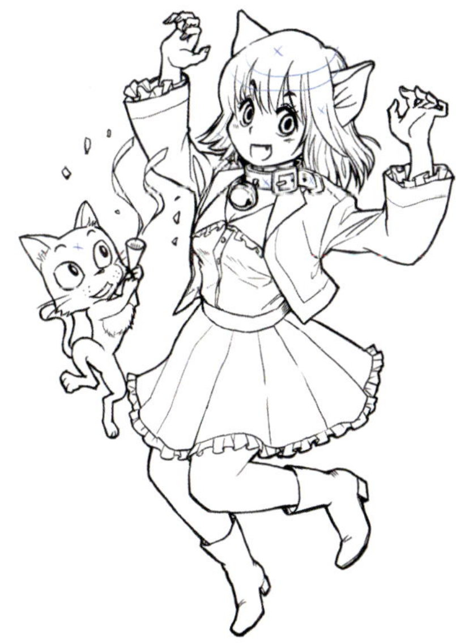

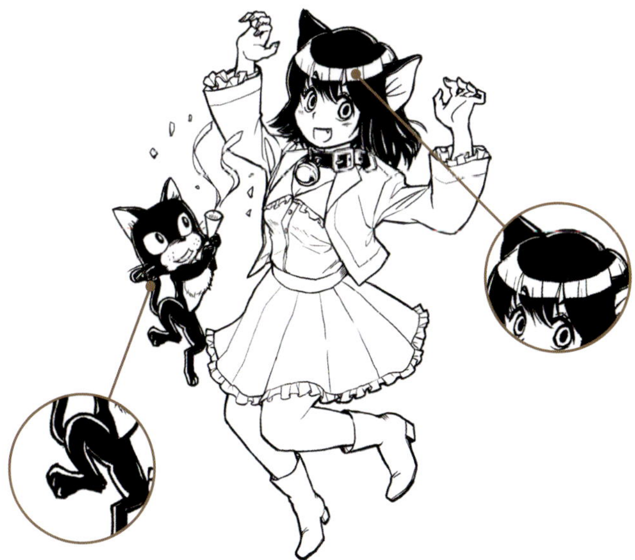

5 Plan the black fill areas and mark them with an 'X' in blue pencil. Mark where the highlights should be, too.

6 Fill in the areas neatly using a brush pen or black marker. Keep 0.5mm of the paper white if the black area has leached into the main body lines.

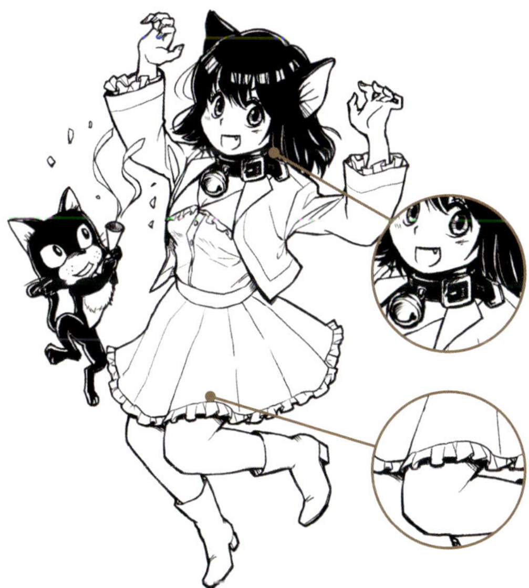

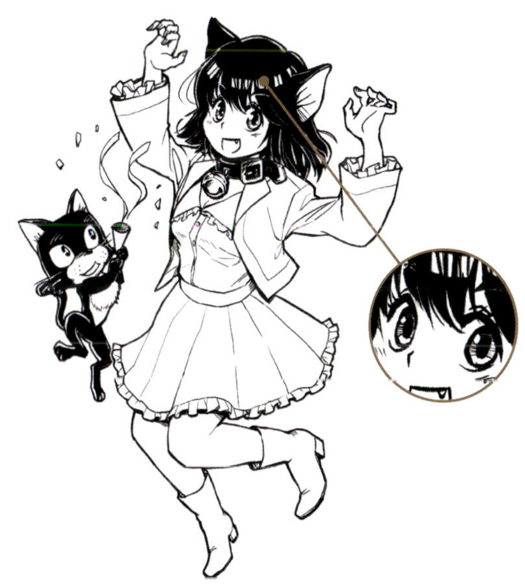

7 Add extra detail in the eyes and hair. Stylize the shapes between the highlights and black fill. Add shadows where they would be natural (see page 106).

8 Add white lines where you need to, as well as for more details in your highlights. Add eye highlights to make your character look more full of life.

Focus on:
Tone

Tone (also called value) is how light or dark on object is, whether it is in colour or greyscale. While there are almost infinite tones of grey, artists generally use between three and five greys.

You can create tone using different pen strokes, such as hatching (using lines), stippling (using dots) and kakeami (see page 108). The tonal value changes depending on how dense the strokes or dots are – when you draw lines or dots closer together, they create a darker value.

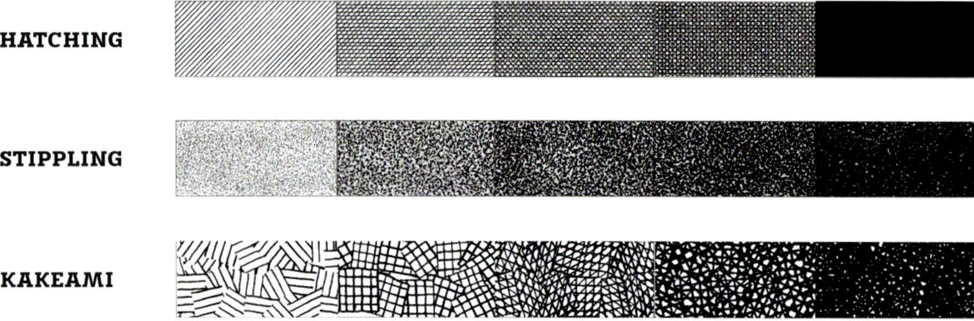

HIGHLIGHTS, SHADE AND SHADOWS

When a light shines on a three-dimensional object, it produces three different tonal values. A pale tone is created on the side in the light, which are the highlights, and a darker tone – shading – occurs on the opposite side. The third area is the shadow cast by the object.

HIGHLIGHTS

To create highlights in areas that are directly lit, leave them white on the paper or use a white pen to add them later. This is best for small amounts.

SHADING

The area opposite the light source should be a grey tone. Gradually change the greys for spherical surfaces, and use a different grey for each surface in a box. Surfaces facing the same direction should have the same tones.

SHADOWS

Objects cast shadows on the surface below them on the opposite side of the light source. If the light is from above, shadows are shorter; if lower, they are longer. Shadows have a sharp edge and are darker than shading. The stronger the light, the darker the shadows and the greater the contrast.

NATURAL SHADING

In soft light, the shading gradually changes.

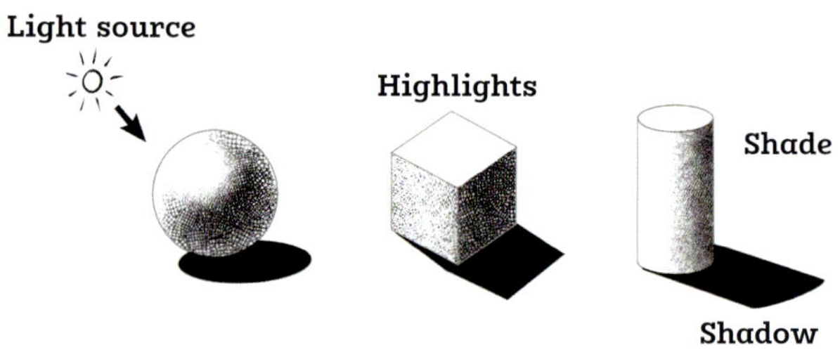

ANIME SHADING

For the stylized shading used in anime and manga, use only three to five grey tones and apply them in sections with sharp edges.

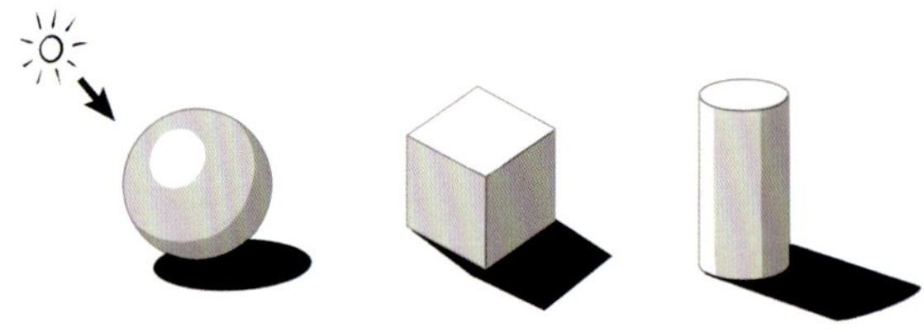

STAGE 4

ADDING GREY TONES

Let's fill in the mid-tones and shading to make your art look like a black-and-white photograph.

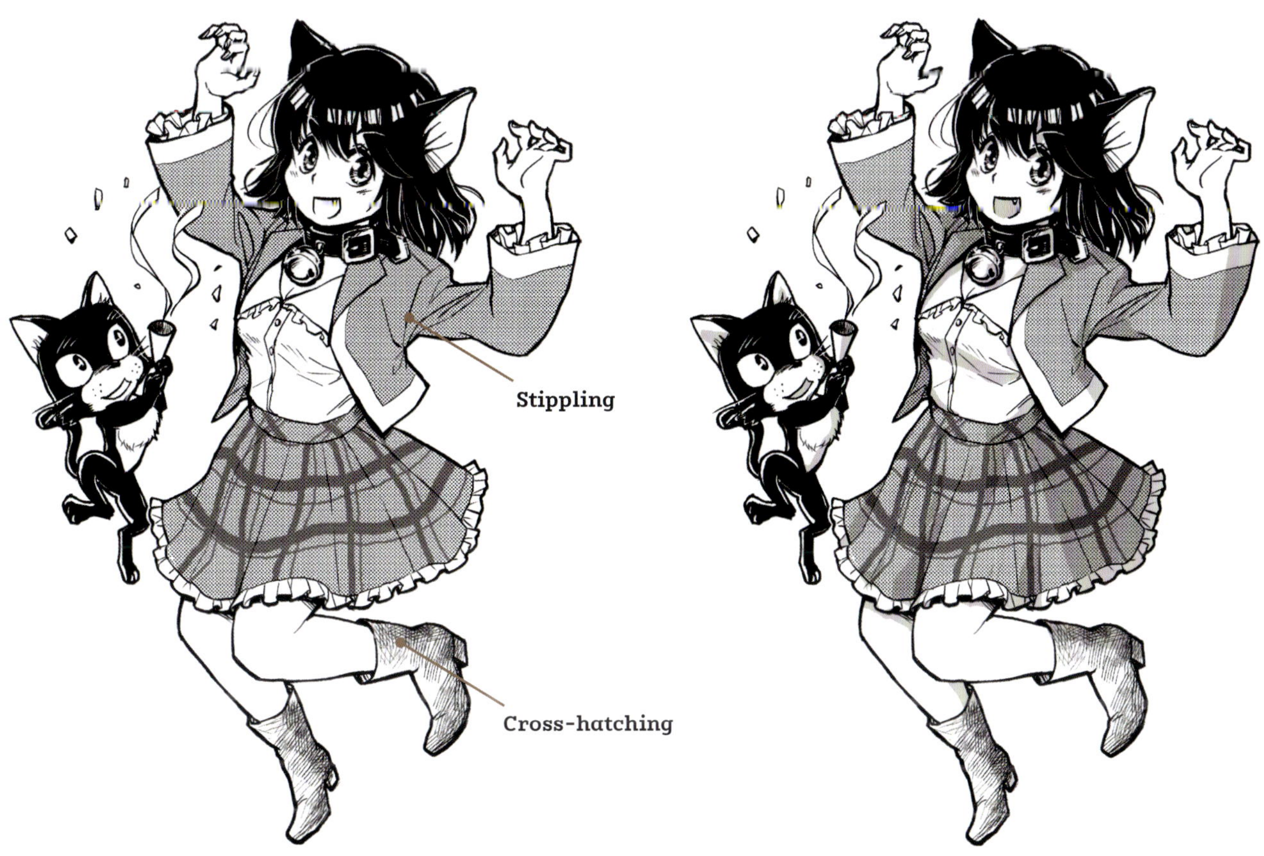

1 By adding mid-tones – one or two greys – you can start to see your drawing feel more three-dimensional. Try using different pen strokes to show a variation of texture and make your image look more fun.

2 I used a light grey marker on top of the mid-tones to create shading, adding further to the three-dimensional look. Think about where the shading should occur in the clothes, such as in the creases in the skirt and under the arms.

TIP

The important thing to bear in mind when creating shade and shadow is having a consistent light source. Once you have decided upon the position of your light source, add shading on the opposite side and shadows beneath the object. You can simplify the shading when drawing cartoons, but it may look flatter.

STAGE 5

ADDING BACKGROUND EFFECTS

Background effects are powerful techniques to help your art stand out and look more attractive. Here are some different examples. Try them out and compare them to how your drawing looked on a plain white background – which one do you like the most?

HANDWRITTEN TEXT

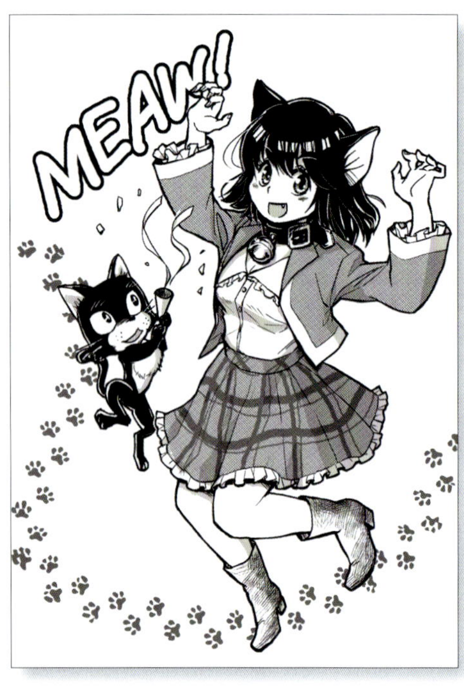

STIPPLING

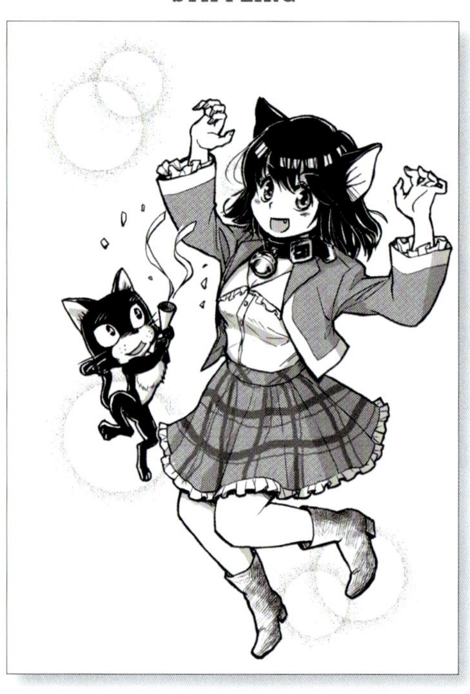

KAKEAMI

The background pattern in this drawing is called kakeami and is popular in comic art. Let's practise making this pattern to master it.

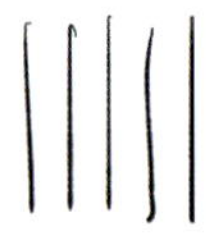

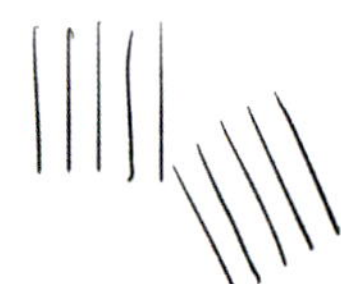

1 Draw five lines inside an invisible square, as if printed on a tile used for a board game.

2 Change the angle of the paper and draw another five lines on a separate invisible tile.

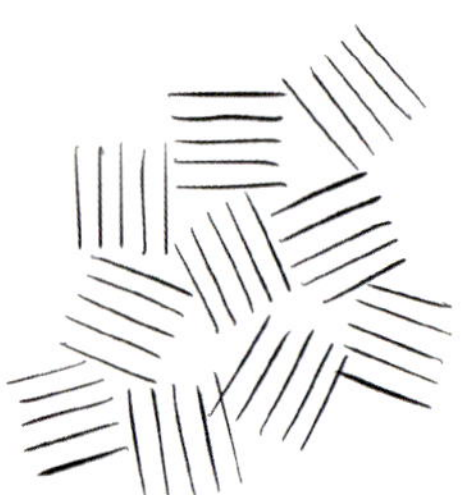

3 Repeat steps 1 and 2 to fill the space and make a pattern around your drawing.

KAKEAMI

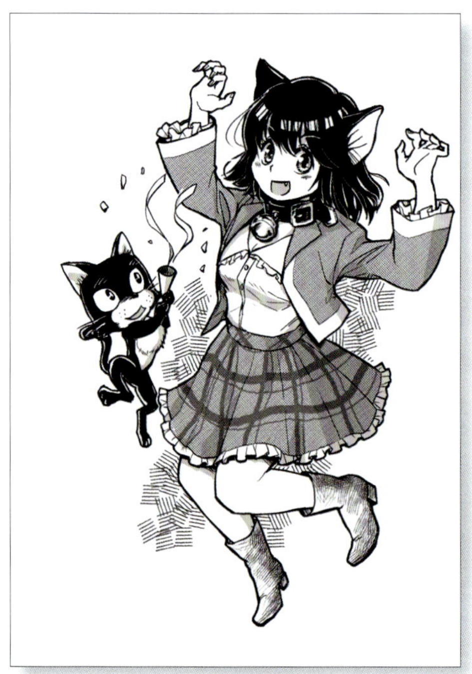

Radial lines

A popular technique for making a manga character stand out or to emphasize its action is to use lines radiating from it. You will need a drawing pin (thumb tack), low-tack tape and adhesive putty to make an anchor point for a ruler.

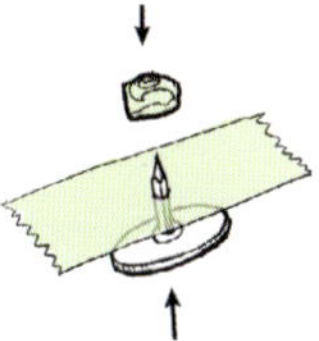

1 With the sticky side of a piece of tape facing down, pierce the centre of the tape with the pin and push the pin up. Cover the pin's sharp point with some adhesive putty or a small piece of eraser.

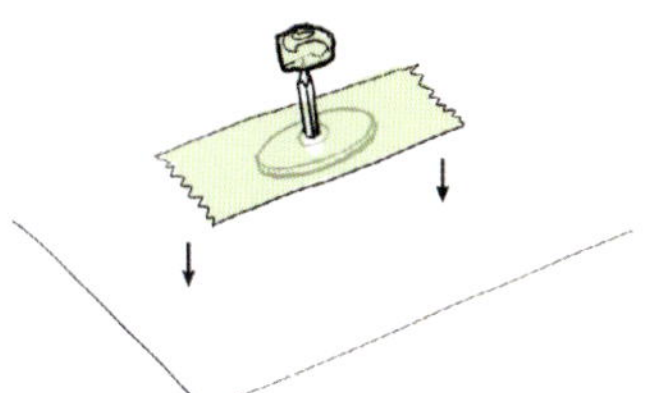

2 Place the pin at the centre of where you would like to draw the radial lines from and fix it to the drawing.

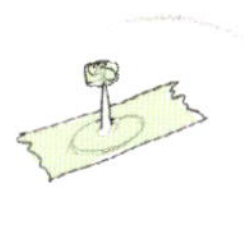

3 Using a pencil, lightly draw a faint oval with the pin in the centre; this is a guide line that you should not draw into as you make the radial lines.

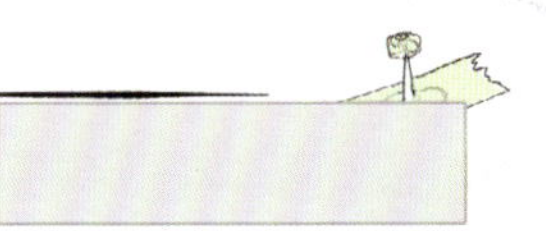

4 Place a ruler with one end against the pin. Draw a line along the ruler quickly, from the edge of the drawing towards the centre. The line should become thinner as it approaches the centre, fading away at the end. Stop at the oval line.

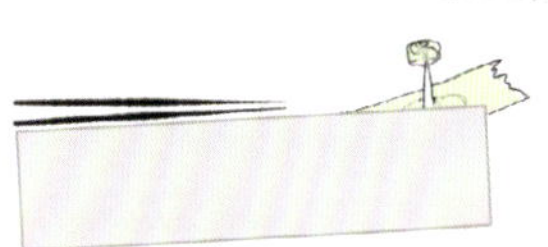

5 Keeping the pin in place, move the ruler around a little, like the hands on a clock, and draw another line.

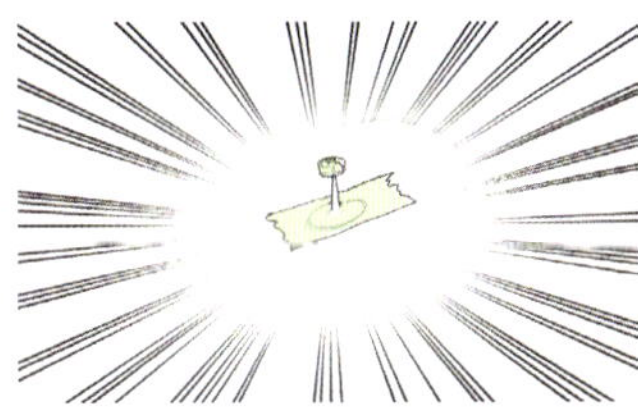

6 Repeat as many times as you need until you come back to the first line.

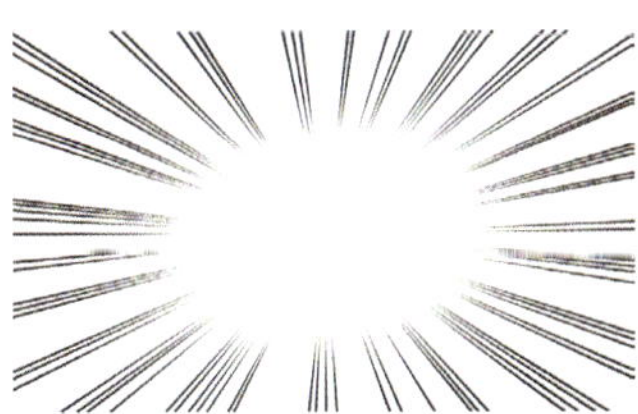

7 Carefully remove the pin and erase the oval line.

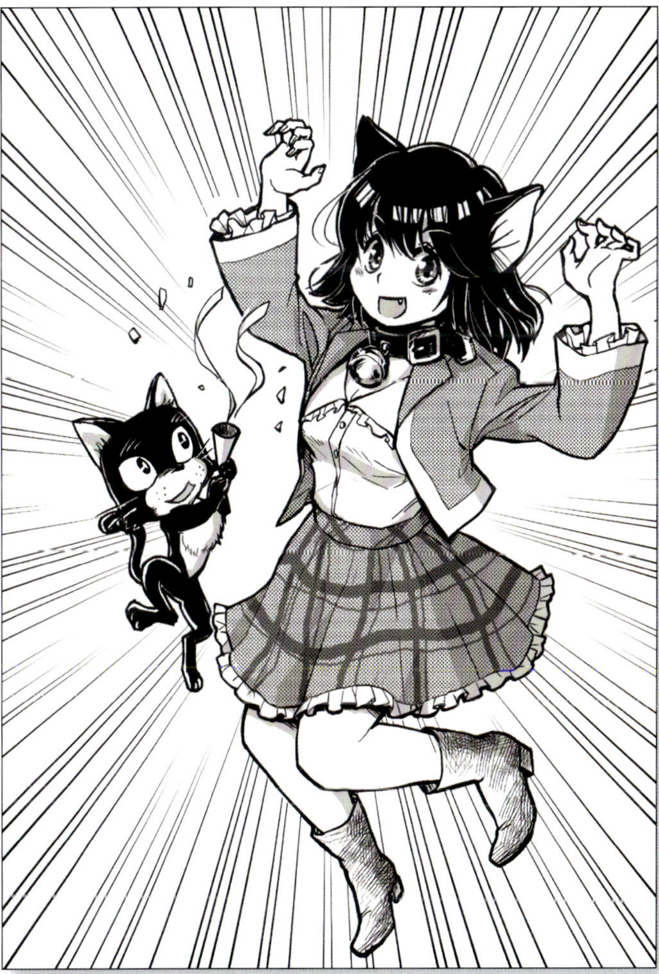

8 Use a white correction pen to clean up where any lines overlap with the main image.

PROJECT 9 DRAW WITH COLOUR MARKERS

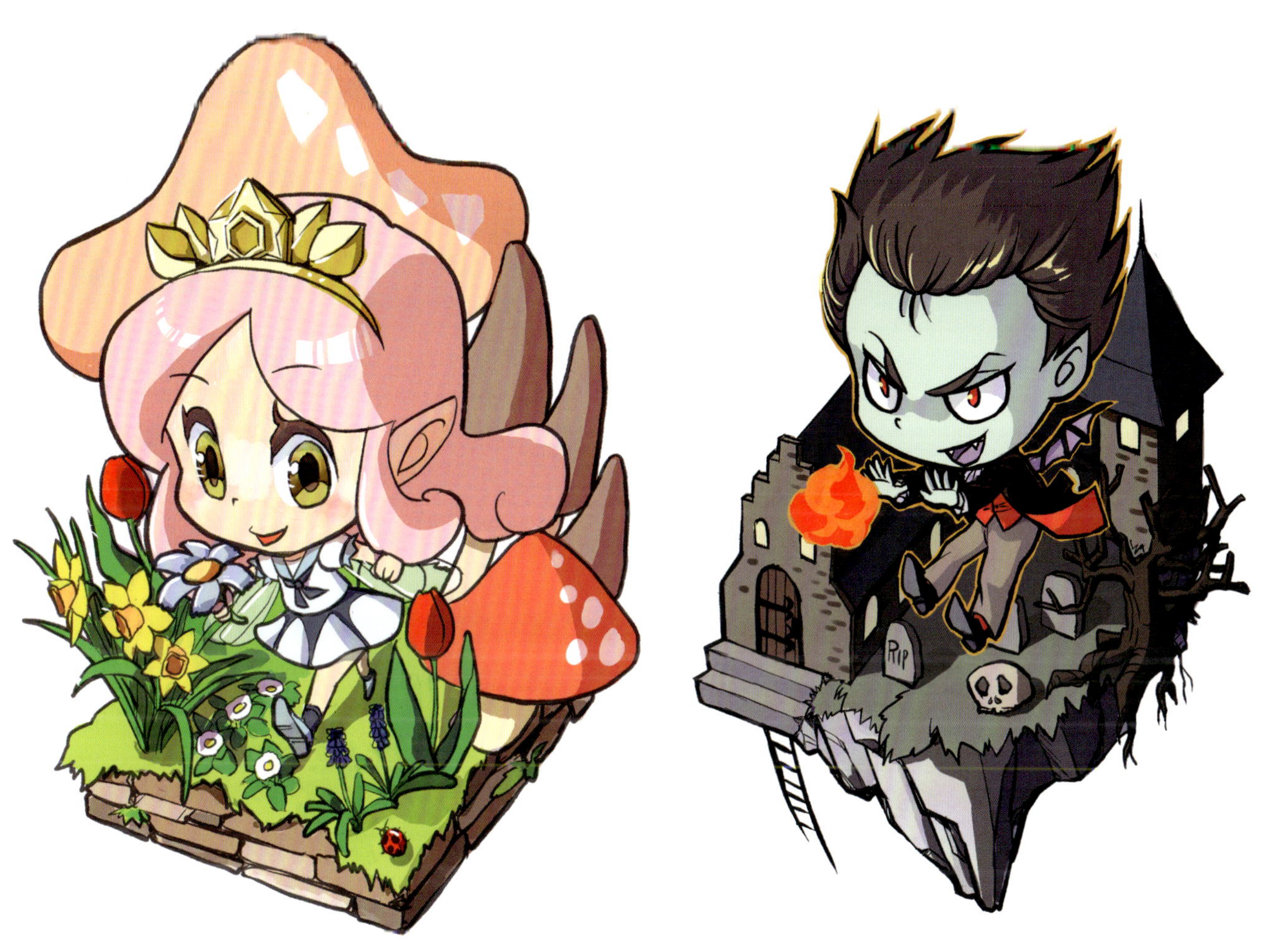

While black and white manga can look dynamic (see pages 98–109), adding colour can really help bring your characters to life. In this chapter, you will learn all about colour theory and how to use colour markers. You will also discover how to create three-dimensional scenes, and you'll find guidance on how to create your own original characters.

Colour theory and mixing

It is best to plan how you will colour your character and background rather than diving straight in. A little knowledge of colour theory will help you in choosing a colour palette (set of colours) for an illustration.

Choosing colours

Create a colour palette for an illustration, starting with just three or four base colours and their tints (lighter or darker versions of the base colour, as shown in the rings of the colour wheel). Choose the theme colour for the character, find a matching colour and include a neutral colour such as grey.

AVOID SIMILAR COLOURS NEXT TO EACH OTHER

Choose your colours carefully, so that people can see all your lines and shapes. Imagine a picture such as 'Crows in a Dark Night'. If the crows and the night sky were painted the same colour, no one would see the birds.

LIMIT STRONG COLOURS

Vivid colours are eye-catching, but they can be too strong and put off a viewer if you use them too much. Limit yourself to one or two, and use less saturation than the other colours.

AVOID PRECONCEPTIONS

Think about the different colours an object can be. Are all leaves green and the sky always a light blue? Not only do different plant species vary in colour, even the parts on the same plant will vary in colour – for example, when lit by different light sources, or when green leaves turn brown.

THE COLOUR WHEEL

When choosing a palette, it is helpful to use a colour wheel. The colours next to each other are related colours that work in harmony. Those opposite are complementary colours that are more vibrant if placed together.

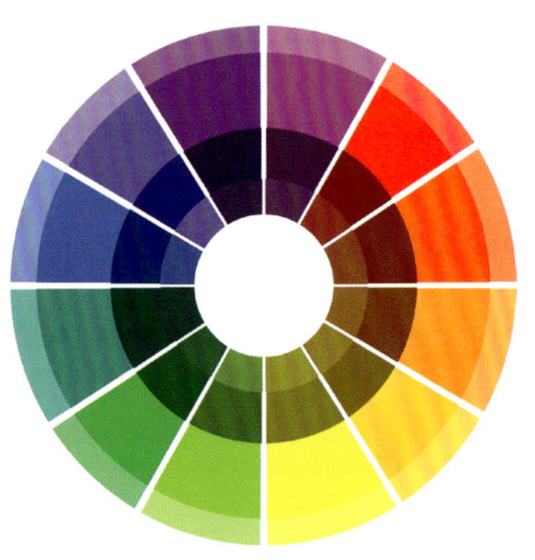

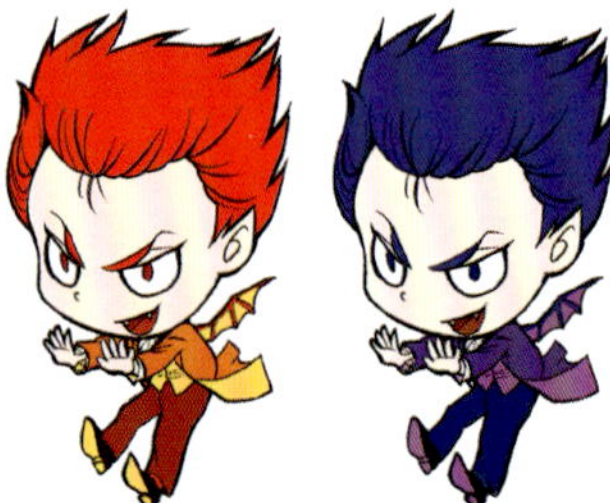

RELATED COLOURS
Colours next to each other on the wheel (here, orange and purple) are safe colours that work in harmony. You can mix them to show gradation.

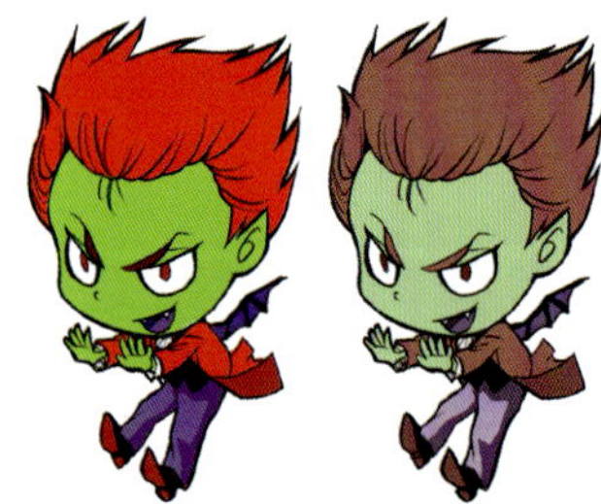

SATURATION
Paint sets often have colours that are more vivid than those in the real world. Learn to use muted colours, which will also enhance the more vivid colours.

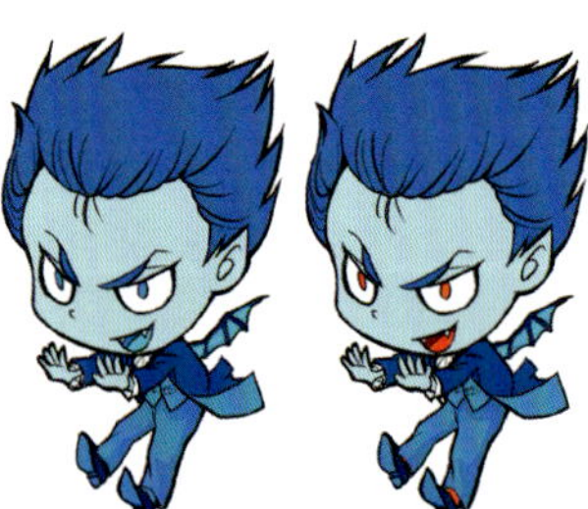

BRIGHTNESS
Using tints is a safe colour choice such as for a monochrome image. Adding a tiny amount of a striking colour can make it seem brighter.

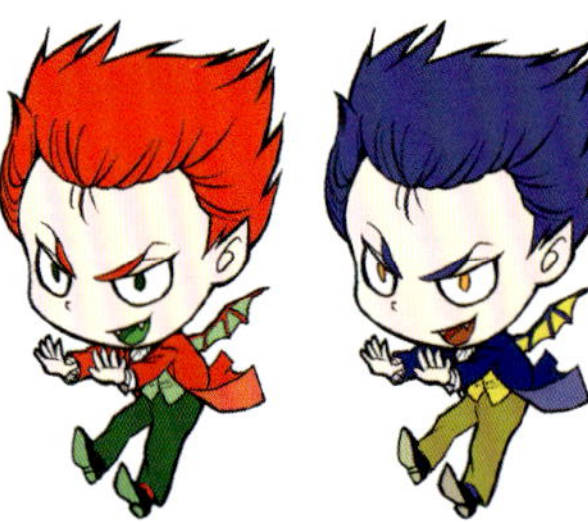

OPPOSITE COLOURS
If you are looking for a sharp and striking colour combination, an effective technique is to use complementary colours on the opposite side of the colour wheel.

How to apply colour

Neatly filling in areas with colour is one of the keys to making your art look great. Carefully fill in all the white gaps and do not go outside the lines.

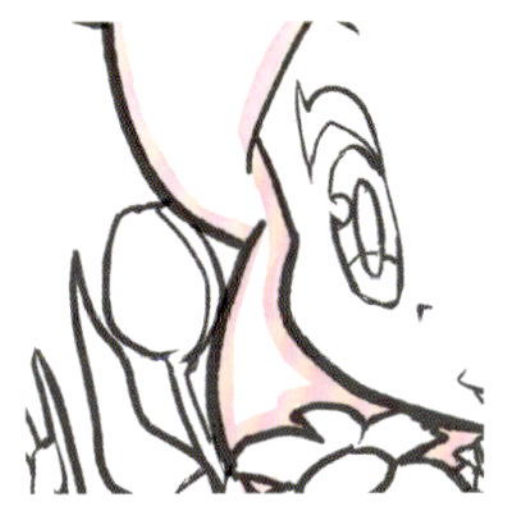

1 Use your colour with a fine tip to carefully trace inside the border of the area to be coloured.

1st coat

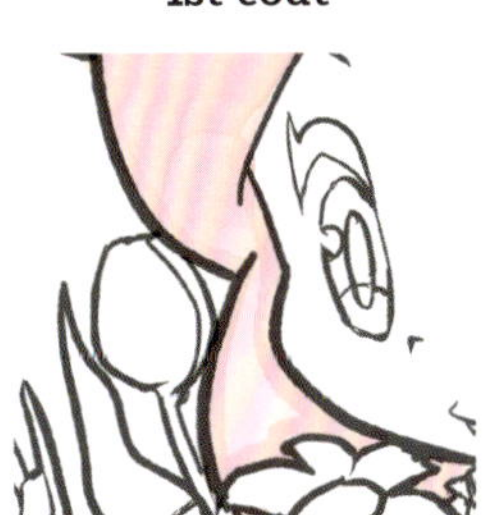

2nd coat

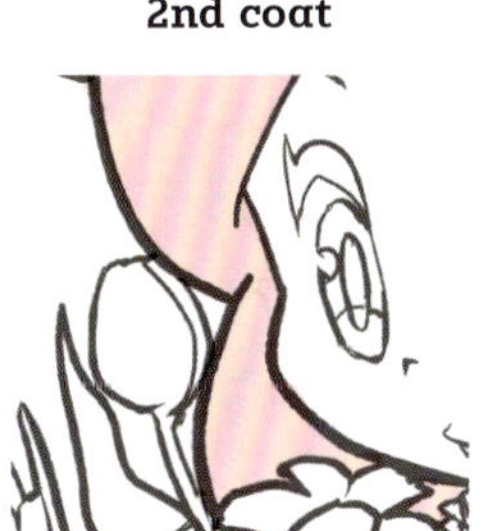

2 Now use the wide part of a flat tip to paint in one direction. This will allow you to colour in quickly and evenly. Apply two coats of colour to eliminate unevenness.

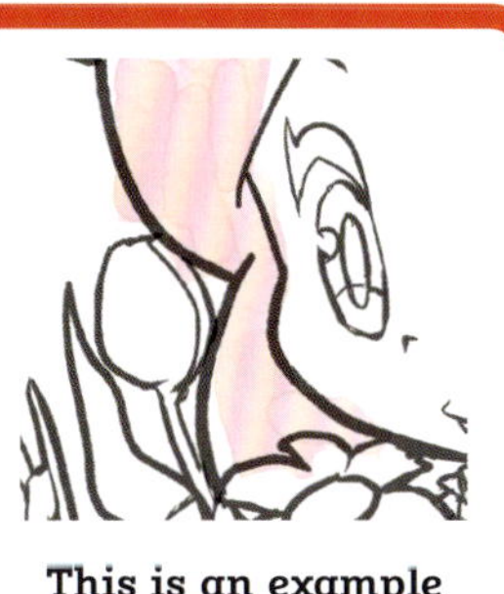

This is an example of bad colouring technique: the colour crosses the lines and there are white gaps. Everything should be filled in neatly.

Colour blending techniques

Mastering how to blend colours will help you make your art more attractive. Blending techniques work best while the first colour is still wet.

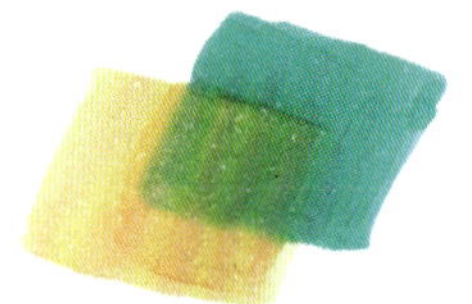

COLOUR MIXING

You can mix colours by placing different colours on top of one another. This is helpful if you can't find the colour you want – for example, try mixing your main colour with light purple or grey to create a shade.

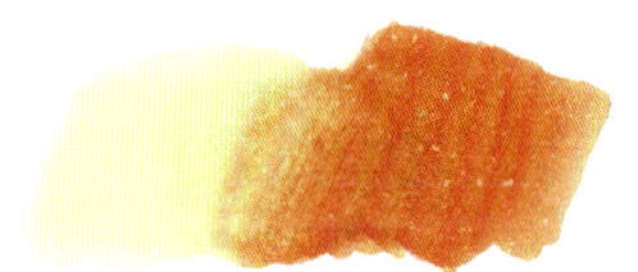

COLOUR GRADIENTS

You can gradually merge two colours to make a beautiful gradient. Draw a colour from one side, then add the second colour from the other side with the two overlapping in the middle. Repeat this with both colours until they merge seamlessly.

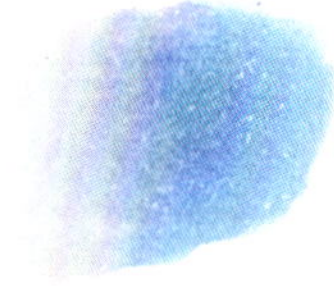

SMUDGING

Use a blender marker (see page 7) to smudge an area and create an attractive effect – it is great for simulating water. Draw on the area with the blender first, then add the colour before the blender dries. This should achieve a light, fading effect.

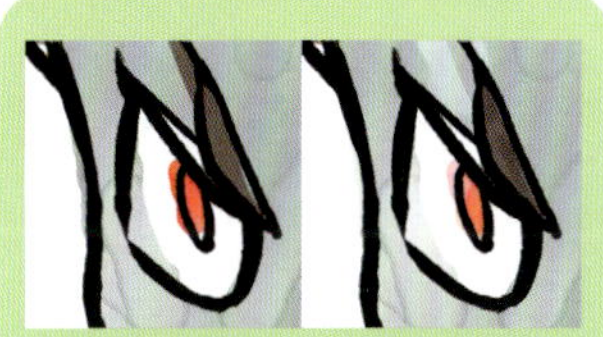

CORRECTION TIP

Blenders can also make it less visible when you have coloured over a line. This is less noticeable than correcting with a white pen and should be tried first.

PRACTISE BLENDING YOUR COLOURS

Before using these techniques on your artwork, practise colour mixing and blending using a base colour, shading colour and a blender marker.

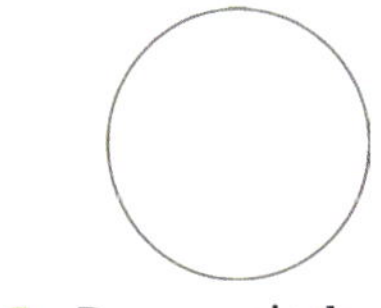

1 Draw a circle.

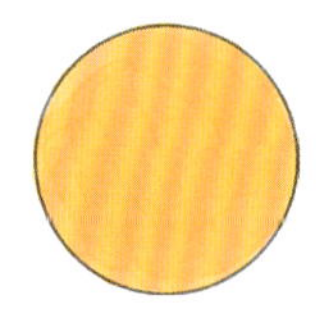

2 Fill it in with a single-coloured marker.

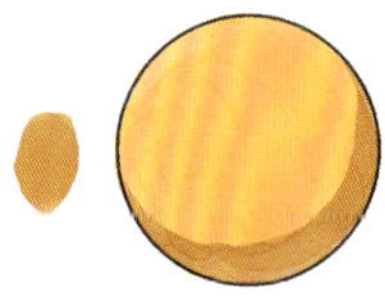

3 Layer a slightly darker colour on the shaded area.

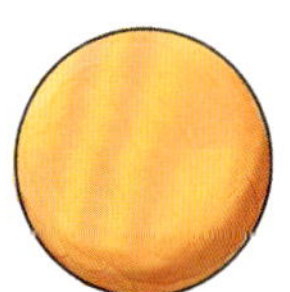

4 Overlay the base colour on the edge of the shade colour to create a gradation.

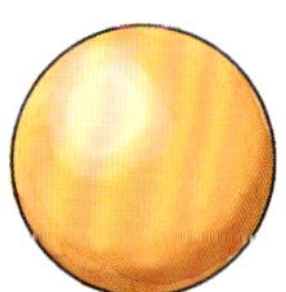

5 With a blender marker, paint over the highlight area and see colour fade.

STAGE 1

DESIGN YOUR CHARACTER

To use your colour markers, you'll need something to colour in! But creating an original character from scratch can be difficult, so here are some suggestions for creating your own unique manga character.

PLANNING YOUR CHARACTER

I find that creating a character sheet with keywords is a great way to develop a new character. You can base your character on an existing one, but even then, you'll still need to come up with changes to make it your own.

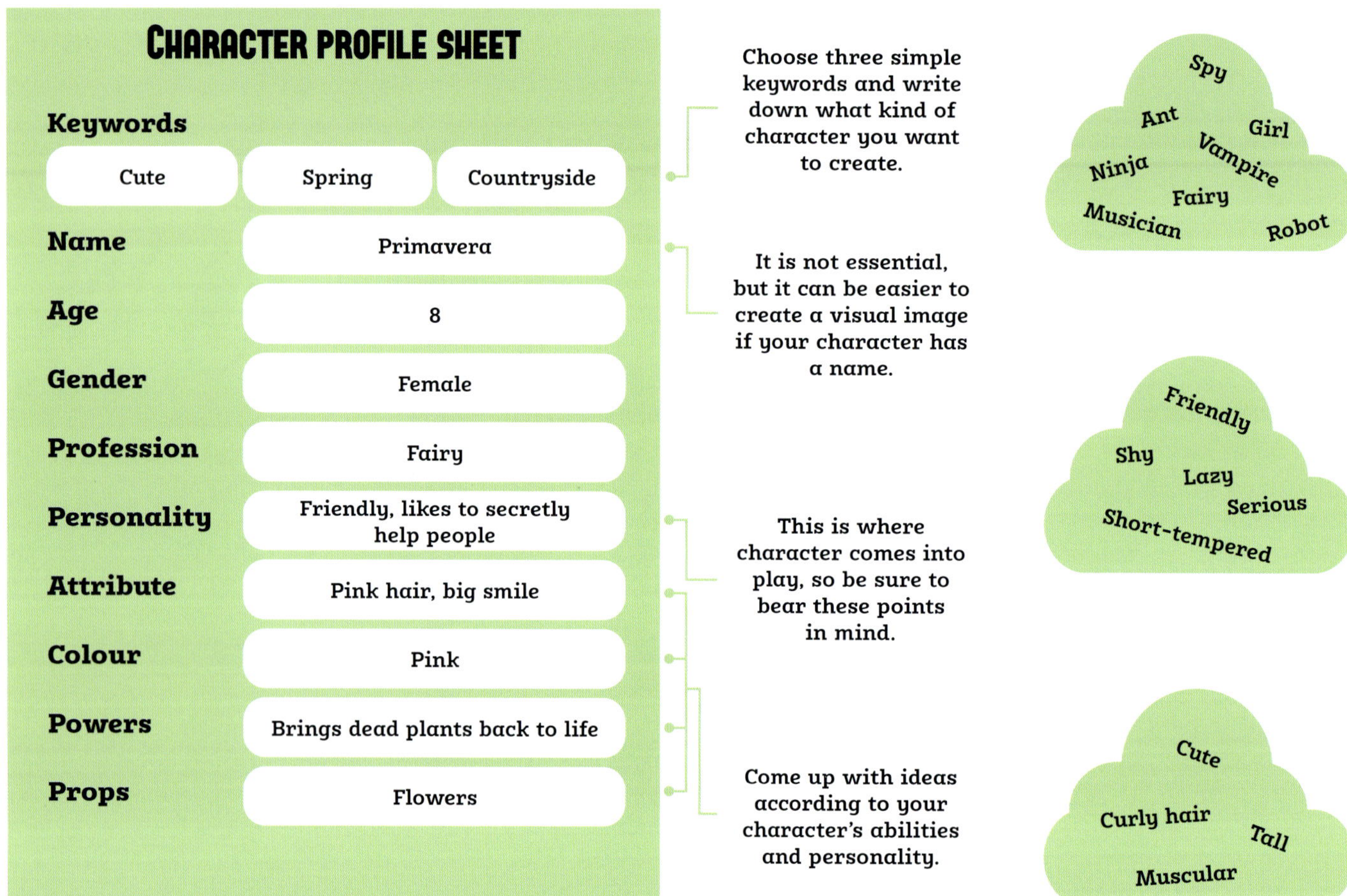

EXPAND UPON YOUR IDEAS

Now that you've brainstormed a character, you can start listing the different things you may wish to draw. Think about not just the character, their clothing and any props, but also what will be in the background to complete a scene. Sketch your ideas to see which fits the vision for your character.

Try to find photographs and drawings of what you intend to draw – these will help you to understand the structure, texture and colour of what you are drawing. It always works better than drawing from only your memory.

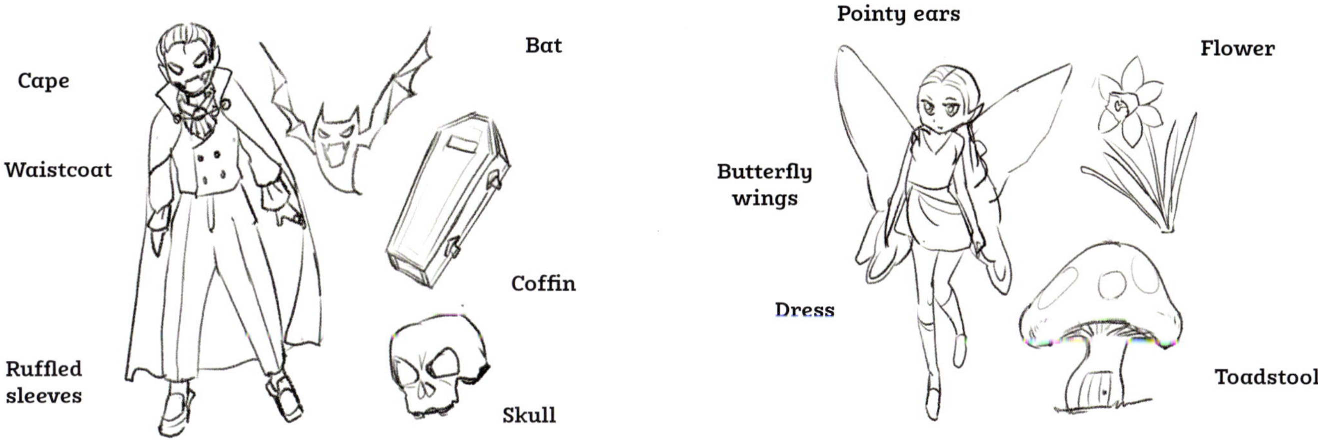

DESIGNING YOUR CHARACTER

Make sketches based on the keywords, profile and the reference. Make multiple idea sketches on some scrap paper and explore every possible design. You don't have to clean up your sketches as this process is just for exploring.

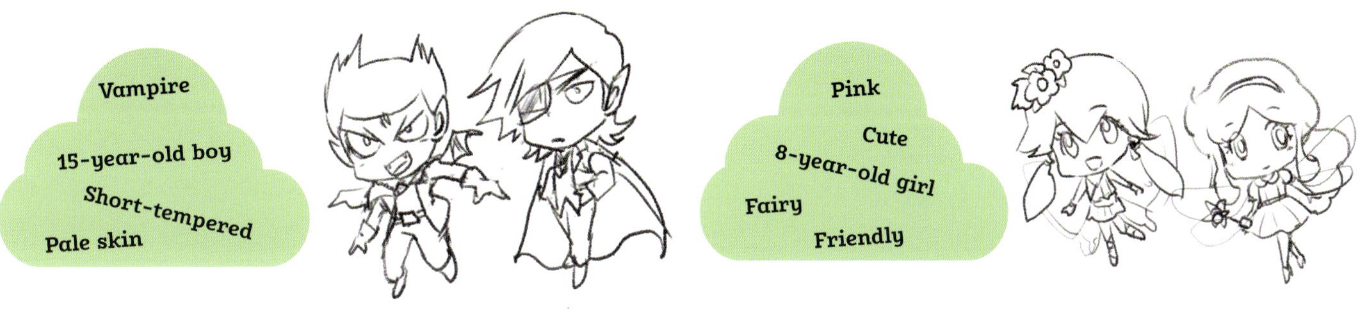

FINISHING YOUR CHARACTER SHEET

It's a good idea to make a neat final design of your character, so you have a reference to copy form, which will help to keep your character looking consistent. Use an A4 (letter-size) sheet of paper to draw full front and back views of your character, along with any props that are key to it.

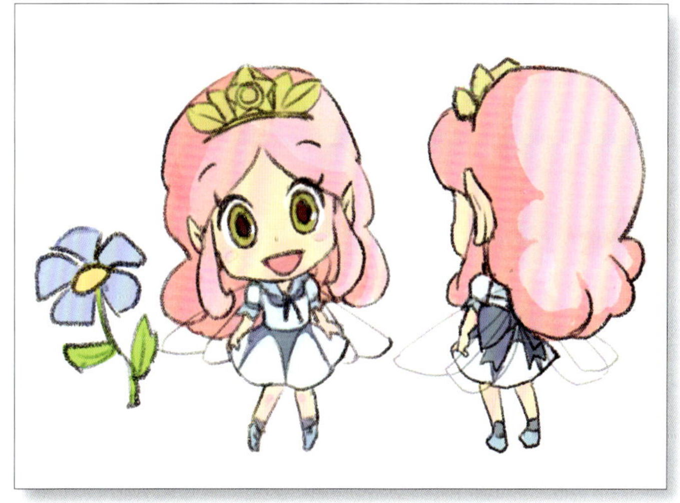

At this point, it's a good time to try out colour combinations to create a palette for your character (see page 112). If you intend to create shading by mixing colours, try them out now (see page 113). You could use the same colour for mixing with your base colours, or use different colours to give you more control over the final colour.

STAGE 2

Draw a 3D Chibi Figure

For this project, we'll be creating a three-dimensional diorama – sort of a miniature theatre set on a stage – with a two-heads-tall chibi character, drawing it from a three-quarter view.

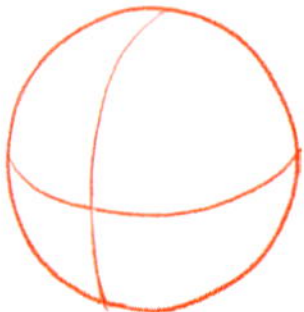

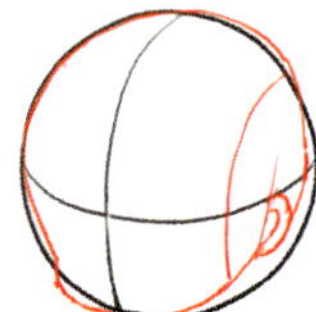

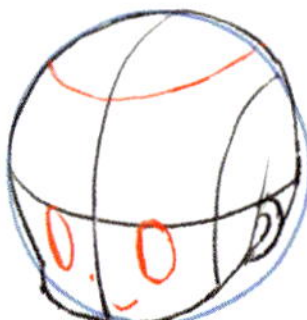

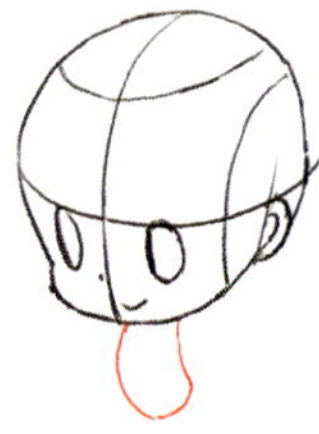

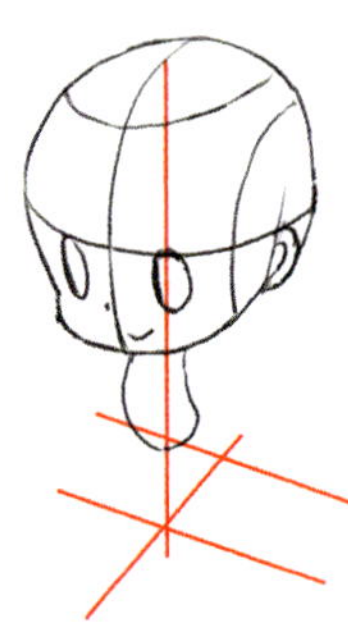

1 Draw a circle and the horizontal and vertical guide lines around the centre of the sphere. Make sure they are curving lines.

2 Add the side guide lines for the edges of the face. Draw an ear below the horizontal line on one side of the face and continue it to the other side, drawing the jaw and chin.

3 Add a pair of eyes underneath the horizontal line, then the nose and mouth. Find the top surface of the head and add a curving line.

4 Add a tiny body, about the size of the face. This is a bird's-eye view, so you can't see the neck at all. The body shape should look similar to a mushroom stalk.

5 Draw a vertical guide line twice the height of the head, starting at the top, and two perpendicular guide lines at its base. Add a parallel line at the position shown.

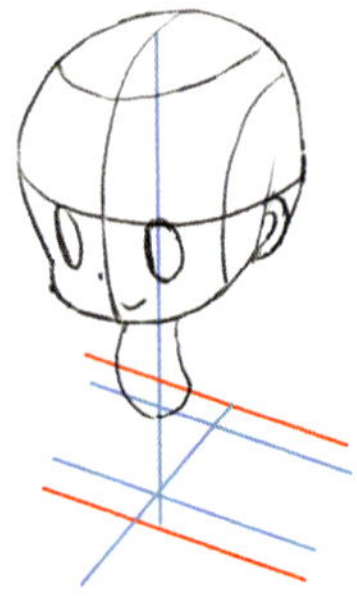

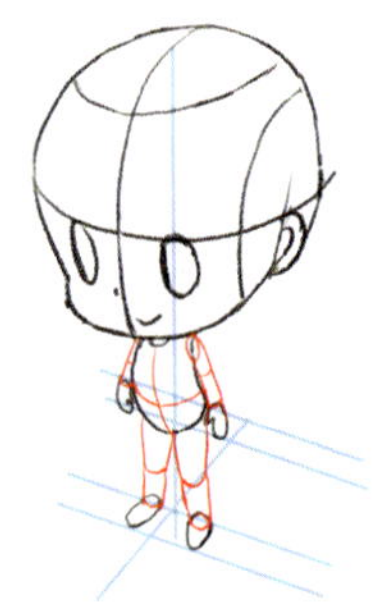

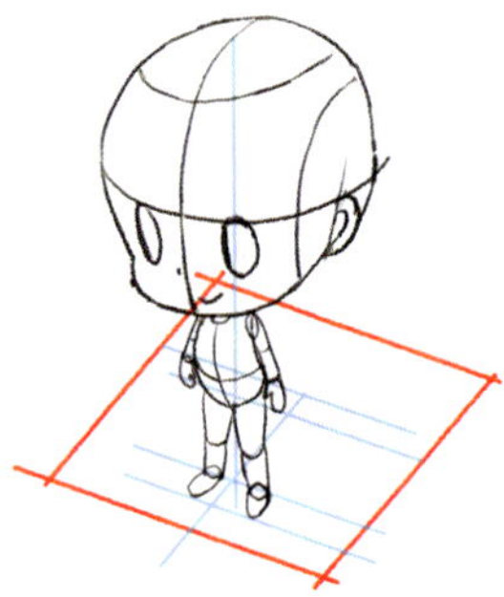

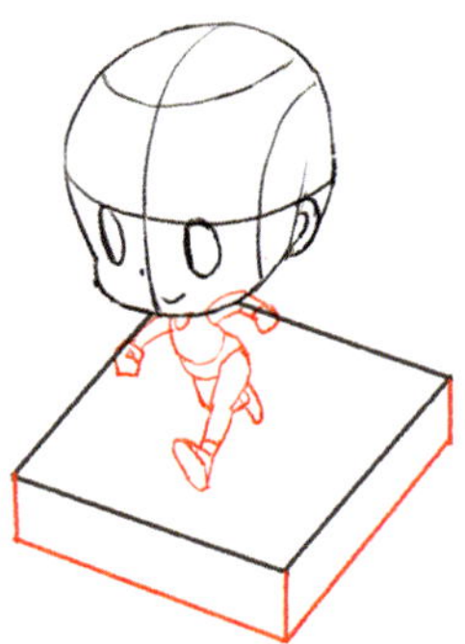

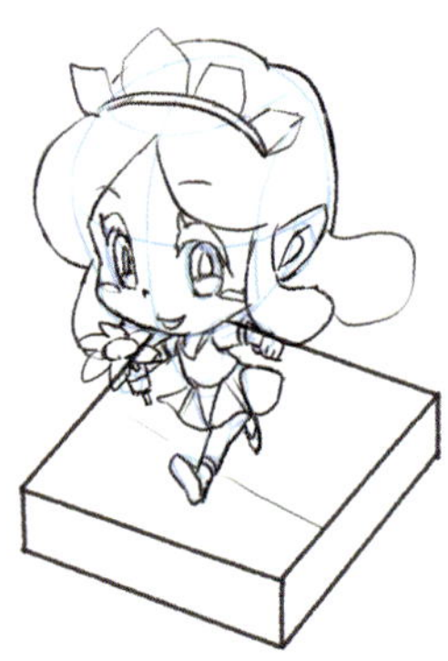

6 Add two more parallel lines as shown above and draw feet and hands between them. Check it looks symmetrical against the central guide lines.

7 Add the limbs by drawing cylinders connected to the body, and add the hands and feet. Add joints and the body central line to complete the doll figure.

8 Now add a base. Draw four straight lines parallel to the perpendicular guide lines drawn in Step 5. The shape will be a parallelogram.

9 Give the base depth. Draw lines down from the corners and join them. Modify the doll's pose for your character. Erase any unnecessary lines.

10 Referring to your character design sheet, turn the doll figure into your character.

STAGE 3

DRAW A 3D DIORAMA

Start with simple forms when creating a three-dimensional background. Create basic shapes by joining cubes, cylinders, spheres, cones, pyramids, tubes, etc. or reshaping them. Assemble everything roughly at the beginning and always wait until the end to draw in detailed shapes, textures, shading, etc. I recommend you start drawing the background and objects for a diorama from the base.

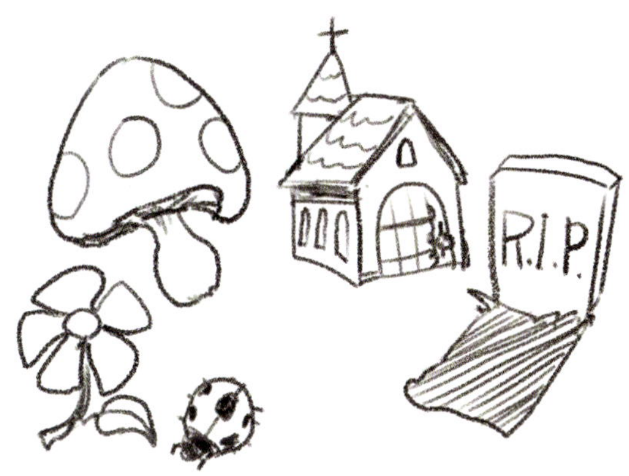

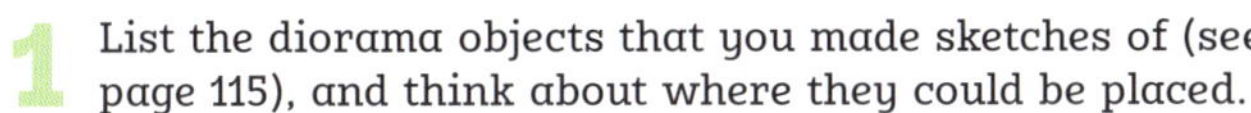

1 List the diorama objects that you made sketches of (see page 115), and think about where they could be placed.

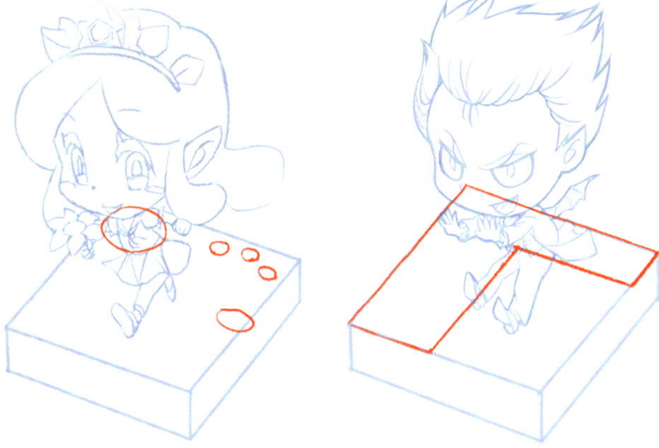

2 Draw the base shapes of the objects and setting for the diorama such as walls or buildings on the stage.

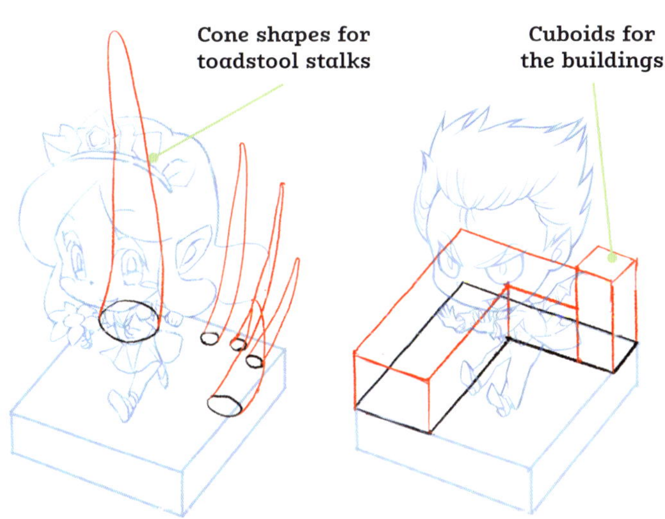

3 Give the shapes height and transform them into 3D forms.

Wide, rounded cone for the top of the toadstool

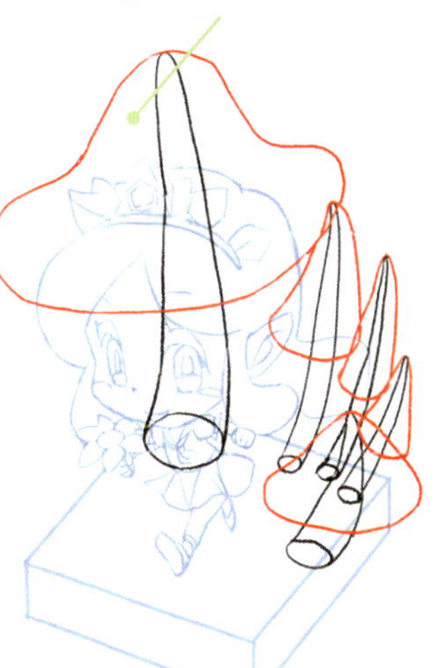

Draw a pyramid for the roof. Make an 'X' on the side walls to find the centre, then draw a vertical line through them to find the apex of the roof.

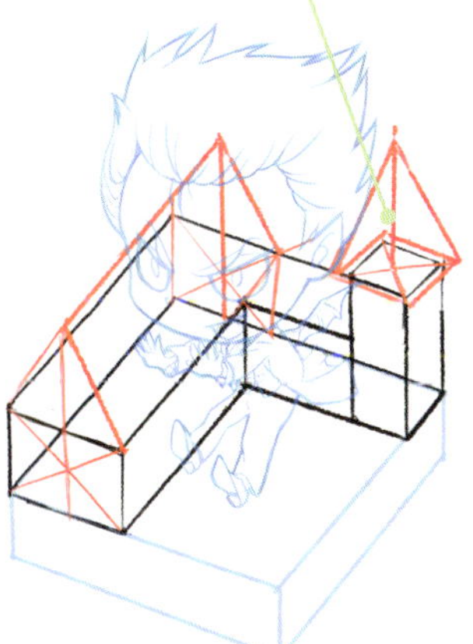

3 Add smaller shapes and add details.

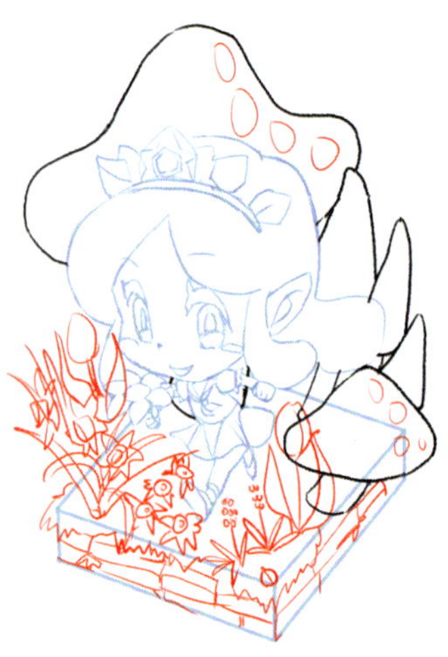

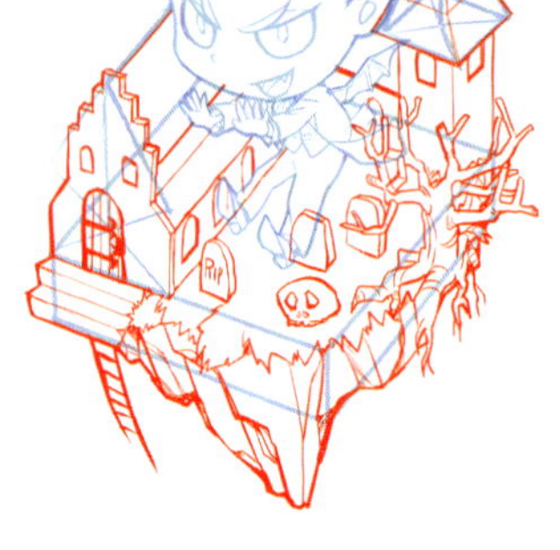
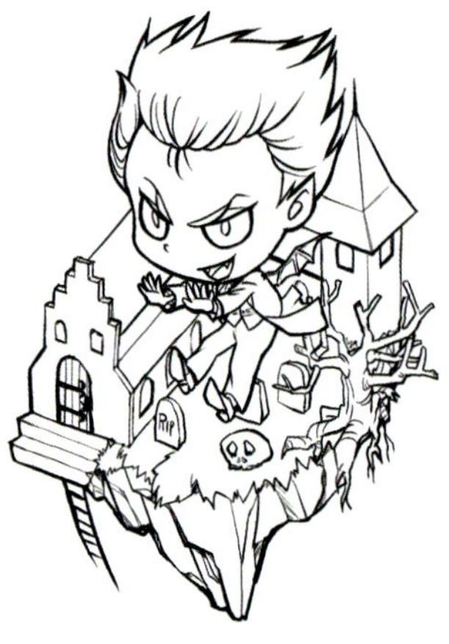

5 Erase the lines that should no longer be visible to make it clear which objects are in front and behind. Add extra props such as rocks, grass, graves, etc.

6 Add all the details and tidy up the lines to ready for inking (see pages 98–109).

Practice: Drawing 3D objects

Drawing a rock

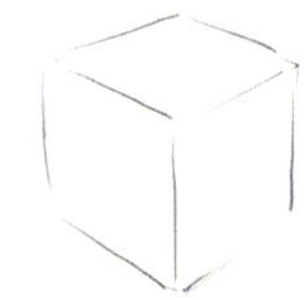

1 Draw a box.

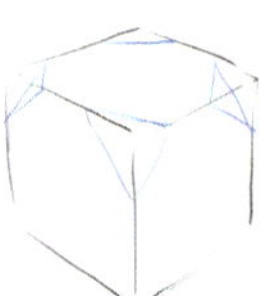

2 Draw in the shapes that you would like to cut off such as these at the corners.

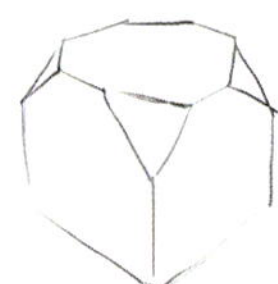

3 Erase any lines that should no longer be visible at the corners.

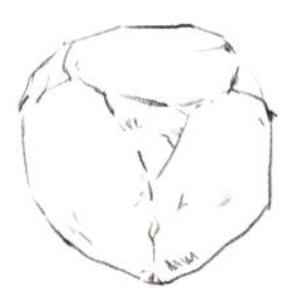

4 Add any details. Adjust the lines so they are organic natural shapes, adding dirt and cracks.

Drawing trees

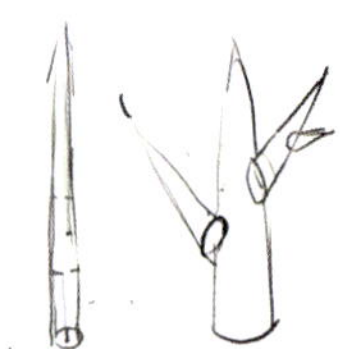

1 Draw a narrow cone shape for trunk. Make branches, which should be smaller cone shapes.

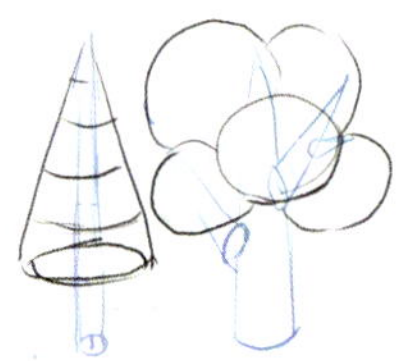

2 Add the main shape for the leaves. Cones or spheres are good for tree canopies.

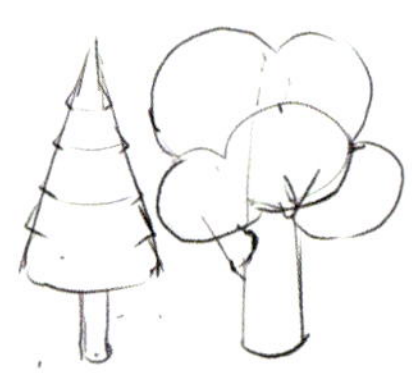

3 Erase any lines that should no longer be visible.

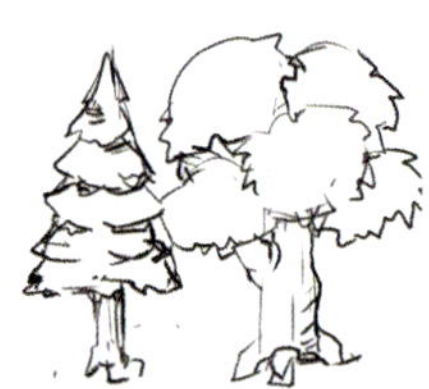

4 Add any details. Adjust the lines so they are organic natural shapes, and add the texture of the leaves and trunks.

STAGE 4

INK YOUR SKETCH

Now that you have a finished pencil drawing of your chibi character and diorama, the next stage is to turn it into an ink line drawing. As you'll be using colour, the approach to inking the sketch differs slightly from making a black and white manga drawing.

Prepare the drawing for tracing (see page 102), then follow Steps 1–3 on page 104 to turn the pencil sketch into an ink line drawing. As we'll be colouring the illustration, you can use sepia or grey ink for the line drawing, which will be softer than black and give a nice finish. At this stage, as this is a colour drawing, don't add any shading or fill in any areas, even if they will be black.

Avoid using copier paper for colour markers because the ink tends to bleed into it. There are specialist comic and colour marker papers available, but I recommend 160-200gsm (60–110lb) card stock, which is inexpensive and easy to find.

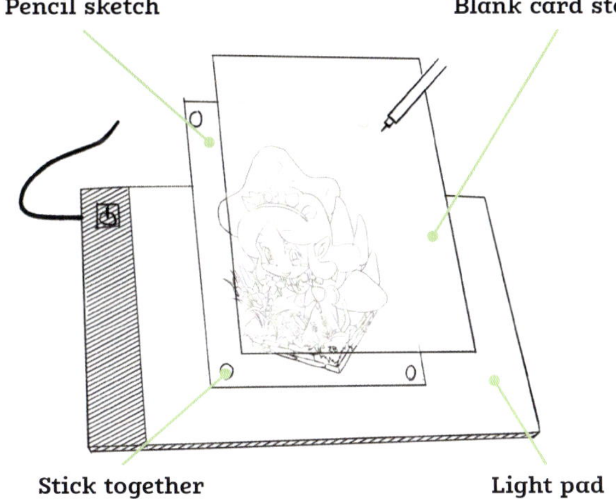

To avoid accidentally filling in areas with colour that you would like to keep white – such as the whites of eyes or highlights on the hair – draw boundary lines around them. Use a faint line in pencil so that you can easily erase it later.

If you are inking directly onto a pencil sketch, remove all the pencil lines when you've finished inking the lines (see step 4 on page 104). Pencil lines don't look professional when they show through colour, and they can darken your markers' tips. It's also important to do this now, because you will not be able to erase them once you put alcohol-based colour marker ink on them.

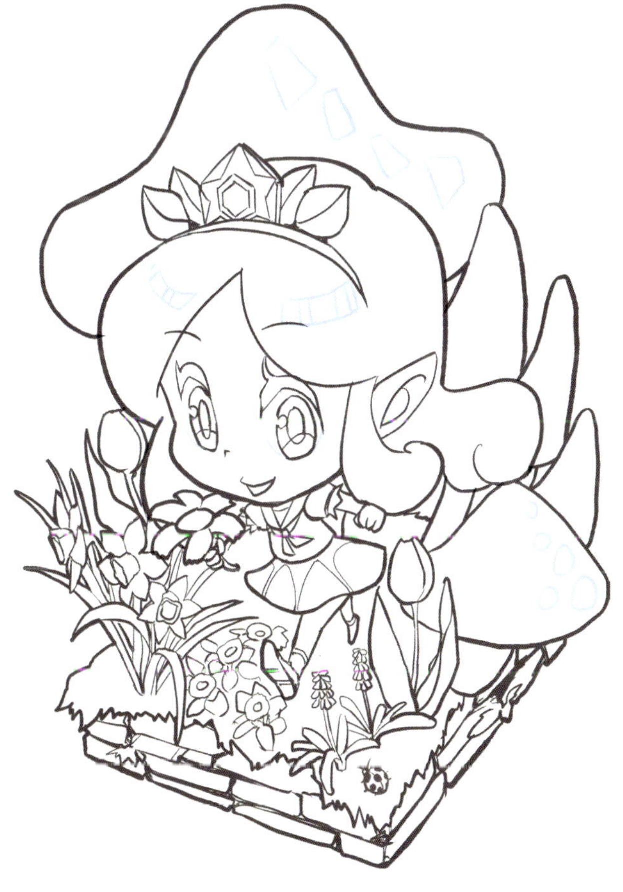

STAGE 5

ADD THE BASE COLOURS

Now let's start applying some colour. Refer back to the colour palette you tried out earlier and check you're happy with it (see page 115).

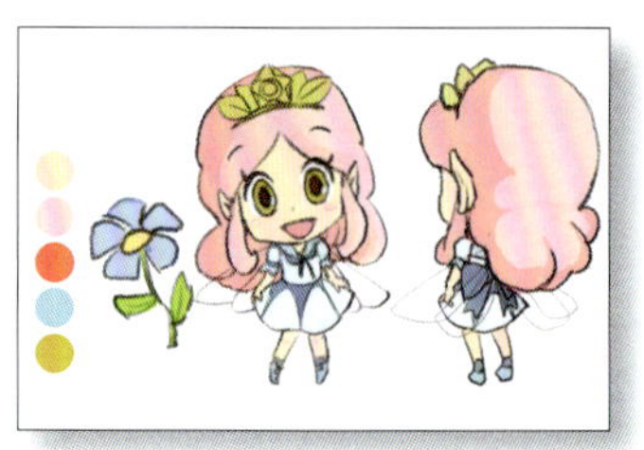

ORDER OF COLOURING

Rather than adding all the colours at the same time, you will need to work in stages. Start with lighter colours and save the darker colours for shading. This reduces the risk of mistakes such as darker colours bleeding through and staining the paper. It is also important because lighter colours can be painted darker later, but darker colours cannot be made lighter.

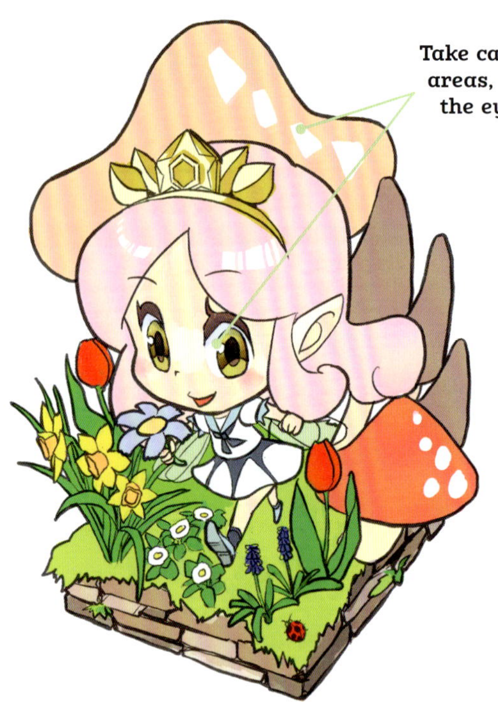

Take care not to colour in white areas, especially the whites of the eyes and any highlights.

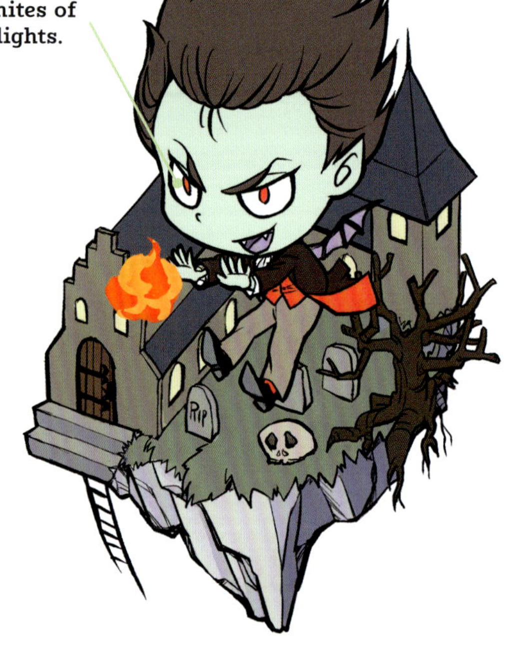

RELATED COLOURS PALETTE

Many colours are used here, but they are coherent because they are a similar tone, sharing a common use of pale, low-saturation colours. The stronger colours appear only in small areas as accents.

COLOUR PALETTE

Similar colours

Pale colours

Stronger colours for accents

CONTRASTING COLOUR PALETTE

If you want the main colours to stand out, choose two contrasting complementary colours (see page 112) and use greys for the rest of the scene.

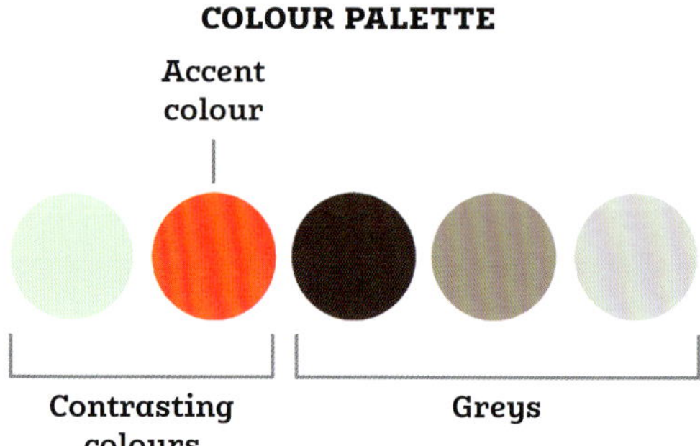

Focus on:
Colouring tips

SKIN TONES

The choice of skin colour is important. Apply a slightly lighter colour for skin than you think you need.

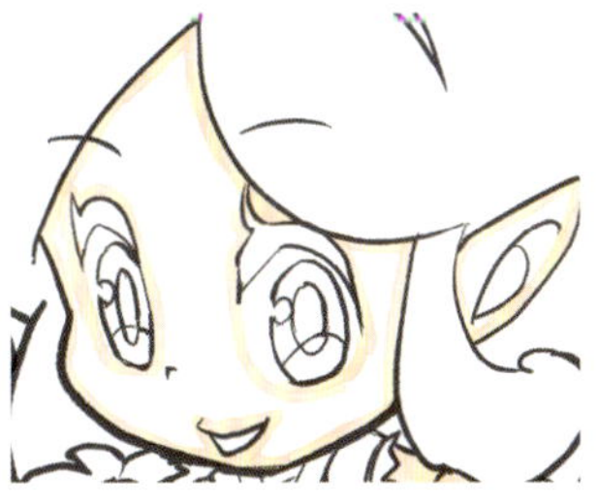

1 Trace the inside of the lines in the skin area and boundary at the whites of the eyes.

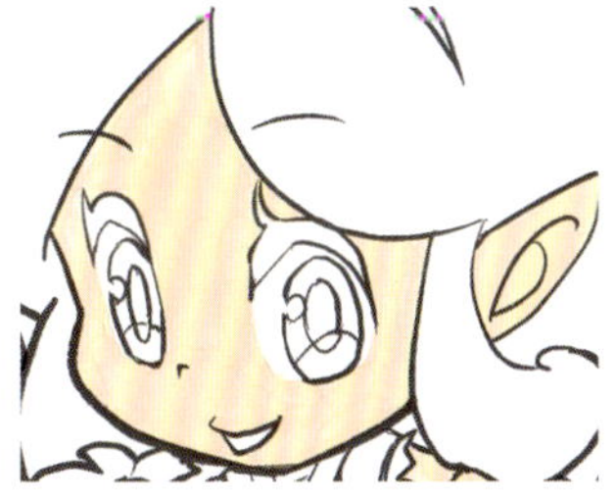

2 Fill in the skin colour, making sure you don't go over any of the boundaries.

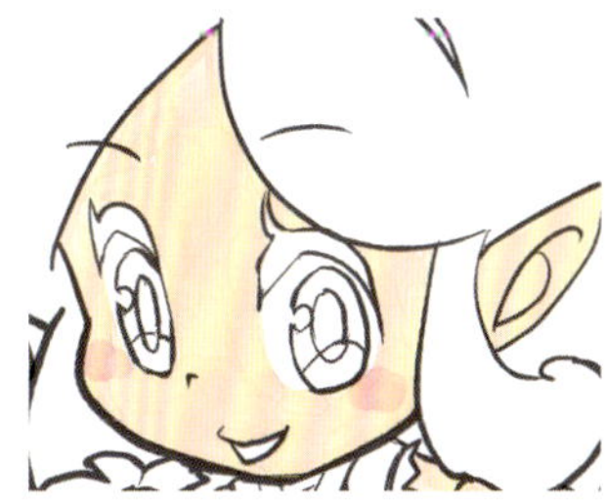

3 For the cheeks, add a pale pink over the skin colour.

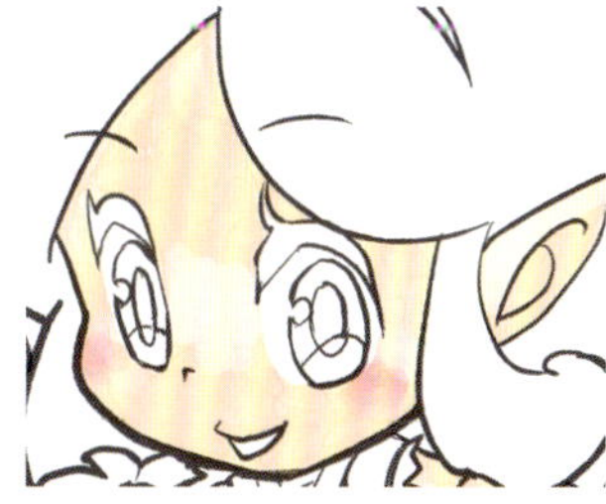

4 You can use a blender marker on the skin colour to create a more attractive skin tone.

COLOURING EYES

Eyes are very important parts of the face to make your drawing look striking. Use two or more colours and blend them to make them sparkle.

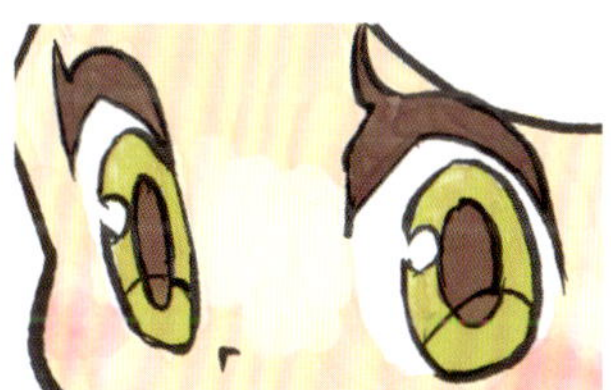

1 Apply the base colour of the eyelashes, iris and pupil.

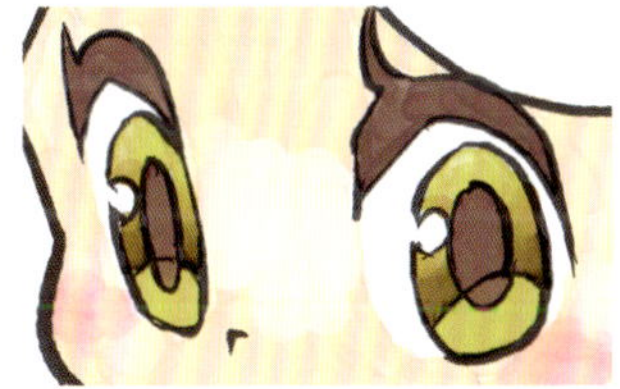

2 Use two more colours to create a gradation of the iris colours.

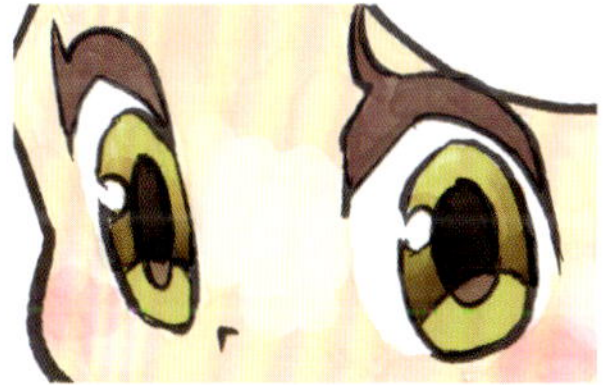

3 Add a darker colour on the pupil (but not on the lower part).

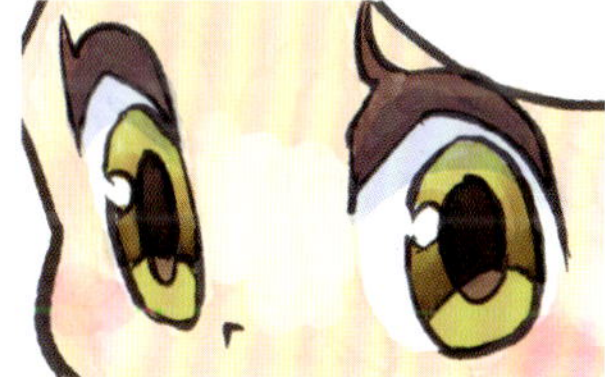

4 Add a shadow on the eye underneath the upper eyelid.

WHITE AREAS

White markers won't be as crisp, so don't colour any areas that should be white. Draw the borders first so you know the limits of what you should colour. Be especially careful not to paint the whites of the eyes when colouring skin.

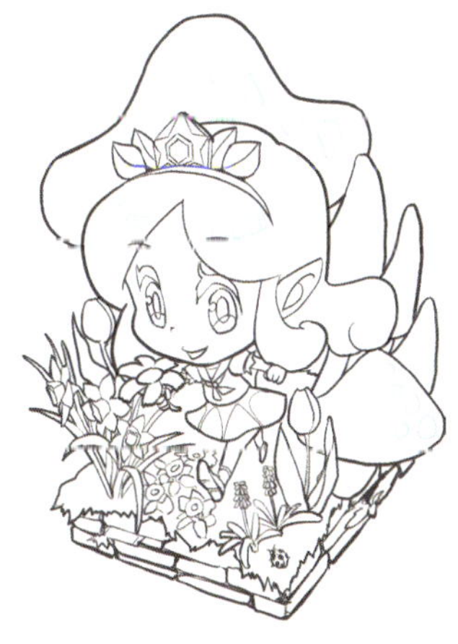

DARK AREAS

If your dark colours are the same colour as the borders, leave about a 1mm ($^{1}/_{32}$in) gap inside the border when colouring. If this white line is too strong, you can fill it with grey.

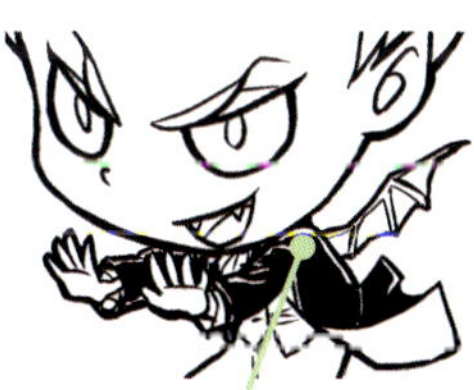

White border

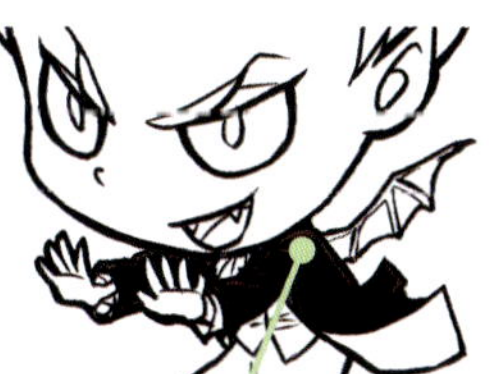

Grey border

ADD SHADING

The base colours alone are perfectly acceptable, but adding shading (see pages 106–7) can make your drawing stand out as if in three dimensions. If you have a lot of dark markers, you can use them to add shading, but if you don't, you can mix colours to create shading.

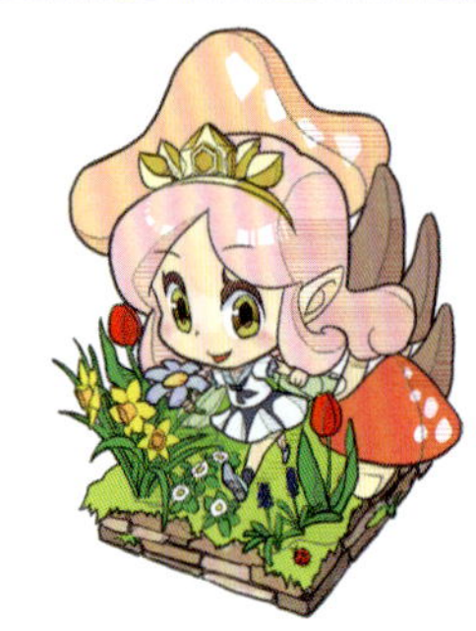

Add very faint pencil guide lines to mark the areas that require shading, then erase them at the end. Once you have got used to it, you can draw lines directly with a shade-coloured marker.

MIXING COLOURS TO CREATE SHADING

The quick and easy method is to simply apply a shade colour over the base colour – the trick is to learn the best colours for shading each base colour. Here, you can see the difference in the finished result, with shadows added with just one colour, or with a different shade colour for each base colour.

SINGLE COLOUR SHADE MIX

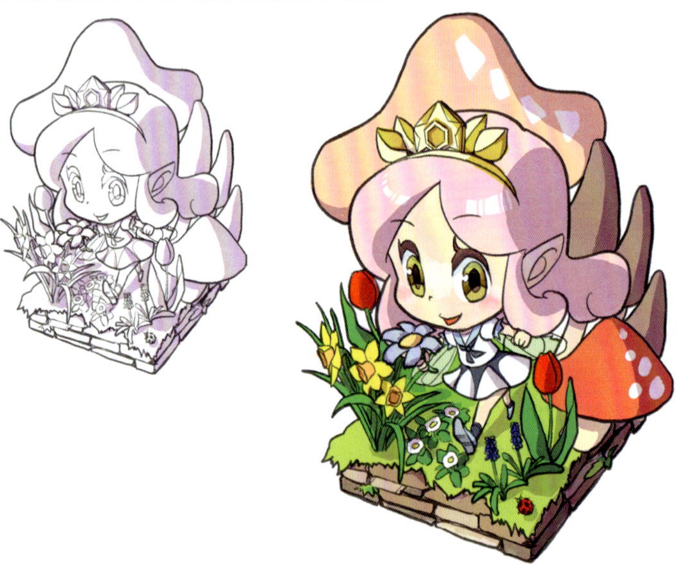

Grey can be mixed with base colours to create shading, but the result tends to look rather muddy. I recommend using a bright purple, which will keep the colours fresh.

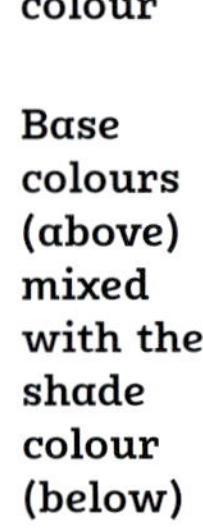

Shade colour

Base colours (above) mixed with the shade colour (below)

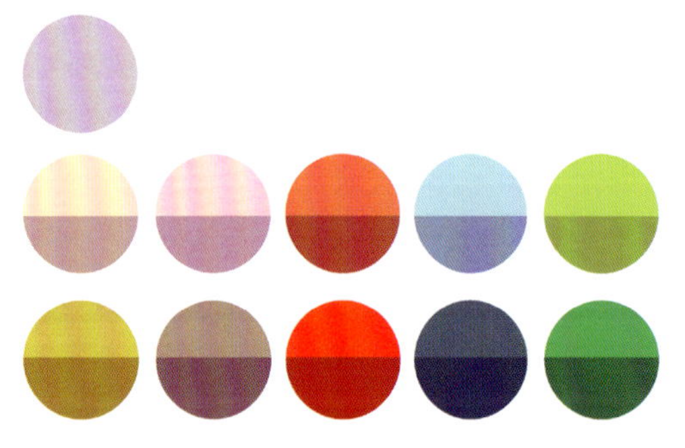

MULTICOLOUR SHADE MIX

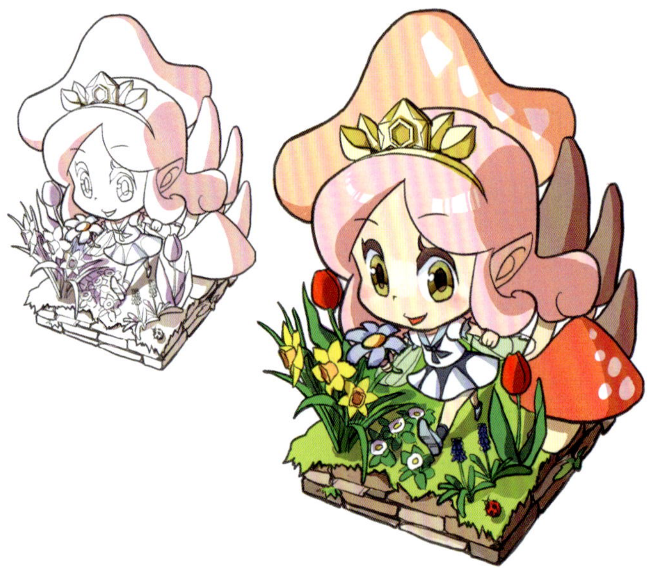

Shadows on warm colours – such as skin tones and pinks – look more natural when a reddish purple is used. Use blue shadows on light blue colours and darker shadows on darker colours.

Shade colours

Base colours (above) mixed with the shade colours (below)

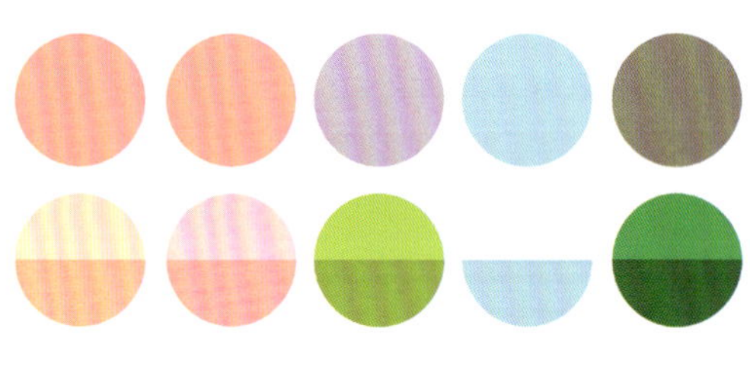

STAGE 7

FINAL ADJUSTMENTS AND TOUCHES

The last stage when creating art is to make final checks. Be methodical and take time to check for any common mistakes, and go over any stages that you found difficult to do. Use the checklist to remind yourself of what you should focus on.

CHECKLIST

- Erase any pencil lines or other working lines.
- Fill in any unintentional white gaps between lines that have been coloured.
- Fix any colour that's overlapping the lines by thinning it with a blender marker, using a white pen, making the outlines thicker or adding a pattern.
- Use two coats of paint or a blender marker to blend any uneven gradation.
- Look to see if the main characters stand out.
- Check there is a sense of depth – add darker tones if needed.

ADDING CONTRAST AND DETAILS

Here, darker grey tones has been overlaid on the background to make the characters stand out. I also added detailing such as bricks.

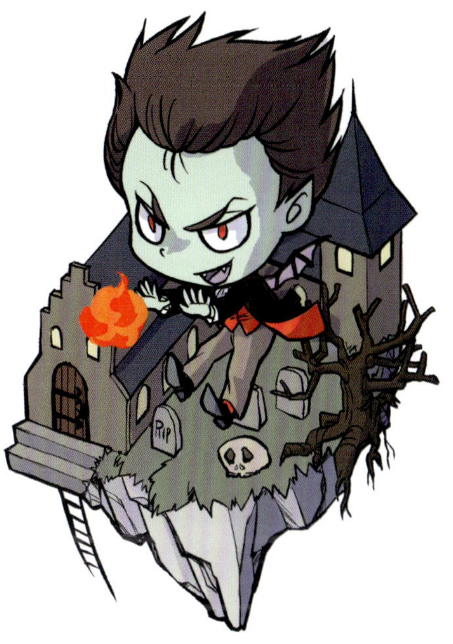

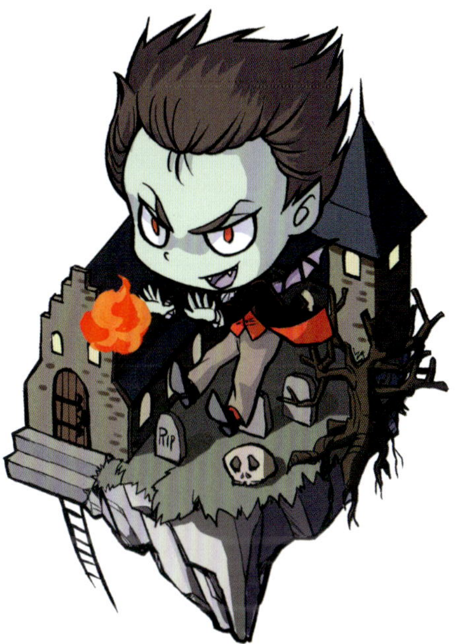

ADDING WHITE

White pens should be used last as they pick up dirt easily. Take care not to apply them to wet ink. Adding sparkle to the eyes and highlight effects can make the drawing more attractive. You can also add a coloured border to make the characters really stand out.

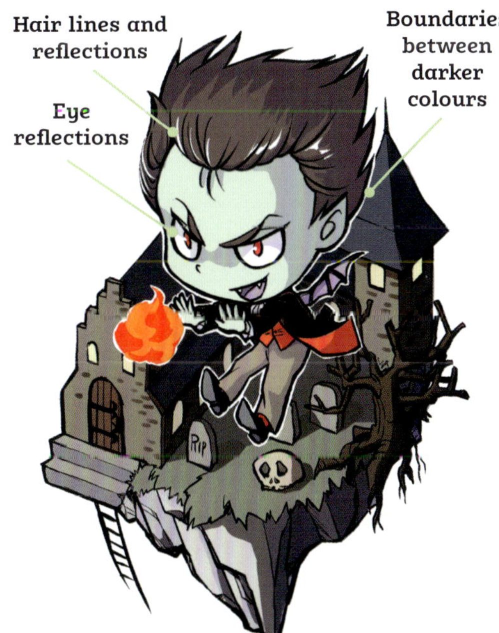

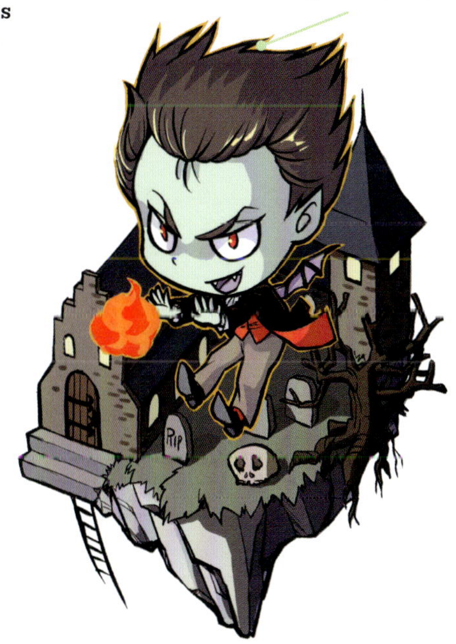

PROJECT 10
DRAW
YOUR OWN SCENES

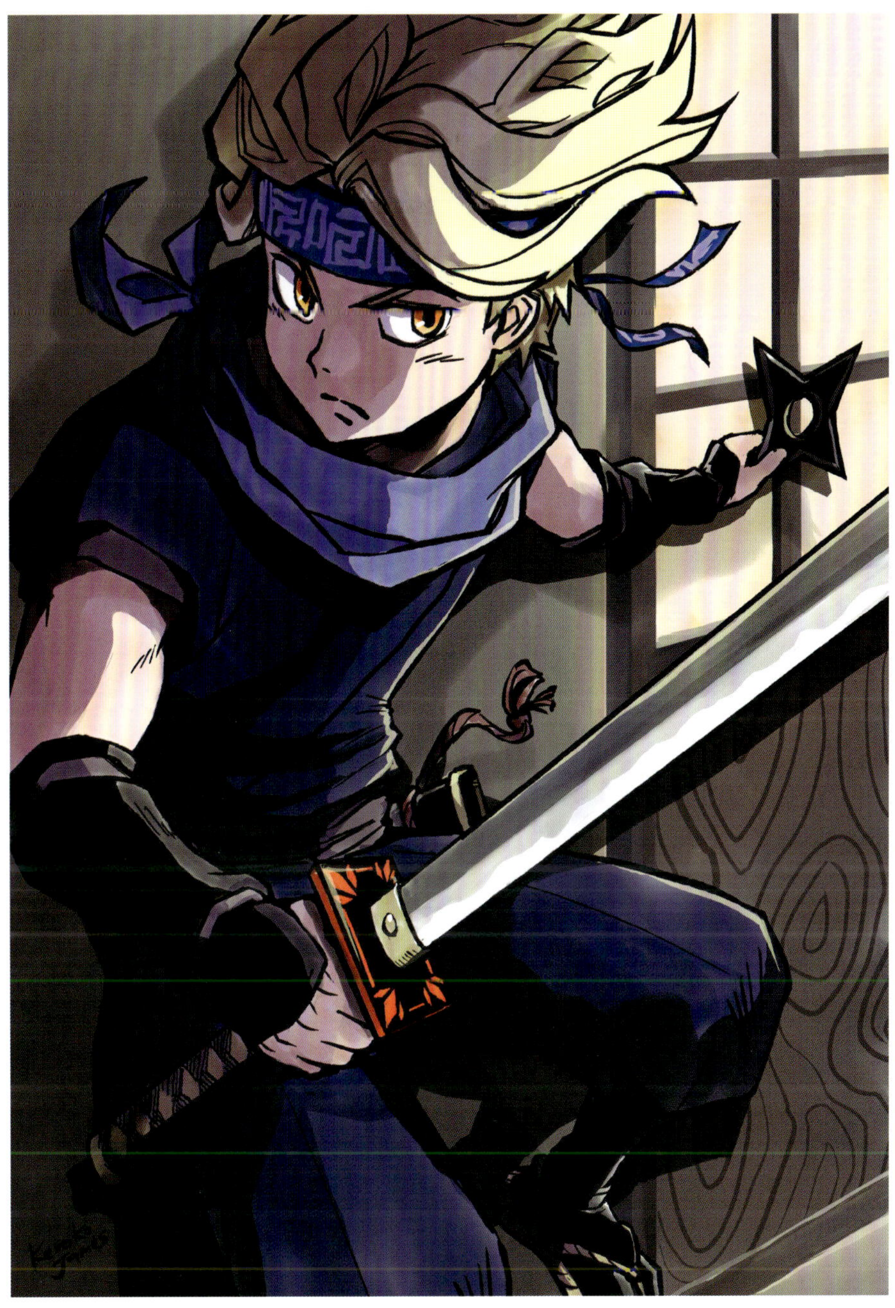

For this final project, you'll learn how to create your own scenes by generating ideas, using thumbnails to develop them into scenes and then using them to create rough pencil sketches and your final artwork. But first you'll learn about two of the most important topics for developing scenes in art: composition and perspective.

Composition

To create a scene, you will need to consider where each object should be in relation to the others – is it at the front or back? Is it next to another object, and if so on which side? You will also need to think about how much of an object you want to see and from which angle.

Framing and orientation

Let's first consider common types of orientation and framing. Portraits are taller than their width and are popular for drawings of people, whereas landscapes are wider than their height and are good for showing characters in scenes with background. However, you can also work with square frames or other shapes. Deciding on the orientation to use will depend on what you want to be seen in the illustration.

You don't always have to fit the whole body of a character in a frame unless that's the only way to explain who they are or what they are doing. If the focus of your drawing is the character, think about what size will show them best. If the character is part of a bigger scene, then make sure you leave enough space for the background. Avoid drawing items too small if you can. Here are some common ways to frame your subject.

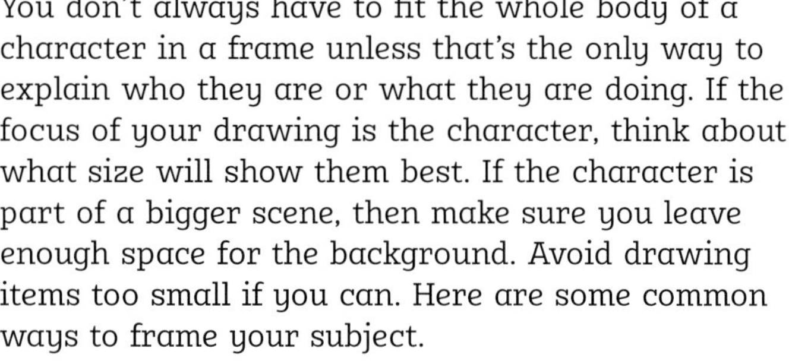

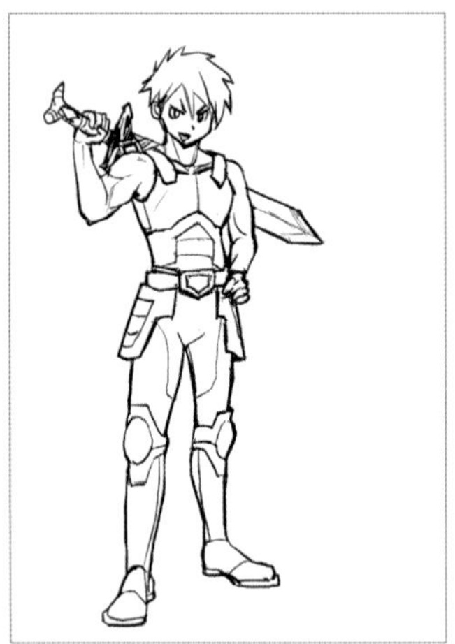

PORTRAIT
Because of the vertical shape of the human body, a portrait orientation is the best choice if you would like to draw a character large. It is also appropriate for other vertical shapes, such as a tower or a skyscraper.

FULL SHOT
This illustration also shows a full-body shot, which is good for when you would like to show full design of the character, such as on covers or posters.

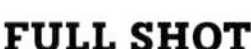

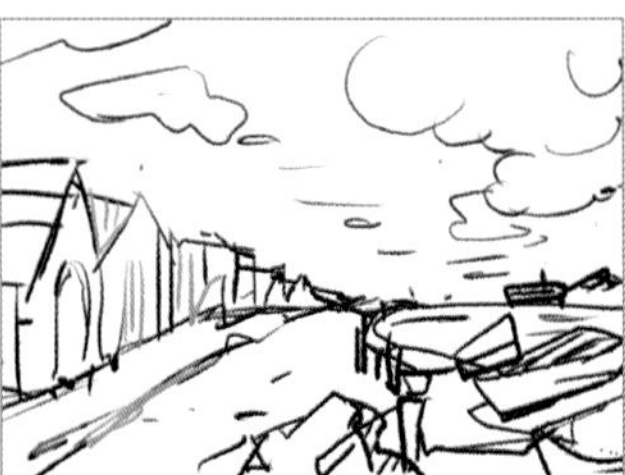

LANDSCAPE
When you would like to depict a panoramic scene, such as a landscape or a city, a landscape orientation makes sense. It is also good to use when you would like to show multiple characters and for big action scenes.

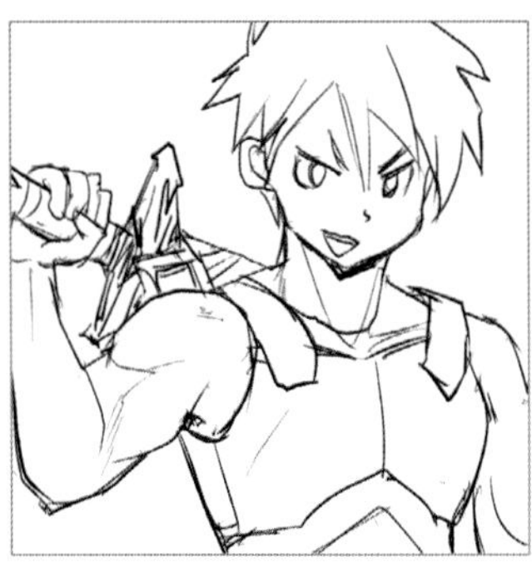

CUSTOM SIZE
Creativity allows anything – you can use any ratio of height to width for framing as long as it fits whatever you are drawing for. Some images need a custom size, such as social media banners and icons.

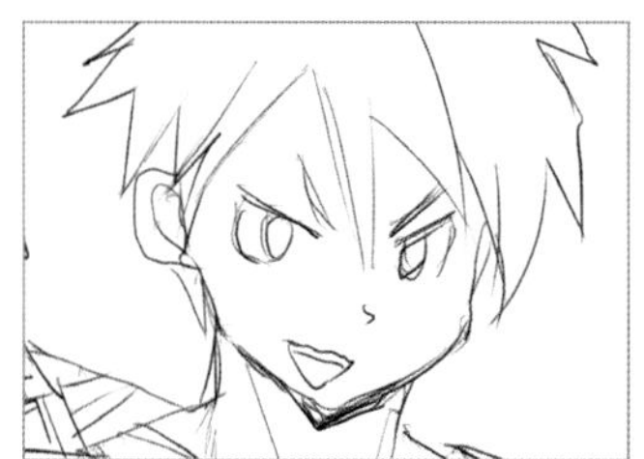

CLOSE-UP SHOT
Coming in close on the subject is used for focusing on a detail or a character's emotion. It can help create powerful, impactful art.

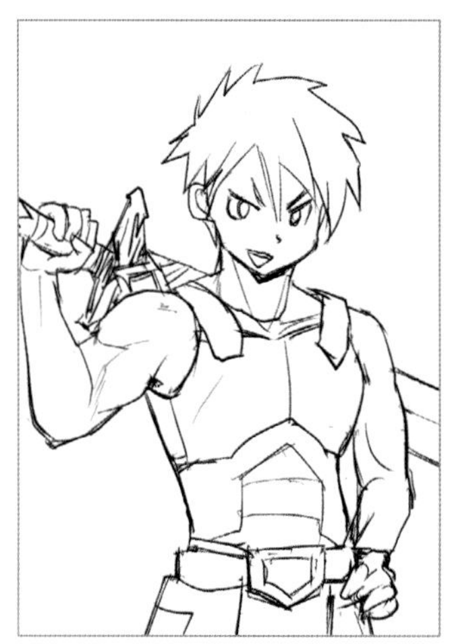

MEDIUM SHOT
Because humans are tall in shape, a head-to-waist or head-to-knee shot is commonly used when drawing a person. If you try to fit the whole body in the frame, the figure will have to be drawn small.

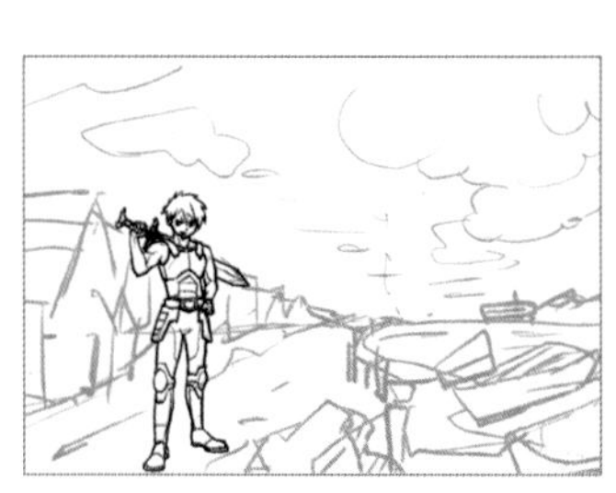

LONG SHOT
Long shots are used when you would like to portray the wider environment or create a more epic scene.

Shaping the composition

The size and positioning of the elements in your artwork will both help the sense of depth in the scene, and how your audience will understand the relationships between the different elements.

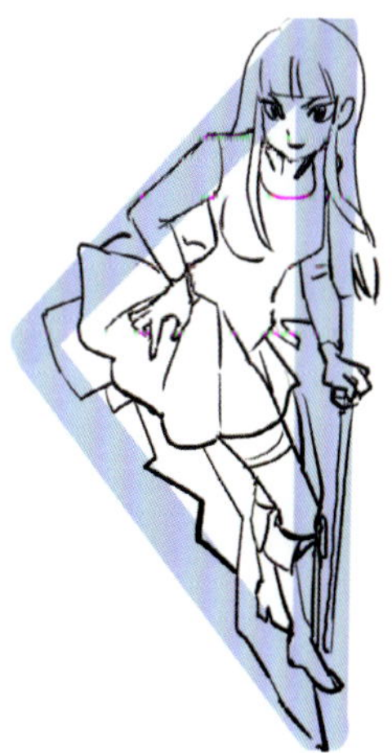

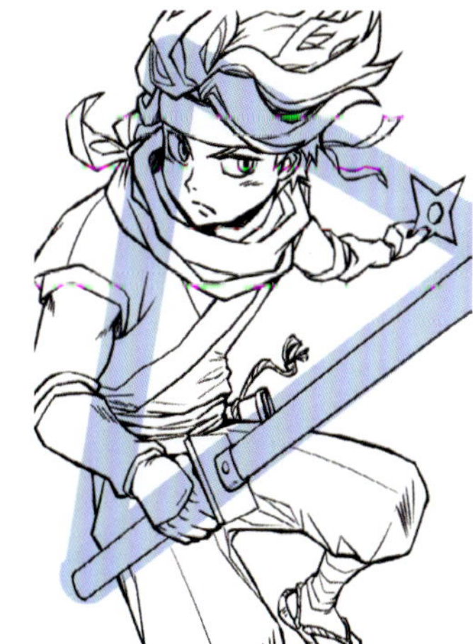

TRIANGLE
A triangle is a good framework to start with when you think about composition because it makes you use diagonal lines in a rectangular frame.

LETTERS
An 'S' shape makes a lovely curve and gives the impression of elegance. You can use other letters such as 'C' curves or 'Y' shapes.

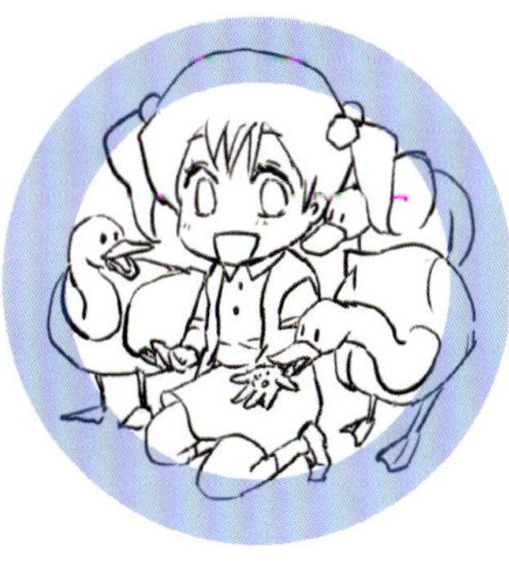

CIRCLE
Using a circle is a good compositional framework if drawing for a young audience, who can find the shape appealing.

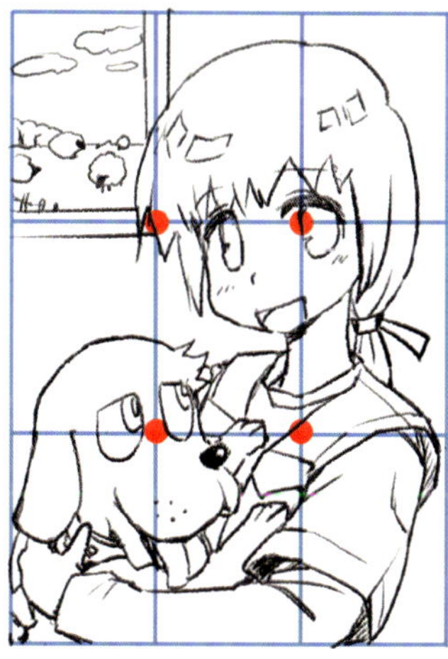

RULE OF THIRDS
The rule of thirds is one of the most important concepts in composition. In it, the scene is divided into a three-by-three grid. To use it, choose as your focal point(s) one or two of the four points where the horizontal and vertical lines intersect. You can also place the horizon line (see page 130) near one of the two horizontal lines. The key point is to avoid symmetry by not putting the focal point in the middle of the frame.

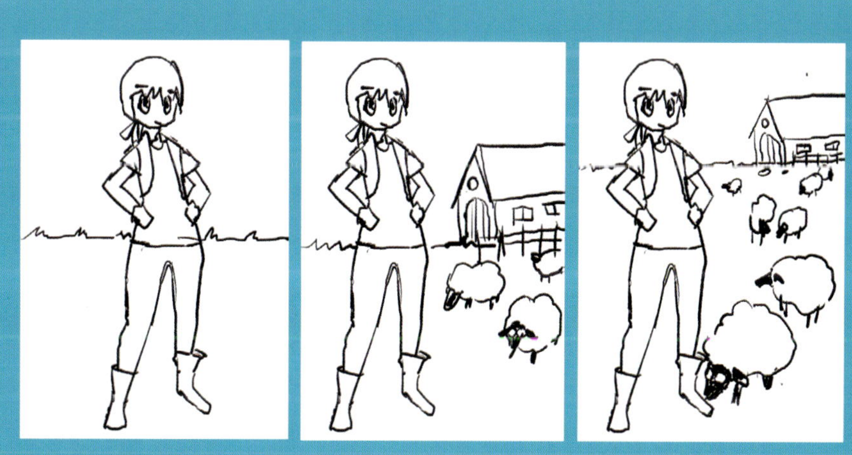

People are more stimulated if they have to look around a whole image, but their eyes stay locked on the centre in a symmetrical composition. The use of right-angled and symmetrical lines (left) looks nice and balanced, and it's fine if your drawing's theme is peace and harmony, but it also looks dull. By moving the character to the left (centre), there is space for the background to breathe. You can also move the horizon line (right) to make the image vertically off-centred.

Camera angle

A more advanced composition technique is to vary the angle in which the audience sees the subject. It is exactly like when you take a photograph: when you look up at something above your eye level, you are using a worm's-eye view, and if you look at something down near your toes, you are using a bird's-eye view.

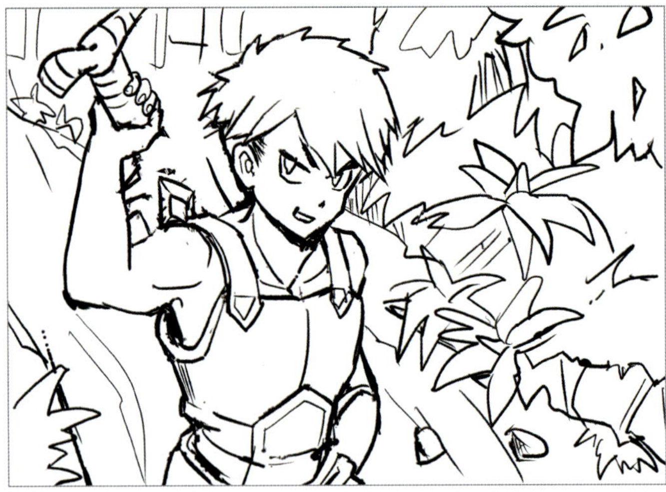

BIRD'S-EYE VIEW
As the name suggests, this is when the viewer is looking down on the subject from a higher angle. One benefit of using this view is that you can make tall figures look shorter, which allows you to draw the head and face bigger and still include the rest of the body.

FOCAL POINTS
The focal point of a scene is the place where you would like to direct the audience's attention. Decide what you would most like the audience to see and use the different compositional techniques to make it the focal point. If you place the focal point in the foreground, it will look very close and detailed. If you place it in the background, the scene will look much calmer, while if the focal point is in the middle ground, it will look balanced.

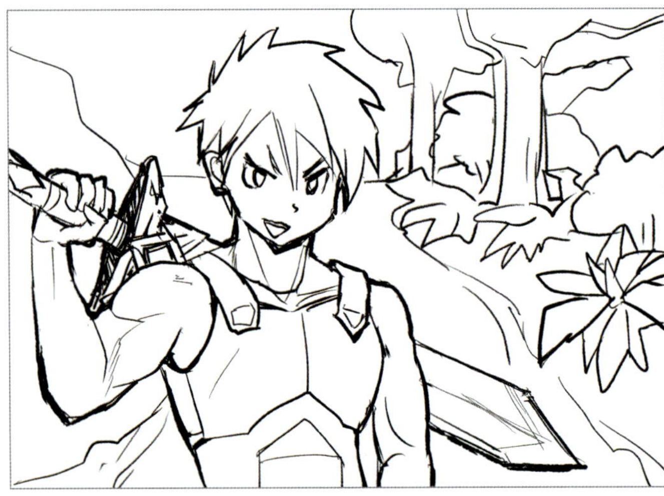

EYE LEVEL
By default, we tend to draw scenes from our eye level, because that is how we normally see the world around us.

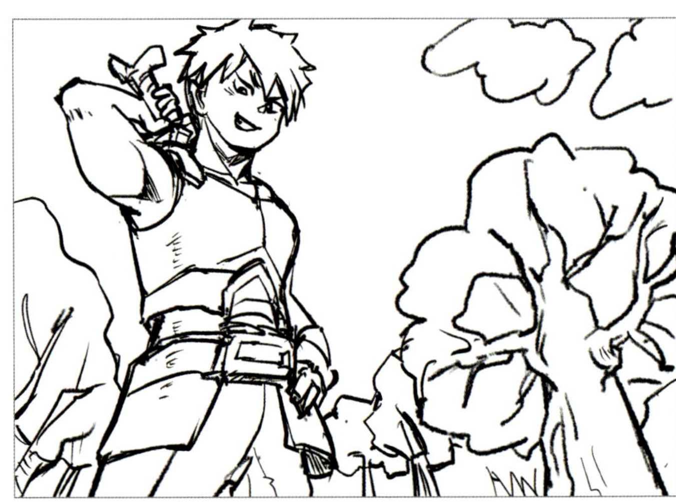

WORM'S-EYE VIEW
As the name suggests, with this view the audience is looking up at the subject. It's a good angle to choose when you would like to draw something big – such as a giant monster – or to create a small child's view of their world.

CREATING DEPTH

Creating a sense of depth is a powerful way to help make your art look realistic. It relies upon dividing the image into three different distances: the foreground, the middle ground and the background. As you plan your composition, remember that closer objects should look larger than those that are far away. Think of the three distances as layers that you can overlap.

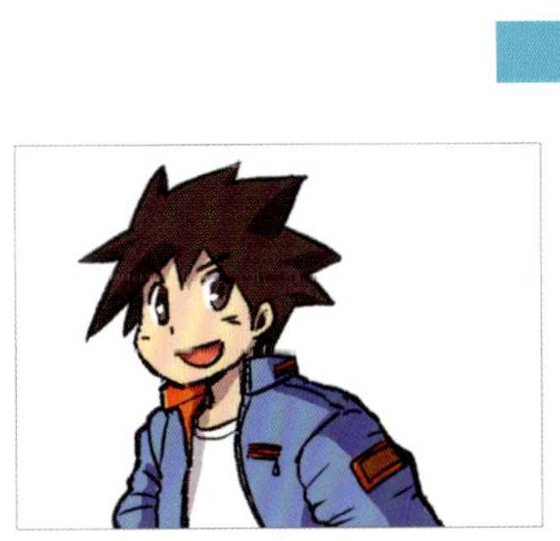

FOREGROUND
Your main characters should normally be positioned in the foreground, as well as objects that are in front of them such as branches or stones. Use thick lines and strong, contrasting colours, and don't forget to add finer details.

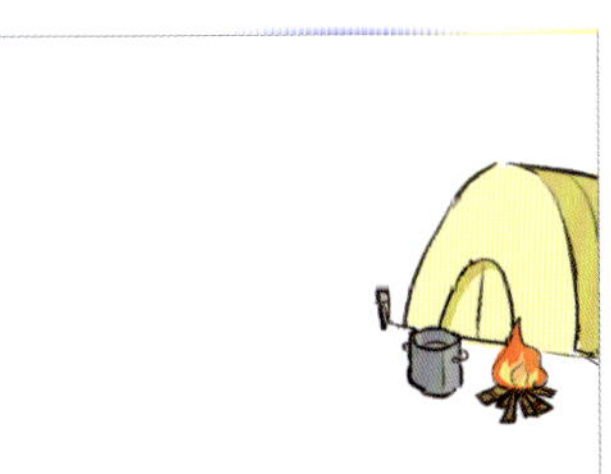

MIDDLE GROUND
Scenery in the middle ground will naturally stand out less than objects in the foreground, but they will stand our more than anything in the background. For objects in the middle ground, use softer lines with milder contrast than those in the foreground, and don't add as many details.

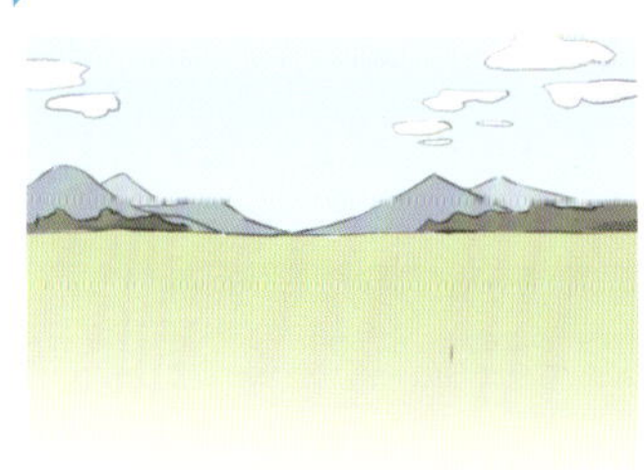

BACKGROUND
Normally the background will be for the landscape such as clouds or mountains. Use faint lines and muted colours with little contrast, and keep details to a minimum.

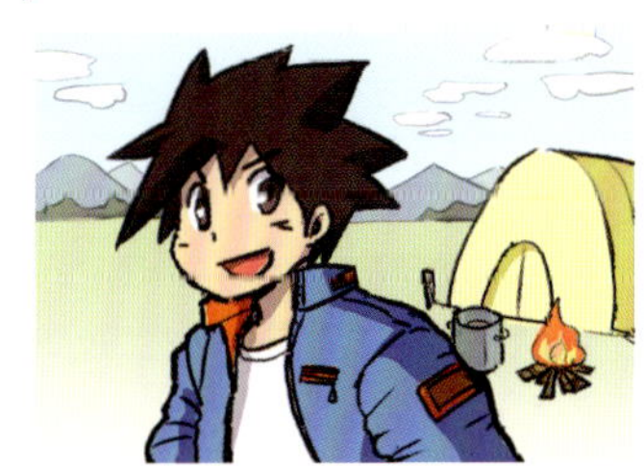

COMBINED
With the layers combined, you can see how the larger character makes the camp site feel like it's further back, and the mountains seem a much greater distance away.

SIZE AND POSITION

The size and positioning of the elements in your artwork will help both the sense of depth in the scene and how your audience will understand the relationships between the different elements.

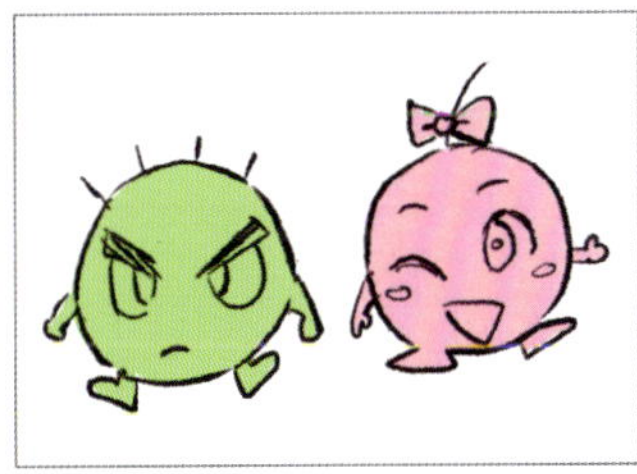

FLAT
When two characters are side by side, the whole scene appears flat.

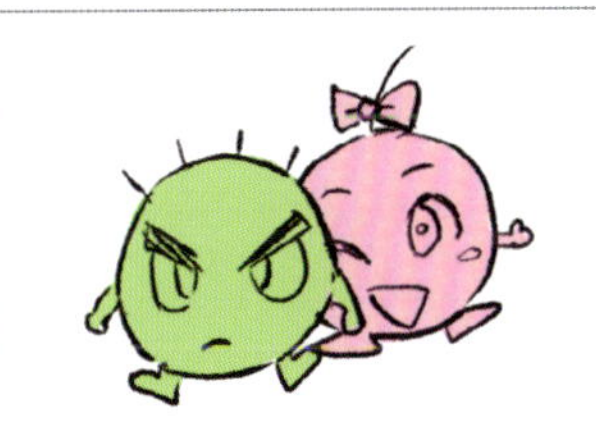

OVERLAPPING
Placing one character so it overlaps the other expresses their positioning in relationship with each other and adds a sense of depth to the scene.

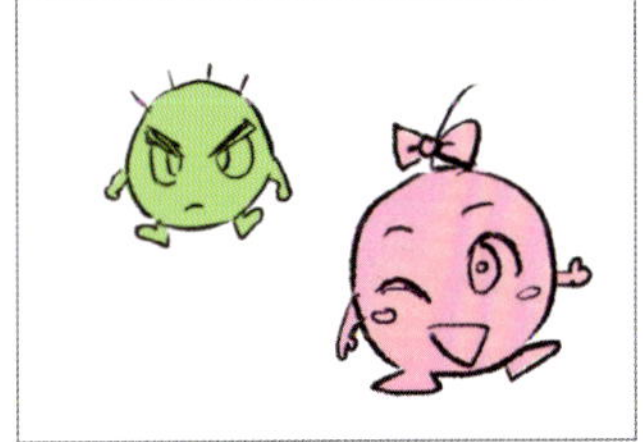

RELATIVE SCALE
Drawing objects in the foreground at a larger scale and positioning them lower in the frame than more distant objects that are smaller and higher up will provide a sense of depth.

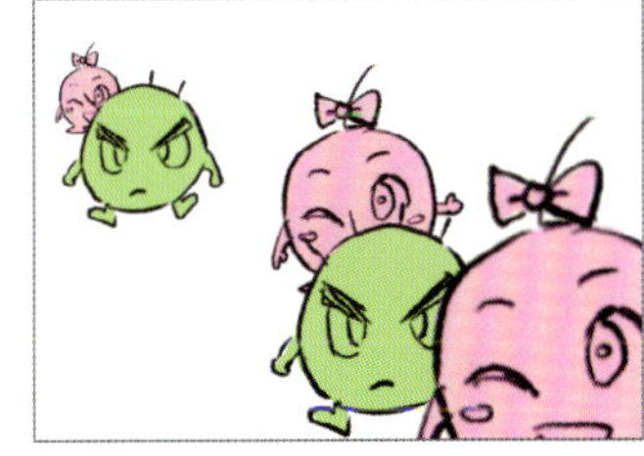

RELATIVE SCALE AND OVERLAP
These techniques can be combined with more objects in the scene, which can also draws the viewer's eye deeper into the picture.

Perspective

If you follow horizontal lines as they recede into the distance, they will merge together. This is known as perspective, and using it when drawing your backgrounds can give your scenes a sense of depth.

One-point perspective

If you wish to draw realistic backgrounds, you will find perspective to be a powerful technique. The easiest way to understand it is to imagine you are looking down a straight railway track. While the rails on either side are parallel and an equal distance apart along the entire length of the track, when you look at the gap between the two rails, it will get narrower and narrower until the tracks meet in the distance on a horizon line. We call that end point the 'vanishing point' (VP). The horizon line is sometimes called the eye level line (EL), because the horizon's apparent position is based on your eye level.

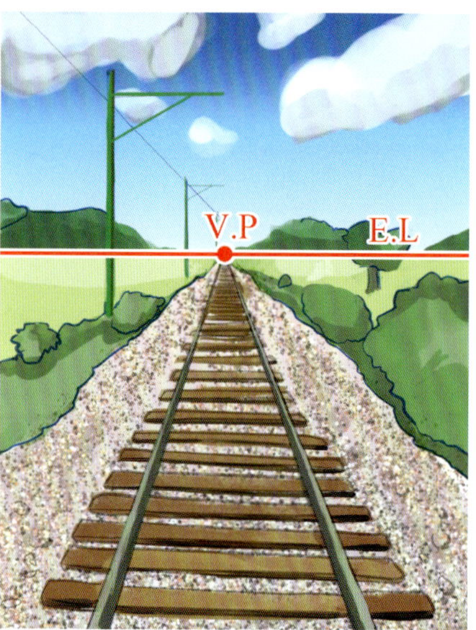

To use one-point perspective in your art, draw faint straight guide lines with a ruler from the edge of the page to the vanishing point. Use these lines to align the elements you draw to give the perception of depth. (There are artworks with two or more perspective points, but they are not normally applied in manga art.)

Practice:
Draw a room with a sense of depth

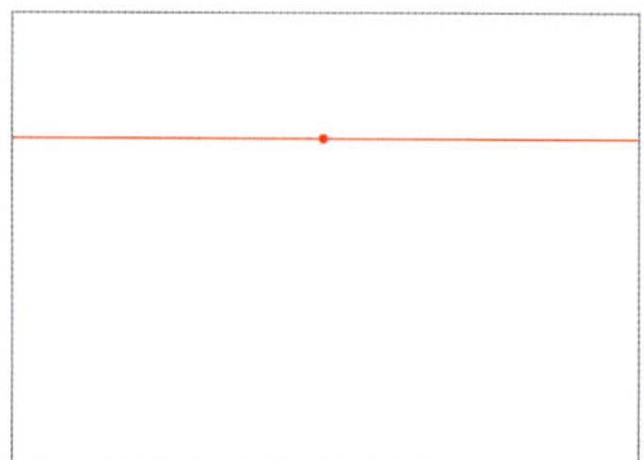

1 Decide on the eye level you want for your drawing and draw the horizon line at it, then add the vanishing point (VP) on the line. You can place the VP at any place on the line, but let's mark it near the centre.

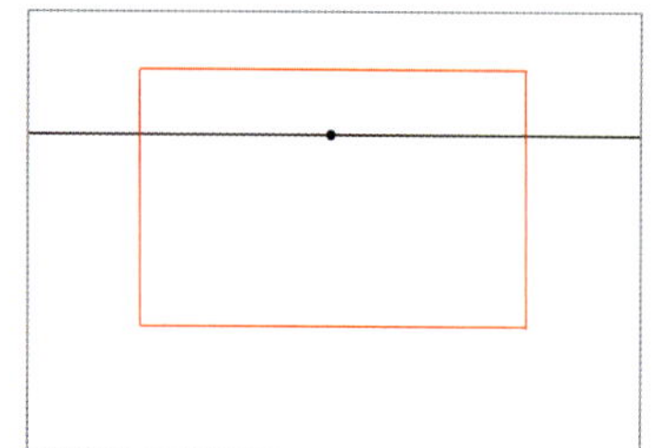

2 Draw a big rectangle for the back wall. The ceiling (the top side of the rectangle) will need to be above the horizon line.

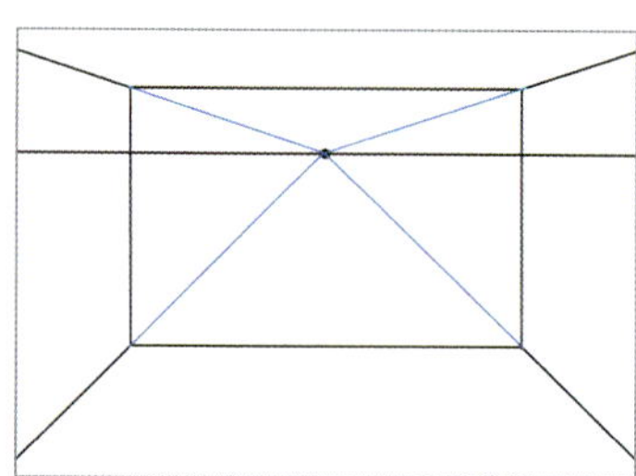

3 Draw four lines from the VP through the corners of the rectangle to the edges of the page, then erase the lines inside the rectangle (but not the horizon line). These lines define the floor, walls and ceiling of the room.

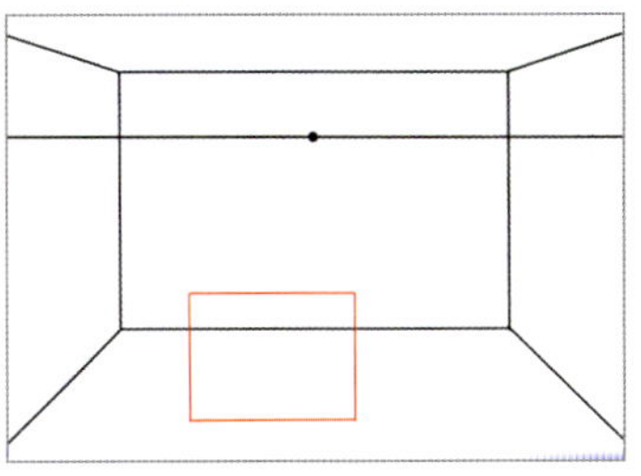

4 To create a desk, draw a small rectangle on the floor.

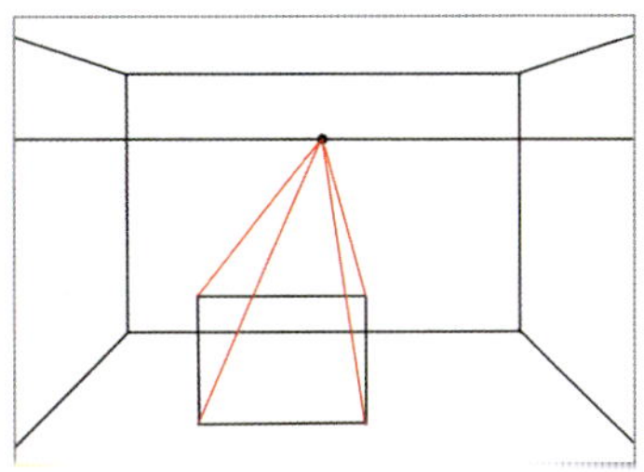

5 Draw four lines connecting the rectangle's corners to the VP.

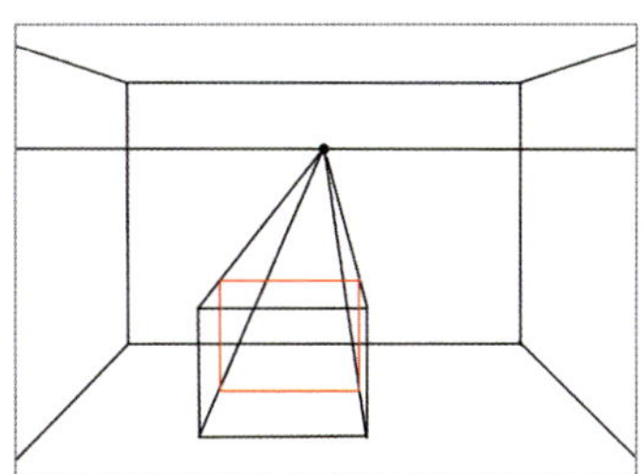

6 Draw a slightly smaller rectangle so that all its sides are parallel to the first rectangle and all four corners are on the guide lines extending to the VP.

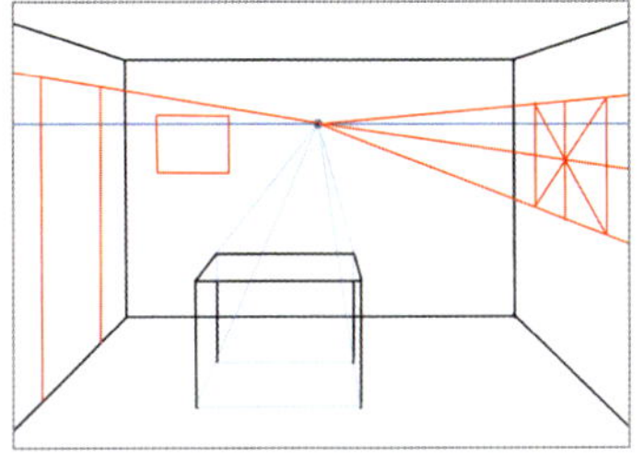

7 Erase all the guide lines, except those that will form the top of the desk and the legs. Add more guide lines extending to the VP to add a door and a window. I also added a rectangle on the back wall for a picture frame.

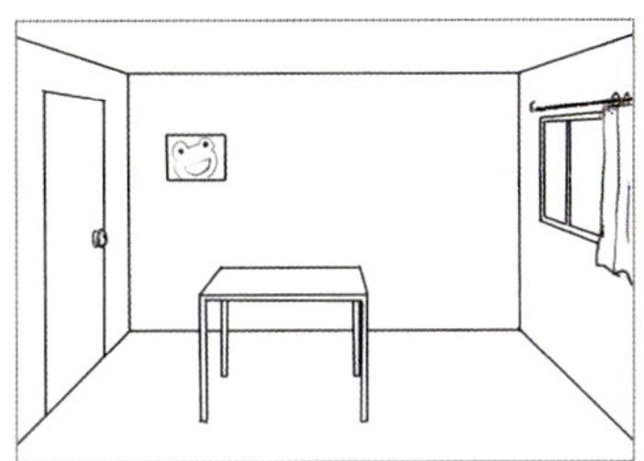

8 Add lines to the table to create the thickness of the tabletop and the legs. Add any other details to the background, such as the door handle, window frame and curtain, and a picture in the picture frame.

BACKGROUND FOR A SCENE

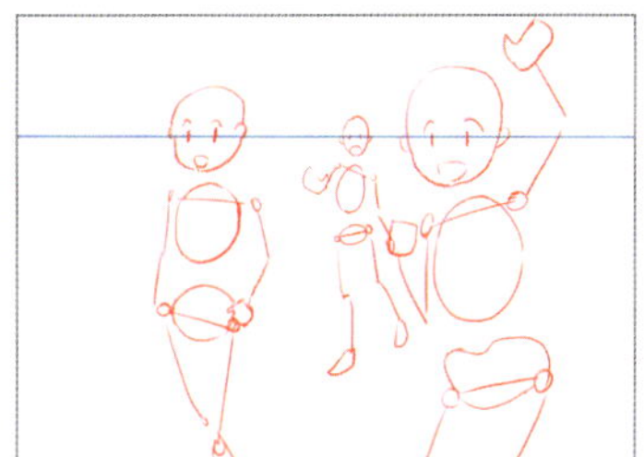

1 Define the eye level and draw the horizon line. Draw stick figures (see pages 44–45) with their eyes at the horizon line. Draw them at different scales and overlap them to give a sense of depth (see opposite).

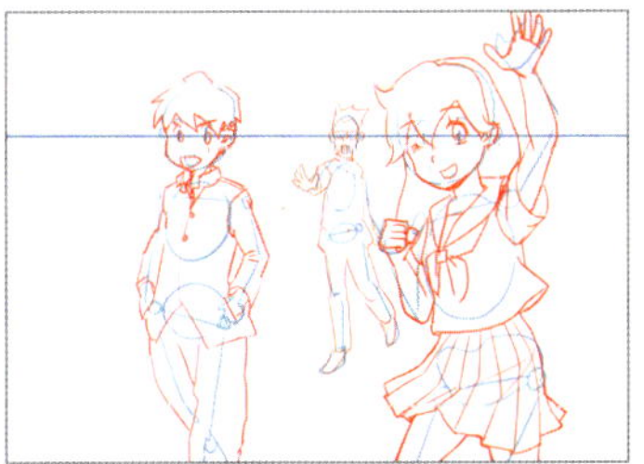

2 Turn the stick figures into doll figures (see pages 46–48) and outline them in the usual way.

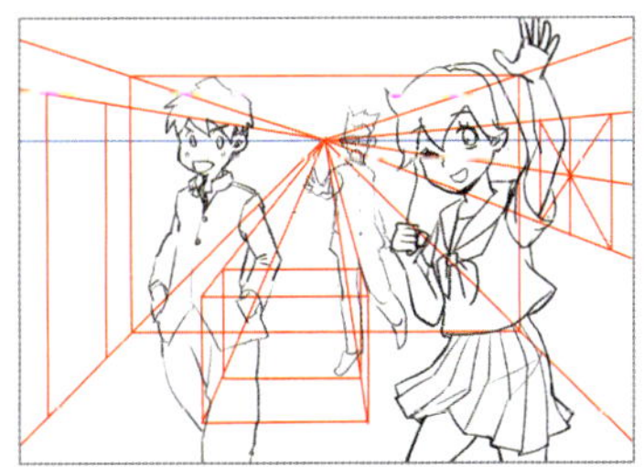

3 Add a VP at the centre of the horizon line. Repeat the previous exercise to add a room and decorations around the characters.

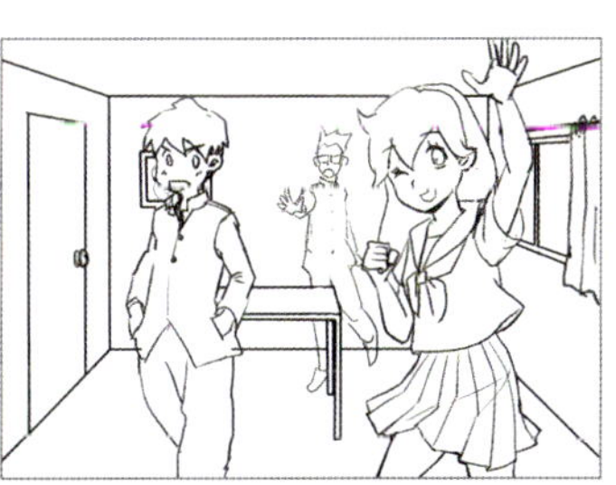

4 Erase any lines that are overlapped by something else and should no longer be visible as well as all the guide lines.

STAGE 1

Planning your own manga scene

Your motivation for making a piece of art may vary; you may have a character you want to draw, or you might want to submit something for a contest, but knowing where to start can be difficult. Here, I've listed different approaches for coming up with a subject to draw.

What do you like to draw the most?

Ask yourself the following questions before you begin. A single answer is fine – just come up with an idea and expand upon it.

I WOULD LIKE TO DRAW A CHARACTER
Many people like a particular manga because of the characters. Design the most attractive and interesting one you can.

I WOULD LIKE TO DRAW A SCENE
People like a strong story. Imagine a dramatic scene and visualize it on paper. If you enjoy the scene, it's always a good start.

I WOULD LIKE TO DRAW A WORLD
An original world can be interesting for your audience. Create a unique setting.

I WOULD LIKE TO DRAW A THEME
You might be given a theme by someone else if you accept a commission. Setting your own theme is also a good way to improve your art.

I WOULD LIKE TO DRAW A MESSAGE
You can place a message in your art such as 'wild forests'. Art can sometimes be a powerful visual communication medium.

What do you want to show your audience?

Once you've come up with a rough idea of a topic, ask yourself some more questions to help you think about your subject in more detail. I have added my answers for this project's art as an example.

WHAT WOULD THE TITLE OF YOUR ART BE IF YOU NAMED AND DESCRIBED IT IN ONE SENTENCE?
Sneaking ninja.
I would like to draw a great ninja character, in an action pose.

WHAT EMOTION WOULD YOU LIKE TO DRAW?
Intensity.

WHO IS THE AUDIENCE OF THE ART?
All ninja fans.

WHAT INTEREST OR ART STRENGTH WOULD YOU LIKE TO SHOW YOUR AUDIENCE?
The attractiveness of my ninja.

Build up your scene

Now that you have an idea and you've established what you want to show your audience, the final brainstorming stage is to establish what will be in your scene.

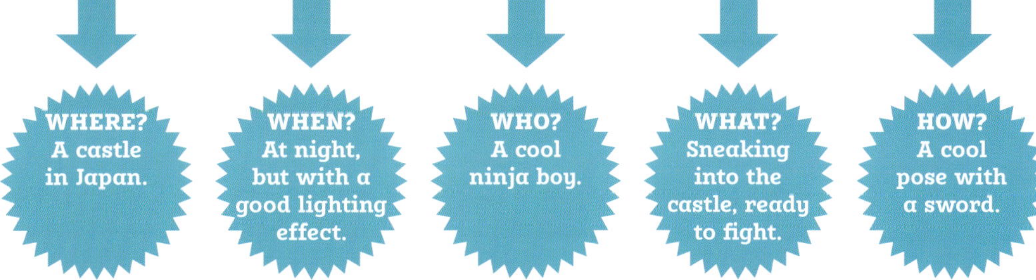

What to do if you still can't think of an idea

Don't worry, it happens from time to time. Instead of sitting in front of a blank page, move your hand and draw something randomly: a circle, a funny face, whatever! It has been scientifically proven that our brains are more active when we are doing something. An idea will come to you!

Collect information and expand upon your ideas

Once you have decided upon your subject, find out more about it and collect visual references. This process is very important for creating art that will make an impact, so don't be lazy. Collect every possible image, and study it until you really get to know your subject and how others have drawn it. Don't forget to note the small details: knowledgeable audiences will love to see them in your art, and it will help them to be convinced by your drawing.

RECORDING IDEAS

I use a notepad to collect my ideas. I use it to make spider diagrams and come up with lists of keywords as I discover more about the subject. I also take a sketchbook with me when I'm researching so that I can draw whenever I'm inspired by, capturing shapes and ideas that I can come back to later. You can also use the camera on your phone or tablet to record what you find. Don't forget to collect any ephemera you find: fliers, stickers, cards and so on can all be kept in your notepad or a dedicated scrapbook for future reference.

WHERE TO SEARCH

There are loads of places you can search for references. Start by doing some research online – as well as websites dedicated to the subject, you'll likely find ideas for films, games, graphic novels and other media that you can watch, play or read. If you're researching art, borrow or buy books about your favourite artists. There may also be galleries near you with art relevant to your subject. But don't limit your research to just art and artists – look at history, science, folklore, fashion or anything else that can provide you with the details that will lift your art to another level.

STAGE 2

ROUGH SKETCHES

Once you've gathered enough research material you can make some preliminary rough sketches based on your notes. These sketches don't need to be polished, just as long as you can understand them later! The ideas and design are more important than the quality of the drawings.

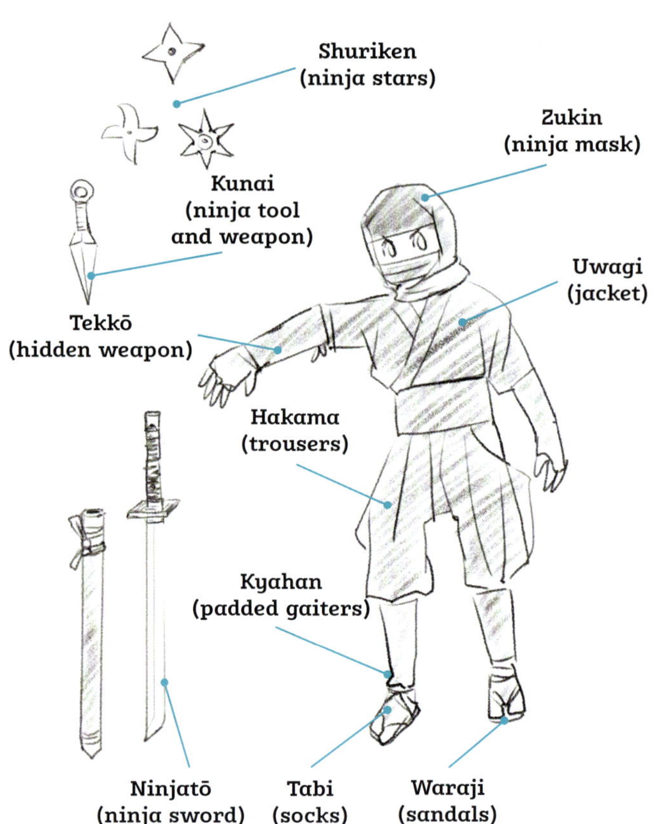

Make a list of all the different elements you could possibly include, then decide which of them are important and which of them could be dropped. Use this final list to create rough sketches, then when you are happy with them, draw them neatly onto a fresh sheet. Try different variations, then ask your friends' opinions about which are the strongest – other people can see things you hadn't thought about and help you improve your scene.

PRACTICE:

DRAW A HAND HOLDING A SWORD

When drawing props, always start with simple lines, shapes and forms, then add details gradually.

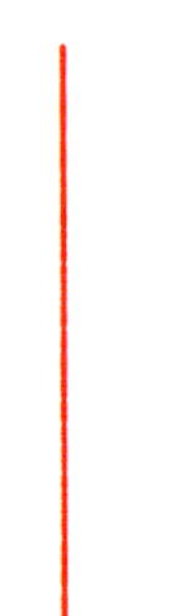

1 Draw a line (use a ruler when drawing a straight object such as a sword).

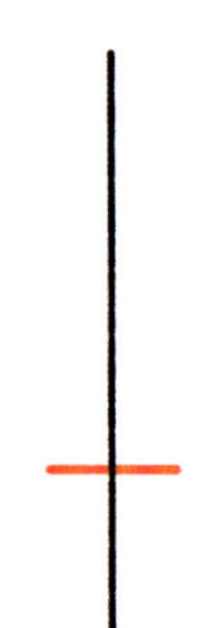

2 Draw the hand guard. This is usually at a right angle to the blade. The handle should be two hands long.

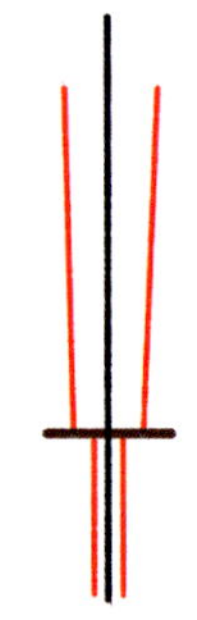

3 Draw the blade and handle. These should be symmetrical straight lines against the first line in Step 1.

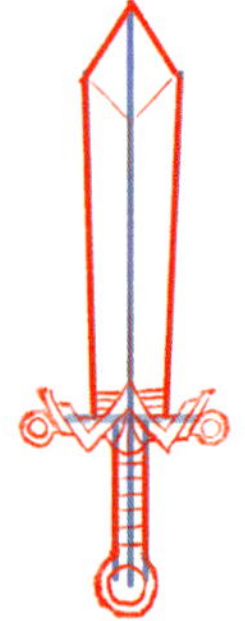

4 Add more shapes and details to decorate your sword.

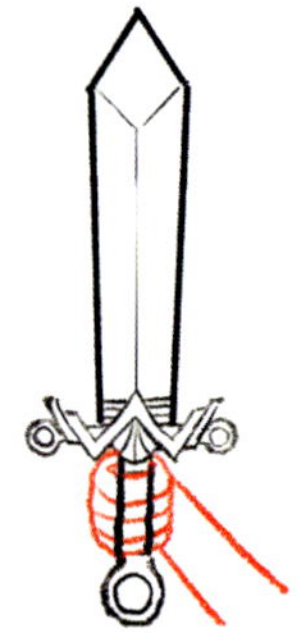

5 To make a hand, wrap a tall doughnut shape around the hand guard. Make four rings for fingers, then attach the arm.

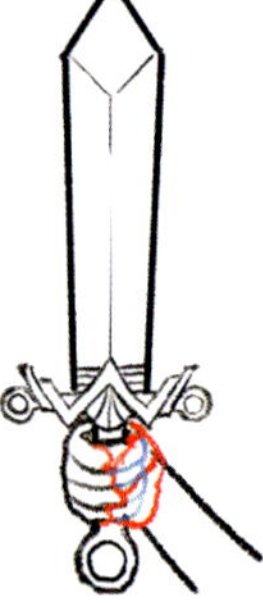

6 Hold a stick and observe where your knuckles, fingertips and thumb are positioned, then mark them on the four rings.

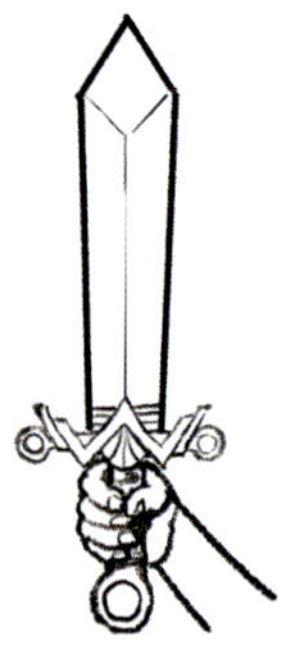

7 Draw the four fingertips and wrap the thumb around from the other side. Adjust your lines and add any details.

STAGE 3

PLAN YOUR COMPOSITION

Now you've finished your sheet of rough sketches, it's time to plan how you will use them in your scene using composition. It's an important stage, so take your time and think carefully about it.

Usually, artists will make small sketches called thumbnails, drawing them in several frames on a sheet of paper to show their ideas. This way, they can try out different compositions to see which work best, and they can discover if there any additional elements that may be needed or any that could be dropped. I recommend using small sheets of paper – cutting two A4 (letter-sized) pages into quarters to make eight small sheets is perfect for coming up with different possible compositions. Compare them and choose the best one.

THUMBNAILS

You do not need to be too accurate in terms of the shapes or details when drawing thumbnails – just sketch simple shapes and silhouettes. What is important are the sizes, poses, positioning and angles of the objects in the composition. Since the thumbnails are just for your reference rather than public display, you can be as creative as you like, and if you get stuck with one sketch, then just try something else until you're happy with the results. You can also use a series of thumbnails to draw a storyboard, which is a plan for drawings when making a comic strip or shots for an animation.

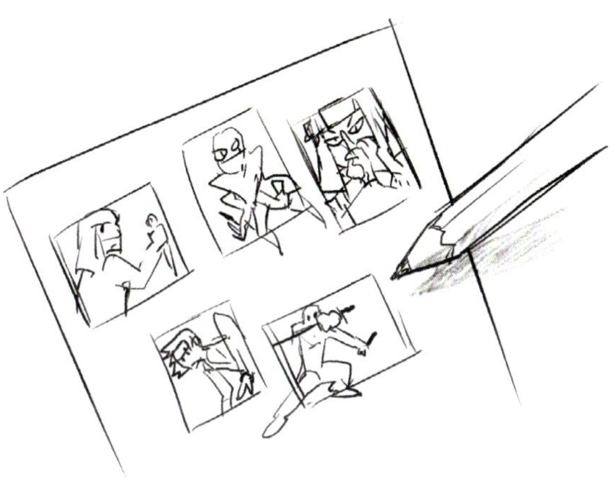

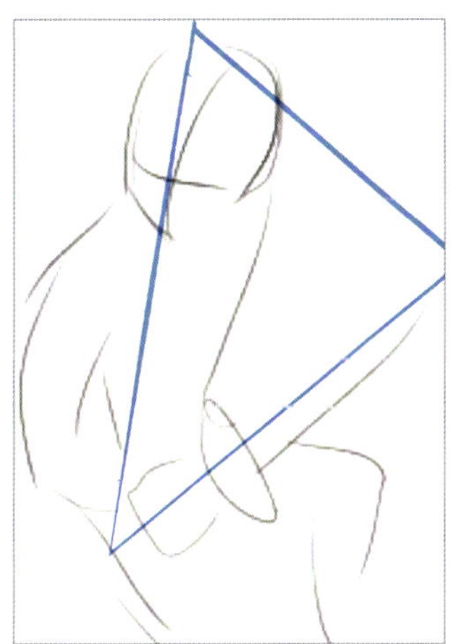

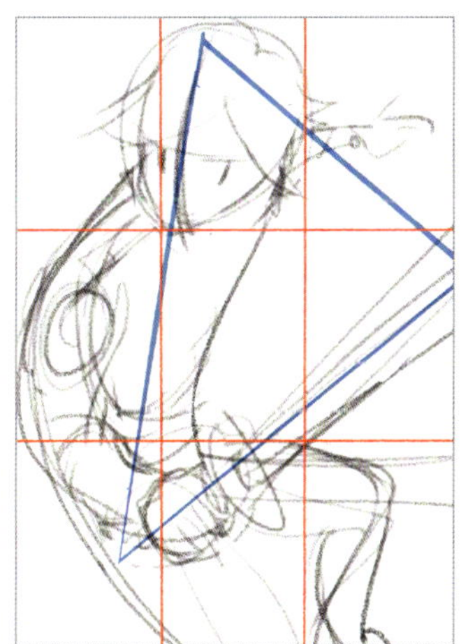

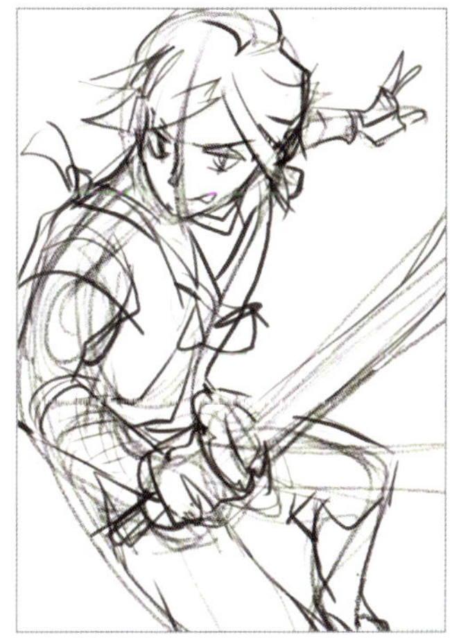

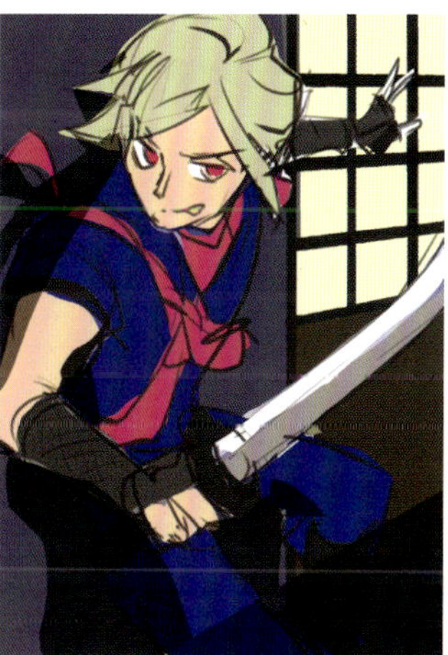

STAGE 4

MAKE THE FINAL SKETCH

Creating a good sketch is critically important for when you trace it to make your final artwork, so take your time on it and use all your skills and creativity to make the strongest possible image. Don't feel compelled to copy your first sketch exactly – I adjusted the position and size of some elements and changed the clothes until I was happy with everything.

COPYING TIPS

- If your original is very rough, don't try to match the exact same shapes.
- Copy the rough shapes and check the proportions are correct before you copy or create the details.
- Draw grid lines to divide your page if it helps with positioning the different parts of your image – for example, you could create a rule-of-thirds grid (see page 127).
- If you find it tricky to draw a good, enlarged copy, use a photocopier to enlarge the image to same size as the final page, then trace it using a light pad.

ENLARGE YOUR THUMBNAIL

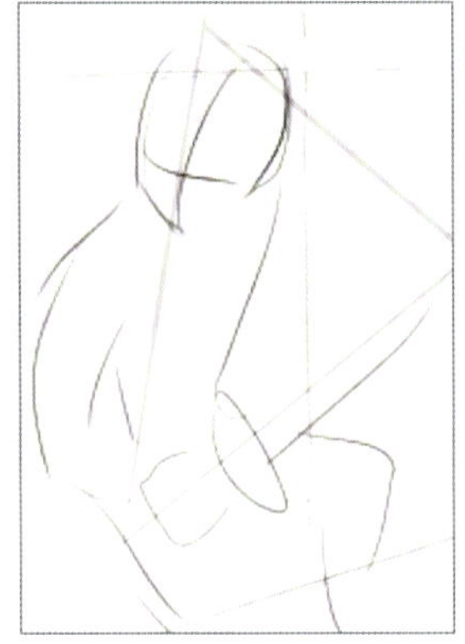

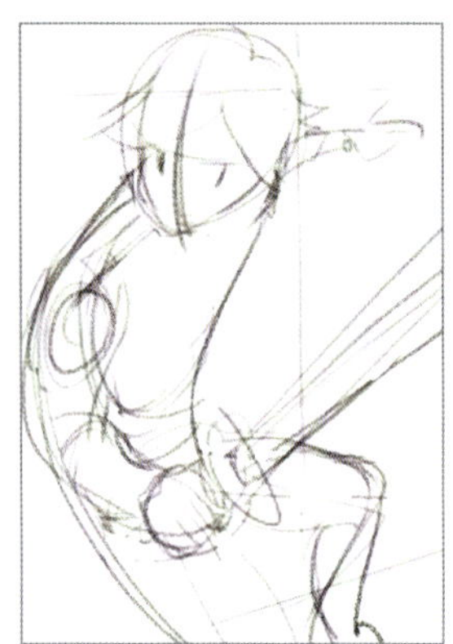

1 Enlarge and copy your thumbnail onto 160gsm (60lb) A4 (letter-size) card stock. Copy the rough silhouette using faint pencil lines, but don't draw detailed shapes. Compare the two and make sure the composition is the same.

DRAW A 3D DOLL SHAPE

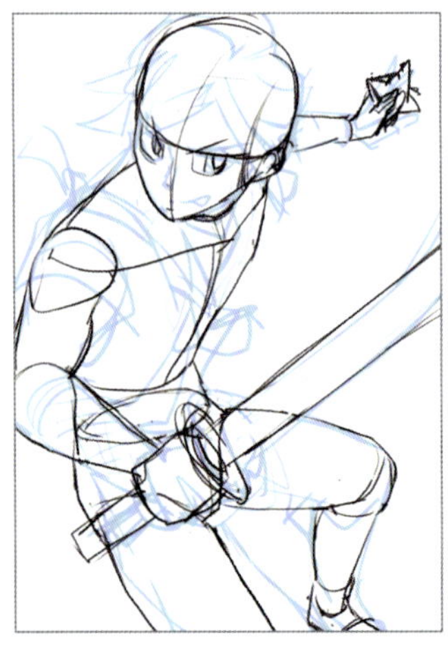

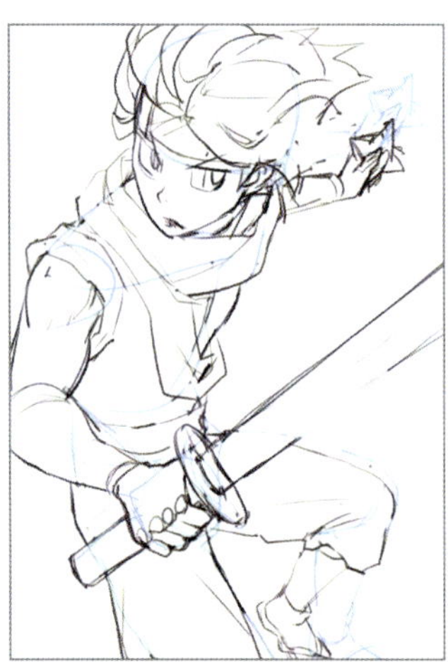

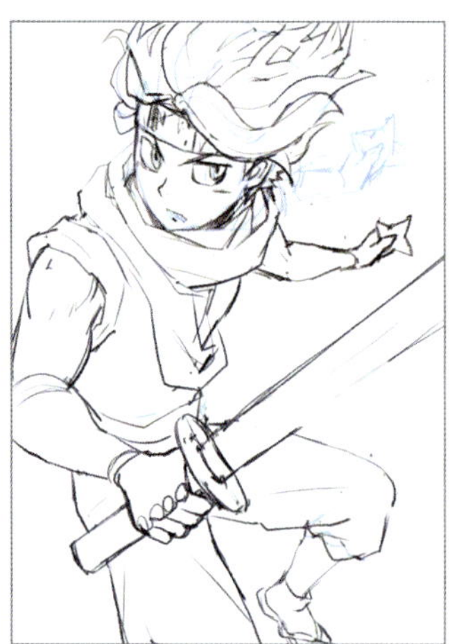

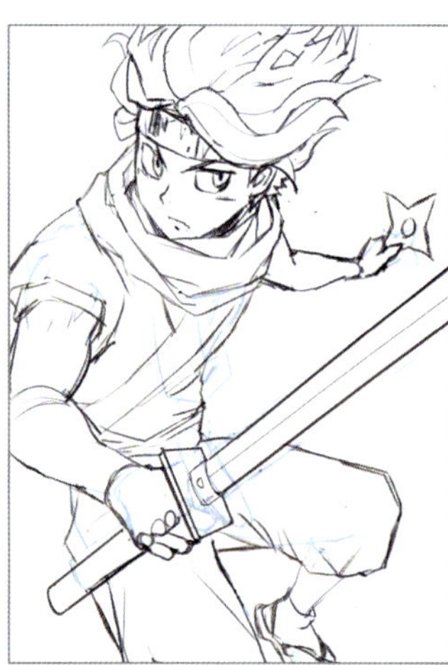

2 To create a strong pose, draw a doll figure over the rough silhouette while considering proportions. Try the pose in front of a mirror and check the angles and limbs of your body against those of your doll figure.

3 Draw your character's design on the doll figure. You may rearrange or add elements if it helps the drawing. I added a bandanna to make the figure look more like a ninja, and I moved the arms and back leg because I didn't like their positions.

4 Draw the facial details and hair. Again, adjust any elements that aren't working – I moved the back arm within the composition triangle.

5 Add the details for the clothing and the sword. I decided to change some elements in the clothes, and I enlarged the shuriken to make it stand out more.

DRAW THE BACKGROUND

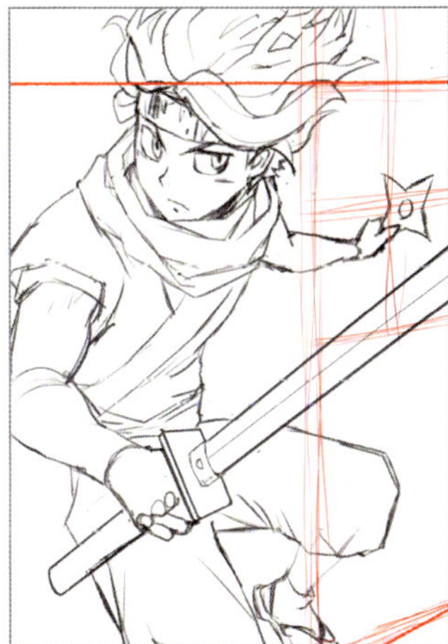

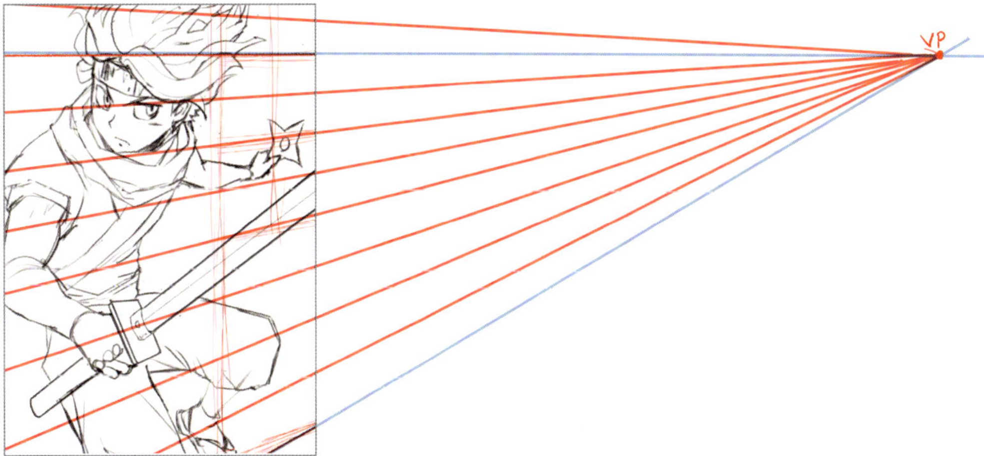

6 To draw the background, draw a horizon line at eye level, then roughly draw the position and angle of a sliding door.

7 The vanishing point is outside the frame, far to the right of the line that forms the base of the door. I drew a grid of lines from the vanishing point back to the frame to help draw the rest of the door accurately.

ADD MORE DETAILS

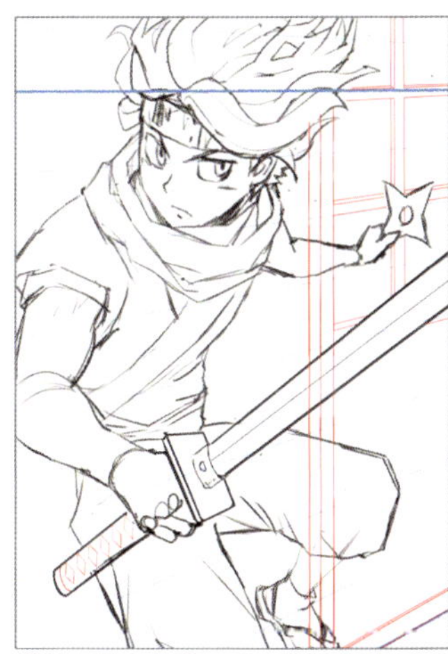

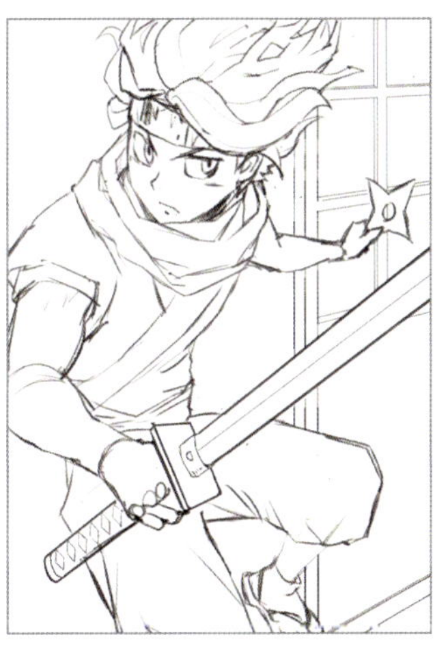

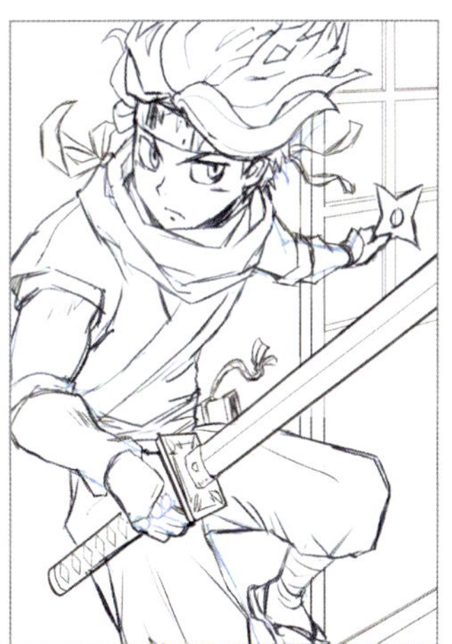

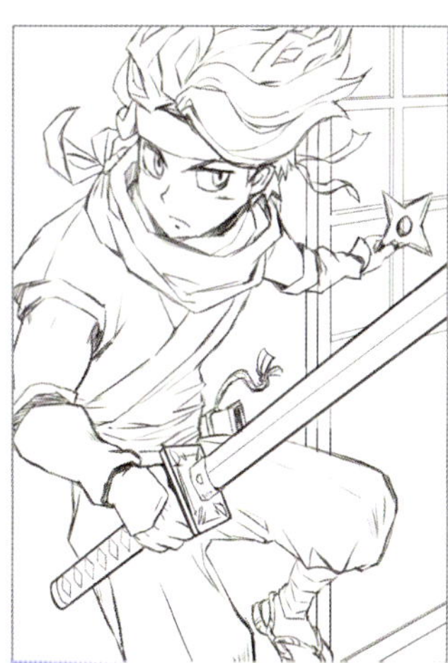

8 Use a ruler to draw the frame of the door over the grid lines.

9 Finally, erase the grid lines.

10 To enhance the sense of movement, I added a cord to the sword and ends to the fluttering bandanna.

11 Tidy up the lines, and your final sketch will be ready for tracing.

TIP

Add more details to objects that are in front or if you want them to catch the eye. In contrast, draw distant objects more simply with less details. This will create a sense of crispness and perspective.

STAGE 5

INK YOUR ART

The next stage is to turn your finished pencil drawing into a drawing with inked lines. The approach is similar to inking a black-and-white manga drawing (see pages 98–109), but you'll need to use different line weights when inking the character and background, and don't use ink to create the shadows.

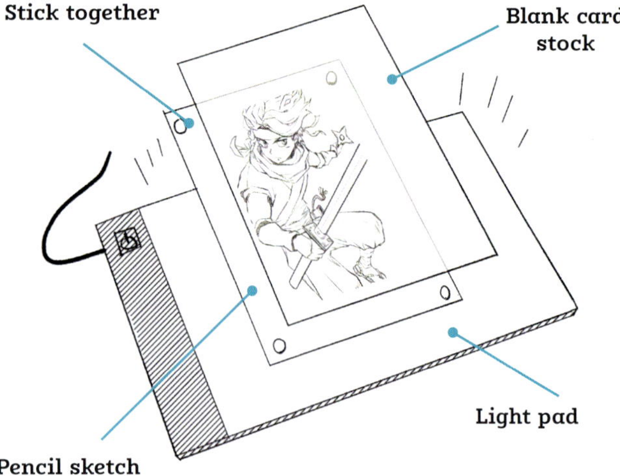

1 Prepare your final pencil work for tracing by placing it on the light pad (see page 102).

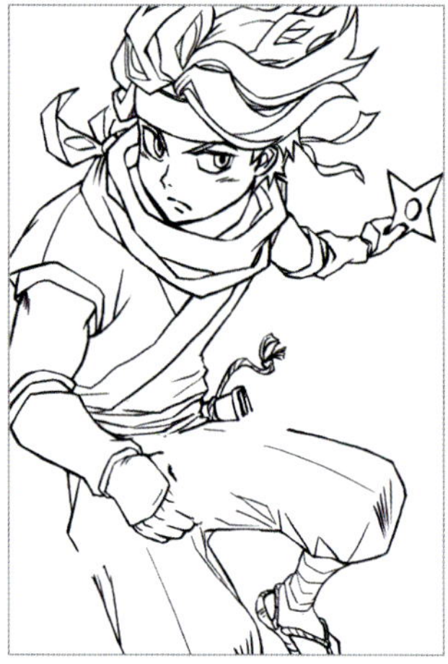

2 Trace the lines of the character. I used a fineliner so that I could vary the line weight depending on the pressure I applied. You may find rotating the paper will help you to draw good lines.

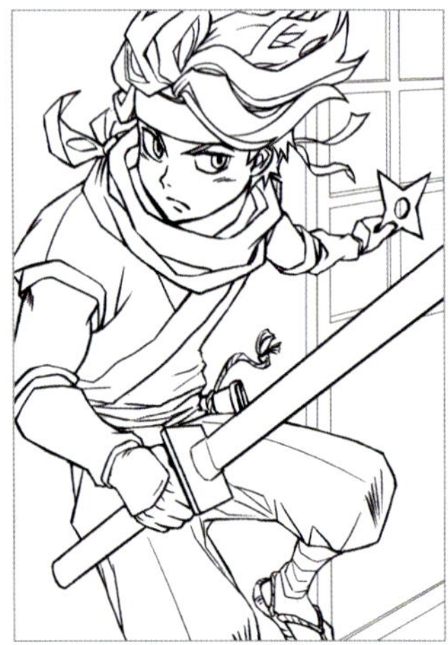

3 Add the background using a thinner fineliner. I use a ruler for manufactured objects such as the sliding door and the sword.

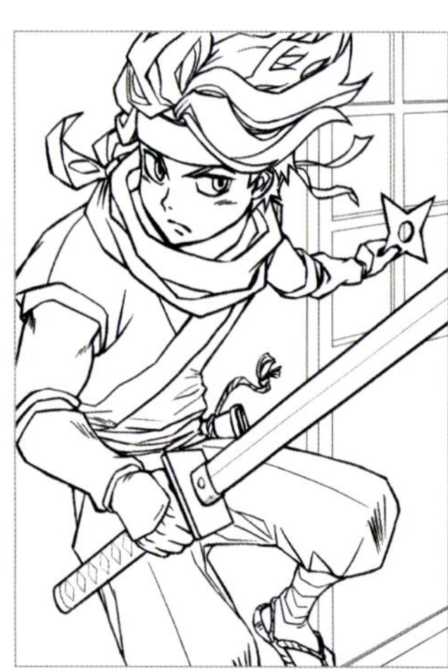

4 Add more details with thin lines, such as the details on the sword and creases on the clothing.

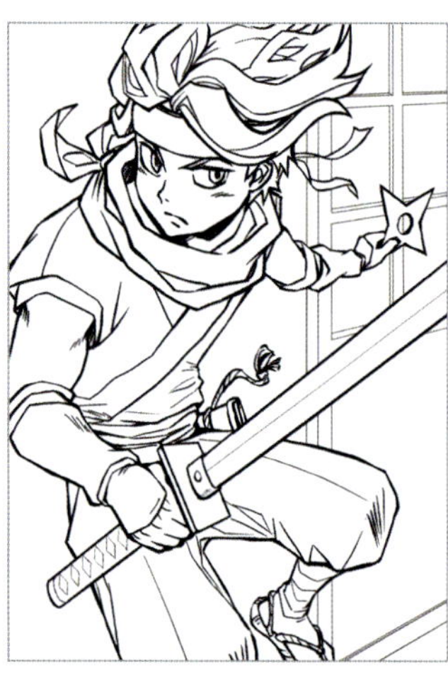

5 Add any black shadows, then add stronger lines to the sides of the shadows, closer objects and the main silhouette. This illustration will be coloured, so other shadows will look better if created with coloured markers. For this reason, don't add any shading.

STAGE 6

COLOUR YOUR ART

Always plan which base colours, shading and highlight colours to use before you start. I recommend making a few photocopies of your inked art and testing your markers on them. Don't colour the whites of the eyes or sword highlights – the paper provides the white.

ADDING THE BASE COLOURS

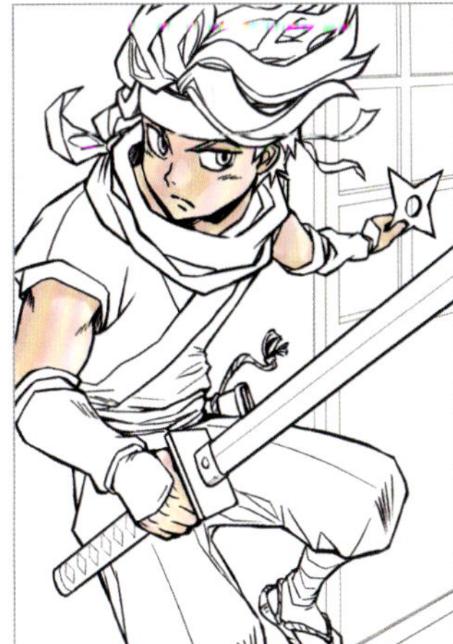

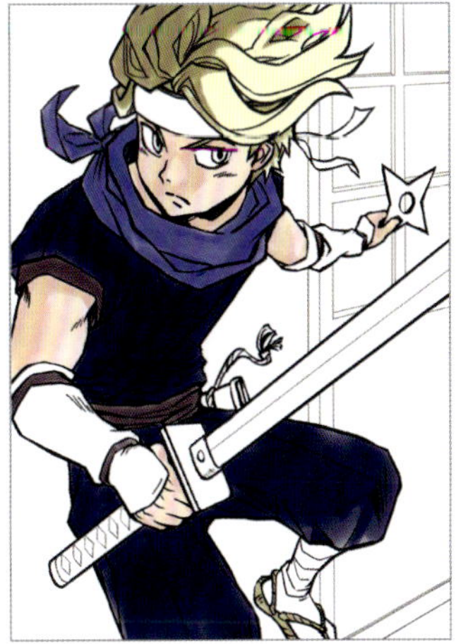

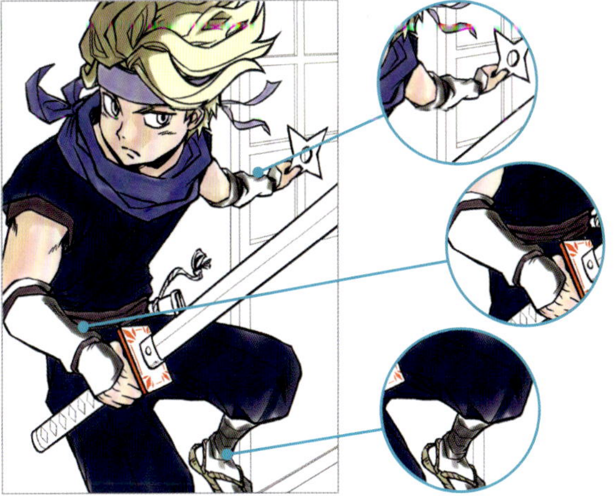

1 Start by adding the skin tone. Use a slightly lighter colour for highlights on the skin, and avoid too dark a colour for shading. I used a blender marker to merge the shade colours.

2 Add the base hair colour, shaded hair colour and all the base colours for the clothing, aside from black.

3 Any areas that are coloured black can't have shading added to them, so instead use a dark grey for the highlights. Add the pattern on the hand guard.

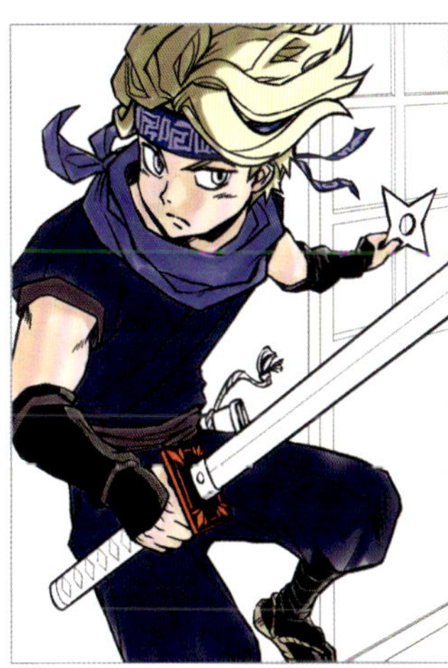

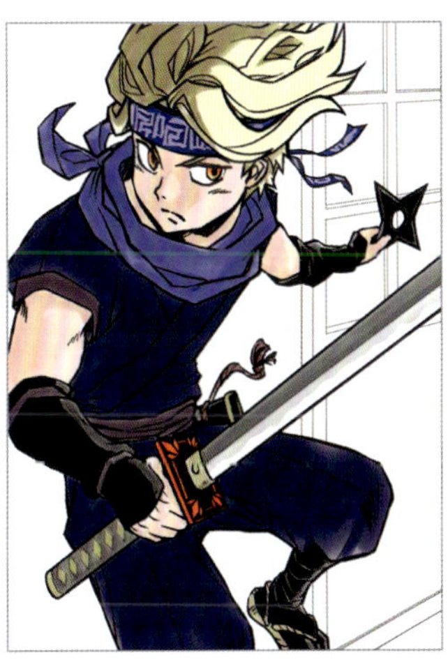

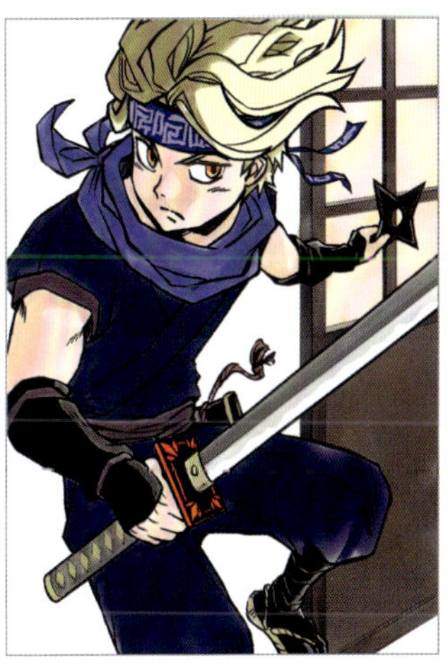

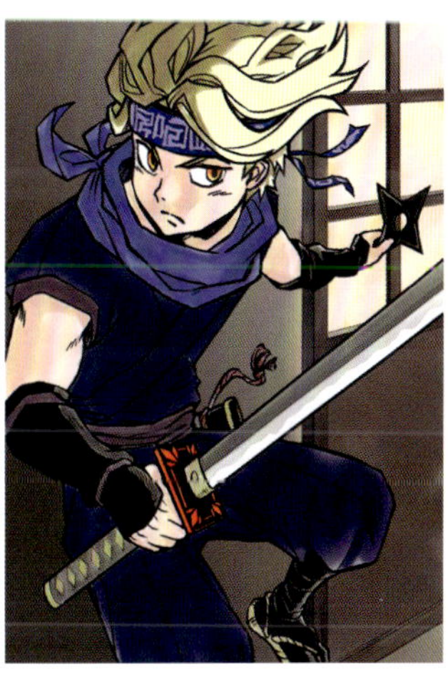

4 Colour the black areas. Add the pattern to the bandanna.

5 Colour the sword, scabbard and shuriken, using two or three colours of grey to suggest metal and leaving areas of the blade white for highlights.

7 Colour the sliding door, then add shading using a similar colour to reduce the contrast so it doesn't distract from the character.

8 Colour the wall and floor with a slight gradation.

STAGE 7

MAKE FINAL ADJUSTMENTS

This last stage can make the difference in turning a good illustration into high-quality art. Examine your drawing and think carefully about what you need to do to make a better final illustration. Possible changes include adjusting the tones, adding fine details such as creases and textures for fabrics, and adding highlights with a white pen or gradation effects with a blender marker.

ADDING SHADING AND SHADOWS

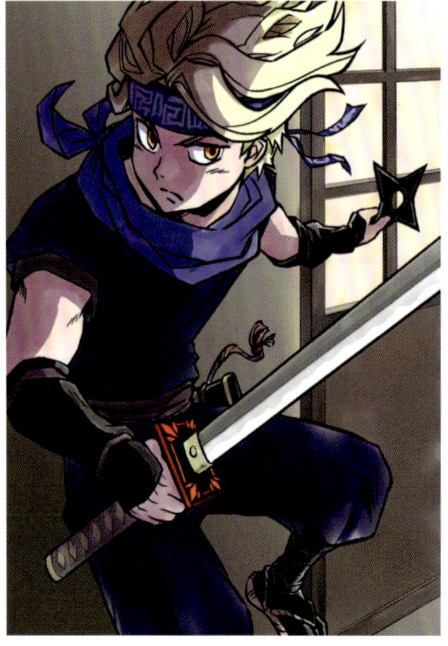

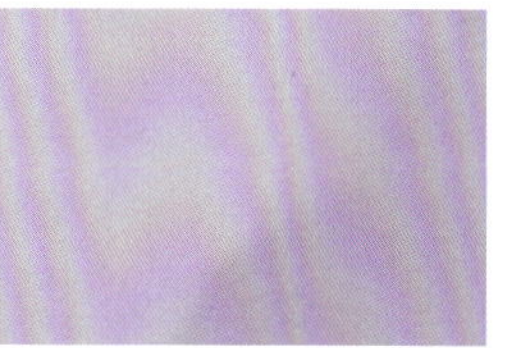

1 Add light purple to all the areas of the ninja that are in light shadows. The light source is the sliding door, so the areas in shadow are on the opposite side of the ninja.

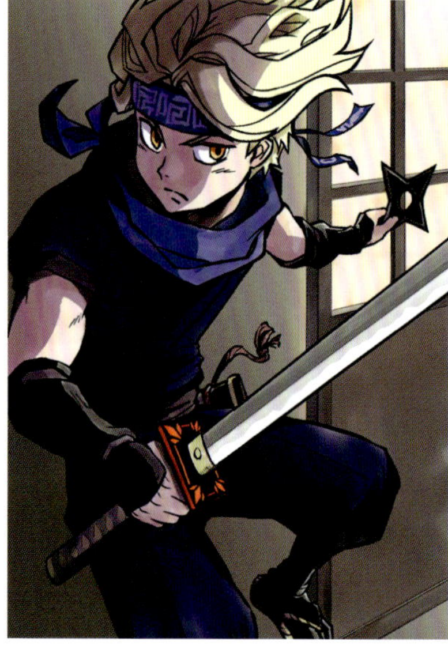

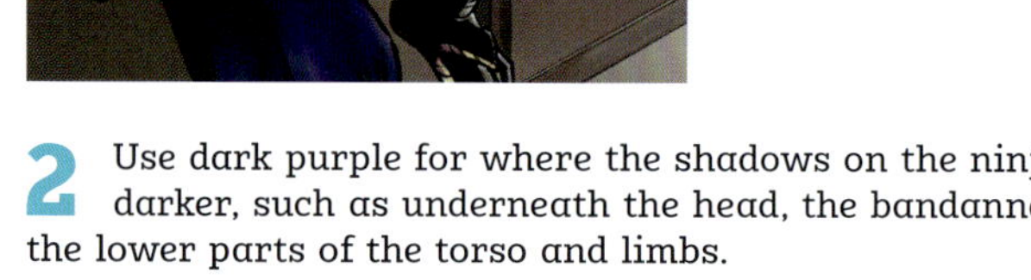

2 Use dark purple for where the shadows on the ninja are darker, such as underneath the head, the bandanna and the lower parts of the torso and limbs.

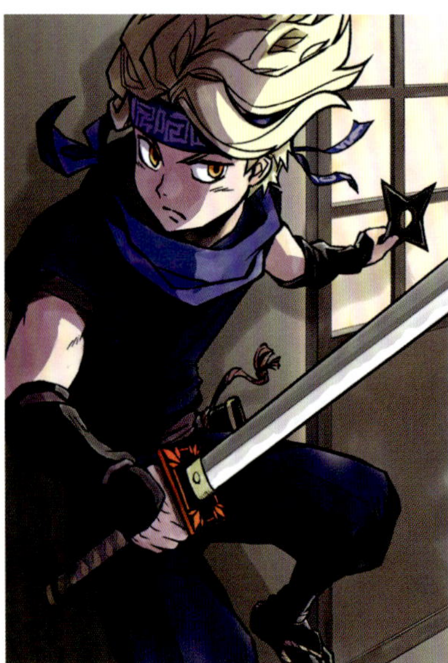

3 Use light grey for the shadow the ninja casts on the wall. Merge the edges with a blender marker.

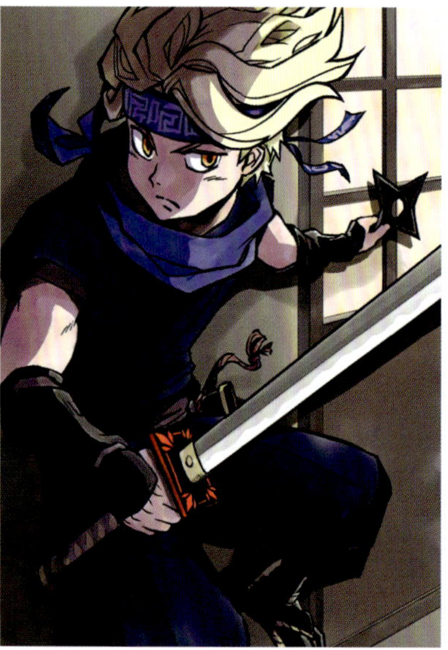

4 To make the picture look even more dramatic, add stronger shadows underneath his arms and legs. This will help make his sword arm stand out.

ADDING DETAILS

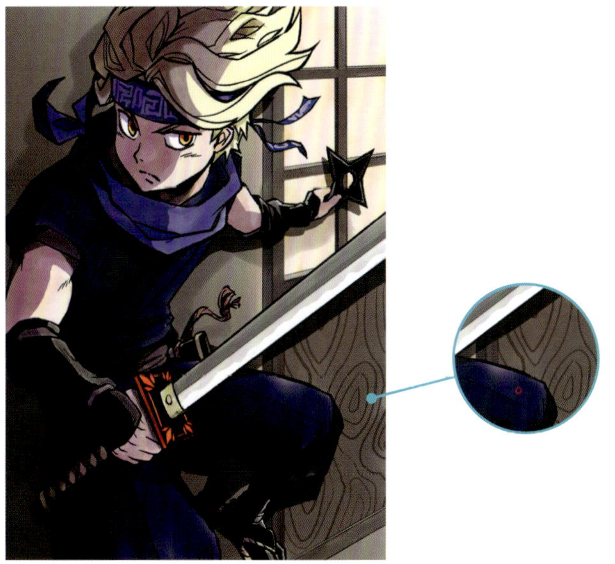

5 Add a pattern to the wood panel in the sliding door to give it some texture.

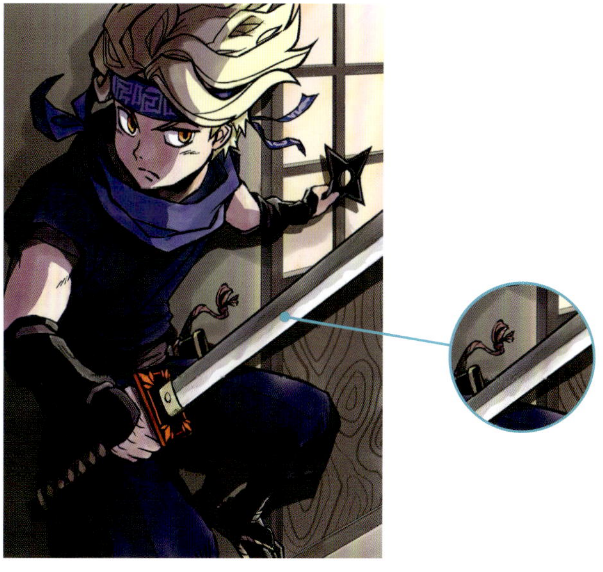

6 Add a subtle reflection on the top edge of the sword using the blue of the clothes and the yellow of the hair.

ADDING WHITE

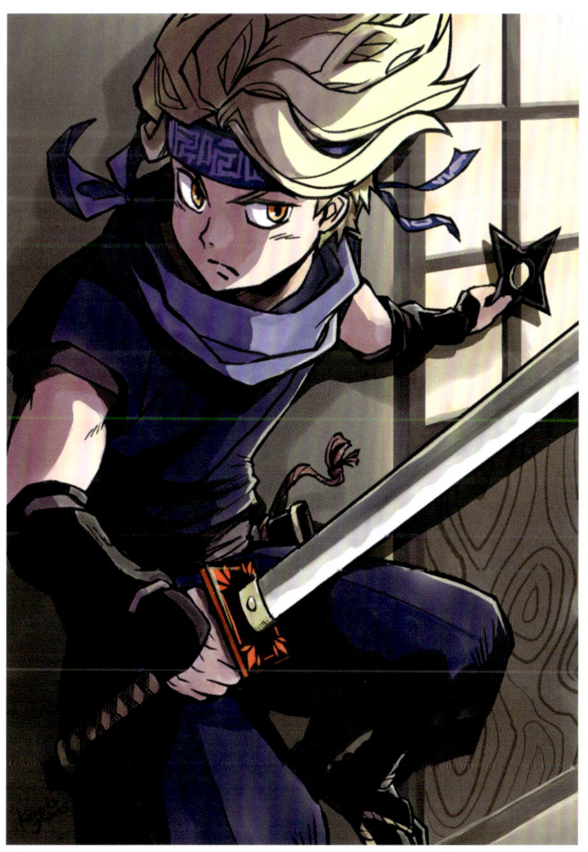

7 I added highlights with an acrylic white pen on the eyes, sword and any fabric close to the light.

FINISH YOUR ART

Step back to look at your illustration from a couple of metres away, so you can judge your art objectively. Check whether the most important elements are clearly visible. Look at the overall balance of the artwork and adjust the tones and colours as you feel you necessary. You should also check for any colour gaps or overlaps and correct them if needed (see page 123).

INDEX

About the Author

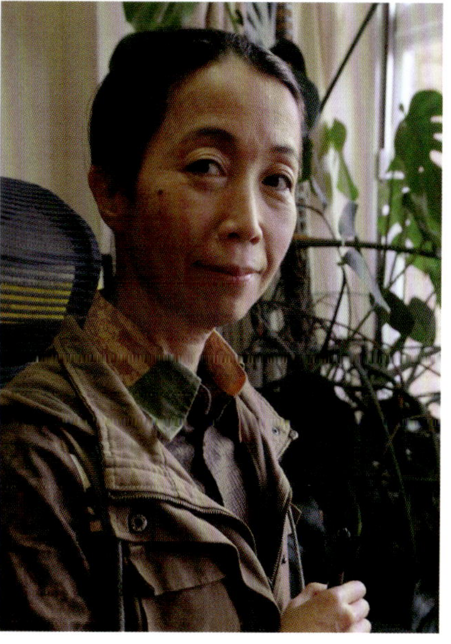

Keroko James is a Japanese illustrator, graphic designer and manga tutor. She was born in Japan and developed a passion for manga and anime culture from an early age. Keroko graduated from Nagoya Zokei University of Art and Design before moving to London in 2006. Since 2016, she has run Froggy Manga (www.froggymanga.com), providing manga drawing classes for children. She has also worked with local authorities to deliver manga workshops in local libraries and youth groups.

Author's Acknowledgements

I would like to send my thanks to everyone at GMC Publications who have been involved, and gave me the opportunity to write this book.

I would also like to include a huge thank you to my husband Jon, who supported me from the start of this project, brushing up my sometimes-clunky English, taking photos and giving me advice. Without him, I would not have been able to finish this book.

Writing this book has not always been easy, partly because it was the first one I'd written, and because it took much longer than planned. During the process, the Covid outbreak forced me to change the way I ran my comics class, and I moved to the suburbs, which changed my circumstances and my environment dramatically.

My gratitude also goes to Tom, Robin and Jonathan for sticking with me through everything, showing patience and perseverence. And although I didn't work with them directly, I would like to send a Japanese thank-you spell, *Arigatō*, to the proofreaders, printers and everyone else involved in producing this book.

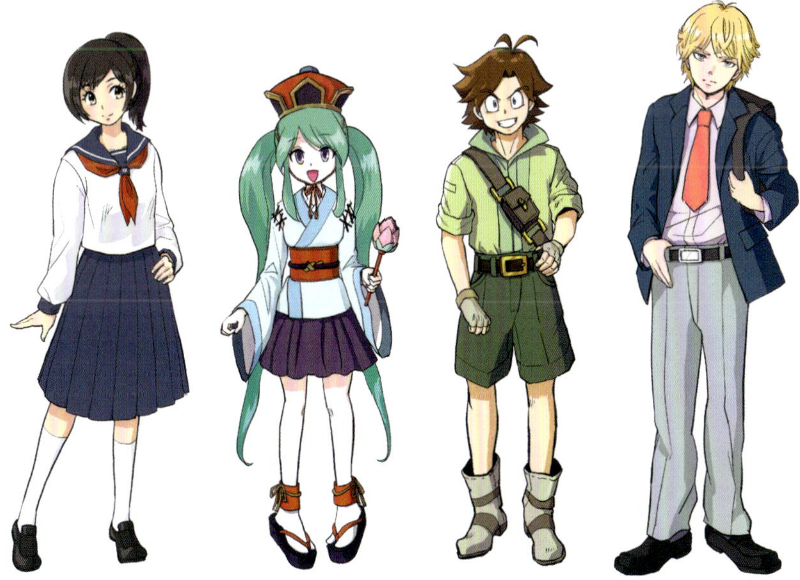

First published 2024 by
Guild of Master Craftsman Publications Ltd
Castle Place, 166 High Street, Lewes,
East Sussex BN7 1XU

ISBN 978-1-78494-637-1

A catalogue record for this book is available from the British Library.

Publisher Jonathan Bailey
Production Jim Bulley
Design Manager Robin Shields
Senior Project Editor Tom Kitch
Editor Theresa Bebbington
Photographer Jon Kaneko-James

Colour origination by GMC Reprographics
Printed and bound in China

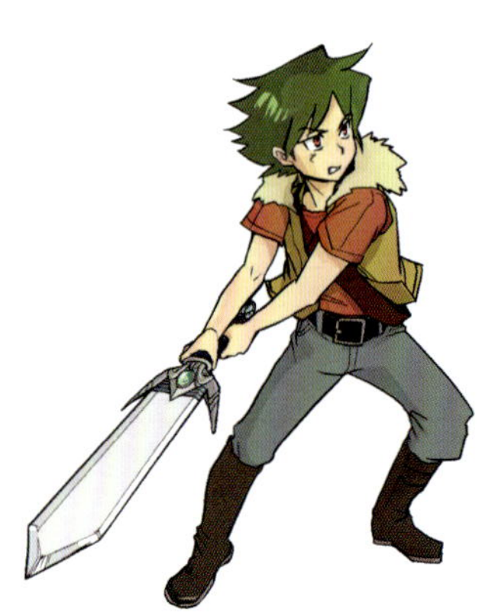
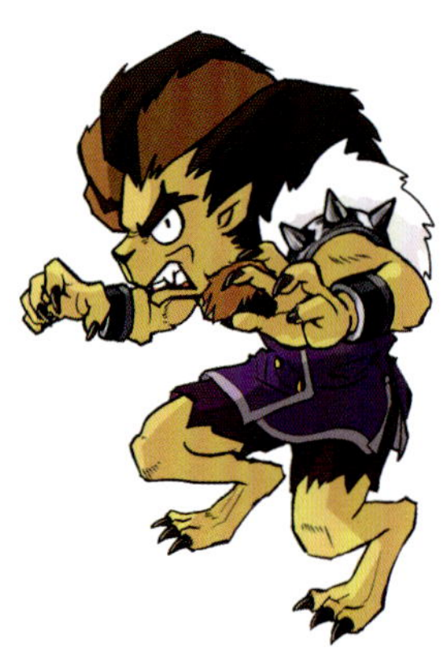
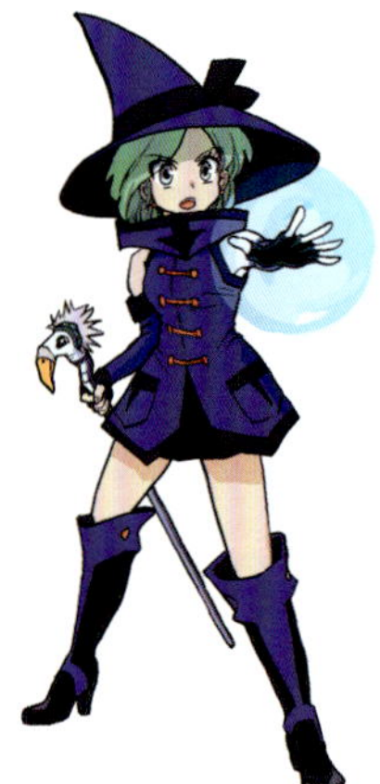
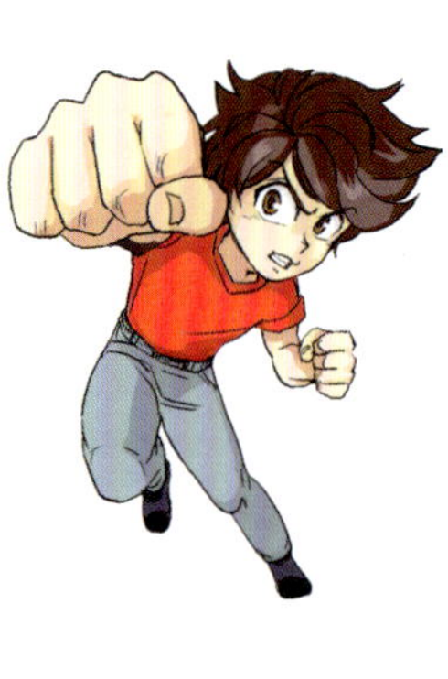

To order a book, contact:
GMC Publications Ltd
Castle Place, 166 High Street, Lewes, East
Sussex, BN7 1XU
United Kingdom
Tel: +44 (0)1273 488005
www.gmcbooks.com